COLLATERAL DAMAGE

COLLATERAL DAMAGE

Americans, Noncombatant Immunity, and Atrocity after World War II

Sahr Conway-Lanz

Routledge
Taylor & Francis Group
New York   London

Routledge is an imprint of the
Taylor & Francis Group, an informa business

Published in 2006 by
Routledge
Taylor & Francis Group
270 Madison Avenue
New York, NY 10016

Published in Great Britain by
Routledge
Taylor & Francis Group
2 Park Square
Milton Park, Abingdon
Oxon OX14 4RN

Printed in the United States of America on acid-free paper
10 9 8 7 6 5 4 3 2 1

International Standard Book Number-10: 0-415-97828-9 (Hardcover) 0-415-97829-7 (Softcover)
International Standard Book Number-13: 978-0-415-97828-6 (Hardcover) 978-0-415-97829-3 (Softcover)
Library of Congress Card Number 2005031055

Library of Congress Cataloging-in-Publication Data

Conway-Lanz, Sahr.
   Collateral damage : Americans, noncombatant immunity, and atrocity after World War II / by Sahr Conway-Lanz.
      p. cm.
   Includes bibliographical references and index.
   ISBN 0-415-97828-9 (hb) -- ISBN 0-415-97829-7 (pb)
   1. Combatants and noncombatants (International law)--History. 2. War victims--Legal status, laws, etc.--History. 3. War crimes--History. 4. United States--Armed Forces--History--20th century. 5. War victims--Moral and ethical aspects. I. Title.

KZ6515.C66 2006
172'.42--dc22
                                           2005031055

Taylor & Francis Group
is the Academic Division of Informa plc.

Visit the Taylor & Francis Web site at
http://www.taylorandfrancis.com

and the Routledge Web site at
http://www.routledge-ny.com

To my parents and Dolores

Contents

Acknowledgments

The help of many made this work possible. This book began as a dissertation at the history department of Harvard University. For their guidance and support along the way, I would like to thank my dissertation advisers Ernest May, Akira Iriye, and Lizabeth Cohen. My other colleagues and friends at Harvard provided both inspiration and a critical, yet sympathetic, first audience for the project's ideas. I would especially like to thank Alexis Albion, Jonathan Conant, Brian Delay, Mark Haefele, Shigeo Hirano, Mike Makovsky, Wade Markel, Neal Rosendorf, Ryan Stanley, Ken Weisbrode, and Brad Zakarin. Two summer research grants from the Charles Warren Center of American History at Harvard University provided early support for this project.

I would also like to thank my teachers outside my graduate program. Felicia Pratto first taught me the joys and rigors of academic research. Barton J. Bernstein's teaching and scholarship provided an initial inspiration for this book. Frank Ninkovich gave crucial encouragement and advice early in the project and helped me to find a publisher at the end. The work of Michael Sherry and Paul Boyer served as intellectual and methodological models for this study. I owe a great many other intellectual debts for this work, and I have tried to acknowledge them adequately in my notes and bibliography.

For their help in facilitating my access to the archival materials that I needed for this project, I am grateful to the staffs at the National Archives, Truman Library, Eisenhower Library, Swarthmore Peace Collection, Naval Historical Center, Andover Harvard Theological Library, and Harvard Law School Special Collections. I would like to thank Charles Hanley for his generous help in sharing documents and his extensive knowledge of the 1950 killings of Korean refugees near No Gun Ri. The librarians at Widener Library, the New York Public Library, and Sterling Memorial Library helped me to track down relevant books and other materials. I would especially like to thank all the staff at Manuscripts and Archives in Yale University's Sterling Memorial Library who provided me with a friendly, stimulating, and supportive professional home while I was putting the finishing touches on this project.

My editor Kimberly Guinta and the staff at Routledge were a pleasure to work with, and I would like to thank the anonymous reviewers for their constructive comments on the manuscript. I am grateful to Dorothy Wells and Joel Rosenthal who helped lead me to Routledge. In addition, I would like to thank Blackwell Publishing, Inc. for granting me permission to republish material from Sahr Conway-Lanz, "Beyond No Gun Ri: Refugees and the United States Military in the Korean War," *Diplomatic History* 29, no. 1 (January 2005): 49–81 that appears in this work in altered form.

I could not have seen this work to completion without the love and support of my family. Dolores believed in me and my ideas, and she has brought countless joys into my life. My parents were my first teachers, and I could not have asked for better ones.

Preface

In the modern world, harm to noncombatants has been central to cross-cultural ideas of what constitutes wrongful political violence. Much of the horror and revulsion inspired by modern warfare, genocide, and terrorism spring from the violence they inflict on innocent bystanders, individuals posing no immediate threat to their attackers. This aversion to harming noncombatants has supported a long-standing and widespread normative belief that noncombatants should and could be provided with immunity from the violence of armed conflict. Noncombatant immunity has served as a fundamental limit on political violence, and many cultures have come to equate deviations from the norm with what it means to commit an atrocity. In the twentieth century, noncombatant immunity has emerged as a basic human right codified in international law.

Yet despite the integral role of noncombatant immunity in cultural understandings of political violence, the subject remains understudied. Most of the work on noncombatant immunity has been conducted either by ethicists and intellectual historians who have examined the idea's development as a part of prescriptive moral theories about the use of force or by historians and social scientists investigating the numerous cases when the norm has been breached. Noncombatant immunity has not received more attention in part because it has been conceived of narrowly as simply a moral idea and, as such, a rather weak restraint on violence in the real world. Many have expressed their skepticism that moral scruples could restrain violence in the face of contrary motives. Indeed, the twentieth century alone has brought so many and such drastic instances of harming noncombatants that it can be difficult to perceive any role that the idea of noncombatant immunity has played in recent history.

However, it is too simple to view noncombatant immunity solely as a moral idea. Shared moral values are one of the reinforcing mechanisms that help to make noncombatant immunity a normative belief, but practical and political considerations also buttress the idea of sparing bystanders. Those using force have often seen harming unthreatening individuals as inefficient and wasteful. They have acted upon the pragmatic belief that attacking combatants directly is the most potent method of reducing the threat an enemy poses. The political utility of atrocity accusations against an enemy can also bolster the idea of noncombatant immunity. Condemning one's opponents as perpetrators of atrocities can mobilize support for your cause and isolate the other side, but if the charges center on harming noncombatants as they often do, the accusers implicitly add their voices to those advocating noncombatant immunity.

It is also inadequate to view noncombatant immunity as simply a notion that places limits on political violence. Constraining violence is certainly one of the ways it can operate, but the idea can contrarily play a role in rationalizing violence. When people perceive the use of force as conforming to some notion of noncombatant immunity, they may more readily accept the violence as justified. In this way, it may facilitate some forms of violence while restraining others.

Finally, it is reductionistic to conceive of noncombatant immunity as a rigidly defined and monolithic idea. Noncombatant immunity has often been a contested notion not only between cultures but within cultures as well. It makes more sense to talk of ideas of noncombatant immunity, and these ideas have changed with time and circumstance. At its core, noncombatant immunity has been the belief that individuals not directly participating in armed conflict should and could be protected from it. However, this basic idea still has left many questions up for debate such as who should be considered a participant, whether conflicting values and interests should be allowed to override these protections, and what responsibilities should belligerents have in keeping noncombatants alive beyond refraining from directly attacking them.

This book seeks to examine how these ideas of noncombatant immunity functioned in this broader sense as contested beliefs that were more than simply prescriptive moral ideas and limits on violence. A comprehensive survey of ideas of noncombatant immunity across all cultures and all history, even modern history, is far beyond the scope of this book. Nevertheless, this study makes a contribution to this larger project by focusing on the United States, a country central to world affairs and warfare in the twentieth century, in a period following World War II when Americans confronted an acute dilemma over noncombatant immunity and attitudes were in flux. This focus allows for the investigation of how local attitudes interacted with transnational beliefs, how these attitudes changed, and how they affected the actual use of force.

The end of World War II opened a period in which Americans confronted their recent experiences with mass killing that left them struggling to define the boundaries between combat and atrocity and between war and genocide. For Americans and their friends and enemies overseas, U.S. incendiary raids and nuclear attacks during the war possessed disturbing similarities to Nazi atrocities. American weapons had indiscriminately killed noncombatants: women, children, and the elderly. Public discussion among Americans in the aftermath of World War II demonstrated that the Vietnam War was not the first time that the problem of civilian casualties in war attracted widespread public attention and that the heated controversy surrounding this subject during the later war owed much to the attitudes that were crystallizing in the post-World War II confrontation with mass killing. In the decade after World War II, Americans carried on a sustained public dialogue over noncombatant immunity reflected in the press, the statements and preoccupations of government officials, and the activities of nongovernmental organizations such as peace groups, veterans associations, and churches. This public discussion debated and ultimately demonstrated a widespread reinterpretation of important elements of the meaning and requirements of conforming to the ideal of noncombatant immunity. The discussion raised questions about the persistence and malleability of notions of noncombatant immunity and about the limits noncombatant immunity could place on violence and the extent of protections to civilians it could provide.

1

Modern War and Mass Killing

On the night of March 9, 1945, more than 250 American B-29 bombers arrived over Tokyo. Each plane carried about six tons of bombs, most filled with a new chemical incendiary called napalm. Dropped in a precise pattern on the city, the fire bombs ignited the largest human-made conflagration ever used as a weapon in war. The bombs fell on a twelve-square-mile rectangle of one of the most densely built-up residential districts in the world, home to more than 1.2 million people. Strong winds whipped the scattered fires ignited by the bombs into a raging firestorm that engulfed entire neighborhoods. The city's residents died by the thousands. When the firestorm subsided more than nine hours later, it had burned out almost sixteen square miles of Tokyo. The destruction was greater than that which the first atomic bombing would inflict on Hiroshima three months later. Tokyo police recorded 267,171 buildings destroyed, leaving more than one million people homeless. Japanese and American officials placed the casualty toll at 83,793 dead and 40,918 wounded. With many schoolchildren evacuated from the city and young men away serving in the military, women, babies, and older men were most of the victims.

The burning of Tokyo was part of a larger campaign of destruction against Japan and Germany in 1945 that the Allies used to help hasten the end of World War II. The British had conducted the first large-scale fire bombing against Hamburg in 1943, which destroyed much of the city and killed an estimated 44,000 people. In early 1945, American planes joined the Royal Air Force (RAF) in showering Dresden with incendiary bombs that ignited another city-devouring firestorm. The incineration of Tokyo began a five month campaign conducted by the U.S. military to burn most of Japan's major cities to the ground. The destruction reached a final climax in August 1945 when American bombers dropped the first atomic bombs on Hiroshima and Nagasaki. The incendiary campaign against Japan devastated 180 square miles of 67 cities, and the entire American strategic bombing effort killed more than 300,000 Japanese and injured an additional 400,000. Most of the victims were civilians.[1]

Killing so many civilians and destroying so much in such a short time was unprecedented in warfare, and this capacity for massive destruction provoked growing concern about the violence of war as Americans became increasingly aware of what their armed forces had done. U.S. weapons, like never before, could inflict death and destruction over wide areas, but this capability made the violence difficult to control. Often times, the weapons did not allow for discrimination between their victims. In the war, American arms had killed women, children, the elderly—noncombatants posing little immediate threat to their attackers. Such harm violated the long-standing and widespread international norm of protecting the innocent from arbitrary injury in war. Western theologians and moralists have called this protection "noncombatant immunity" and the destructiveness of the Second World War proved to be one of the greatest challenges that the norm had ever faced.

The contradiction between new massively destructive methods of warfare and noncombatant immunity was made more acute in 1945 because the world had begun to learn the full extent of the killings carried out under the Nazi regime. With the revelations of Nazi genocide, peoples around the world had a fresh and horrific example of the slaughter of civilians. The Holocaust would emerge as the epitome of inhumane atrocity in the twentieth century. Some, including Americans, saw unsettling similarities between American methods of warfare in the bombing campaigns of 1945 and the German atrocities. Both killed the innocent arbitrarily. The victims were "innocent" in the sense that they posed little direct threat to their assailants and were "arbitrarily" killed in that the victims died because of their nationality, creed, or simple geographic location and not specifically because of any actions they had taken or hostilities they had held against their killers.

The contradiction between new methods of war and noncombatant immunity and the resemblance, even if vague, between American and Nazi actions proved unsettling to many Americans and others in the shadow of U.S. military power. These developments disturbed Americans' perceptions of themselves as a humane people. They also jeopardized the United States' international reputation as a humane nation, an image that American leaders hoped could help forge a coalition in the emerging Cold War. However, the dilemma was more than a question of American image and identity. Because of American international influence buttressed by its military might and possession of nuclear weapons, how the United States dealt with the contradiction had far-reaching implications for the world.

1.1 The Tradition of Noncombatant Immunity

In the twentieth century, noncombatant immunity had become a small part of what it meant to be humane. Protection from violence that one did not participate in had become a human right and sparing noncombatants in war had become a human responsibility. Violating this right had become a quintessential atrocity. The idea of noncombatant immunity has found purchase in so many diverse religions, cultural traditions, and ways of reasoning that one can call it an international normative value in the twentieth century and arguably much earlier. However, the idea has been a contested one and has taken various forms. One can see a basic form among ancient peoples and more recent small-scale societies. The custom of sparing the lives of women and children in order to enslave them or incorporate them into the conquerors' families may have been motivated by self-interest, but it has saved many from death. Prohibitions against killing noncombatants developed early in many of the major religious traditions around the world. Ancient Hindu texts depicted war as a fight between equals and identified classes of people who should be spared including bystanders, who did not participate in combat, and those fleeing the battlefield.[2] Early rabbinical Jewish law placed limits on warfare to protect noncombatants and restrain general devastation such as allowing noncombatants to escape a besieged city and prohibiting the destruction of trees.[3] Medieval Islamic jurists agreed that noncombatants who did not take part in fighting such as women, children, monks, the elderly, the blind, and the insane should not be harmed.[4] Confucianism's preference for avoiding excess in attaining military victory was reflected in a Manchu imperial decree of 1731 that threatened death to soldiers "who oppress the people, native or foreign, on a line of march, by forcing them to buy or sell, plundering, destroying buildings, or violating women."[5]

Many Americans in 1945 found themselves inheritors of the European tradition of noncombatant immunity. The historian James Turner Johnson has traced this tradition to two sources in the Middle Ages, one Christian and the other secular. The Catholic church advocated a "Peace of God" to help limit the ravages of medieval warfare, especially those that harmed the church. The Peace of God urged that protection from war's violence be given to people who had nothing to do with war-making, such as clerics, monks, friars, pilgrims, travelers, merchants, and peasants as well as their animals, goods, and lands. Secular customary practice and the chivalric code also limited the means of fighting. According to these conventions, war was a contest between equals, and the harming of those presumed helpless, such as women and children, was dishonorable.

By the sixteenth century, Christian theologians, most notably the Spaniards Francisco Victoria and Francisco Suarez, integrated these religious and secular customs into a more intricate doctrine of just war. Their writings addressed two distinct but interrelated questions: *jus ad bellum* or the requirements for the legitimate initiation of war, and *jus in bello* being the legitimate methods for war's conduct. They drew on the writings of Augustine, Thomas Aquinas, and canon law to elaborate *jus ad bellum* while the medieval conventions on sparing the peaceable and helpless became an important element of *jus in bello*. In the seventeenth and eighteenth centuries, European scholars incorporated just war doctrine into the first systems of international law they created. In the legal thought of Hugo Grotius, John Locke, and Emmerich de Vattel, noncombatant immunity became a central principle of a secular exposition of *jus in bello*. Like the Peace of God, Grotius, Locke, and Vattel bestowed immunity on individuals based on their function during war. If individuals did not directly participate in the prosecution of the war, they did not deserve to be harmed by its violence. Locke and Vattel extended this reasoning to apply to physical structures such as churches and fine buildings that were not used in the war.[6]

The European version of noncombatant immunity and the other diverse sources of the norm shared a few simple ideas but left a number of central questions open to dispute. Noncombatant immunity in its simplest form was the notion that those not participating in the fighting of a war should and could be protected from the war's violence. This simple idea begged the questions of who should be considered a participant in war, whether this protection should be abandoned in the face of conflicting values, and what responsibilities should belligerents have in keeping noncombatants alive beyond refraining from their purposeful slaughter. For instance, should those who manufacture the soldiers' weapons or those who pay taxes that support a war effort be considered completely innocent of waging war? Should noncombatants be spared at the risk of soldiers' lives or the risk of prolonging the fighting? Must soldiers avoid attacking segments of an enemy's economy, like its food supplies, because these are necessary to prevent starvation among noncombatants?

Americans had debated questions like these before. Noncombatant immunity had a long tradition in North America. Back to the seventeenth century wars in New England between English settlers and Algonquian Indians, both sides appear to have held noncombatant immunity as an ideal. Some indications suggest that the Algonquian way of war included a general practice of avoiding indiscriminate killing. Likewise, the English struggled to reconcile their fighting with the ideas of *jus in bello* that the writings of Victoria and Grotius were elaborating at the time.[7]

Limiting harm to noncombatants, however, would give rise to controversy in later American wars. During the American Civil War, northerners clashed over the policy of "hard war" against the south. Harsh Union methods such as burning private property met with criticism in the north and became a national political issue in the 1864 presidential elections.[8] The wars with Indians in the west after the Civil War also led to protest over what some white Americans saw as the Army's indiscriminate use of force. Reformers, who hoped to change Indian policy, condemned the massacre of Indian men, women, and children, and attracted support in the press and Congress.[9] Controversy over the treatment of noncombatants during the Philippine War resulted in a congressional investigation and the trial and punishment of

American officers. A general, who reportedly had planned to burn the entire island of Samar, was convicted for his conduct during the later phase of the pacification campaign that the U.S. military conducted in the Philippines from 1899 to 1902 to suppress the independence movement there.[10] Americans had long struggled with the problem of noncombatant immunity.

1.2 The Challenge of Total War

However, the last year of World War II marked a watershed in the history of noncombatant immunity in the United States and for the world. Americans confronted the question of whether they accepted the prospect that the violence of war would be unlimited, at least in the sense of being unrestrained by the customary distinction between combatant and noncombatant. Not only did the events of 1945 leave Americans facing the uncomfortable tension between their country's participation in mass killing and simultaneous revulsion at Nazi atrocities, but three broader historical trends had helped to deepen the contradiction between massively destructive methods of warfare and the norm of noncombatant immunity. By 1945, older ideas about the mobilization of entire nations for war had combined with the mechanization of warfare to pose the greatest challenge noncombatant immunity had faced among Americans. These merging trends severely complicated the question of what were legitimate targets for war's violence and provided rationales and opportunities for deciding that virtually all of an enemy's society contributed in some way to the war effort and was open for destruction as a military target. Yet, as these trends were combining to threaten noncombatant immunity, a third development suggested the resilience of the norm. In the face of the changing character of warfare, governments began in the mid-nineteenth century to construct a body of international law that attempted to codify customary protections for civilians.

The idea of total war, the vision of entire nations at war, had long threatened to render noncombatant immunity obsolete, but this threat had been largely an abstract one until technology changed the way wars were fought in the twentieth century. Although a twentieth century expression, "total war" has become the common term encapsulating the earlier ideas of a nation in arms and people's war that emerged from the American and European revolutions of the late eighteenth and early nineteenth centuries. According to these nationalistic doctrines, war was no longer the sole domain of military professionals and warrior elites. An entire people would fight for their nation. American and French revolutionaries held up the citizen soldier as an ideal and called for a nation in arms with universal military service for men. The related notion of a people's war envisioned a similar program of popular mobilization. The popular uprising and prolonged guerrilla struggle in the face of Napoleon's attempt to place his brother on the Spanish throne provided a vivid example of a people's war, a mass movement from beneath which revolutionaries would continue to promote as a means to rid a people of an illegitimate regime.

These grandiose visions of mobilization left little room for the notion of innocent noncombatants uninvolved in the fight. Popular warfare cut through the traditional divisions of class, sex, and age that had separated soldiers from noncombatants. When the French Republic proclaimed the *levee en masse* to raise a citizen army against the revolution's enemies, it declared that "every French person must stand ready to serve and support our armed forces." A role in the war effort would be found for everyone, the revolutionary government believed. Young men would fight; husbands would forge weapons and transport supplies; wives and daughters would make tents and uniforms and care for the wounded; and old men would publicly exhort the Republic's cause to boost morale.

Although these new ideas spread beyond the enthusiastic revolutionaries who promoted them and helped states to raise large armies in the nineteenth century, popular war remained largely a theoretical threat to civilians because of the way wars were then fought. The mobilization capacities of nineteenth century states were not great, and, as a result, much of the public in fact had little involvement with war efforts. Even when civilians made vital contributions to a war, militaries had few means to strike at an enemy's civil society before the land and naval forces defending it had been defeated. Civilians might be vulnerable in a people's war or if guerrilla warfare continued after an enemy's forces had occupied their lands, but this type of fighting was comparatively rare. While ideas of popular warfare undercut the perceived innocence of civilians, war's violence remained confined largely to soldiers. Most of the suffering that nineteenth century wars inflicted on civilians came from the much older threats of sieges, pillaging, and blockades.[11]

The ideas of popular war became much more dangerous for noncombatants when a technological revolution in warfare began in the mid-nineteenth century, which culminated in the devastation of World War II. Over this period, the mechanization of warfare posed a dual threat to civilians. The growing importance of industry, transportation, and communications in warfare, and hence the workers that kept these complex systems running, reinforced the notion that many civilians were not uninvolved innocents. Factory-produced supplies and ammunition flowed more swiftly and reliably along railroad lines to larger armies making these soldiers more deadly. However, the mechanization of warfare also threatened civilians through the dramatic expansion in firepower it made possible. The weapons of war advanced phenomenally in their capabilities to kill and destroy over large areas. As firepower grew, the violence of war became radically more difficult to control. In the late nineteenth and early twentieth centuries, armies acquired new weapons that could fire more quickly and kill at greater distances and over larger areas. The machine gun was first widely used in the American Civil

War. The Maxim gun, the standard machine gun of the British army in World War I, fired 500 rounds a minute, and in 1918, the German army introduced a machine gun that fired 1,000 rounds a minute. By World War I, innovations in artillery gave armies the capability to hurl massive barrages miles in front of them. The enormous German 420 mm mortar, nicknamed "Big Bertha," could launch a shell over nine miles. The French 75 mm howitzer could fire fifteen rounds per minute to a range of five miles. In a single day in September 1917, the British fired off one million artillery shells.[12]

As technological and political change undermined noncombatant immunity, the custom demonstrated its resilience. Beginning in the second half of the nineteenth century, a series of international conventions on the conduct of war gave formal legal sanction to aspects of the general custom of noncombatant immunity. In 1864, international delegates signed the first conventions on the treatment of the sick and wounded in war. The convention applied to members of armed forces, but it bestowed a neutral or noncombatant status on injured soldiers and those taking care of them and introduced the red cross as a symbol denoting immunity from attack. The Hague conventions of 1899 and 1907 formulated a set of international rules of warfare including prohibitions against illegitimate means. Article 22 stated, "The right of belligerents to adopt means of injuring the enemy is not unlimited." Other articles forbade the bombardment of undefended towns, villages, dwellings, or buildings and asserted that "all necessary steps must be taken to spare, as far as possible, buildings dedicated to religion, art, science, or charitable purposes, historic monuments, hospitals, and places where the sick and wounded are collected, provided they are not being used at the time for military purposes." Despite the qualifications, the Hague conventions identified segments of societies that deserved protection from war's destruction. Although specific mention of civilians as a protected class in international humanitarian law would wait until after World War II, the general principles that those not participating in combat should be spared from further harm and that the means in war had customary limits had found expression in international law before World War I.[13]

The Great War demonstrated, like no war before it, the deadly potential of mechanized warfare and brought the world the closest to a truly total war it had yet been. For four years, armies of millions of young men marched against enemy guns across a wasteland of trenches and fortifications in Flanders and northern France. The slaughter of soldiers was appalling. On the first day of the Battle of the Somme, the British Army suffered 60,000 casualties. The war killed eight-and-a-half million men in uniform and wounded twenty-one million. Although the violence of the war was not confined to the battlefield, soldiers were still the principle victims of warfare, something that would change with World War II. Estimates have placed noncombatant deaths in the First World War at six-and-a-half million. The new technology of that war favored the static defense over the mobile offense and produced a bloody stalemate that confined the fighting to a relatively small area, but devoured soldiers by the thousands.[14]

World War I further demonstrated international sensitivity to the killing of noncombatants. When Germany invaded Belgium, France and Britain supplemented their armed resistance with a barrage of atrocity charges. In 1915, the British government published the Bryce Report, which accused the German army of a systematic campaign of atrocities in Belgium intended to terrorize the civilian populace into passivity. According to the report, one of the Germans' primary crimes was the killing of noncombatants. The report created a sensation in the international press and attracted wide attention among Americans. The German government defended itself with a report claiming its military had conducted legitimate reprisals against civilians who had taken up arms to resist the invasion.[15] Americans also clashed with Germany over the boundaries of noncombatancy when the German navy embarked on a policy of unrestricted submarine warfare. German attacks against neutral and unarmed merchant ships, such as the *Lusitania,* which sank killing 1,200 passengers, outraged Americans and helped to propel the United States into the war on the side of the Entente.

After the war, revulsion at the slaughter of soldiers in the trenches inspired military leaders to search for a way to prevent future stalemates and reintroduce mobility into war, but their search accelerated modern warfare's threats to noncombatants. A few military theorists speculated that the tank and airplane, which had appeared on the battlefield during the First World War but had not realized much of their potential, offered the means to avert a bloody stalemate. The tank promised an end to static trench warfare. Thick armor protected the tank against machine gun fire and shrapnel, allowing it to slash through trench lines and barbed wire.

While the tank offered the potential to expand the battlefield on the ground through maneuverability, the airplane inspired enthusiasts to envision entirely new ways of fighting wars. Not only could the airplane be used as flying artillery to support soldiers on the ground, visionaries proclaimed air power a weapon to attack a country's will and industrial capacity to wage war. The specialized bomber would fly over the frontlines and strike war industries and vulnerable cities. It would provide the capability to attack an entire nation, which ideas of total warfare were encouraging many to believe had become intricately involved in war-making. Militaries first used bombers extensively in World War I. German zeppelins and airplanes bombed British cities killing more than 1,400 people and disrupting some industrial production. The British launched attacks against German cities that far exceeded those that they had suffered.[16] However, these attacks were a pale shadow of the devastation that airplanes would inflict in the next world war.

The relatively limited effects of aerial bombardment in World War I did not prevent enthusiastic speculation about air power's role in future wars, and some of the visions were dark, indeed, for civilians. One of the most notorious promoters of air power, the Italian General Guilio Douhet, focused attention on the question of whether civilian populations themselves were a proper target for aerial attacks. Writing in the 1920s, he believed World War I demonstrated that future wars would be fought by entire peoples and, with the rise of great air forces, civilian populations could no longer be sheltered from attack. Thinking of wars as clashes between nations and not simply their militaries, Douhet went beyond advocating the destruction of industry or even the urban infrastructure of cities and openly contemplated bombing civilians in order to end wars swiftly. He saw great potential for devastating an enemy nation with airplanes loaded with poison gas and incendiaries. In such a war, he wrote, "There will be no distinction any longer between soldiers and civilians." He admitted that the choice of what targets to bomb was a difficult one, but he believed that attacking civilian populations directly could generate panic and the loss of will to continue the war. "Mercifully," he wrote, "the decision will be quick in this kind of war, since the decisive blows will be directed at civilians, that element of the countries at war least able to sustain them."[17] Others were not so sure that the bomber would be a blessing.

Fears that the airplane would introduce indiscriminate killing of civilians gave rise to unsuccessful attempts to formulate international law regulating aerial bombardment. During the winter of 1922–1923, distinguished jurists and a host of technical advisors drafted a set of rules for air warfare at the Hague. Article 22 of the rules reads, "Aerial bombardment for the purpose of terrorizing the civilian population, of destroying or damaging private property not of military character, or of injuring noncombatants is prohibited." Another provision banned the bombardment of "cities, towns, villages, dwellings, or buildings not in the immediate neighborhood of the operations of land forces." The rules listed examples of what constituted legitimate military targets such as armed forces themselves, factories producing distinctly military supplies, lines of communication, and transportation used for military purposes. Although the 1923 Hague draft rules offered protections for civilians, countries refused to adopt them in legally binding form. The rules reflected concern that changes in military technology posed new threats to the norm of noncombatant immunity, but their abandonment suggested that formal international law on its own lacked promise for ameliorating the dangers.[18]

Some Americans hoped that the dangers were exaggerated. The military specialists charged with integrating the airplane into the U.S. armed forces optimistically minimized the threat that the bomber posed to noncombatant immunity. The doctrine of air warfare formulated for the growing American air force largely avoided the extremes of Douhet's vision. In the 1920s, officers at the Air Corps Tactical School considered using the airplane to strike directly against civilian populations, but by the 1930s, Air Corps planners had supplanted this thinking with a doctrine of precision bombing which targeted vital components of an enemy's economy. The planners readily accepted industries that supported war production as legitimate military targets for attack. Bombers theoretically would destroy critical industries such as oil, steel, electrical power, and transportation. The planners speculated that civilians would suffer from these attacks and that the bombing would undermine civilian morale, but the mass killing of noncombatants would not be a direct aim of the precision attacks. The Army Air Force (AAF) plan for air war drawn up in 1941 embodied this strategy of precision bombing and recognized the disadvantages of bombing cities. Nevertheless, the plan included the contingency that American bombers might strike residential areas as a final blow to a sufficiently demoralized civilian population in order to conclude the war swiftly.

Even though the authors of the precision bombing doctrine acknowledged that world opinion condemned the bombing of cities and civilians, they justified their strategy largely on the grounds of efficiency. They reasoned that bombers were expensive, and so their use could only be justified against the most valuable industrial targets. They also judged that industrial economies were highly interdependent and, therefore, vulnerable at critical choke points in production and supply, and that civilian elements of the economy were those that posed the least immediate threat to friendly armed forces. American air men's thinking about air war before World War II, while hardly moralistic, conformed comfortably with noncombatant immunity.[19]

As international tensions increased in the late 1930s, statements by U.S. officials reinforced the expectation that Americans would continue to uphold the custom of noncombatant immunity. The American government repeatedly criticized the fascist states for bombarding civilians. The State Department condemned Japanese bombing of civilians in 1937 and 1938. Secretary of State Cordell Hull denounced the Fascist bombing of Barcelona in 1938, asserting, "No theory of war can justify such conduct." Several months later, he organized a "moral embargo" that discouraged U.S. sales of aircraft to countries who used them to bomb civilians. The same year, the Senate issued its own "unqualified condemnation of the inhuman bombing of civilian populations." When Germany invaded Poland in 1939, President Franklin D. Roosevelt urgently appealed to all sides in the hostilities to publicly affirm that their armed forces "shall in no event, and under no circumstances, undertake the bombardment from the air of civilian populations or of unfortified cities." Alluding to earlier air attacks, he said "ruthless bombing" had killed and maimed thousands of defenseless men, women, and children and had "profoundly shocked the conscience of humanity." Roosevelt feared that hundreds of thousands of "innocent human beings" would be harmed if the belligerent nations sunk to "this form of inhuman barbarism."[20]

When the United States entered World War II, it adopted an official policy of precision bombing in accordance with its air force's doctrine on air power and in line with the official sentiments expressed in the late 1930s. Leaders of the American air force, sensitive about their public image, appreciated the comfortable fit between precision bombing and public sentiments against attacking civilians.[21] However, the war would demonstrate that the policy of precision bombing could not prevent mass destruction. As American bombers joined British forces in attacks against Axis-occupied Europe, the two air forces agreed on a division of labor. The RAF would attack urban areas by night, and the U.S. AAF would attack selected targets deemed vital to the enemy's military effort by daylight. The RAF had found that their planes had difficulty accurately bombing small targets without suffering unacceptable losses and had shifted to targeting entire urban districts including residential areas.[22] The AAF encountered similar operational difficulties that undermined the distinction between American precision bombing, which seemed to promise greater immunity for noncombatants, and British area bombing, which left very little room for it. Weather, enemy air defenses, and equipment and techniques not sufficient to provide expected bombing accuracy made bombing attacks hard to control.

However, operational constraints were not the only forces that broke down the distinction between precision bombing and area bombing. The hope that bombing could demoralize civilian populations and hasten surrender tempted the AAF into attacks on smaller towns and urban areas of marginal industrial importance. Organizational interests also drove the AAF toward more indiscriminate destruction. Its leaders wanted to demonstrate the importance of the AAF's contribution to fighting the war. Often unable to provide evidence that bombing had destroyed particular targets, the AAF pointed to statistics on sorties flown, tons of bombs dropped, and acreage destroyed, which served as surrogate measures of the AAF's contribution to the war effort and a justification of its costs. Boosting these statistics became a way of adding to AAF prestige even when the results hardly constituted a precise use of force.

Shifts in target selection as the war progressed, likewise, increased the risks for civilians. With the Allies' Normandy invasion, American planes increasingly directed their attacks against transportation targets, such as railroad yards, and these targets were usually located in the midst of cities and towns. In the Pacific, General Curtis E. LeMay's Twenty First Air Force adopted fire-bombing and area destruction as an alternative means of pursuing the goal of precision bombing. Precision attacks had produced disappointing results against Japanese industries. Because small and widely scattered workshops fed manufactured parts to larger factories, LeMay sought to disrupt production by destroying the urban areas containing both the small workshops and the larger factories. The burning of Tokyo and other Japanese cities was the result. By 1945, American air power in Europe and Japan was demolishing entire sections of cities and killing thousands of civilians in the process. Warfare against an entire society, total war, had become a practicable strategy.[23]

Despite the city-destruction in which the country's armed forces were engaging, American leaders insisted that the United States was continuing to adhere to a policy of precision bombing, and few on the side of the Allies questioned the attacks on cities during the war. Shortly after American planes joined the RAF in burning Dresden in February 1945, Secretary of War Henry L. Stimson assured the public: "We will continue to bomb military targets and . . . there has been no change in the policy against conducting 'terror bombings' against civilian populations." When asked about the burning of Tokyo at a press conference, an Air Force spokesperson General Lauris Norstad denied that there had been any change in the Air Force's basic policy of "pin-point" precision bombing.[24]

During the war, the bombing of cities generated little sustained discussion. One of the most prominent debates in the American press was sparked in 1944 by an English pacifist Vera Brittain who attacked Allied policy as "massacre by bombing." Her article, which appeared in the American pacifist journal *Fellowship,* but attracted the notice of the *New York Times,* criticized the bombing of cities and was preceded by an introduction signed by twenty-eight clergymen and antiwar activists. However, many of the reactions to Brittain's essay condemned her position and the controversy soon faded.[25] Between the reassuring official statements and the scarcity of dissent, Americans were not forced during the war to confront the challenge that the new massively destructive methods of warfare posed to noncombatant immunity.

1.3 The Atomic Bomb

The atomic bombings of Japan, however, focused American attention on the dilemma of killing noncombatants, and the sudden end of the war freed Americans from exigencies that restrained debate, dissent, and self-doubt. Reaction to the atomic bomb and the destruction of Hiroshima and Nagasaki revealed disagreement and uncertainty over noncombatant immunity. On the one hand, concerns about harming civilians did not prevent the use of the atomic bomb from being popular, and a few Americans appeared ready to discard the notion of noncombatant immunity entirely. On the other, a vocal minority protested against the new weapon precisely because it killed civilians indiscriminately.

The atomic bomb inspired extensive public discussion and widespread anxiety. It captured the attention of most Americans at least momentarily and remained a prominent topic in the media for several years as Americans tried to puzzle out the implications of this massively destructive technology of war. The historian Paul Boyer has suggested that the revelation of the atomic bomb was "a psychic event of almost unprecedented proportions." According to a 1946 opinion study from the Social Science Research Council, 98 percent of the adult population knew of the atomic bomb.[26]

The advent of the atomic bomb introduced multiple problems for Americans to consider, not the least the fear that the weapon might one day be used against them. However, the killing of noncombatants was one of the central dilemmas the new weapon raised. The attention that the atomic bombings attracted meant that the details of the devastation of Hiroshima and Nagasaki swiftly became public knowledge. Unlike the conventional city bombing, which the press had passed over quickly and had treated in terms that ignored or obscured civilian deaths, the atomic bombings produced thousands of words and images in the media that made it difficult for Americans to deny the harm that U.S. weapons had done to noncombatants.

Initially, President Harry S. Truman attempted to minimize the impression that civilians had been attacked with the atomic bomb. In his announcement of the first atomic attack, he referred to Hiroshima as "a Japanese Army base." Several days later, Truman elaborated, "The world will note that the first atomic bomb was dropped on Hiroshima, a military base. That was because we wished in this first attack to avoid, insofar as possible, the killing of civilians."[27] However, relatively quickly Americans came to acknowledge that the atomic bombs had killed large numbers of civilians and completely devastated large parts of two cities. One example of this acknowledgement of civilian suffering was John Hersey's 1946 essay "Hiroshima." Originally appearing in the *New Yorker*, the essay described the experiences of six Hiroshima residents during the attack and as a book became a best seller.

While knowledge of the mass killing became difficult for Americans to avoid, concerns about harming civilians did not prevent overwhelming approval of the use of the atomic bombs, even when Americans understood that cities had been the targets. Opinion polls from 1945 bare out this attitude. A Gallup poll in August revealed that 85 percent approved of the use of the atomic bomb against Japanese cities. A poll for *Fortune* magazine conducted by Elmo Roper suggested that most Americans were not remorseful over the destruction of Hiroshima and Nagasaki. The poll asked a representative sample of Americans to select the statement that best described their attitude toward the atomic bombing of Japan. Fifty-three and a half percent chose the statement: "We should have used the two bombs on cities, just as we did." Only 4.5 percent believed, "We should not have used any atomic bombs at all." A slightly larger minority of 13.8 percent selected the statement: "We should have dropped one first on some unpopulated region, to show the Japanese its power, and dropped the second one on a city only if they hadn't surrendered after the first one." However, 22.7 percent of respondents agreed with the sentiment: "We should have quickly used many more of the bombs before Japan had a chance to surrender." This sizable minority of "disappointed savagery," as *Fortune* magazine called it, desired even greater devastation of Japan. They did not reject noncombatant immunity explicitly, but their response suggested profound indifference.[28]

In their reactions to the atomic attacks, some Americans did appear ready to discard any notion of noncombatant immunity. One wrote the *Washington Post* to ask why Allied soldiers should die before Japanese women and children. The writer believed, "It's just as wrong for [the soldiers] to die as for civilians to die." Another letter to the *Louisville Courier-Journal* praised the use of the atomic bomb and urged the annihilation of all life in Japan. "The life of one of my sons or any other American boy is worth the life of everything that walks, creeps, or crawls in Japan," it said. "I think they should drop enough atomic bombs to destroy all life in Japan and leave it a desolated waste." These sentiments for extermination followed similar expressions from the war. A December 1944 Gallup poll found that 13 percent of respondents favored the killing of all Japanese. In April 1945, the chairman of the War Manpower Commission Paul V. McNutt told a public audience that he favored "the extermination of the Japanese in toto." When asked to clarify whether he meant the Japanese military or the people as a whole, he admitted that he meant all Japanese. A week later he told the press that his comments were his personal views and not official policy. A minority of Americans had considered leaving the norm of noncombatant immunity behind completely and turning the war into a purposeful extermination of an entire people.[29]

More common than people who expressed their own indifference to noncombatant immunity were those who concluded that the devastation of World War II demonstrated that the American people no longer saw the value of protecting civilians. This belief manifested itself among those disturbed by the killing of civilians, not by those insensitive to it, but this thinking encouraged a perception that Americans had abandoned noncombatant immunity. In an August 1945 editorial for *U.S. News and World Report*, David Lawrence saw a change in values. "A few decades ago man did not think it fair or sportsman-like to attack non-combatants," he wrote. "War was reserved for armies and navies." ABC radio commentator Raymond Gram Swing worried that the shift in values was not a temporary wartime lapse. Swing felt that almost a year after the war "there has been no snapping back to the prewar attitude of condemning a war waged against civilians, no nationwide or worldwide campaign to restore the thinking of past times." Writing in 1947, David Lilienthal, the chairman of the Atomic Energy Commission (AEC) believed restraints on violence had become a thing of the past. "All ethical limitations of warfare are gone, not because the means of destruction are more cruel or painful or otherwise hideous in their effect upon combatants, but because there are no individual combatants," he wrote in his diary. "The fences are gone." To many Americans in the late 1940s, the boundaries placed on the violence of war that had offered protection to noncombatants appeared irretrievably lost.[30]

However, other Americans protested against the atomic bombings precisely because they had destroyed cities and harmed innocent civilians. Church leaders, the religious press, social critics, and peace organizations were the main sources of these sentiments. Two weeks after Hiroshima, thirty-four prominent Protestant clergy wrote President Truman to protest the destruction. One of the signers, Henry Emerson Fosdick questioned the justification of the attacks in nationally broadcast sermons. "Saying that Japan was guilty and deserved it, gets us nowhere," the minister declared. "The mothers and babies of Hiroshima and Nagasaki did not deserve it." The historian Robert C. Batchelder has concluded that Catholic theologians and journals were "nearly unanimous in condemning the bomb's use." Their revulsion at killing noncombatants was the primary reason. In March 1946, a commission of Protestant theologians and scholars chaired by Robert L. Calhoun presented its report "Atomic Warfare and the Christian Faith" to the Federal Council of Churches. The report concluded that the attacks against Japan were "morally indefensible" and pointed to the "indiscriminate slaughter of noncombatants" as an important reason for this verdict.

The social critic Lewis Mumford and the pacifist leader A. J. Muste took their condemnations of the attacks one step further. They compared the use of the atomic bombs with the crimes of the Nazis. Mumford labeled the massively destructive methods used by the Allies, including the atomic bomb, "genocide," a word newly coined to describe the extermination of peoples that the Nazis had undertaken. Muste put it bluntly in his 1947 book *Not by Might*: "If Dachau was a crime, Hiroshima is a crime." To Muste, this was final proof that war must be abandoned because of its atrocious character. In their criticism of the nuclear attacks, this vocal minority upheld the norm of noncombatant immunity, and some urged the abandonment of massively destructive war as the means to preserve it.[31]

Calling the atomic attacks on Japan "genocide" evoked powerful sentiments against killing the innocent, which the full revelation of Nazi atrocities had reinvigorated. While Americans discussed the implications of nuclear weapons, the Allied governments established war crimes tribunals to hold Axis leaders accountable for harm against noncombatants. The killing of innocent civilians would become the international epitome of evil and symbolize the cruelty of an enemy that the Allies had sacrificed so much to defeat. During the war, the scope of German atrocities had slowly been revealed to Americans. In November 1942, the State Department had gathered enough evidence that it authorized Rabbi Stephen Wise, a prominent American Jewish leader, to announce that Germany was conducting a policy of extermination against the Jews. The Allied War Crimes Declaration, the following month, and the Moscow Declaration, a year later, condemned German atrocities and pledged the Allies to try the perpetrators. American liberation of the Buchenwald and Dachau concentration camps in the spring of 1945 attracted extensive media attention and gave many Americans their first view of what would later be known as the Holocaust. In 1945, Americans generally did not see Nazi atrocities as a special crime against Jews as they increasingly would in the 1960s and as the term "Holocaust" would come to denote. Instead, Jews were seen as one out of many groups of civilians slaughtered by the Nazi regime. This panoply of murder composed a picture of general German barbarism in the war and made the Nazis almost universally reviled as the archmalefactors of the twentieth century.[32]

War crimes trials played an important role in vilifying the Nazis and their Axis collaborators. In 1945, the Allies established an international tribunal in Nuremberg to prosecute the twenty-two surviving Germans that the Allies believed to be the most responsible for the war and its atrocities. Eighteen were indicted for war crimes which included murder or ill-treatment of civilians in occupied territory, plunder of public or private property, and wanton destruction of cities and towns. Eighteen were charged with crimes against humanity, which the Nuremberg tribunal's charter defined as "murder, extermination, enslavement, deportation, and other inhumane acts committed against any civilian population." At the conclusion of the trial in 1946, eleven of the defendants were hanged, all convicted of crimes against humanity and all but one convicted of war crimes. During the three subsequent years, the formerly allied countries held trials of thousands of German war criminals in their own zones of occupation. The United States held twelve subsequent trials in Nuremberg, which convicted 1,814 Germans of war crimes and executed 283.[33]

A parallel set of trials occurred in Asia. From 1946 to 1948, the International Military Tribunal for the Far East tried twenty-eight Japanese military and civilian leaders for engaging in a conspiracy to commit atrocities. The prosecutors charged they had unleashed the "wholesale destruction of human lives, not alone on the field of battle ... but in the homes, hospitals, and orphanages, in factories and fields; and the victims would be the young and the old, the well and the infirm—men, women, and children alike." Between 1945 and 1951, several thousand more former Japanese soldiers were found guilty of committing atrocities and war crimes by military tribunals throughout Asia.[34]

The charge of "victor's justice" haunted the postwar trials. To some the dividing line between Axis crimes and Allied actions that killed innocent civilians was not clear. Justice Radhabinod Pal of India, in his dissenting opinion at the Tokyo trial, argued that the allied powers' use of the atom bomb was the nearest equivalent in the war in Asia to the Nazis' "policy of indiscriminate murder."[35] Conscious of the snares of hypocrisy, none of the tribunals had prosecuted any of the defeated for promiscuous bombing of civilians. Although the war crimes trials perpetuated the notion that the killing of innocent civilians was an atrocious crime, Americans were left with the challenge of clearly distinguishing their actions during the past war and their strategies for fighting a future war in an atomic age from the crimes of the Nazis and their confederates.

As during the interwar period, international law appeared to lack promise in providing Americans with immediate deliverance from their dilemma. The late 1940s saw two developments in international humanitarian law that addressed harm to noncombatants in war, but beyond reinforcing an international norm against attacking civilians, they did not hold much promise, to those few Americans who paid attention to them, of resolving the problems of massively destructive war. From 1945 to 1949, the United States cooperated in the drafting of four new Geneva Conventions on war victims, and in 1948, the United Nations completed the writing of a Genocide Convention which the U.S. Senate took under consideration.

The four Geneva Conventions of 1949 were the result of almost four years of international negotiation and effort led by the International Committee of the Red Cross (ICRC). The ICRC wanted the conventions to codify further the rights of war victims and the responsibilities that belligerent nations had to them. Three of the Geneva Conventions of 1949 updated the nineteenth century Red Cross Conventions on the treatment of the sick and wounded in warfare and the Geneva Convention of 1929 on prisoners of war. The fourth convention introduced an entirely new body of law on the protection of civilians in time of war. It delineated duties of occupying powers such as ensuring adequate food and medical supplies for civilians, established elaborate rules for the management of civilian internment camps, and prohibited pillaging and collective punishments against occupied civilian populations. The new convention did little to address the threat that increased firepower posed for noncombatants. It contained a provision for the voluntary establishment of neutralized zones, in which noncombatants could be gathered, that belligerents were to grant immunity from attack when the zones were completely free of military activity. However, proposals raised by the Soviet Union to ban weapons of mass destruction under the conventions failed to gain support. The United States signed the four new conventions along with forty-four other governments by the end of 1949, but in the American press, the Geneva Conventions received little attention. What notice they did receive reflected skepticism that the new laws could do much to mitigate the horrors of modern war.[36]

Written in 1948, the U.N. Convention on Genocide gained a public hearing by a subcommittee of the Senate Foreign Relations Committee in early 1950. The Genocide Convention, which sought to outlaw the destruction of national, racial, or religious groups whether in peacetime or in war, reinforced the international norm that civilian populations should not be indiscriminately killed. However, the Senate did not ratify the Genocide Convention in 1949, and the convention remained unratified by the United States until 1988. Ratification did not fail out of insensitivity to the horrors of genocide. It failed because of objections to the wording of the convention that raised concerns that the law would usurp American domestic law, be applied against white

Americans' treatment of African Americans in the south, and not be applicable to the brutal Soviet treatment of political and class groups in the Soviet Union. Its failure, though, illustrated the lack of promise that international law by itself held for solving Americans' dilemma over noncombatant immunity.[37]

1.4 Contested Boundaries between Combat and Atrocity

The dilemma, which the events of 1945 made so visible, left Americans in the years following the war struggling to define the boundaries between combat and atrocity, between war and genocide. Countervailing circumstances buffeted Americans and their attitudes toward the protection of civilians. New massively destructive methods of warfare had apparently helped to win the war, and these new weapons held the promise of bolstering American security in peacetime. However, the American government had committed itself to punishing its enemies for killing innocent civilians. At the time that the norm of noncombatant immunity faced a challenge to its continued relevance and practicality like it had never faced before, the Holocaust made the killing of the innocent the international epitome of atrocity. Americans appeared torn by uncertainty and contradictory attitudes toward noncombatant immunity. Two groups offered opposing solutions to the dilemma, one suggesting the abandonment of noncombatant immunity and the other abstention from massively destructive methods of war. However, both groups appeared to be small, if vocal, minorities, whose potential influence remained unclear.

This dilemma inspired a decade-long series of public discussions among Americans about noncombatant immunity. From these discussions emerged an uneasy reconciliation of the norm with American methods of warfare. The leading participants in these exchanges were not theologians or philosophers. These discussions of values occurred among a broader public attuned to international affairs and among officials attentive to public opinion. This foreign policy public consisted largely of nongovernmental organizations such as peace groups, veterans associations, and churches and their supporters as well as journalists reporting on international affairs and their readership.

Historians have started to examine the problem of noncombatants in warfare.[38] Histories have explained the prelude to the dilemma of 1945 and have begun to examine aspects of its legacy, but none has made noncombatant immunity in the crucial period after 1945, when Americans struggled to evaluate what they had wrought in war, a focus of their study. Works on the history of the just war tradition and international humanitarian law have described the intellectual and institutional development of the idea of noncombatant immunity. How broader publics engaged and practiced noncombatant immunity has not been a central project of this literature.[39]

The early history of bombing cities has attracted close scholarly attention. Several works have focused on strategic bombing through the end of World War II,[40] but this scope misses a broader military and cultural significance of the aerial destruction of 1945. Americans at the time, and since, have largely found strategic bombing so unsettling precisely because it kills noncombatants and destroys property indiscriminately. The bomber was a novel technology, capable of massive destruction and difficult to control, but so were the tank, napalm, and the atomic bomb. What charged their use with such cultural and political significance was the norm of noncombatant immunity.

Works on early American attitudes toward the atomic bomb offer explanations for why Americans came to accept such a frightening weapon. They argue that many Americans began to hope that the weapons would never be used and yet provide security for the United States either through deterrence or agreements on the international control of atomic energy. These works also emphasize that the acceptance of nuclear weapons was eased by hopes that the peaceful use of atomic energy would bring vast benefits. This literature does not consider how Americans attempted to reconcile even these weapons of mass destruction with the norm of noncombatant immunity.[41]

Although the problem of civilian casualties has attracted consistent attention in studies of the Vietnam War, the works have treated the issue simply as a feature of that war and have not placed it in a broader historical context.[42] American concern over civilian casualties did not originate with the Vietnam War nor did that war constitute the greatest challenge for American adherence to the norm of noncombatant immunity in modern times.

Other histories have gone too far in depicting the threat that the developments of World War II posed for the norm. These histories have suggested a moral revolution or a cultural shift during the war in which Americans came to accept attacks on civilians and therefore, in effect, the abandonment of noncombatant immunity.[43] The dilemma of 1945 left an important legacy, but that legacy was not a moral revolution in which Americans abandoned a normative belief in noncombatant immunity.

In the decade after World War II, Americans attempted to reconcile massively destructive methods of warfare and noncombatant immunity instead of abandoning either one. They valued both the security that they believed their deadly arsenal provided and their identity as a humane people. Through public dialogue, Americans fashioned an uneasy reconciliation that fit their interests but also accommodated international constraints. The reconciliation followed two paths: one that perpetuated older ideas in the face of changing circumstances and another which introduced a significant change in American thinking about noncombatant immunity. As they had during the war, many Americans tenaciously clung to the optimistic assumption that violence in war could still be used in a discriminating manner despite the increased destructiveness of weapons. In effect, they continued to deny a contradiction between the American way of war and noncombatant immunity, placing their faith in the ability to control and direct precisely the violence of modern war. However, this denial of a dilemma was no longer enough. The Korean War and the hydrogen bomb made it difficult to ignore completely that American military action had inflicted or would inflict massive harm on civilians. Therefore, in the early 1950s, a new American interpretation of noncombatant immunity emerged which incorporated elastic definitions of a "military target" in war, but more significantly made intent the dividing line between justifiable and unjustifiable action. It became common for Americans to claim that any harm the United States inflicted on noncombatants was unintentional, a tragedy the responsibility for which was diffuse. The notion of atrocity for Americans had shrunk. Only the calculated killing of people uninvolved in the fighting of wars remained generally condemned as inhumane and indefensible.

The rest of this book examines the unfolding of these two dominant modes of reconciliation in the decade after World War II. Chapters 2 and 3 establish that by the late 1940s, few Americans advocated abandoning either noncombatant immunity or massively destructive techniques of war, a reluctance which left many struggling to reconcile the two. Chapter 2 examines the "Revolt of the Admirals" in 1949 and the discussion surrounding this widely publicized criticism of U.S. war plans by top-ranking admirals in congressional hearings. The public discussion revealed that almost no one was willing to claim that attacks against noncombatants were a legitimate method of warfare. Chapter 3 focuses on the public discussion generated in early 1950 by news that the U.S. government was proceeding with the development of the vastly more destructive hydrogen bomb. This discussion demonstrated substantial public support for the new weapon despite continuing concerns about how instruments of such massive and indiscriminate violence could be reconciled with the avoidance of harm to noncombatants.

Chapter 4 is the first of two chapters which illustrate the persistence of the optimistic notion that violence in war could still be employed discriminately despite increasingly destructive firepower. It focuses on the discussion and implementation of the bombing of North Korea in the first year of the Korean War and on the failure of U.S. armed forces to manage Korean refugees, a failure which contributed to such incidents as the shooting of civilians by American soldiers near No Gun Ri. The chapter argues that American concerns over noncombatant immunity initially imposed significant limits on violence in the Korean War, but these restraints still left Koreans highly vulnerable and faded as the war progressed. As the war became more destructive, an expansive definition of what constituted a "military target" helped to sustain optimistic American views of the war. The vague distinction between military and civilian segments of an enemy society allowed American military and civilian officials to stretch the term "military target" to include virtually every human-made structure. This expanded definition made it easier for the American public to ignore the widespread destruction and to believe that their armed forces were not attacking civilians.

Chapter 5 examines the introduction of tactical nuclear weapons to the American public in 1951. These weapons, in theory, promised to be arms for use against an enemy's military, rather than for the obliteration of cities. The chapter argues that the optimism of many Americans about their ability to control any war's violence was so strong that they believed that even nuclear weapons, the epitome of mass killing, could be tamed and used only against military targets. Americans did not simply hope to avoid the use of nuclear weapons; many came to believe that the weapons, even used in a future war, could be made to conform to a notion of noncombatant immunity and, therefore, made less horrible.

Chapters 6 and 7 depict the increasing importance that intentions gained in rationalizing harm to noncombatants. Chapter 6 argues that many Americans found it difficult to deny that U.S. weapons contributed to the vast civil destruction caused by the Korean War, but most hesitated to hold their country responsible for the harm. Instead, they emphasized evidence of American intentions to avoid injuring civilians such as the relief aid that the U.S. government and American charities were offering to war victims and the advance warnings to civilians of air attacks. Chapter 7 examines public reaction to the incorporation of thermonuclear weapons into the American arsenal in the mid-1950s. Most acknowledged these vastly more destructive hydrogen bombs would kill many civilians if they were used, but the country's increasing dependence on these weapons did not strip Americans of their attachment to noncombatant immunity nor even of their optimism that violence in war could still be used discriminately. What this dependence did do was reinforce the belief that the culturally significant distinction was not whether U.S. weapons actually killed civilians, but whether Americans intended to kill civilians with their weapons.

The final chapter explores the extended legacy of America's confrontation with the dilemma of modern war and mass killing. Optimistic denial, elastic definitions of military targets, and the importance of intention permeated discussion throughout the second half of the twentieth century and beyond. They infused discussions of nuclear strategy from the late 1950s onward, the Vietnam War, and post-Cold War U.S. interventions in the Persian Gulf, Afghanistan, and Iraq. The controversies surrounding civilian casualties in the Vietnam War had their foundations laid with the uneasy reconciliation of U.S. military policies with the norm of noncombatant immunity. Moreover, the form that the reconciliation took obscured a torturous question. Americans largely avoided discussing the disturbing likelihood that a conflict existed between the preservation of American soldiers' lives and those of noncombatants.

In accommodating the international norm, the American reinterpretation of the noncombatant immunity placed some limits on the use of violence. One clear limit manifested itself in Americans' unwillingness to accept the idea that civilian populations themselves were legitimate targets in war.

However, the limits on violence provided meager protection for civilians caught in the midst of American wars, and the reinterpretation of noncombatant immunity helped to justify violence as well. When Americans believed their armed forces did not intend to harm noncombatants and attacked only military targets, they remained more accepting of war's violence. Collateral damage became, to many, an unfortunate but acceptable cost of war.

2

The "Revolt of the Admirals" and the Limits of Mass Destruction

The destruction that the United States had inflicted upon Japan and Germany during World War II raised questions about Americans' continued commitment to the tradition of noncombatant immunity, both for contemporaries and those who have looked back on this period. There were good reasons for this uncertainty. Following the war, the country armed itself with a growing arsenal of atomic weapons. Americans' talk was not more reassuring than their behavior. For four years after the war, it was difficult to tell from what Americans said publicly that they had not abandoned the custom of sparing civilians in war. However, public comment provided a hazy view of the issue during this period. After the initial tumult over the atomic bomb had died down in 1946, public attention had not been sharply focused on the problem of noncombatant immunity and so clear expressions of sentiments were rare.

This changed in the fall of 1949. At that time, a dramatic set of congressional hearings, sparked by disagreements over military strategy and rivalry among the armed services, provoked another examination of the contradictions between noncombatant immunity and massively destructive methods of warfare. The hearings and the public comment on them revealed that few were willing to advocate attacks on noncombatants as a method of warfare or to propose the abandonment of noncombatant immunity. Although it had taken several years after the war to become clear, World War II had not ended Americans' support for the norm of noncombatant immunity.

2.1 The Specter of Irrelevance

In the years right after World War II, it was not difficult to form the impression that noncombatant immunity had lost its relevance for Americans. The atomic air offensive was becoming the heart of American notions of security in a post-war world. Many Americans placed their hopes in the bomber and the U.S. monopoly on atomic weapons to defend their nation. In theory, the awful power of the atomic bomb, solely in American hands, would deter a war or ensure that the United States would triumph if a war did break out.

Therefore, Americans had strong motivations to focus on the destructive power of the weapon and to neglect its disturbing implications. Not surprisingly, awe at the atomic bomb's destructive power overshadowed the few expressions of concern over the potential threat to noncombatants. According to the logic of the American atomic monopoly, the more destructive the weapon, the more secure the United States would seem.

Air power was the second leg of U.S. security in the post-war world, and its growing importance became an additional sign of the ambiguous American commitment to noncombatant immunity. After the war, the Air Force struggled to become an independent military service coequal with the Army and the Navy in the U.S. military establishment. One of its strongest rationales for independence was the Air Force's ability to carry out strategic air warfare: attacks in which airplanes inflicted damage on an enemy far behind the battle lines. If planes independently of land and sea forces could harm or even defeat an enemy nation, an air service deserved autonomy, the airmen argued. The destructive power of the atomic bomb enhanced the perception that strategic air warfare would inflict grievous injury on an enemy and be an important element in achieving a military victory.

In 1947, the National Security Act unified the Army and Navy within a single organization, the National Military Establishment, which was later renamed the Department of Defense. The Air Force effectively achieved its goal of independence by obtaining equal status with the two other services within the National Military Establishment. In its new role, the Air Force came to enjoy a popularity that challenged the privileged position that the Navy had traditionally occupied with the Congress and the public. Since the Soviet Union was a great land power with a weak navy, the Air Force and its strategic bombers offered an attractive alternative to the creation of a large land army or navy to provide security in the face of increasing tensions with the Soviet Union. However, the popularity of the Air Force in part rested upon the belief in a uniquely powerful and effective atomic bomb.

The Air Force's rise to prominence encouraged loose talk that seemed to contradict a continued commitment to noncombatant immunity. Out of enthusiasm for their cause, Air Force leaders and their boosters emphasized the destructiveness of air power and encouraged a popular notion that American plans to fight the next war required the obliteration of enemy cities and their civilian populations. Most Air Force statements that discussed the strategic air offensive proposed for the next war referred to its goal as the destruction of the enemy's "war-making capacity." However, some official statements elaborated on the potential for devastation that air power possessed. In late 1945, just weeks before he would become the commanding general of the Air Force, Carl A. Spaatz wrote in *Collier's* magazine that future wars required "smashing the enemy's whole organism" and that a successful offensive "must be total in every way, designed to destroy an enemy's home base and spare him nothing."[1]

The Air Force's civilian leaders made similar public statements. Secretary of the Air Force W. Stuart Symington suggested the complete devastation of the United States' next enemy in a war. At the commencement of the Air War College in 1949, he said, "But should we ever be committed again to war, we must make sure that the end of those hostilities leaves little likelihood that the enemy's military threat will soon rise again, phoenix-like, from the ashes. We must destroy the enemy's war-making capacity for a long time to come...." The destructive power of strategic bombing would be crucial in achieving this national objective, Symington said, and his phoenix simile left much room for imagining the total devastation of an enemy country.[2]

An extreme statement of the American intent to target enemy civilians appeared in a series of articles that William Bradford Huie wrote for *Reader's Digest*. Huie was an enthusiastic supporter of the Air Force, and his articles claimed that he had close ties with some of the top generals in that service. In one of his articles, Huie urged that to prevent a war, the Soviet Union should be warned of the dire consequences it would face if it attacked the United States or one of its allies. Huie wanted the Soviets to know that "a staggering proportion of the inhabitants of Russia's key cities — millions of persons — can be killed or maimed in the first raids" and that the United States could do to Russia "what Rome did to Carthage." Huie was worried that the Soviet generals did not adequately understand what the United States was willing to do to protect itself. He was concerned by "the ominous intelligence that some of the Russian generals are not even convinced that we *will* [emphasis in original] employ the atomic weapons against civilians."[3]

The official statements and those purporting to be official, which suggested that the United States had adopted a policy of attacking noncombatants, provided a basis for a broader popular notion that the U.S. military planned to attack cities and civilian populations in a future war. In early 1949, this popular notion appeared in radio news broadcasts. ABC's Ray Henle commented, "Many Americans — probably most Americans — believe that our military forces are in a position to blast Russia to pieces, if she dared to attack us, that we got a big pile of atomic bombs, that we could shower down on Russian cities, from our huge bombers, and literally wipe those cities off the map...."[4] The notion was also reflected in the comments of R. E. Lapp, a physicist who became a frequent commentator on atomic warfare in the press. In an interview in *U.S. News and World Report*, Lapp said, "It is well known that the war plans [of the United States] are based upon an atomic blitz of Russian cities."[5] A United Press (UP) story in March 1949 contributed to the notion that American war plans targeted Soviet cities. The article reported that military planners had selected seventy "strategic targets" in Russia as possible objectives in the event of a war. It also noted that "by coincidence or not" the Rand-McNally world atlas identified seventy Russian cities which had a population of 100,000 or more.[6] From this tentative suggestion that the United States might be targeting cities, others quickly began writing as if cities were in fact the targets.[7]

Reinforcing the assumption that cities would be the targets of American atomic weapons, military authorities avoided discussion of the use of the atomic bomb against an enemy's military forces in the field. Since American military leaders assumed that atomic bombs would be scarce for years to come, they did not view the atomic bomb as a tactical weapon in the late 1940s.

A vague definition of the term "strategic bombing" buttressed the impression in many minds that the phrase denoted attacks on cities and noncombatants. In public discussion, strategic bombing was often contrasted with tactical bombing or the tactical use of air power. With the reluctance of military professionals to draw a precise distinction between tactics and strategy, the new term suffered from an imprecise definition. For example, Lieutenant General George C. Kenney was unable to give a congressional committee any definition of "strategic bombing" when asked to in public hearings. Since General Kenney was the head of Strategic Air Command (SAC), the new branch of the Air Force responsible for strategic air warfare, his inability to define the new term demonstrated just how vague its meaning was. The Joint Chiefs of Staff (JCS) had defined "strategic air warfare" in 1948, but this term was rarely used in public discussions.[8] Without a standard definition of "strategic bombing" and with the ambiguous official statements about the destructiveness of air power, many equated the phrase with area bombing and attacks on cities and civilian populations as such. Writing in an Air Force journal, a British air power booster J. M. Spaight felt the problem of the conflation of "strategic bombing" with attacks on civilians had become acute enough to constitute a reason for coining a new term free of such connotations to replace "strategic bombing."[9]

2.2 A Critique of Strategic Bombing

Spaight had good reason to worry. Since the war, a small group of critics had led an increasingly vocal challenge to the Air Force's cherished mission of strategic air warfare. Much of the criticism stemmed from rivalry between the military services, which gave impetus to disagreements over the best strategy for fighting future wars. However, as one of their central arguments, the Air Force's critics pointed to the negative consequences of attacks on civilians, which they believed strategic bombing entailed. This theme in the critique of strategic bombing hinted at the cultural power that the norm of noncombatant immunity retained.

Only days after the end of World War II, Hoffman Nickerson, a former Army major and writer on military affairs, attacked the Allies' use of air power in the war with a scathing chapter in his book *Arms and Policy, 1939–1944*. In 1942, Nickerson had provocatively labeled strategic bombing "baby-killing" in a *Harper's Magazine* article. In his book, he employed arguments about the undesirability of harming noncombatants to challenge the value of strategic bombing. He contended that it was doubtful that the bombing of cities had saved Allied lives or that "baby killing" could achieve a peace for the victor better than the one that preceded the conflict. The atomic bomb, while certainly more terrifying, was only another implement for "baby killing" to Nickerson.[10]

Nickerson was a lonely voice in 1945, but by 1949, criticism of strategic bombing against cities had spread in the United States. An emerging international dialogue on noncombatant immunity had encouraged this trend. In the international community, Americans were exposed to supposed friends and potential enemies who questioned the strategy of bombing cities and condemned the atomic bomb as an implement of extermination.

The intersection of controversy in Britain over strategic bombing with the undercurrent of criticism in the United States helped to broaden American discussion of the issues. After the war, the British confronted their own ghosts about the bombing of civilians. They went through a process of questioning the wisdom of the RAF's policy of targeting residential districts of German cities and towns in nighttime bomber raids. This process spawned a number of books in the late 1940s, which questioned the effectiveness of strategic bombing and condemned the aerial destruction of cities and their civilian inhabitants. Three books in particular attracted attention in the United States: B. H. Liddell Hart's *The Revolution in Warfare*, J. F. C. Fuller's *The Second World War*, and P. M. S. Blackett's *Fear, War, and the Bomb*. In arguing that the tremendous new powers of mechanized warfare had transformed interstate conflict for the worse, the military strategist Liddell Hart lamented that air operations in the Second World War had "produced such a wholesale massacring of civilians as to recall the practice of barbarian times." J. F. C. Fuller largely agreed. Major General Fuller, an expert on tank warfare, asserted that the destruction of urban areas and the industry of Germany and Japan had been wasted effort and not essential to the defeat of those countries. The politically senseless destruction of cities and the slaughter of civilians betokened a reversion to barbarism and the decline of religion that Fuller blamed as much on Britain and the United States as on Germany, Russia, and Japan. P. M. S. Blackett, a Nobel laureate in physics, disparaged the effectiveness of the atomic bomb as a weapon of war and claimed that Americans had accepted attacks on civilians as a method of warfare while the Soviets and their military had repudiated such tactics.[11]

The Soviets had indeed attempted to distance themselves from massively destructive methods of warfare. Far behind the United States in the development of strategic air power and lacking the atomic bomb, the Soviet Union found it easy to denounce nuclear warfare and aggressively support noncombatant immunity. As Soviet-American relations deteriorated, the Soviet Union added a line to its propaganda. Supplementing its accusations that the leaders of the United States were warmongers, the Soviets began to suggest that Americans planned to use atrocious means to win their imperialistic wars. The opening salvo in this campaign came in the summer of 1949 at the conference called by the ICRC to update the Geneva conventions on war victims. The Soviet delegation to the conference introduced a resolution that said, "The use in the event of future war of a bacteriological or chemical means of war as well as atomic weapon or any other weapon intended for the mass extermination of populations is incompatible with the elementary principles of international law and is contrary to the honor and conscience of people."[12] The resolution was defeated at the conference and the entire incident received minimal press attention in the United States,[13] but the Soviets continued to condemn American methods of warfare into the early 1950s to the increasing consternation of American officials concerned about their country's international image.

Throughout 1949, criticism of the bombing of noncombatants attracted an increasing amount of attention in the American mainstream press. Marshall Andrews, a writer on military affairs, wrote two articles for the *Washington Post* in January criticizing the strategy of city bombing. David Lawrence, the founder and editor of *U.S. News and World Report* and a syndicated columnist, criticized the U.S. military's overreliance in its war plans on the use of atomic bombs against cities. The military editor for the *New York Times* Hanson W. Baldwin began to doubt whether a strategy to destroy Soviet cities and civilians in a future war could be reconciled with American national objectives. Likewise, the prominent columnist and commentator Walter Lippmann questioned the efficacy of the strategic bombing of cities in winning a war and contended that the destruction of civil society caused by such methods would hamper the establishment of a lasting peace.[14]

With this undercurrent of criticism, some of the supporters of strategic air power sought to revive the notion of precision bombing and to distance air power from the methods of area bombing and the indiscriminate destruction of cities. While many of the air power boosters in the late 1940s chose to emphasize the destructive potential of the atomic bomb and ceased to mention any need for continued precision or discrimination in strategic bombing, two books appeared in 1948 and 1949 that argued for the importance of strategic bombing again took up the theme of precision air strikes that had been so prominent during the war. J. M. Spaight, who had served as principal assistant secretary in the British Air Ministry during World War II and wrote prolifically in support of air power, believed that air power could disarm an enemy by destroying its war potential. This could be done through precision attacks against the enemy's transportation network and oil supplies. Spaight argued that general attacks against cities and civilian populations, which critics of air power called inhumane and wasteful,[15] would be unnecessary. In his extended analysis of the effectiveness of strategic air power, Stefan T. Possony, a professor of political science who had served as a consultant to the Air Force, also argued that selective bombing was superior to "total bombing." Total destruction of an enemy would only be a liability to the victor, he argued.[16]

This continued support for precision bombing was fed in part by the reports of the United States Strategic Bombing Survey. This survey of the use of Allied air power against Germany and Japan employed hundreds of civilian specialists and military personnel for more than a year and produced over 200 reports. The reports emphasized the vital contribution that strategic bombing made to the Allied victory, but they raised plenty of questions about the effectiveness of strategic bombing, especially in its more indiscriminately destructive form of area bombing. The survey questioned the effectiveness of area bombing and demonstrated that even precision bombing against industry had not produced significant results in Germany until after the Normandy invasion in 1944. The reports concluded that attacks on the oil industry and transportation were the most effective.[17]

The denigration of strategic bombing and the condemnation of attacks on noncombatants found ready acceptance among many of the same peace organizations and religious periodicals that had disapproved of the atomic bombings of Japan. The well-established Christian peace organization the Fellowship of Reconciliation through editorials in its journal *Fellowship* continued to condemn as atrocities the destruction of Hiroshima and Nagasaki and their thousands of men, women, and children. *Christian Century* published an article that questioned whether the destruction of cities could lead to lasting peace and *Catholic World* ran another that argued that war with atomic weapons used against Russian cities would kill more innocent people than guilty ones. *Christian Century* also printed editorials that condemned the immorality of total wars fought indiscriminately against entire populations. Editorials of the Jesuit magazine *America* in the summer of 1949 condemned the use of atomic bombs against cities and their innocent civilian populations. One of the editorials claimed that the use of atomic bombs was not inherently evil. It stated that the weapon could be used justifiably against military targets like fleets or military encampments, but that the "'one bomb — one city' doctrine ... will mean America's moral suicide."[18]

Even before the fall hearings, a few in the Truman administration and Congress took notice of the growing criticism of strategic bombing. Budget Director Frank Pace, Jr. wrote Truman a memo in April 1949 questioning whether "unrestricted" atomic warfare was consistent with national policy. He doubted that the American public would support a nuclear war unless the United States was attacked. Representative Edith Nourse Rogers of Massachusetts introduced Marshall Andrew's January 23 *Washington Post* article into the *Congressional Record*. On June 27, 1949, Senator Ralph E. Flanders of Vermont proposed Senate Joint Resolution 112 prohibiting the use of the atomic bomb except in retaliation for an atomic attack. The resolution based the prohibition on the conclusion that "the atomic bomb, like biological warfare and whole-sale poisoning, is not properly a military device directed against the armed forces of the enemy, but is rather a means for the mass murder of civilians…." However, the resolution received a cold reception. Senator Brien McMahon, who chaired the Joint Congressional Committee on Atomic Energy that was to consider the bill, predicted that the resolution would never reemerge from the committee. He considered the bill "not helpful."[19]

Air Force leaders initially responded to the criticism of strategic bombing by trying to suppress it instead of disputing the charges publicly, dismissing the critics as cranks and anti-Air Force propagandists. One civilian consultant writing on behalf of the Air Force to another government agency characterized the critics of strategic bombing in this way: "I believe that, on investigation you will find that Fuller is a notorious crank; that Liddell-Hart has been discredited since the fall of France in 1940; that Lawrence follows the Navy-League anti-Air Force party line and is recognized as a spokesman of the most extreme Navy viewpoint; and that Baldwin is not far behind Lawrence." The more obscure critics the Air Force could simply watch closely, but those who possessed more prominent outlets for their views provoked the Air Force leadership into action. After Marshall Andrews wrote his January 1949 articles for the *Washington Post*, Air Force Secretary Stuart Symington and Director of Public Information for the Air Force Stephen F. Leo arranged a meeting with Andrews and Philip L. Graham, the publisher of the *Post*. Symington and Leo gave Andrews the "wire brush treatment" in the meeting and convinced Graham not to publish any more of Andrews' articles on strategic bombing and military policy. Andrews had to wait a year and publish his views as a book instead. There was also a rumor that Hanson Baldwin and Walter Lippmann were being investigated for their criticism in the *Atlantic Monthly* of strategic bombing.[20]

David Lawrence aroused the wrath of General Curtis E. LeMay who had taken over as head of SAC. Lawrence's criticism of strategic bombing prompted LeMay in early September 1949 to detail his director of public information to compile a critique of Lawrence and his charges and then distribute it to the public information officers at all the SAC bases. The intention was to convince local newspapers to discontinue Lawrence's columns on the Air Force and "to cut into his livelihood as a writer." These actions met with success in at least one case with the *Omaha World-Herald* and had enough of an impact to prompt Lawrence to write a letter of protest to LeMay.[21]

2.3 The Revolt of the Admirals

In the fall of 1949, the critiques of strategic bombing emerged from relative obscurity to become a national issue. Congressional hearings in October resulting from a dispute between the Navy and the Air Force over new weapon systems attracted national attention to the lingering post-war criticisms of strategic bombing and brought the issues of noncombatant immunity back into public focus. In the hearings, the top admirals of the Navy used arguments against indiscriminately destructive methods of war to attack the Air Force and one of its prized weapons programs. The admirals decried what they labeled the "atomic blitz" as an unsound strategy for fighting a future war and attacked the Air Force's new B-36 intercontinental heavy bomber as a symbol of this flawed strategy. The public discussion surrounding the hearings frankly confronted the question of harming innocent noncombatants in war. With the question squarely faced, reassurances predominated: almost no one, including the Air Force and the supporters of air power, advocated harming civilians as a method of warfare. The level of attention the issue of noncombatant immunity received in the press, even though it was quickly eclipsed by other concerns, suggested a significant amount of interest on the part of the American public in the problem. The public controversy compelled a clarification of the loose and ominous talk about the destructive uses of air power and marginalized those who persisted to advocate frankly an abandonment of the norm of noncombatant immunity and the adoption of destroying cities and killing noncombatants as a method of warfare.

Rivalry between the Navy and the Air Force produced the October hearings at which the critique of strategic bombing and the problem of noncombatant immunity temporarily took the spotlight. By 1949, the unification of the armed forces under the National Security Act of 1947 had not produced harmony. Tensions flared among the services because of competition over the roles and missions each service would perform in future wars and over shares of a shrinking military budget. Many in the Navy feared that it might lose its aviation and Marine ground forces in the process of unification, while officers of the Air Force and Army sought to prevent Navy encroachment on the military roles and missions for which they believed their services were especially suited. The president's proposal of a military budget under $15 billion for 1950 and strong congressional support for a larger air force threatened the roughly equal division of funds between the three services which had governed the armed forces' funding since unification.[22]

The Navy's concerns over unification and the defense budget reached greater heights with the cancellation of the construction of a new type of flat deck aircraft carrier in April 1949. The Air Force had promoted the argument that this new "super" carrier was unnecessary because it duplicated the strategic bombing capabilities that the Air Force possessed and the Secretary of Defense Louis A. Johnson agreed. The Navy reacted strongly to the decision. John L. Sullivan, the secretary of the Navy, resigned in protest. Senior officers vented their dissatisfaction in the press by attacking the Air Force's reliance on long-range airplanes for strategic bombing. They believed that the canceled super carrier and the planes it could transport provided a prudent alternative to Air Force bombers. Fleet Admiral William F. Halsey, Jr., in an interview claimed that based on the results of the last war, the Air Force's long-range bombers could not conduct pinpoint bombing and were therefore unable to destroy much of value. Rear Admiral D. V. Gallery in a belligerent *Saturday Evening Post* article attacked the Air Force's notion of strategic bombing which he termed the "atomic blitz." In condemning the strategy, he appealed to the sympathy felt for innocent noncombatants among his audience. He wrote: "[T]he atomic blitz is a war against the common people. The atom bomb is a weapon of indiscriminate destruction and mass slaughter. You 'win' an atomic war by destroying so many cities and killing so many little people that their leaders finally decide to give up."[23]

The immediate origins of the hearings stemmed from concern over Navy morale in the face of the super carrier cancellation, but even more from charges of corruption surrounding the procurement of the Air Force's intercontinental bomber, the B-36. The House Armed Services Committee under the chairmanship of Carl Vinson called hearings to investigate the corruption charges but adopted a wide-ranging agenda because of concerns over Navy morale, the cancellation of the super carrier, and the criticisms of strategic bombing as a national strategy. An initial set of hearings in August examined B-36 procurement and found the corruption charges were groundless, but the hearings were closed before the Navy had received a chance to testify. With growing concerns about Navy morale, the committee called a second set of hearings to give the Navy leadership a chance to comment on the rest of the initial agenda.

The new set of hearings on unification and strategy, which the press would label "The Revolt of the Admirals," were convened on October 6 to hear the Navy's testimony. The Navy's second witness, Admiral Arthur W. Radford, commander in chief of the Pacific Fleet, began a barrage of criticism. For a week, the highest-ranking officers of the Navy would criticize the B-36 and the method of warfare that they believed it represented. The admirals would charge that the implementation of unification had resulted in the undervaluing of the Navy and Marine Corps in the planning for future wars and in their exclusion from important Department of Defense decisions.

Radford's testimony presented an overview of the case that the Navy had assembled. A primary element of that case and one that attracted a good deal of attention in the press was its critique of the bombing of cities and civilians as a strategy of warfare. Radford warned the committee against the danger of U.S. reliance on what he termed an "atomic blitz" strategy of bombing enemy cities that would prove both ineffective in winning a war and morally objectionable to the American people. The admiral claimed that the B-36 was a symbol of the atomic blitz because it was designed to bomb its targets from altitudes so high that its strikes would only be accurate enough for "mass area bombing of urban areas." Radford condemned the folly of a "war of annihilation," which he implied the Air Force advocated. Many military men, Radford claimed, rejected this theory of warfare "on the grounds that it will fail to bring victory." He pointed to this difference of opinion over the bombing blitz as "the root of our principal troubles in unification." Radford rejected the notion that the threat of an atomic blitz would serve as an adequate deterrent and argued that even if carrying out such bombing could bring a military victory, it would be "Pyrrhic" and "politically and economically senseless" because of the high costs it would impose on achieving a stable and lasting peace. Radford concluded, "In my opinion the American people, if they were well informed on all factors involved, would consider such a war morally reprehensible."

Radford's statement before the committee was not a model of forensic clarity. He structured his talk in accordance with the seven-item agenda that the committee had adopted for its investigation, which helped to obscure what he claimed was his main argument: the inadequacy of an atomic blitz strategy. Although all of his responses to the agenda items at least obliquely related to his central argument against the atomic blitz, he devoted only a few paragraphs of his thirteen-page talk to explicating his critique of the atomic blitz of cities. He spent most of his talk explaining why the B-36 was an inferior weapon system and how a danger existed that tactical air support and carrier aviation was being neglected due to an overreliance on the atomic blitz. In the talk, his supporting arguments overshadowed what he claimed was the "heart" of the matter.[24]

During questioning after his prepared statement, Radford received a chance to clarify his critique of the atomic blitz. Radford stated that he believed in "strategic bombing" and the need for the Air Force, but said, "It is a matter of emphasis and it is a matter of accuracy. I don't believe in mass killing of noncombatants." After another question, Radford admitted that while he did not feel this way during the war, he now condemned what the U.S. bombing had done during World War II based on what he learned from studies completed after the war. Chairman Vinson then cut off this line of discussion by calling it "too theoretical" and then changing the subject. But Vinson could not prevent the congressmen from returning to Radford's critique of the atomic blitz. In response to later questions, Radford said, "I feel very strongly, however, that this committee must differentiate in strategic bombing between the bombing of purely military targets and mass area bombing, which has a great effect on the peace following a war." He followed this comment up with the claim: "I feel that the mass bombing of cities in general whether it is done by ordinary bombs or atomic bombs, is the question which this country as a nation has to evaluate — whether the American people really support war fought in that manner."[25]

After a series of witnesses provided technical information that supported the Navy's case against the B-36, Rear Admiral Ralph A. Ofstie on October 11 gave the strongest and most detailed statement criticizing the atomic blitz strategy. Ofstie contended "strategic air warfare, as practiced in the past and as proposed for the future, is militarily unsound and of limited effect, is morally wrong, and is decidedly harmful to the stability of a postwar world." He equated strategic bombing with "attacks on cities" and argued that it was not an effective way to fight a war nor in accordance with the national objectives of the United States.

The admiral offered several ways in which strategic bombing did not further American national objectives and the issue of noncombatant immunity featured heavily in them. He claimed that strategic bombing could not prevent the invasion of Western Europe, and using atomic weapons to "liberate" conquered territory hardly promised an acceptable response: "Are we to atomize or otherwise destroy such urban and industrial areas, where friendly peoples outnumber the invaders in a ratio of perhaps 50 or 100 to 1?" Ofstie also asserted that strategic bombing, as then practiced, "unavoidably includes random mass slaughter of men, women, and children in the enemy country," even though he claimed that the "intent of wholesale extermination of enemy civilians" did not enter into the official definition of strategic air warfare. The admiral viewed World War II as illustrative of this fact. The Allies did not initially intend to attack cities or noncombatants, but they eventually resorted to "area bombing of cities" because of the "inherent inaccuracy of high altitude bombing." He continued, "I am sure that the moral force of the people of this country is in strong opposition to military methods so contrary to our fundamental ideals. It is time that strategic bombing be squarely faced in this light; that it be examined in relation to the decent opinions of mankind." Finally, he argued that the destruction caused by strategic bombing imposed a heavy cost upon a post-war peace. Again, he pointed to World War II and the economic burden that the U.S. faced in rebuilding Germany and Japan. He feared that the effects of another war "attended by large-scale destruction of the homes and cities" of the belligerents would be devastating for the world economy. Ofstie offered as an alternative to the atomic blitz a return to precision bombing against narrowly delineated targets such as oil, shipping, and other forms of transportation with weapons better suited to do this than the B-36.

At the end of his presentation, Admiral Ofstie reiterated his point about the conflict between indiscriminate bombing and American values. He said, "Our country has had a long history in support of measures for the amelioration of the effects of warfare. If we now consciously adopt a ruthless and barbaric policy toward other peoples, how can we prevent the breakdown of those standards of morality which have been a guiding force in this democracy since its inception? The concept of indiscriminate bombing attacks on nonmilitary targets undermines these accepted standards and if it is initiated may destroy them."[26]

The questioning of Ofstie by the committee was brief. W. Sterling Cole, a senior member of the committee, began his questions with a statement of lavish praise for Ofstie's testimony. Cole personally endorsed and commended the admiral's "very calm, dispassionate, and profound" consideration of this "very vital problem" to the American public, and he complimented the presentation as "one of the finest military papers that has ever come to my attention." The comment of another congressman captured the essence of Ofstie's statement: "True strategic bombing is hitting specific targets, not innocent people." One Air Force observer wrote in his notes about the hearings: "Admiral Ofstie's statement seemed to make a strong impression on the Committee, including those members friendly to the Air Force cause."[27] Admiral Ofstie had placed concern over indiscriminate destruction at the center of his testimony and appealed to the public's aversion to harming noncombatants in war.

Four senior admirals, who testified after Ofstie, reinforced the Navy's critique of strategic bombing and its reaffirmation of noncombatant immunity. Fleet Admiral William F. Halsey, Admiral Thomas C. Kinkaid, Admiral Raymond A. Spruance, and Fleet Admiral Chester W. Nimitz all testified that area attacks on cities and civilian populations were less effective than precise and selective attacks on military targets. Kinkaid and Nimitz also repeated the concern about the post-war costs that use of strategic bombing would impose on the victor. Kinkaid reiterated the charge that "unlimited strategic bombing" was morally indefensible without elaborating on his reasoning and inaccurately suggested that "terrorizing bombardments" of cities were prohibited under the Washington Treaty of 1922.[28] Spruance argued that the United States in conducting a war should distinguish between the people in enemy countries and their leaders if its goal was to create a free world. When questioned whether it was "practical" for modern day bombing to attack "with the least possible damage to innocent civilians and people that have no direct connection with the war," Admiral Halsey said that he thought it was.[29]

On October 13, the Navy finished presenting its case with the testimony of its top officer Admiral Louis E. Denfeld. Unlike Radford, the Chief of Naval Operations did not emphasize the dispute over the atomic blitz strategy as the primary source of controversy. Instead, he depicted the dissatisfaction within the Navy as a result of the improper implementation of unification which had placed barriers to the Navy properly fulfilling its military role.[30]

Although the Navy presented other issues in the hearings, its critique of strategic bombing figured prominently in the Navy's testimony before the House Armed Services Committee. The critique objected to practices of the last war; emphasized selectivity and the need for accuracy in hitting military targets instead of cities and civilian populations; and provided military, political, economic, and moral reasons for continuing to provide noncombatants with immunity in war. The Navy's case rested on the assumption that the members of Congress and the public would care about protecting noncombatants.

During the week of Navy testimony, the questions of a few representatives did hint at some reservations over noncombatant immunity, but even those who appeared less attached to the idea suggested that Americans in general were reluctant to harm innocent noncombatants in war. In questioning Admiral Radford, both Representatives Melvin Price and Overton Brooks raised the possibility that the mass bombing of cities might be necessary to win a war if the enemy chose to use such tactics. Nevertheless, they admitted that Americans condemned the mass bombing of cities. As Congressman Price chastened Radford at one point, "No one favors mass bombing, Admiral."[31]

Congressman Paul J. Kilday, although acknowledging the tragedy of noncombatant deaths in war, offered a rationale for the loss of life. In the hearings, he twice brought out the claim that the killing of civilians was a regrettable but unintentional and unavoidable result of warfare. Under Kilday's questioning, a Navy commander conceded that even an amphibious assault using conventional weapons would result incidentally in the killing and injury of many civilians. In an exchange with Admiral William H. P. Blandy, Kilday took his argument further and claimed that the killing of civilians was "an incident of warfare that has always existed." For Kilday, if wars were to be fought, one had to accept that civilians would perish, and the idea that the deaths were unintended and unavoidable should ease one's acceptance. This idea of the legitimacy of inflicting unintended noncombatant deaths in war would become increasingly common in public discussions among Americans in the years to come.

Admiral Blandy had testified the evening following Ofstie's contentious statement. He had provoked Kilday by introducing a particularly charged phrase into the hearings that reduced the problem of noncombatant immunity to stark terms. Blandy had referred to the problem of "the killing of women and children" in war and this struck a raw nerve with Kilday. Kilday complained, "The thing I regretted was to see in these hearings emphasis being placed on the killing of women and children."

Kilday received little satisfaction from Blandy, however, because the admiral refused to concede to Kilday's claim that the killing of noncombatants was an immutable historical constant of warfare. Blandy acknowledged that a few civilians had been unintentionally killed in the landing at Vera Cruz in 1914, but contended that they were not killed in such great numbers as during World War II. The admiral said he had read books that stated that Britain "at least" had a policy of destroying workers' homes during the last war. Blandy also argued that new weapons had led to greater harm to civilians, and Kilday conceded that the killing of civilians was greater because "your operations are greater; they cover a greater extent...." The admiral said his point was that he would avoid the killing of noncombatants "if there were any possible way to avoid it." When Kilday continued to insist that killing noncombatants had always been incidental to warfare, Blandy replied that bombing the deep interior of an enemy country without fighter escort, from high altitudes, and sometimes by radar would be "far more likely to kill innocent people than ...

to destroy worth-while objectives...." Blandy had asserted that certain choices could still be made about the waging of war that could significantly affect the degree to which noncombatant immunity was preserved.[32]

Admiral Blandy, though, was conflicted over the issue of noncombatant immunity. He was not an unreserved defender of the concept and his testimony did not fully conform to the argument that the rest of the Navy witnesses had offered. Unlike the other naval officers, Blandy admitted that he would be willing to kill women and children in war under certain circumstances. When questioned by Congressman Dewey Short, he said, "I am thankful that I have never been called on to take the lives of women and children in war. And I would have the same natural repugnance against it as anyone would have. But if I felt, or my superiors felt that, it was unavoidable in war operations to preserve the freedom of this country, I would do it." Short responded to this uncomfortable statement with the optimistic comment: "Well, from the testimony of Admiral Radford, Admiral Ofstie, and yourself, you all follow the same pattern. I judge that we should not have indiscriminate bombing — blasting urban populations, wholesale slaughter — but, rather, precision bombing on military targets." Blandy repeated his ambivalent comment to Kilday in their discussion of killing women and children. "I would only do it if it were the only way to preserve the freedom of this country, which I think is worth a great deal not only to this country but to the world." For Blandy, the preservation of a great value could justify harm to noncombatants, but his testimony left open the question of what kind of situation might present a clear and necessary choice between the abstraction of American freedom and the deaths of enemy civilians.[33]

The issue of destroying enemy cities and harming civilians as a method of war attracted extensive attention in newspaper coverage despite the fact that the Navy testimony ranged over multiple complaints.[34] For most of the two weeks between October 6 and October 20, the hearings were front page news. The degree of prominence, which the issue of attacks on cities and noncombatants attained, varied between newspapers, but most considered this Navy charge significant and newsworthy. The *New York Times*, *Washington Post*, and *Baltimore Sun* gave prominent and extensive coverage to the issue from the time of Radford's testimony.[35] Other newspapers were slower to give prominence to the Navy charge of the dangers of bombing cities and noncombatants. The *St. Louis Post-Dispatch*, *Philadelphia Bulletin*, and *Cleveland Press* treated the charge as one among many criticisms until the testimony of Admiral Halsey, a hero of World War II, repeated some of the points that Radford and Ofstie had commented on in more depth. The papers then gave the issue prominent treatment.[36] After Halsey's testimony, the *St. Louis Post-Dispatch* headlined its article on the hearings with "Mass Bombing of Red Cities by B-36s Would Be Costly Mistake, Says Adm. Halsey."[37] For the *Detroit News* and *Houston Chronicle*, the Navy criticism of bombing cities did not appear at all in their coverage of the hearings until Halsey's testimony but then received prominent treatment if only for one day.[38]

As another indication of the attention that the issue of harm to noncombatants generated, the testimony of Ralph Ofstie received much more prominence in the newspapers than his prestige and rank of rear admiral merited in the company of so many war heroes and the top ranking leadership of the Navy. His arguments against attacking noncombatants attracted the close attention of the *New York Times* and *Washington Post*. The October 12 headlines of the *New York Times* coverage of the hearings included "Random Slaughter of Civilians Violates Our Ideals, Ofstie Tells House Inquiry." The paper also printed the full text of Ofstie's statement before the committee, an honor it did not bestow on any other Navy witness.[39] Ofstie's testimony was also the focus of a retrospective article and a W. K. Kelsey column in other newspapers.[40]

The problems posed by bombing cities and civilians attracted the attention of a number of editorial pages and columnists. The *Washington Post* and *Philadelphia Bulletin* each devoted an editorial specifically to the issue of attacks on civilians, the *Bulletin*'s editorial entitled "The Barbarity of Bombing."[41] Columnists Richard Moley, W. K. Kelsey, David Lawrence, and Paul Jones each sympathetically addressed the criticism of attacking cities.[42] In the *Philadelphia Bulletin*, Paul Jones' column decried what he saw as the decision that Americans had reached to destroy enemy cities if war were to come again. He said that the United States was not entitled to such broad claims of self-defense that it could indiscriminately kill noncombatants. These were the horrifying tactics of Tamerlane and Genghis Khan. Caustically, he described the path that he felt Americans had followed: "The bomb-sight experts used to say they could drop a bomb in a pickle-barrel. Then this notion was amended to mean that they could hit a pickle factory. And now we seem to claim that it's the same thing if we just blast everyone who has ever eaten a pickle."[43]

Not all newspapers placed great emphasis on the Navy's arguments against attacking cities in their coverage of the hearings. The arguments were reported in the *Los Angeles Times, Boston Post, San Francisco Examiner,* and *Chicago Tribune,* but received no special prominence. The *Chicago Tribune* carried only brief references in three of its articles. In these papers, any special significance that the Navy witnesses wanted to impart to this critique of strategic bombing was lost in the welter of other accusations that the Navy made in the hearings.[44]

The extent of newspaper attention to the Navy's attack on city bombing suggested that American newspapers believed the issue of noncombatant immunity still to be important and of interest to their readers. Although the extensive newspaper coverage did not necessarily equate to broad public interest in the issue, it does provide indirect evidence of a continued public concern about noncombatant immunity. Certainly, the idea was not being ignored.

2.4 The Air Force's Response

On October 18, the Air Force had its chance for rebuttal. It offered only two witnesses, the Secretary of the Air Force Stuart Symington and Hoyt S. Vandenberg, the Air Force Chief of Staff, but their testimony and questioning lasted a day and a half. Symington and Vandenberg reassured the committee and the public that contrary to the Navy's charges the Air Force did not favor the mass bombing of civilians as a strategy of war. However, their testimony expressed some ambivalence toward the idea of noncombatant immunity that paralleled a diversity of views within the Air Force on the subject.

The differing Air Force views were illustrated clearly in the process of drafting the statements that Symington and Vandenberg would present in the hearings. General Orville A. Anderson, commandant of the Air War College and a veteran of interservice feuds with the Navy, prepared drafts for the secretary and chief of staff that argued that moral considerations should not influence military planning. His drafts claimed that the Navy's contention that strategic bombing was immoral constituted the charge "uppermost in importance." The drafts contained the premise that the best way to argue publicly against the charge of immorality was to say that humanitarian values had to give way before the need for the defense of a nation and its beliefs. After asserting that civilians living around "vital military targets" could not provide the targets with immunity, he wrote, "In war the humanities must be adjusted to the needs of this nation to insure its own survival." In another draft, he included a long quote from Lord Arthur Tedder, General Dwight D. Eisenhower's deputy commander during World War II, which argued that moral beliefs would not hinder the use of the atomic bomb when nations were fighting for their lives and beliefs.[45]

The statements that Symington and Vandenberg actually delivered in the hearings rejected Anderson's approach to refuting the Navy's criticism. Instead of asserting that traditional American beliefs about not harming noncombatants would have to bend to the realities of modern war, the statements assured that the Air Force did not intend to deviate from the tradition of noncombatant immunity. However, when questioned by the committee, Symington did reveal some ambivalence toward the protection of noncombatants.

Secretary Symington's prepared statement before the committee contained much to reassure the public that the Air Force did not advocate abandoning noncombatant immunity. He assured the representatives that the Air Force did not plan any such "atomic blitz" for the next war as the Navy witnesses had described. Although he claimed that strategic bombing against "the heart of the enemy's war-making power" would minimize the loss of American soldiers' lives, he did not offer this benefit as a justification for taking enemy civilian lives. Instead, he said bluntly, "It has been stated that the Air Force favors mass bombing of civilians. That is not true. It is inevitable that attacks on industrial targets will kill civilians. That is not an exclusive characteristic of the atomic bomb, but is an unavoidable result of modern total warfare." While Symington acknowledged that enemy civilians could not be completely protected, he was careful to point out that "industrial targets" and not cities or their civilian populations would be the objects of attack. Even if civilians were no longer safe in modern war, the Air Force speaking through its civilian chief did not join with those who advocated intentional attacks on noncombatants.[46]

The questioning of Symington at the hearings revealed a more ambiguous attitude toward noncombatant immunity. In several exchanges with congressmen, Symington twice dodged explicitly endorsing the killing of civilians as a method of war but then agreed with another congressman who offered justifications for such harm. The first exchange began when Congressman Short acknowledged that Symington's prepared comments had reassured him. He said, "I am glad that you stated in your testimony that you do not believe nor does the Air Force believe in massacre or indiscriminate bombing of civilian populations, although we did have that in the last war." When Short followed this comment up with a provocatively phrased question about killing civilians, Symington refused to endorse such killing and instead deferred to the opinions of military leaders. Short asked, "So that if it was necessary to drop atomic bombs indiscriminately on cities where women and children would be slaughtered in wholesale fashion you would subscribe to it, of course." Symington replied, "No. I would say that I would rather not commit myself to subscribing to any policy which the military people felt would lose American lives and result in the loss by America of a war." Again, Symington had asserted that his overriding concerns were the preservation of American lives and victory in war, but he had refused to offer these as explicit justifications for killing civilians.[47]

Later in the session, Congressman Leroy Johnson again raised the subject of killing civilians. He asked, "Your idea of the strategic bombing allocated to the Air Forces is long-range bombing on definite military targets; is that correct?" Symington replied less than definitely, "I would think so, yes, sir." Johnson then asked whether Symington thought there had been any "indiscriminate bombing" in the last war. Symington dodged the question and the implications that an affirmative answer would have revealed: "To the best of my knowledge, I know of no indiscriminate bombing. I don't know exactly what you mean by indiscriminate bombing. I would rather have that question for the military." Johnson tried to clarify his question: "Well; in bombing Germany, the bombing was more or less indiscriminate in that they laid out a pattern of bombing and they unnecessarily killed a great many civilians. That is what I am talking about." This time the committee chairperson recommended that Johnson ask the military men this question, but then Symington interjected a last point. He argued that he could not see the difference between "trying to stop the functioning of a man on a lathe building a bomber to attack the United States, and trying to stop a soldier." Some civilians were part of an enemy's war machine and in no sense innocent noncombatants. Johnson agreed that munitions workers would constitute "a military target." Although the two could agree that the mechanization of warfare had resulted in some civilian workers clearly becoming part of any war effort, Symington's comment did not reveal what he thought about attacks on enemy civilians not involved in war industries. He did not offer a justification for killing "innocent" noncombatants nor did he assert that innocents no longer existed in a total war.[48]

Representative Charles H. Elston, who questioned Symington immediately after Johnson, was the only individual in the hearings who bluntly suggested that American soldiers' lives were more valuable than those of enemy civilians and that, therefore, bombing noncombatants was a legitimate practice. Elston said: "It is infinitely better, of course, that a number of civilians be killed in enemy countries than a few American soldiers be killed. For example, the killing of tens of thousands of people in the bombing of Hiroshima and Nagasaki perhaps saved the lives of a great many American soldiers." Symington replied that he thought President Truman had once told him the bombings had saved a quarter of million American casualties. Elston followed up by saying, "So you can't just say that in every case it is wrong to bomb civilians." Symington responded: "I don't see how it could be, sir. If civilians are going to be killed, I would rather have them their civilians than our civilians."[49]

Despite his unqualified reassurances in his prepared statement that the Air Force did not favor mass bombing of civilians and despite his two earlier attempts to dodge the appearance of justifying the killing of innocent civilians, Secretary Symington agreed with Elston's legitimatization of the practice. This might have been a glimpse of Symington's personal, as opposed to public, sentiments on noncombatant immunity. He may not have placed much, if any, significance in protecting enemy civilians given other circumstances like the threat to American lives, but it is possible that because he and his advisors in the Air Force feared the public reaction to a blunt disavowal of noncombatant immunity, he adopted a reassuring tone for most of his testimony. After agreeing with Elston, the secretary, under additional questioning, again avoided an opportunity to justify attacks on civilians and refused to comment on what had been said at the hearings about the "morality of war."[50]

The testimony of Air Force Chief of Staff Hoyt Vandenberg returned to the theme of reassurance and raised none of the ambiguities about bombing civilians that the questioning of the secretary had. Vandenberg defended the concept of strategic bombing incorporated into current American war plans. He said the concept was not exclusively an Air Force idea but had been approved by the JCS. He argued that curtailing American long-range strategic bombing capabilities would rob the United States of a deterrent to war and would abandon a counterbalance to the Soviet Union's large land army.

Although the general purposely avoided an explicit discussion of the issue of bombing cities or civilians, he did contend that the B-36 was capable of precision bombing. An Air Force consultant, who had been responsible for organizing the Air Force's testimony at the hearings, had proposed a more direct response to the charge that the Air Force favored killing noncombatants be included in General Vandenberg's statement. The response made clear that the alternative to killing enemy noncombatants was harm to American soldiers, but this argument was left out of the Air Force chief's testimony. Instead, Vandenberg implied that the targets of strategic bombing would be armament industries when he argued that abandoning strategic bombing eliminated the opportunity to choke off an enemy's war-making power at the source and destroy his weapons before they could be employed.

The general also reassured the committee that the Air Force could bomb with precision. Although he admitted that high-altitude bombing was difficult, he said that bombing methods were constantly improving and recent tests had convinced him that the "necessary accuracy can be consistently attained." Again, when he was later questioned by the committee, Vandenberg assured them that definite improvements had been made in bombing equipment since the last war which would mean that bombing from 40,000 feet with the B-36 would not, as a congressman had asked, "necessarily involve mass bombing of civilians." Vandenberg was being quite optimistic in his assurances since the Air Force had not extensively tested the bombing accuracy of the B-36.

None of the questions concerning the bombing of civilians that Symington asked the committee to address to the generals were broached with Vandenberg. Possibly concerns about military secrecy, which the general voiced in his statement, chastened the representatives. Vandenberg said that the discussion of strategy that the hearings had conducted publicly was harmful to U.S. security. Several influential senators had also spoken out against the public airing of the Navy's complaints. Vinson as chairperson might have also discouraged further questions on these issues more subtly than he had earlier in the hearings.[51]

Several days earlier in a closed session, General Vandenberg had reassured members of the Joint Congressional Committee on Atomic Energy, some of whom also served on Vinson's committee, about Air Force attitudes. The controversy over strategic bombing had led the committee into "a general discussion of the morality of war" during which one senator emphasized several times that, in the final analysis, the killing of noncombatants was unjustifiable and Vandenberg stated that "the popular notion that the U.S. Air Force entered into the spirit as well as the operation of mass bombing in Europe was unfounded, and that its sole targets were strategic planst [sic] and transportation facilities, and that unfortunately civilian workers or nearby residents were killed."[52]

The Air Force's reassurances coincided with another optimistic theme that appeared in the hearings. The witnesses and representatives addressed the question of the compatibility of the use of atomic weapons with the preservation of noncombatant immunity. The admirals were divided, the Air Force did not speak directly on this question, but the committee members who spoke on the issue were quite optimistic about the ability to reconcile atomic weapons with sparing noncombatants. Admiral Nimitz was the sole outspoken pessimist at the hearings who imagined that the use of the atomic bomb would necessarily result in large-scale harm to noncombatants. He claimed that the atomic bomb "cannot be pinpointed — it must be used in area bombardment and the chances are that its greatest damage will fall on noncombatants, many of whom will be women and children not engaged in the war effort."[53] In contrast, Admirals Radford and Blandy believed that if employed properly, atomic bombs could be used in precision bombing of military targets that would avoid extensive harm to civilians.[54] Likewise, Congressmen Short and Cole repeatedly tried to clarify in the hearings that the Navy's critique, which condemned the mass slaughter of noncombatants, attacked a particular type of bombing, "indiscriminate bombing" or "area bombing," and not the use of atomic weapons in and of themselves. The representatives implied that atomic weapons could be used in a manner that discriminated between combatants and noncombatants and that there was no inherent incapability between using atomic weapons and maintaining some form of noncombatant immunity.[55] The dominant sentiment of the hearings suggested the possibility that even the new weapons of mass destruction did not have to be implements for the mass slaughter of civilians. This sentiment would become popular among many American leaders and a segment of the public in the early 1950s as the U.S. nuclear arsenal expanded.

Following the Air Force's presentations, the testimony of General Omar N. Bradley, the chairperson of the JCS, marked a turning point in the hearings as well as in the media's coverage of the proceedings. Bradley gave one final response to the Navy's critique of strategic bombing and the killing of civilians, but as Admiral Denfeld had done in his statement, Bradley focused most of his strongly worded criticism of the Navy's complaints, and hence much of the public attention, on the issue of unification. Like Symington and Vandenberg, Bradley defended the effectiveness of strategic bombing in winning and deterring wars. He also provided some reassurance that the U.S. military had not abandoned the notion of noncombatant immunity. He defined strategic bombing not as attacks on cities but on "the war-making capacity or potential of an enemy nation." He said, "I do not advocate a wanton destruction of cities or people" and that "in carrying out any of our missions from the squad on the battlefield to the bomber deep into enemy territory, we Americans will seek to achieve maximum effectiveness against the enemy's armed forces, with minimum harm to the nonparticipating civilian populace." However, his reassurances were qualified, and they left unclear what constituted "wanton" destruction and how much was a "minimum" of harm. Bradley admitted that attacks on the war-making capacity of an enemy might kill noncombatants: "It is obvious that workers live near factories and that if you bomb the factories, you may bomb the people." To Bradley, the important element in justifying any harm done to noncombatants was that Americans would not inflict the harm intentionally.

However, Bradley's reassurances were qualified in other ways as well. He conceded, "you may win the war, and lose the peace" but argued that "military planners must plan to win" because of the high cost of losing. His testimony also suggested the possibility that attacks on civilians could help win a war efficiently, a conclusion which most of the admirals led by Ofstie and Radford had wanted to discredit. Bradley claimed that "any great injury you can inflict upon the morale of that nation contributes to the victory." This claim was not equivalent to advocating attacks on noncombatants. After all, he could have been referring to numerous ways of undermining enemy morale including destruction of their armed forces or war industries. Nevertheless, despite the fact that Admiral Halsey had argued during the hearings that attacks on civilians would strengthen enemy morale,[56] one conceivable way of harming a nation's morale and a method that occurred to U.S. military leaders during World War II was to inflict suffering and terror on enemy civilians through the bombing and destruction of civilian homes, families, and basic necessities like food and heating fuel.[57]

Bradley closed his discussion of strategic bombing on another ambiguous note. After his reassurance that Americans sought to minimize harm to enemy noncombatants, he said: "I am reminded, however, that I don't believe a Communist ideology and the dictatorship it fosters, has any such humanitarian outlook about war. They will sacrifice human life at the slightest provocation, and would be inclined to sacrifice our lives even more quickly. I might suggest that if our attacks are only in retaliation for an attack made upon us, the American people may feel that strategic bombing is both militarily and morally justified." Even though he did not mention attacks on noncombatants directly, the statement did imply that the United States would be justified in attacking Communist-bloc civilians if the Soviet Union attacked American civilians first. Bradley's final comment on strategic bombing also included the vague comment, "As far as I am concerned, war itself is immoral."[58]

Despite Bradley's mixture of reassuring and ambiguous comments, he had not offered explicit justifications for attacking noncombatants nor clear rejections of the idea of noncombatant immunity. Like Symington, his acknowledgments that attacks on civilians should be avoided may not have reflected his own deep convictions but instead his concession to what he perceived as public sentiment on the issue. Nevertheless, his statement, like the Air Force statements and the Navy's arguments, reaffirmed a notion of noncombatant immunity. Participants in the hearings agreed that civilians workers in war industries could no longer be considered noncombatants and how much of a city and its industry could be legitimately bombed remained vague, but almost all of the participants agreed that noncombatants still deserved some form of protection. Congressman Elston was the sole participant in the hearings who explicitly justified the purposeful killing of civilians in war. If those who believed that noncombatant immunity had become inconsequential in the age of total war were in the majority, they had kept quiet during these public hearings.

Most of Bradley's testimony did not address the issue of strategic bombing but instead strongly criticized the Navy witnesses for opposing unification of the armed forces. He called the admirals "fancy dans" and berated them for not being team players.[59] After General Bradley's testimony, the hearings continued for two more days, but discussion in the hearings and in the press turned away from the Navy's criticism of strategic bombing. Bradley's attack on the Navy for resisting unification helped to shift the locus of attention to restoring interservice unity and resolving problems in the implementation of unification. After Bradley's testimony, public consideration of noncombatant immunity receded, but it had already attracted a significant amount of attention outside the committee room.

The hearings had put the Truman administration on the defensive in public. President Truman avoided involvement in the controversy and the State Department sought to portray it as a technical squabble. At his press conference on October 13, Truman refused to comment when asked about the Navy's testimony generally and refused again when asked specifically about Radford's and Ofstie's charges that the Air Force plan for "strategic atomic warfare" was immoral. Truman's evasion was hardly surprising considering he did not place much stock in the Navy's critique of the atomic blitz. He wrote a member of the House Armed Services Committee that the dispute in the hearings was a matter of indiscipline in conforming to unification: "As soon as we get the cry babies in the niches where they belong, we will have no more trouble." The State Department issued cautionary guidance on the hearings to its overseas media outlets such as the Voice of America. The guidance recommended minimum treatment of the controversy and suggested that coverage should depict the hearings as a "democratic expression reflecting technical differences between branches of armed services."[60]

The press included reminders that the Soviet Union sought to further its international standing by charging that the United States planned to attack civilians. Soviet Foreign Minister Andrei Vyshinsky described the American interservice controversy as an argument over the best way of "exterminating the greatest possible number of Soviet human beings in Soviet cities." An article in the *Philadelphia Bulletin* worried that the hearings probably had Soviet propagandists' "tongues hanging out" with the Navy's charges of "our 'barbaric' policy of planning, in war, 'a random mass slaughter' of innocent men, women and children." The *Washington Post* reported on the unwitting assistance that the admirals were giving to the Soviets in Germany. "Soviet-line" newspapers there had devoted considerable attention to the hearings and had been "hammering away at the theme that, while the Soviet army and air force attacked only 'military targets' in Germany during World War II, the 'Anglo-American imperialists' concentrated instead on the 'deliberate slaughter of women and children, calculatedly seeking to destroy urban areas and industry to eliminate future competition.'"[61]

2.5 The Public Reaction

The press coverage of the hearings reflected a variety of reactions to the criticism of strategic bombing, but the issue of harm to noncombatants received significant attention and few were willing to justify such harm in war. Many in the press treated the issue of harm to noncombatants as a dilemma in need of a resolution. They sought to preserve American security in an era of massively destructive weapons without completely abandoning the tradition of noncombatant immunity. Some supported the admirals' contention that the solution was a return to precision bombing such as Hanson Baldwin in the *New York Times*. The *Washington Post* editorial page drawing on the criticisms of Fuller and Blackett had adopted this position even before the admirals' testimony but reiterated it during the hearings. A *Post* editorial expressed its reassurance at Secretary Symington's "categorical statements of policy" that the Air Force did not favor the mass bombing of civilians. However, it was still concerned that high-altitude bombing with the B-36 could turn attempts at precision bombing into "indiscriminate saturation" and suggested that a civilian board of experts review U.S. military strategy to ensure that strategic bombing would further American national objectives in a war.[62]

Other voices in the media called for measures beyond a return to precision bombing to avoid the horrors of slaughtering noncombatants. Few supported the proposal of the Soviet Union to outlaw the atomic bomb because of its potential for harm to civilians,[63] but others looked to some form of arms control as a solution. Despite the stalled negotiations over the international control of atomic energy since the American proposal of the Baruch plan in 1946, Chester I. Barnard, president of the Rockefeller Foundation, was optimistic about the possibility of an agreement with the Soviets. He believed that international control would do much to alleviate the menace of "indiscriminate annihilation of civilian populations." Swayed by the admirals' testimony, W. K. Kelsey, whose columns ran in the *Detroit News*, initially saw a solution to indiscriminate destruction in disarmament to make wars more difficult to start and in a pledge not to bomb enemy cities unless American cities were bombed first. However, in a second column, Kelsey's confidence in a course of action wavered because he could not decide between the arguments of the Navy and Bradley's claim that the threat of the atomic bomb deterred war.[64]

The *Saturday Evening Post* was greatly disturbed by the prospect of "total" wars that would involve the United States in indiscriminate attacks on civilians, but was vague about a solution. Using Admiral Ofstie's testimony as a point of departure, a November editorial was critical of American attacks on civilians and the destruction of enemy economies in the last war. It was not optimistic that the United States would change its practices in the future given what it saw as the importance of seeking unconditional surrender in wars fought by democracies: "We fear terribly that what we do in a new war will be as wrong and stupid as much of what we did in the last one…." So the *Saturday Evening Post* placed its hopes in perpetual peace but implied that the peace would be cemented by the threat of military force.[65]

Others were more explicit in claiming that deterrence offered a solution to the dilemma. Henry H. Arnold, the retired commander of the Army Air Forces during World War II, commented in the *New York Times* that the potential destructiveness of future wars meant that the United States must not let another occur. Arnold wrote, "Modern wars with the scientific devices invented for more effective means of spreading death and destruction would have thrilled Ghengis Khan." On an ABC radio broadcast, William L. Laurence, a science reporter for the *New York Times*, argued that the potential to devastate cities would be an important deterrent to war, and a column by the military commentator George Fielding Eliot in the *St. Louis Post-Dispatch* emphasized the importance of deterrence.[66] Although deterrence, based on the threat of annihilating cities and civilians, might be seen as a rejection of noncombatant immunity because the idea supposed that one would actually carry out the threat if need be, deterrence could provide comfort to those concerned about the killing of noncombatants. If deterrence succeeded, no war would break out and no civilians or anyone else would be killed.

In reacting to the hearings, many acknowledged the severity of the conflict between massively destructive wars and the tradition of noncombatant immunity but avoided offering a solution. The *Nation* printed an editorial that expressed its concern over the morality of the atomic blitz but like the *Saturday Evening Post* did not suggest a clear answer. The editorial pages of the *Baltimore Sun*, *Philadelphia Bulletin*, and *Detroit News*, the columnist David Dietz, and an article in *Collier's* magazine agreed that the problem called for solution by military or civilian experts. The Catholic magazine *Commonweal* felt a different type of expertise was required. Sympathetic to the Navy's criticisms of attacks on civilians, its editorials identified the crucial question as whether atomic bombs constituted "evil means" in warfare because they might make "random mass destruction of non-combatants not lamentably incidental but actually essential to military operations." The editorial concluded that moralists were those best qualified to answer the question.[67]

Telford Taylor agreed that strategic bombing and atomic bombs raised moral issues that Americans would have to confront. Brigadier General Taylor, who had served as the U.S. chief prosecutor at the Nuremberg war crimes trials, did not believe, however, that the issues should be left to specialists. In a

November article for the *Washington Post,* he argued that the issues required broad public discussion, and he identified specifically what he believed the crucial issues to be. He contended that "area bombing" and not simply the use of atomic weapons constituted the heart of the issue. Area bombing had as its object "to level the cities attacked and cause the maximum loss of civilian life and property." Taylor rejected the idea that atomic bombs were tactical weapons that could be used discriminately against specific military targets and equated their use, at least in their present form, with area bombing, as the use of fire bombs against Japan had been. He gently criticized Symington and Bradley for implying at the hearings that American atomic bombs in a future war would only be used against war industries and their workers. The most difficult question to answer, Taylor proposed, was not whether the U.S. should use the atomic bomb if the Soviet Union were to launch an atomic attack against the United States, but whether the U.S. should use the bomb in less desperate situations. Taylor believed Bradley was probably right that Americans would put aside any moral qualms and agree that use in retaliation was morally justified, but in less dire situations, the question of use was more difficult. Although Taylor did not provide an answer, he did suggest a number of considerations that impinged on the problem. He believed that the customs of war could not prohibit weapons or practices that had substantial military value, although he pointed out that not all ruthless and destructive methods delivered practical gains. Based on the experience of World War II and the war crimes trials that followed it, there appeared to be no basis in international law to claim that area bombing was criminal, but Taylor argued that international morality had as its foundation enlightened self-interest and that the current potential for "race suicide" increased the pressure for a minimum of international law to hinder the destruction.[68]

Not all of the press expressed concern over the issues of noncombatant immunity considered in the hearings. Some ignored the question of reconciling noncombatant immunity with modern warfare like *Life* magazine, the *Cleveland Press*, and *Houston Chronicle*, and others seemed confused by the questions the admirals had raised like *U.S. News and World Report* and *Newsweek*.[69] The coverage of the *Los Angeles Times* and *Boston Post* portrayed the controversy as a relatively minor technical squabble that could be cleared up by a committee.[70]

A segment of the media expressed little concern about the prospects of the United States harming noncombatants and hinted at justifications for such harm, but shied away from openly advocating attacks on noncombatants. The pages of *Time* magazine reflected a relative lack of sensitivity about bombing cities and civilians, concluding that General Bradley "had all but blasted the Navy admirals' case."[71] The admirals' arguments were lost on the columnist Bob Considine who complained about their attacks on the B-36. "It ain't bombing us," he wrote. Writing for the *Nation,* Fletcher Pratt, a commentator on military affairs, suggested that the reality of total warfare was undermining the moral rationale for protecting civilians. Pratt criticized the admirals for making "a rather bad point when they talked about the immorality of the atom bomb." He wrote, "The fact that many of the people hit would be civilians has not a great deal of meaning in this age of really total warfare, when a woman at a lathe in a factory is as important as a man at the front, and neither can operate without the other." His article left unclear what his attitude would be toward an enemy civilian who contributed little or nothing to the fighting of the war, but clearly, he believed noncombatant immunity was losing its relevance.[72]

The news coverage of the *St. Louis Post-Dispatch* also demonstrated little concern over harm to noncombatants. Although the newspaper gave significant attention to the Navy's protests against harming noncombatants, its coverage reflected little distress over the possibility. With the close of the hearings, the *Post-Dispatch* devoted an entire article to the issue of attacks on noncombatants entitled "Admirals Say Atomic Bombing Is 'Immoral.'" Although the article clearly conveyed the admirals' charges, it was not sympathetic to them. The article commented, "Admirals are not supposed to have consciences, but Rear Admiral Ofstie appears to be tormented by a conscience." It closed with Admiral Blandy's admission that he would kill women and children if it was necessary to preserve the security of the country.[73]

Although some in the press did not appear particularly sensitive to the issue of noncombatant immunity in their coverage of the hearings, it was uncommon that press coverage contained any defense of the strategy of attacking noncombatants in war or suggested that noncombatant immunity was an outdated principle in the atomic age. The absence of the justification of attacks against civilians was surprising given that the Soviet Union had exploded its first atomic bomb in September. With the Soviets armed with the new weapon of mass destruction, it was curious that more Americans did not justify their country's potential attacks on civilians on the grounds that the Soviets were planning similar attacks. General Bradley mentioned retaliation as a justification for the use of strategic bombing and the atomic bomb in his testimony and a few newspapers chose to include this comment in their coverage.[74] However, Bradley did not specifically justify attacks on noncombatants.

Only much less prominent voices made such arguments. A letter to the editor of the *Washington Post* responding to Admiral Radford's argument against bombing cities took this position. It contended that the United States had to assume that the next war would begin with a surprise atomic strike against American cities. Therefore, "the only preventive, failing an effective system of international controls, is to have the machinery for instant retaliation — to have *in being* the means by which great numbers of atomic bombs may be suddenly dropped upon the cities of Russia or upon the cities of any other nation that may have the bomb." Even this argument might have been as much an argument for deterrence as one advocating attacks on civilians.[75]

Defense of the military benefits of attacking civilians also did not appear often in the public discussion of the hearings despite so many of the participants claiming to be hardheaded pragmatists. Appeals to the logic of total war — that attacks on civilians would hamper war production — were rare. In a review of P. M. S. Blackett's *Fear, War, and the Bomb,* which appeared after the hearings, Carl Kaysen was one of the few who explicitly pointed out the possibility that the harm atomic bombs inflicted on civilians could enhance its effects against enemy war industry. He wrote, "Horrible as it is, the possibility that mass killing of civilians in sufficient magnitude in air raids can add a new dimension to the effectiveness of bombing must be examined." He concluded that the great radius of destruction of the atomic bomb would increase the effectiveness of area raids against cities.[76] The scarcity of some of the more obvious justifications for attacking noncombatants in the public discussion of the hearings suggested that few were willing to challenge the perceived norm that it was wrong or unwise to harm civilians in war.

The objections that a few representatives offered in the hearings to the admirals' position against bombing cities and civilians received almost no attention in the press. For example, the *New York Times* did not report Congressman Elston's justification of attacking noncombatants even though it printed part of Secretary Symington's more moderate response to the representative.[77] Although the opposition to the admirals in the hearings from Representatives Price, Kilday, and Brooks did not attract the attention of the press, a news conference that these three held on the hearings was considered newsworthy. The three defended the B-36 even before the rebuttal from the Air Force was heard. However, they chose to hedge their opposition to the Navy's attacks on city bombing. As Congressman Price put it, "I don't want to bomb cities. No one does. But the intercontinental bomber is here and we'd better have one because the other fellow is going to."[78] Apparently, justification of attacks on noncombatants attracted less attention in the press than disavowals of such attacks.

One exception to this trend proved the rule that sentiments that could be construed as justifying attacks on civilians were marginal in American thinking or at least uncomfortable for Americans to hear. The Communist *Daily Worker* emphasized the pieces of Secretary Symington's testimony and his questioning by representatives that suggested the legitimacy of attacks on noncombatants. Like Soviet propaganda, the *Daily Worker*'s coverage of the hearings primarily stressed the intent of American leaders to start a war with the Soviet Union,[79] but the charge that American leaders planned a ruthless and savage war against noncombatants also figured prominently. The headline for the report of Symington's testimony read, "Mass Slaughter Defended by Air Force Head." The article included none of Symington's reassuring statements but did contain his statement that attacks on industrial targets would inevitably kill civilians. To support its sensational headline, the article also quoted

Congressman Elston's proffered justification of saving American soldiers' lives in exchange for the killing of enemy civilians.[80]

Even though much of the concern voiced over noncombatant immunity emerged from the more liberal and leftist segments of the press during the hearings controversy, the conservative press also acknowledged the sentiments against the purposeful killing of civilians in war. The editorial pages of the *San Francisco Examiner* and the *Chicago Tribune*, newspapers which had devoted little attention to the Navy's charges against attacking civilians, paid oblique tributes to a perceived norm supporting noncombatant immunity. On October 18, the day that Secretary Symington began presenting the Air Force's rebuttal, the *Examiner*, a Hearst paper, printed a full-page editorial entitled "The Massacre of Children." The editorial described in words of moral outrage the Soviet killing of an entire student body of a school in the Donetz Basin as part of their scorched earth policy during their retreat before the Germans in 1941. The editorial admitted that the Soviets feared that the students would be recruited as soldiers by the Nazis but belittled this justification and called the action "the final depravity of indiscriminate murder." The editorial said that the massacre should be remembered by Americans to remind them of "what an evil thing is Russian Communism." With its references to "children" and "indiscriminate," the editorial portrayed the students as innocent victims of war and its strident condemnations of the Soviets attempted to draw on its readers' agreement that such killings were especially atrocious. The article was premised on the idea that killing noncombatants was worse than the general tragedy of death in war.[81] In December, the *Examiner* printed a long article by Karl H. Von Wiegand which expressed concern about the decline of world morality and which viewed the waging of war against women and children as a sign of this trend.[82]

The *Chicago Tribune's* tribute to noncombatant immunity was much more begrudging, but it was an acknowledgment of an international norm supporting the idea nonetheless. In late October and November, the newspaper printed three editorials that repeated the theme that American civilian and military leaders would be executed for war crimes if the United States were to lose a future war. The first of these editorials specified that one of the crimes of which American leaders would be guilty was conducting war with the "utmost brutality." The editorial equated this with the use of the atomic bomb against civilians. These editorials of a newspaper, long an advocate of isolationism, were much more disturbed by the recent elaboration of international law on war crimes than by the prospect of Americans killing civilians in war. However, the editorials did perceive international support for noncombatant immunity.[83]

Despite the extensive public discussion of noncombatant immunity that they sparked, the October hearings with the Navy's attacks on strategic bombing produced no dramatic change in defense policies. Admiral Denfeld was dismissed as chief of naval operations, but the B-36 continued to be procured, no super carriers were ever built, no change was made in basic American strategy for the next war, no revision of the unification law undertaken, and the defense budget would have to wait for the Korean War for substantial increases. However, the hearings did provide evidence that many Americans still valued the tradition of noncombatant immunity. Although generalizations about the cultural attitudes of millions of Americans must remain speculative, the public discussion surrounding the hearings did demonstrate several concrete occurrences suggestive of broad American attitudes. Much of the press believed the issue of noncombatant immunity to be newsworthy and significant for their readers, many journalists expressed their own concerns about harm to noncombatants, and almost no one publicly advanced the view that attacks on noncombatants were a legitimate method of warfare, few suggesting even that it was a regrettable but necessary tactic in war. Instead, the optimistic belief that the United States should and could continue to discriminate between combatants and noncombatants and that the distinction would offer significant protection to civilians dominated public discussion surrounding the hearings.

Journalists were not the only ones who believed the public was concerned about the protection of civilians in warfare. The admirals included the issue in their testimony precisely because they believed that it would garner public support and not out of a long-standing principled commitment to the idea. During the hearings, the Navy's "moral" arguments met with a good deal of skepticism in the press as to their sincerity. Although he may not have been insincere in his testimony, Admiral Ralph Ofstie, who was responsible for injecting most of the criticism of city bombing into the hearings, appears to have had no long-standing principled attachment to noncombatant immunity.

What the admiral did have was a long history of conflict with the Air Force over the most efficient use of air power. Ofstie had served as the senior naval officer on the United States Strategic Bombing Survey of Japan in 1945 and 1946. His arguments during the survey with the senior representative of the AAF, General Orville Anderson, became notorious.[84] Ofstie believed that the experience of World War II had demonstrated that oil production and storage facilities and transportation systems like shipping and railroads were the only lucrative targets for systematic bombing. He viewed these targets as requiring precision bombing attacks and dismissed the campaign by the Air Force's heavy bombers to destroy Japanese urban and industrial areas as unnecessary, inefficient, and costly. Ofstie felt these views had not been adequately conveyed in the Summary Reports of the European and Japanese Strategic Bombing Surveys because of undue Air Force influence on the survey directors.[85] Surely, it was no coincidence that the precision attacks against oil and transportation were the kind of operation to which the Navy and its carrier-based planes could make a significant contribution in future wars. The admiral's interpretation of the use of air power in World War II conformed to his service's interests in the competition for defense funding and prestige.

Taking advantage of the confusion over the meaning of the term "strategic bombing," Admiral Oftsie by 1948 was trying to convince his colleagues that the phrase meant simply mass attacks on urban and industrial areas. According to his semantics, "strategic bombing" did not include precision air attacks on oil and transportation targets. In an April 1949 memorandum to the Office of the Deputy Chief of Naval Operations for Air, Oftsie wrote that strategic bombing "is essentially based on the wholesale destruction of urban and industrial areas and the civil populace of the enemy rather than direct attack on his active military machine." These distinct precision attacks the Navy was prepared to undertake. This innovative definition of strategic bombing solved a number of problems for Oftsie and the Navy position on air warfare. It allowed Oftsie and other navy advocates to claim that the Navy had no interest in undertaking strategic bombing operations and was, therefore, not violating interservice agreements on roles and missions that had assigned strategic bombing to the Air Force. It also allowed Oftsie to criticize unreservedly "strategic bombing" and adopt moralistic arguments against the practice that were new to the admiral's thinking. But Oftsie's creative interpretation of strategic bombing certainly contributed to the confusion over what precisely the admirals were criticizing.[86]

Although Oftsie came to equate the Air Force's strategic bombing mission with mass attack on the industry and civilian populace of an enemy country, until the late summer of 1949 he based his arguments against reliance on this strategy, arguments which circulated in internal Navy documents, on efficiency in fighting a war and on the post-war costs of such a strategy. It was not until it appeared that the Navy would receive a public hearing on national military strategy before a congressional committee that Oftsie added a new moralistic element to his arguments that stressed the tragedy of killing innocent noncombatants. Oftsie appears to have had no long-standing personal commitment to noncombatant immunity based on any aversion to harming innocents. In a 1948 memorandum to the Navy's General Board, he fully supported the use of "weapons of mass destruction" under conditions advantageous to an American war effort even when they resulted in massive destruction of urban areas. He wrote that if the U.S. undertook a preventive war against the Soviet Union, an idea which he supported, a "reasonable" plan of operations would "knock hell out of Moscow with atomic bombs … [and the] same for the major urban and industrial areas." He went on to describe the atomic bomb as "our best shot in the locker. Certainly we will use it, under all conditions, unless some one in high places is screwball."[87]

Oftsie was not alone among the Navy witnesses at the October hearings who lacked a long-standing principled commitment to noncombatant immunity. Admirals Radford and Halsey also possessed less than consistent views on the subject. In his long career, which included serving under Eisenhower as the chairperson of the JCS, Radford never again raised publicly the subject of attacks on cities or civilians. Halsey's public statements during World War II, which included the rallying slogan "Kill Japs, kill Japs, kill more Japs," inspired one historian to label his rhetoric "exterminationist" and bordering on the advocacy of genocide.[88]

Admiral Ofstie introduced into his arguments against strategic bombing a moralistic condemnation of the harming of innocents out of a belief that it would have a favorable public reception and would be a useful tool in the Navy's debate with the Air Force. A September radio broadcast by ABC commentator Elmer Davis helped to propel Ofstie to emphasize the Air Force's plan to attack cities. In a memorandum, Ofstie criticized Davis for endorsing Air Force "propaganda" and noted that "it is of interest particularly that Mr. Davis has mentioned *cities* [emphasis in the original] (in other words, area targets) as the objective of area attack." Ofstie concluded the memorandum by saying that he should answer this point in his talk before the House Armed Services Committee.[89]

After his testimony, Ofstie was both pleased over the public reception of the moralistic aspects of his talk and concerned that his Air Force opponents might be able to undermine his arguments by challenging his lack of commitment to them. He wrote his friend James A. Fields, a naval historian, about the hearings: "My own part in this business … has been very well received and may have some little influence among church people because of introducing the moral issue. However, I am damn sure that Orville Anderson and his cohorts will attempt some devastating retort and perhaps highly effective, such, for example, as stating that I haven't been inside of a church for the last thirty years."[90] Since his testimony on the immorality of harming civilians did not stem from long-standing personal convictions, Ofstie had included it because he believed that the American public still valued this idea even in the new atomic age of total war.

Ofstie did place limits on the moralistic arguments that he would use against the Air Force. He purposely avoided the use of the term "genocide" in the construction of his congressional testimony. Writing to Admiral Gallery, a confederate in the public attack on strategic bombing, Ofstie warned him away from introducing the emotionally charged term "genocide" into public statements. He worried that the term could backfire because of the current international consideration of the U.N. Convention on Genocide. He explained that according to a legal aide of Admiral Radford, the Soviets supported the Genocide Convention out of a desire to use it to justify executing captured American aircrews that might bomb Soviet cities. He concluded, "It would therefore have been bad news had I brought genocide into the picture when it could just as well be covered by the simple statement 'bombing of urban areas.'"[91] The *Daily Worker* printed the charge that the bombing of

Hiroshima and Nagasaki was a form of genocide around the time of the hearings, but otherwise the new and highly charged term remained out of the hearings controversy.[92]

It would be unfair to characterize the Navy witnesses' use of arguments that drew on the tradition of noncombatant immunity as cynical and insincere. The admirals may have honestly believed in their testimony at the time. However, the Navy's charges were not the reflection of long-standing personal convictions on the part of Navy leaders, but were instead an attempt to appeal for public support against Air Force influence by invoking popular arguments.

2.6 The Air Force Clarifies its Position

Although this strategy did not result in any clear victories for the Navy, it did have an effect on the Air Force and its boosters. Some in the Air Force, concerned about public sensitivity to noncombatant immunity, worked to clarify that their service did not advocate attacks on noncombatants. An exchange of letters in early 1950 between an influential Air Force consultant W. Barton Leach, a Harvard law professor and Air Force reserve general, and the Library of Congress's Legislative Reference Service nicely illustrated this attempt at clarification. The Legislative Reference Service was a research agency that provided Congress with impartial information so that its members could carry out their legislative responsibilities. One of the service's pamphlets on national defense planning published in September 1949 had come to Professor Leach's attention in the wake of the hearings. As the man who had been responsible for organizing the Air Force's testimony at the hearings, he was not happy with what he saw. The pamphlet included a discussion of air power that claimed that the advocates of strategic bombing — and the pamphlet strongly implied that the Air Force was one of these advocates — supported attacks on civilians and cities as a method of warfare. The pamphlet also described objections to this type of strategic bombing that closely resembled the Navy's arguments before the House Armed Services Committee.[93]

On behalf of the Air Force, Professor Leach wrote a harsh letter to the director of the Legislative Reference Service about the pamphlet. Leach claimed that the pamphlet "does not attain any reasonable standard of accuracy and objectivity." He objected to the implication that the Air Force adhered to the "Douhet theory of urban area bombardment" and asserted, "It ought to be known to any person professing expertness in this field that the American concept of strategic bombing is one of attack on selected industrial target systems, such as petroleum production and aircraft manufacture." Implying that Navy propaganda had misled the author of the pamphlet, Leach referred the director to the published testimony of the recent hearings as well as documents that the Air Force had produced in response to the hearings and suggested that the pamphlet be withdrawn and replaced with a new study incorporating this additional information. The director responded to Leach by pointing out that at the time of the preparation of the pamphlet, the documents that Leach recommended as clearly stating the Air Force's position had not existed.[94] The episode illustrated both that a researcher attempting to be impartial in the middle of 1949 had difficulty not depicting the Air Force as favoring attacks on noncombatants and that the Air Force viewed the October 1949 hearings as a clarification of its official position on the issue.

The journal of the Air Force's Air University displayed additional attempts at clarifying the Air Force's attitude toward noncombatant immunity. General Orville Anderson, the one who had drafted the elaborate and unused responses to the Navy's moral arguments against strategic bombing, wrote an article entitled "Air Warfare and Morality" for the winter 1949 issue of the journal. Anderson's article was quite a contrast to his draft statements. Instead of justifying attacks on noncombatants as he did in his drafts for the hearings, Anderson, like his superiors, attempted to distance the Air Force from the advocacy of attacks on civilians. The general dismissed as "fallacious" the argument that "strategic bombing kills the innocent population and is not directed against legitimate military objectives." He admitted that the total nature of modern war had made the distinction between combatants and noncombatants difficult to discern and the difference between soldiers and workers in war industry nebulous. He also claimed that, with the importance of industry to warfare, the physical infrastructure of cities had become a legitimate military target. However, he believed that children and other noncombatants could be spared, as in World War II, through warnings of attack and the evacuation of cities. Although Anderson alluded to arguments about the importance of preserving American values and the lives of their soldiers, he did not call for the abandonment of noncombatant immunity or for attacks on civilians as a lesser evil. According to Anderson, the Air Force would only attack military targets and undertake precautions to avoid harming noncombatants.[95]

A second article in the *Air University Quarterly Review* by a military chaplain asserted that, based on his review of moral theologians, modern war was not inherently evil but that direct and intentional attack on noncombatants was immoral. The use of nuclear weapons, he claimed, would be justified if they were targeted against military objectives and adequate warnings were provided to noncombatants in areas surrounding the target.[96] This view of the morality of war conformed neatly with General Anderson's arguments and an Air Force that would pursue precision bombing against military targets. Other Air Force officers tried to project this image of the Air Force in other military journals and the wider press.[97]

A few public statements demonstrated the continued variance of opinion within the Air Force, especially at the lower levels, on the issue of attacks on noncombatants. For example, a December press release from the Public Information Office of the Headquarters of the Eighth Air Force in Fort Worth ensured that despite the magnitude of destruction that atomic weapons would inflict, the airmen would have "no qualms" about dropping the bomb. The release, which contained interviews with B-36 crew members and was sent to the UP as an article authored by Jud Dixon, emphasized that the B-36s would be attacking "military targets" and that the bombardiers would be striving for perfection in delivering the bombs accurately on target. However, the flyers did not dodge the question of potentially harming civilians. One captain said, "To save one American city, I'd help destroy 10 or a hundred of an enemy's." Another tail gunner, when confronted with the prospect of killing civilians who lived around a military target, put it this way: "Well, that is a chance we will all have to take. Anyway, I'd rather be over there dropping bombs on their military installations and letting the enemy civilians take a chance — because I know an enemy nation won't give us that consideration — they'll just knock hell out of our civilians and everything else."[98] The Navy's attacks on strategic bombing may have made much of the Air Force's leadership more sensitive to the issue of noncombatant immunity, but not all in the service were so affected.

It was not only Air Force officers who felt it necessary to clarify their stance on the protection of noncombatants in the wake of the October hearings. The aircraft designer Alexander P. de Seversky, one of the Air Force's biggest civilian boosters, authored another book on air power that appeared in mid-1950. The book included a chapter entitled "The Fallacy of Killing," which explained that the proper use of aerial bombardment was not to kill people, either soldiers or civilians, but to deprive the enemy of weapons and the will to wage war by destroying industry and the material means to live a "normal existence." Although Seversky believed that the collapse of the civilian population's morale would hasten a nation's capitulation, he specifically said that this demoralization would not be accomplished by "attacking people directly." Instead of indiscriminate slaughter, air power should be used for the precision bombing of industry.[99]

Seversky's earlier writings had been much more ambiguous on this point. Although his widely sold 1942 book *Victory Through Airpower* had included the argument that the precision bombing of industrial targets was needed to undermine civilian morale instead of "random" bombing of cities, much more prominent in the book were his depictions of the massive destruction of future wars. In his first chapter, Seversky described a terrifying vision of a future air attack against the United States. The "whole nation" was the target. It was "paralyzed by bombing and incendiarism and wholesale slaughter." The story concluded with the statement: "The aim of total war is total destruction: to obliterate the United States as a modern nation."[100] In a *Reader's Digest* article in February 1946 about the atomic bombings of Hiroshima and Nagasaki, Seversky again was ambiguous in his stance toward indiscriminate destruction. While claiming that the destructive power of the atomic bomb had been exaggerated, he praised the destruction of Hiroshima. He wrote, "It was one of those cases when the right force was used against the right target at the right time to produce the maximum effect."[101] After the 1949 hearings, Seversky, like the Air Force leaders he supported, was more cautious about appearing to advocate attacks on civilians and the indiscriminate destruction of cities.

The public discussion generated by the Revolt of the Admirals demonstrated the endurance of ideas of noncombatant immunity and the marginal position of those who supported attacks on noncombatants. Previous histories of the 1949 hearings have emphasized the dispute's significance for service relations in the short term,[102] but the hearings represented the beginnings of a broader American reinterpretation of noncombatant immunity. The Navy's admirals had injected arguments about the imprudence and immorality of indiscriminate destruction into their criticism of Air Force strategy with the hope of evoking public sympathy. The reaction in the press suggested that the admirals had struck upon an issue that still troubled Americans and made their leaders defensive. Confronted publicly with charges of planning to annihilate cities and innocent civilians, leaders of the Air Force and their supporters backed away from supporting attacks on noncombatants. A large segment of the press across a broad social spectrum from pacifist and religious periodicals to the middle class *Saturday Evening Post* expressed concern over harming noncombatants in war. Even the vehemently anti-communist Hearst newspapers and the conservative *Chicago Tribune* made nods to the tradition of noncombatant immunity. Only a few solitary voices like Representative Elston advanced arguments justifying American attacks on noncombatants. Even in the age of total war, Americans clung to the tradition of preventing harm to noncombatants. However, their commitment to massively destructive methods of warfare had limits, as discussion of the new hydrogen bomb would soon show.

3
The Hydrogen Bomb and the Limits of Noncombatant Immunity

Senator Edwin C. Johnson believed in maintaining strict secrecy surrounding the American atomic energy program. He served on the Joint Congressional Committee on Atomic Energy and appeared in a televised debate on November 1, 1949, to defend continued secrecy. So he was indignant when journalists later accused him of revealing in his televised remarks one of the government's biggest atomic secrets. During the debate, the senator from Colorado had said that American scientists were working on a "super bomb" one thousand times more powerful than the bomb dropped on Nagasaki. At first, Johnson's indiscretion attracted no notice until Alfred Friendly made the remark the focus of a November 18 report in the *Washington Post*. By early January, the syndicated column of Joseph and Stewart Alsop had spread word of the super bomb around the country, and Johnson's revelation began grabbing headlines.[1] The new weapon was soon christened the "hydrogen bomb" because its explosive power came from the thermonuclear reaction of the fusion of hydrogen atoms. The media attention surrounding the hydrogen bomb in the winter of 1949–1950 again brought the problem of noncombatant immunity before the public.

The October 1949 unification and strategy hearings had demonstrated that Americans were not ready to disavow noncombatant immunity. However, public discussion of the hydrogen bomb would reveal the limits of their concern over harm to noncombatants. Like with the Revolt of the Admirals, this discussion showed that few were willing to justify attacks on noncombatants, but concern over noncombatant immunity did not extend much further. Although some opposed the new weapon out of their desires to prevent the killing of noncombatants, most voiced their approval of the tremendously destructive bomb. Security, which many Americans believed the new weapon would enhance, outweighed concern over massive destruction. Debate over the hydrogen bomb revealed that those who were willing to abandon war, or at least its most destructive weapons, for the sake of sparing noncombatants occupied almost as marginal a position among the American public as those who accepted waging war against civilians. As the October 1949 hearings had revealed the limits of Americans' tolerance for massive destruction, the hydrogen bomb controversy expressed the limits of their pursuit of noncombatant immunity. Unwilling to forfeit either noncombatant immunity or massively destructive methods of warfare, most Americans were left with a troubling dilemma, which in early 1950 saw only fledgling attempts to find some satisfactory resolution.

3.1 The Secret Government Debate over the Hydrogen Bomb

The super bomb had been on Senator Johnson's mind because he had become embroiled in a secret government debate over whether to devote maximum effort in the atomic energy program to hydrogen bomb development. Like the Revolt of the Admirals, this internal dispute revealed concerns over indiscriminate destruction, but these considerations were voiced by officials who were not playing to a public audience. Some who opposed building the new weapon of mass destruction feared that it was an implement of genocide, but this was a minority view, and the dispute in general demonstrated the limits of concern over noncombatant immunity. The debate within the government foreshadowed the broader public discussion that would shortly follow.

The internal government dispute began in October 1949 when Lewis L. Strauss, a member of the AEC, suggested the acceleration of the thermonuclear weapon program as a response to the Soviet explosion of its first atomic bomb. Controversy broke out when the General Advisory Committee (GAC), a group of science advisors to the AEC, recommended against implementing Strauss' proposal. The committee, composed of nine atomic scientists and industrialists including the wartime head of the Los Alamos laboratory J. Robert Oppenheimer and Harvard president James B. Conant, raised concerns about the indiscriminate destructiveness of thermonuclear weapons as part of its argument against developing them. The main body of the committee's report said the new bomb "is not a weapon which can be used exclusively for the destruction of material installations of military or semimilitary purposes. Its use therefore carries much further than the atomic bomb itself the policy of exterminating civilian populations." A dissenting minority recommended that development should be undertaken if the Soviet Union refused to abandon building the weapon, but both the majority and minority recommendations expressed fears about the destructiveness of the bomb. The majority conclusion said that with the weapon's unlimited destructive potential it "might become a weapon of genocide." The minority put it this way: "By its very nature it cannot be confined to a military objective but becomes a weapon which in practical effect is almost one of genocide." Both recommendations raised the even more frightening prospect that the new weapon could pose a threat to the survival of the human race and stressed that development of the bomb would have adverse political effects abroad.

The minority recommendation concluded, the hydrogen bomb "is necessarily an evil thing considered in any light."[2]

One of the GAC members, Lee A. DuBridge, president of the California Institute of Technology, wrote AEC chairman David Lilienthal a more extensive explanation of his views on the hydrogen bomb. The letter concluded with an argument on the "moral question." He wrote, "But certainly our moral position in the eyes of our own people and the people of the world is not enhanced by the development of a weapon whose sole advantage over other weapons is that it will kill more civilians or wipe out larger cities. One need not argue that an A-bomb is moral and a super is immoral. But whatever moral position we have come to occupy by virtue of our present program can only be worsened by making a great forward step in the production of weapons of mass destruction — weapons of terror. If our moral position is already bad why not make it better rather than worse?"[3]

By a three to two majority, the AEC concurred with the recommendation of its scientific advisory committee against development of the hydrogen bomb. However, the AEC majority in its report to the president did not place particular emphasis on the destructiveness of the weapon in its objections to development. Instead, it argued that the new bomb would not add to American military strength and would threaten American efforts for peace with the Soviet Union.[4] Faced with a conflict among his advisors, Truman appointed a special committee of the National Security Council (NSC) composed of the chairman of the AEC, the Secretary of Defense, and the Secretary of State to consider the issue.

As the State Department became involved in the consideration of the thermonuclear program, the contradiction between weapons of mass destruction and the tradition of noncombatant immunity attracted attention within the agency. In mid-December, R. G. Hooker, Jr., a member of the Policy Planning Staff, drafted a paper on "The Moral and Ideological Implications of U.S. Policy on the Use of the Atomic Weapon." He argued that the United States should renounce first use of atomic weapons in a future war and rely on them only as a retaliatory measure if an enemy should employ them first. Hooker listed as one of the benefits of this position: "It would also show that we do not propose in the event of war to conduct it with weapons the principal victims of which are civilian populations." He devoted much of the paper to discussing the mistake that the Nazis committed in waging war against the entire Soviet people during World War II, instead of attempting to drive a wedge between the people and their leaders. Hooker feared that the United States would make the same mistake in the next war if it relied on nuclear weapons.[5]

Hooker had little influence within the State Department and even less in the administration, but his boss George Kennan, the director of the Policy Planning Staff and architect of the policy of containment, also took an interest in the problem of atomic weapons and attacks on noncombatants. In October,

Kennan had begun the preparation of a long paper on the subject of the international control of atomic weapons. By January 20, he had completed a seventy-nine-page analysis that included consideration of the question of building the hydrogen bomb and the problem of noncombatant immunity. After reading an earlier draft of the paper, the Assistant Secretary of State for United Nations Affairs John D. Hickerson described the analysis as "permeated with the assumption that the use of the atomic bomb is morally wrong."

In the paper, Kennan argued that there existed a vital difference between nuclear and conventional weapons. He wrote, "The distinction lies in the way in which a weapon can be applied. Largely, the conventional weapons of warfare have admitted and recognized the possibility of surrender and submission. For that reason, they have traditionally been designed to spare the unarmed and helpless non-combatant, who was assumed already to be in a state of submission when confronted with military force, as well as the combatant prepared to lay down his arms." Kennan concluded that this possibility of surrender was fundamental to warfare because it recognized that war should be a means to a political end, an end that "at least did not negate the principle of life itself." Kennan did allow that if an enemy were to use massively destructive weapons against the United States, the country might need to reply in kind as the "price of survival," but, like Hooker, he believed that the United States should not initiate the use of atomic weapons.[6]

Kennan may have felt strongly about the problems of the destructiveness of nuclear weapons, but by early 1950 he had lost the stature that he had once possessed in the administration. On January 1, 1950, Paul H. Nitze replaced him as director of the Policy Planning Staff. Kennan's paper on international control did not become a formal Policy Planning Staff report because Nitze and other members of the staff did not entirely agree with the substance of the paper. Nitze, although sensitive to the political ramifications of reliance on weapons of mass destruction, placed this as only one among several factors he weighed in considering the decision to accelerate the hydrogen bomb program. In a memorandum on the thermonuclear weapon program, Nitze wrote that one important consideration was "that emphasis by the U.S. on the possible employment of weapons of mass destruction, in the event of a hot war, is detrimental to the position of the U.S. in the cold war." However, he concluded that the AEC should accelerate its program on the bomb to test its feasibility because he believed it to be essential that the United States not lag behind the Soviets in this technology. As a concession to his concerns about the U.S. position in the Cold War, he proposed that the new weapon, if feasible, not be stockpiled until a review of national security was completed.[7]

Kennan and Hooker like the members of the GAC represented a minority within the government concerned enough about the genocidal potential of the hydrogen bomb to consider foregoing the development or use of the weapon. Their beliefs were not widespread, however, especially not among those with the final responsibility for making military and foreign policy. Secretary of State Dean Acheson placed little importance on the moral issues raised by the hydrogen bomb and their political implications. Acheson directed the State Department staff working on the question of the hydrogen bomb away from attempts to answer any "ultimate moral question." The moral questions should be examined, he believed, but only as one among many considerations. In his memoirs, Acheson wrote that he never understood the logic of the moral arguments against the hydrogen bomb and that he did not find them persuasive under critical examination.[8]

Others in the administration offered arguments that dismissed worries over the new bomb's potential effects on enemy noncombatants. Lewis Strauss defended his proposal against any moral objections. He wrote in a memorandum to the president that "all war is horrible" and that the Soviet Union would not be restrained by moral scruples in pursuing the new weapon. "A government of atheists is not likely to be dissuaded from producing the weapon on 'moral' grounds," he argued.[9]

The chairman of the Joint Congressional Committee on Atomic Energy, Brien McMahon, also discounted the "moral" arguments against the hydrogen bomb and believed that the killing of noncombatants might be avoided. In a confidential letter to the president, McMahon acknowledged that war with thermonuclear weapons would be horrible, but he offered a number of arguments for why it would still be justifiable. To the GAC's claim that the weapon was genocidal, he offered the solution of warning civilian populations before the use of the bomb. Although he did not explicitly advocate attacks on civilian populations as a reprisal, he did contend that lack of the ability to retaliate "in kind" against an attack on American cities would lead to defeat and possibly "utter annihilation." He followed this argument with the contention that modern warfare itself was "genocidal," and not any particular weapon used to fight it. To the claim that use of massively destructive weapons would leave such chaos and resentment that a lasting peace would be difficult to achieve, McMahon admitted that this might be so but believed that "our first duty consists in doing what is necessary to win." To him, the virtues of the thermonuclear weapon in winning a war, which the senator detailed at some length in this letter, outweighed the costs of massive destruction.[10]

The JCS also believed that the military value of developing the super bomb outweighed any other "social, psychological, or moral objections" to the weapon. By the middle of January, the JCS had prepared a long memorandum for the Secretary of Defense, which addressed, point by point, the objections that the GAC report and Dubridge's letter had raised. The memorandum praised the military utility of the thermonuclear weapon: "Such a weapon would improve our defense in its broadest sense, as a potential offensive weapon, a possible deterrent to war, a potential retaliatory weapon, as well as defensive weapon against enemy forces." In the opinion of the JCS, the bomb had the potential to be decisive in a conflict. In rejoinder to the assertion that the super bomb was not a military weapon because it would be directed at the destruction of large cities, the memo insisted that the U.S. military did "not intend to destroy large cities *per se*; rather, only to attack such targets as are necessary in war in order to impose the national objectives of the United States upon an enemy." The memo stated that those sympathetic to the United States would understand that building the hydrogen bomb was necessary to sustain American leadership in the world, and this understanding would, therefore, minimize the political ramifications of development. As a final response to the arguments of the GAC, the memo observed, "In addition, it is difficult to escape the conviction that in war it is folly to argue whether one weapon is more immoral than another. For, in the larger sense, it is war itself which is immoral, and the stigma of such immorality must rest upon the nation which initiates hostilities."[11]

Strauss, McMahon, and the Joint Chiefs all mentioned the potential for the use of the hydrogen bomb as a tactical weapon against an enemy's armed forces. McMahon suggested that this type of use would avoid the problem of inflicting large numbers of civilian casualties. Their statements showed that since 1945, the idea that atomic weapons might not be used solely against cities, their industries, and their populations had gained more credibility within the American government and military as production of atomic arms increased and the weapons became less scarce.

To the defenders of the hydrogen bomb within the government, the military benefits of the new weapon outweighed any of its political or moral liabilities. War itself was immoral and genocidal, not a particular weapon. However, the defenders offered concessions to concerns over harm to noncombatants. Civilians could be warned and nuclear weapons might be used against enemy military forces instead of cities. The Joint Chiefs' formulation that the U.S. military did not intend to destroy cities per se echoed the comments of Representative Kilday and General Bradley during the "Revolt of the Admirals." The JCS did not intend to destroy cities, but cities might be destroyed in the pursuit of other objectives. This position allowed for the justification of massive destruction while still condemning attacks on noncombatants. Killing noncombatants and destroying civil societies could be condemned as evil and rejected as a goal, but such harm could be rationalized as an unintended and tragic cost of pursuing other legitimate goals.

Beyond provoking defenses of the morality of the hydrogen bomb, the concerns of the GAC and those within the State Department over the weapon's destructiveness had no effect on Truman's decision to accelerate the thermonuclear program. With Secretary Johnson backing the views of the JCS, Acheson unconvinced by the objections to the bomb, and Lilienthal realizing that opposition to the two secretaries would be futile, the special committee recommended unanimously to speed along the thermonuclear program.

Neither the special committee nor President Truman found the GAC concerns over the destructiveness of the hydrogen bomb significant enough to outweigh the perceived need to stay ahead of the Soviet Union in the arms race.

3.2 Truman's Public Announcement

The special committee recommended that Truman make a brief statement to the public since Senator Johnson's indiscretion had led to growing interest and some wild speculation concerning the weapon. On January 31, 1950, Truman announced that he had directed the AEC to proceed with its work on all forms of nuclear weaponry including the hydrogen bomb. He said that it was his responsibility to ensure that the country was able "to defend itself from any possible aggressor." He assured the public that the work would be carried out "on a basis consistent with the overall objectives of our program for peace and security" until a satisfactory regime for the international control of atomic energy could be implemented.[12]

Truman's announcement met with broad approval among Americans and most gave no more than passing consideration to the "moral" issues raised by the new weapon. They were satisfied that development of the bomb would add to American security. A public opinion poll taken around the time of the president's announcement reflected strong support for the decision with 73 percent of respondents approving of proceeding with the hydrogen bomb. Congress and newspaper editorial pages also expressed their approval. Based on a survey of public opinion conducted by its correspondents in cities across the nation, the *New York Times* described the consensus on the hydrogen bomb in this manner: "It's a nasty business, but we can't afford to let the Russians get the jump on us."[13]

As news of the weapon and its implications for warfare spread through the media even before the president's announcement, many Americans understood that the hydrogen bomb was indeed "nasty business." Many in the press made it clear that the hydrogen bomb would be a weapon used against cities.[14] People began to raise what they termed the "moral" issues surrounding the development of the super bomb. The public discussion of these moral issues was often so vague that it was difficult to discern specific concerns, but several did appear consistently. Some considered the moral issue to be that building the hydrogen bomb would provocatively contribute to an arms race that could lead to war. Others thought the bomb raised moral issues because of its great destructiveness regardless of whether it was used to destroy soldiers or civilians. Still others worried the weapon confronted the world with the ultimate moral question in posing a threat to the survival of the human race. However, many took the "moral" issue of the hydrogen bomb to be the harming of noncombatant populations.

As the potential destructiveness of the hydrogen bomb became apparent, a few feared, as the government's scientists had, that the new weapon that many saw as a guarantor of American security could not be easily distinguished from the atrocious methods of the Nazis. The controversy over the hydrogen bomb occurred at the same time that the Senate was considering the U.N. Genocide Convention, and for some, these issues intermeshed. This minority questioned whether a bomb that could destroy 100 square miles might be an instrument of genocide comparable to the crimes of the Nazis. The political gossip columnist Drew Pearson broadcast on his radio program in the middle of January a largely false rumor that David Lilienthal resigned his position with the AEC in part because of his opposition to the hydrogen bomb. Pearson claimed that Lilienthal equated the bomb with "genocide — a mass killing of mankind" and charged that Lilienthal was working to rally the churches in opposition to the new weapon. Editorials in the religious magazines *Commonweal* and *Christian Century* compared the hydrogen bomb to the butchery of the Nazis and questioned whether use of the weapon constituted genocide under the proposed convention. An article in the Progressive Party's weekly the *National Guardian* likewise compared the new bomb to Nazi atrocities. Letters appeared in newspapers that also associated the hydrogen bomb with genocide and Nazi crimes.[15]

The Senate hearings on the Genocide Convention also briefly touched upon the hydrogen bomb. The associate secretary of the peace organization the National Council for the Prevention of War, James Finucane, raised the subject in his testimony. In professing his support for the Genocide Convention, Finucane asked the Senate to consider resolving the inconsistencies that building the hydrogen bomb posed for American adoption of the convention. He claimed the new bomb "is a pure and simple genocidal weapon" and that its use would fall under the definition of genocide offered in the law. The last witness at the hearings, David Whatley, a Washington DC lawyer, commended Finucane's point and spoke out against the "mass murder of civilians by area bombing," referring to Admiral Ofstie's statement in the unification and strategy hearings. The statements were not well received by Senator Brien McMahon and Senator Henry Cabot Lodge, Jr., but the UP did send over the wire a February 1 statement on the contradiction between the hydrogen bomb and the Genocide Convention by the National Council for the Prevention of War, and several newspapers ran the story. A month after the hearings, a congressman inserted a pastor's sermon into the *Congressional Record* that said that use of the hydrogen bomb would make a "travesty" of the Genocide Convention.[16]

The Soviet Union attempted to use the hydrogen bomb's association with genocide against the United States. Soviet radio said the H-bomb decision was comparable to the Nazis' path and a *Red Star* article charged that American leaders were "now yelling that they have superbombs that can substitute for Maidenek and Auschwitz." The *Daily Worker* echoed this line in the United States. The paper called the hydrogen bomb an "instrument for the wholesale incineration of civilian populations" and a weapon outstripping "the wildest dreams of the SS and Himmler himself."[17]

However, there was very little negative reaction to Truman's decision on the hydrogen bomb around the world. Prime Minister Jawaharlal Nehru of India commented: "If we have come to the conclusion that the world is a bad show let the hydrogen bomb put an end to it. Otherwise put an end to the hydrogen bomb." Nehru's reaction was uncommon, though. A State Department telegram reported that the Japanese, although alarmed at the implications of the hydrogen bomb, "apparently do not question morality of President's decision and are realistic enough to appreciate factors which made decision necessary."[18] Western European governments generally agreed with Truman's decision on the weapon.

Beyond those who worried about the genocidal nature of the hydrogen bomb, a segment of the American public did evidence a serious concern about the increased threat to noncombatants that fusion weapons would pose. However, the concern was far from a dominant sentiment. A number of letters to the editorial pages of newspapers and to President Truman and other government officials reflected this concern. One woman wrote to the *New York Times*, "The H-bomb will erase not a village but an entire country from the face of the earth without any discrimination between soldiers and noncombatants."[19] In an unpublished poll by the National Opinion Research Center taken right before Truman's January 31 announcement on the hydrogen bomb, 37 percent of the respondents felt that the United States would not be justified in using atomic bombs against Russia if it attacked one of our Western European allies. Of these respondents, almost half gave their reasons for being opposed as "Too destructive, inhuman," "Should never be used," or "Shouldn't use it first."[20] Only 11 percent mentioned "fear of retaliation" and 4 percent "fear world destruction."[21]

A belief in the prudence of distinguishing between the Russian people and their rulers reinforced concerns about the hydrogen bomb's indiscriminate destructiveness. Before Truman's announcement, Wallace Carroll, a specialist in psychological warfare, had written an article for *Life* magazine that warned Americans against committing the same mistake that the Nazis had in fighting the Russians. Carroll argued that millions of Soviet citizens could be turned against their government through propaganda and psychological warfare, but that unwise use of atomic weapons would alienate those potential allies. He cautioned against a war of "total destruction" and suggested that if any atomic weapons had to be used that warnings be issued to the civilians first.[22] After the president's decision on the bomb, the columnists David Lawrence and Malvina Lindsay expressed similar reservations. Lawrence raised concerns that American possession of the hydrogen bomb and threats of "extermination" contributed to the international climate of fear and made attempts to split the Russian people from their Communist masters more difficult. Lindsay blasted the stupidity of American Cold War policy, which failed to distinguish more clearly between the Soviet police state and the Russian people. She said that, after all, the United States could not just exterminate all 211 million Soviet citizens.[23]

The small pacifist movement in the United States added its voice to the opposition to the hydrogen bomb and placed the weapon's potential to kill innocent noncombatants at the center of its criticism. The Christian pacifist Fellowship of Reconciliation, the secular War Resisters League, and the newly formed Peacemakers movement believed the hydrogen bomb buried the just war tradition once and for all. These pacifist organizations concluded that the new fusion bomb, because of its indiscriminate destructiveness, marked a decisive development in modern warfare that foreclosed the possibility of future just wars.[24] In 1950, the pacifists drew on a sentiment, which had been growing among religious leaders in the late 1940s, that questioned the just war tradition. Two years earlier, a report of the first meeting of the World Council of Churches held in Amsterdam declared the traditional notion of just war obsolete.[25]

Peace activists held a number of small protests against the hydrogen bomb, but the demonstrations fell far outside the mainstream of American sentiment. At a vigil against the hydrogen bomb in New York City, Reverend Donald Harrington commented, "That people who show concern over the moral implications of the hydrogen bomb are regarded as objects of curiosity is a sad comment on the world's desperate needs. There ought to be so many people interested in this that it would be commonplace."[26]

Although opposition to the hydrogen bomb was marginal in the United States, it was not a sentiment found only on the liberal end of the political spectrum. In an article on the hydrogen bomb in the Christian fundamentalist newsletter *Bible News Flashes*, an accusation that the Truman administration harbored hundreds of Communists and the speculation that the Bible foretold of the hydrogen bomb accompanied this criticism of the atomic bombing of Japan: "Without a shadow of doubt the greatest 'war crime' in the history of the world was the atomic bombing of Hiroshima and Nagasaki where tens of thousands of unsuspecting and helpless women, children and innocent babes had their lives snuffed out and where tens of thousands of others exposed to the burning rays died, days, months, and years later in indescribable torture. To what depths the human race has descended. Demon-actuated men are now determined to annihilate the human race."[27]

Despite their appearance across the political spectrum, public concerns over noncombatant immunity, which the hydrogen bombs evoked, had clear limits. Indeed, many Americans seemed unconcerned about the issues. One columnist was astounded that the "monstrous weapon" produced "no sensation anywhere" comparable to the reaction to the atomic bomb. *Time* and *Life* magazines both ran articles commenting on the public's willful avoidance of the issues raised by the new weapon.[28]

Religious leaders provided some of the examples of the muted reaction. The Federal Council of Churches in America could not agree upon a common position on the hydrogen bomb and so issued a compromise statement and established a commission to study the weapon's implications. The compromise statement said that some on the council opposed the construction of hydrogen bombs that "could be used only for the mass destruction of populations" and that others supported building the weapon because "our people and the other free societies should not be left without the means of defense through the threat of retaliation." The suggestion of Harold E. Stassen, president of the University of Pennsylvania, for an interfaith conference between Protestants, Catholics, and Jews on the hydrogen bomb never came to fruition.[29]

Limits to concern over noncombatant immunity were also apparent among the hydrogen bomb's advocates. Some who supported President Truman's decision sought to defend the new weapon against charges that its development was unwise and immoral. A common defense was to stress the necessity of or the lack of choice in developing the weapon because the Soviets would inevitably construct it. The *New York Times* science writer William L. Laurence reported that some unnamed scientists believed that the lack of choice meant that no moral values were involved in the decision to proceed with the hydrogen bomb since moral questions implied the possibility of choice. Another common claim was that the hydrogen bomb was no more horrible than the weapons of war that preceded it. The editorial page of the *New York Times* saw Americans' moral qualms over the hydrogen bomb as a credit to them and expressed the hope that war could be made more "orderly" and less "messy" and that "the verb to *annihilate* will be turned over exclusively to exterminators of vermin, to whom it properly belongs," but it also argued that the world did not face any new increase in the cruelty of warfare. The fire raids of World War II or the sacking of cities thousands of years ago were as hideous as either the actual atomic bomb or contemplated hydrogen bomb. Others questioned American qualms because they believed that the Soviets would not have similar moral reservations. The columnist Dorothy Thompson believed that the Communist form of warfare needed to be more closely scrutinized. She argued that only one form of warfare had been morally stigmatized and not the form practiced by the Communists even though it "atomizes the whole of human society, causing as great or greater terror, death, homelessness, and vast migrations of peoples as the other."[30]

A few of the arguments offered in defense of the fusion bomb came close to explicitly justifying attacks on noncombatants. Some suggested that the possession and possible use of the hydrogen bomb could be a lesser evil than the consequences of not building the weapon. The physicist Frederick Seitz in an address to the American Physical Society urged physicists to overcome any moral qualms and work harder on atomic weapons. Although he did not specify the moral dilemmas confronting scientists, he contended that these concerns were outweighed by the threat to western civilization and its most important ideals. An editorial from *Commonweal* expressed its revulsion at the destruction of cities in World War II and the atomic bombings of Hiroshima and Nagasaki, but refused to condemn Truman's decision to build the hydrogen bomb. It argued, "To rely on inferior weapons would be to expose ourselves to unnecessary slaughter and to abandon Western Europe, and perhaps eventually our own country, to a dictatorship that tramples basic human rights and makes life unendurable."[31]

Several rationalized the hydrogen bomb by appealing to grim reciprocity in war. If the Soviets used atomic weapons against civilians, then the United States would be justified in retaliating in kind. "It would not be pleasant to live in a world which our own country was compelled to slaughter millions of people in other countries by the use of the H-bomb," an editorial in the *New York Times* concluded. "It would, however, be just a little pleasanter than having our own people slaughtered by H-bombs thrown in from outside." Lewis Strauss also made public statements that implied that attacks on noncombatants in retaliation for a Soviet attack were justified. In a speech that he later turned into a *Life* magazine article, Strauss acknowledged the evil of attacking civilians. He wrote, "The destruction of civil populations is abhorrent whatever the means or weapons used — no matter how 'orthodox.'" However, he maintained, "If our country is subjected to a new and more horrible Pearl Harbor with atomic bombs or hydrogen bombs, or our national existence seriously endangered by some other new and terrible form of warfare, then and under those circumstances we would be justified in using every weapon we possessed to insure the preservation of our freedom and our way of life." In these and other statements, he also emphasized Soviet atheism and what he claimed to be their denial of the "existence of moral law."[32]

Since the expectation that the Soviet Union would eventually possess the hydrogen bomb was so prominent in explanations for why the weapon needed to be developed, it is surprising that Americans did not more often explicitly advocate the possible need for attacks on Soviet civilians in retaliation for a Soviet attack on Americans. The more common, but vague, mentions of the importance of the hydrogen bomb in "retaliation" against Soviet aggression, for "defense," or in "winning" a war against the Soviets might have contained the implication that Soviet civilians would be attacked, but explicit support for such attacks was rare.

This was even more surprising because attention to how the United States should defend itself against an atomic attack once again brought forward the possibility that strikes against civilian populations might be a devastatingly effective method of warfare. George Fielding Eliot, a writer on military and foreign affairs, wrote an article for the *American Legion* magazine in February 1950 on civil defense that considered this possibility. In arguing for the dispersal of American urban population and industry, he suggested that "two or three well-placed bombs dropped on the heart of Detroit, killing or injuring perhaps a quarter or a third of the population of that city and putting the city out of business as a going concern, would do more damage to American auto-motive production than the same number of bombs dropped with precision on the local Ford, Chrysler and Dodge plants." Such a discussion, which depicted the Soviet Union as the theoretical perpetrator of the attacks, did not necessarily translate into advocacy of American attacks against enemy non-combatants, but it was not a farfetched implication that what could work for the Soviets could work for the United States.[33]

Those who accepted attacks on cities and civilian populations and believed noncombatant immunity had become a thing of the past did exist, but they rarely expressed their opinions publicly. One example was William L. Borden who in 1950 was serving on the staff of the Congressional Joint Committee on Atomic Energy. Borden wrote a top-secret memorandum about the value of the hydrogen bomb to his boss Representative Sterling Cole who was initially skeptical about the value of the new weapon. Cole had given speeches that gently implied the hydrogen bomb might be more immoral than lesser weap-ons because it was more indiscriminate in its effects. Borden argued that the use of the hydrogen bomb against a city like New York would be militarily effective even though the city did not contain many factories or installations that contributed directly to the support of the armed forces. The "destruction of New York," he claimed, would demoralize everyone in the United States, thereby improving Soviet chances for victory. The harm to the civilian popula-tion would also be important. "Moreover, even in terms of the narrowest mili-tary logic, destruction of New York would reduce our supply of soldiers and workers," Borden wrote. "It would also, through population attrition, tend to prevent post-war American resurgence and revenge in the event of a Soviet victory."

Borden contended that the maintenance of a distinction between military and nonmilitary targets could be "wishful thinking" now that total war, which he linked to totalitarianism, had been invented. He wrote, "Certainly if the last war is any indication, a mental picture of A-bombs dropping neatly upon bases and munitions factories and largely avoiding damage to civilians is far removed from reality." In his memo, Borden did include a nod to the tradition of noncombatant immunity. He claimed that "moral objections" to the use of nuclear weapons could be met "in part" by providing warnings to populations living in target areas through radio broadcasts or leaflets. However, since Bor-den based his arguments for the utility of the hydrogen bomb in part on its capacity for killing civilians, it is doubtful that this comment was anything more than a superficial acknowledgment of the need to pacify potential critics. Borden's true interest in warning civilians may have been its potential to pro-voke mass evacuations and disrupt the Soviet war effort, which he went on to describe briefly in his memorandum.[34]

As the public discussion surrounding the unveiling of the hydrogen bomb demonstrated, American concern for noncombatant immunity had its limits.

Few Americans openly advocated foregoing the most powerful and indiscriminate explosives that humankind had invented. However, support for the bomb did not translate into open rejection of noncombatant immunity. Acceptance of massively destructive techniques of warfare existed uneasily alongside widespread avowal of the illegitimacy of attacking noncombatants.

3.3 Searching for Reconciliation

Some Americans, who believed the hydrogen bomb should be developed, were troubled enough by the contradiction between the new weapon and noncombatant immunity that they sought some form of reconciliation. A new effort at establishing the international control of atomic energy, negotiations on which had been stalled since 1946, offered a way of acquiescing to the development of the hydrogen bomb in the short term while holding out a hope that its use could be avoided. Many Americans looked to this option to resolve their dilemma. Senator Brien McMahon proposed offering $50 billion in economic aid to the world, including the Soviet bloc, if all nations would agree to international control with adequate inspections. Senator Millard E. Tydings of Maryland called for a world disarmament conference to eliminate both nuclear and conventional military forces. The editorial pages of the *New York Times*, *St. Louis Post-Dispatch*, *Detroit News*, and *Cleveland Press* endorsed further efforts to achieve international control and disarmament. Appalled at the potential for slaughter in modern war and convinced that neither side could win one, the *Detroit News* was not satisfied with the "distinction between mass destruction and that aimed at the fighting man or the war worker and his tools." The distinction had never much appealed to the widow of the slain soldier, it said, and "saturation" bombing from World War II and the World War I naval blockade of food for civilians had already undermined the distinction. Therefore, the paper declared war itself immoral and advocated world disarmament in order to end the practice but accepted the need for the construction of the hydrogen bomb until agreement could be reached.[35]

Liberal and religious journals like the *New Republic*, *Nation*, and *Christian Century* endorsed a new attempt at international control as an alternative to a war of extermination and the destruction of whole populations. Walter M. Horton in the *Christian Century* was even optimistic about eliminating war or at least its most destructive methods, pointing out that the Navy's top admirals had recently protested against the growing indiscriminate destruction of warfare. Likewise, the National Council of Presbyterian Men adopted a resolution that urged the President "to continue the efforts by the United States to bring together all nations of the world to control all physical forces of warfare designed to destroy civilians en masse."[36] However, President Truman and Secretary Acheson soon made clear that the United States would make no new proposals or undertake any additional efforts on behalf of international control. Although the hope remained that horror at the prospect of the hydrogen bomb could convince the Soviets to agree to the old American terms for international control, the prospects for agreement were dim.

A number saw hope in a fantastic form of deterrence that would not require formal international agreement to secure peace. While some believed that the hydrogen bomb would be an additional deterrent to Soviet aggression, which would be used if needed, a number sought to harness the weapon's power to deter without condoning the weapon's use. They believed the bomb to be so terrible that nations would be scared into peaceful ways, even though they believed that the weapon was too horrible to use. An editorial from the Jesuit magazine *America* took some solace from this notion. "This ghastly weapon cannot be designed primarily for use against an aggressor," it said. "Its real purpose must be to forestall aggression, to ward off war so that we may have the political and economic *opportunity* to build up a peaceful world." A column by David Lawrence asked, "Does the United States really mean to use the hydrogen bomb some day or do we merely intend to threaten its use so as to force an agreement assuring international control of atomic weapons?"[37] This form of deterrence, which separated the weapon's power to deter from an intention to use it, was problematic because if the hydrogen bomb was so terrible, then it might weaken the American will to employ it. If the United States was unwilling to use the horrible weapon, then an aggressor had nothing to fear from the fusion bomb. For those who were anguished over the prospect of the hydrogen bomb's use against noncombatants, deterrence backed by an unusable weapon provided a questionable resolution.

A group of scientists proposed an alternative plan that sought to cultivate a limited form of deterrence that would prevent the new weapon from ever being used in war. Twelve physicists, most of whom had worked on the atomic bomb, proposed that the United States pledge not to be the first to use the hydrogen bomb in any future war and to reserve its use only for retaliation if another country were to employ the weapon. The scientists accepted Truman's decision to proceed with the development of the bomb because they believed that American possession of it might deter its use by others, but they asserted that no country had the right to use the weapon against another. They claimed that the bomb "is no longer a weapon of war but a means of extermination of whole populations" and its use "would be a betrayal of all standards of morality and of Christian civilization itself."[38]

Hans A. Bethe, who had been the head of the theoretical division at Los Alamos and had made important contributions to understanding the thermonuclear process in stars, became the spokesman for this proposal. He elaborated on the moral issues that made the plan imperative on Eleanor Roosevelt's television show and with articles in *Scientific American* and the *Bulletin of the Atomic Scientists*. Bethe argued that while the atomic bomb could still be used against military targets, the hydrogen bomb could only mean "a wholesale destruction of civilian populations." He characterized the broader American conflict with the Soviets as one over means that would become meaningless if the United States adopted methods comparable to the butchery of Genghis Khan. The technological trend that set the United States on the path to the hydrogen bomb, Bethe saw, as motivated by humane intentions. After the slaughter in the trenches of World War I, American military leaders had replaced war by soldiers with war by machine in order to conserve life as much as possible. However, the hydrogen bomb had carried the end to its absurd extreme in which "in place of one soldier who would die in battle, [the hydrogen bomb] kills a hundred noncombatant civilians." Bethe also offered a rejoinder to the contention that the new bomb was no more immoral than any other weapon. The thousandfold increase in destructive power over the blockbuster that the atomic bomb represented placed that weapon in a new moral category, which motivated Americans to seek international control. The hydrogen bomb, projected to be one thousand times more powerful than the atomic bomb, likewise created yet another correspondingly worse moral problem.[39]

Although the scientists' no first use proposal received a fair amount of newspaper attention,[40] the idea received only a few isolated endorsements. Henry A. Wallace of the Progressive Party, the theologian Reinhold Niebuhr, the editorial page of the *Philadelphia Bulletin*, and Senator Ralph Flanders, who had introduced the congressional resolution to ban the use of the atomic bomb in 1949, opposed the first use of the hydrogen bomb against an enemy. Some lack of sympathy for the pledge stemmed from a misunderstanding of what the scientists were proposing. A *Houston Chronicle* editorial entitled "Atomic Confusion" only contributed to the befuddlement surrounding the hydrogen bomb by dismissing the scientists' proposal because, it claimed, American leaders had already stated that the United States would not use the atomic bomb first. Apparently, the newspaper was thinking of governmental statements that the country would not use the atomic bomb for aggression but only as retaliation against nations who attacked the United States or its allies. However, this official stance left open the possibility that the United States would use nuclear weapons in retaliation against a conventional attack. The editorial had mistaken these statements for a pledge not to use the new weapons first.[41]

A few in government such as Robert Oppenheimer and George Kennan did support a no-first-use pledge, and the subject was considered during the broad review of national security policy undertaken on the recommendation of the NSC special committee which advised Truman to accelerate the thermonuclear weapon program.[42] The review produced the Cold War manifesto NSC-68 in April 1950, which contained an influential statement of the ends and means of the American struggle against international communism. NSC-68 rejected a no-first-use pledge, and the United States never offered one. The twelve physicists' attempt at reconciling the possession of weapons of mass destruction with a commitment to noncombatant immunity had little future.

William Laurence offered a different type of reconciliation that did not foreswear or seek to avoid the use of the hydrogen bomb. He was one of the enthusiastic defenders of the thermonuclear bomb against the charge that it was a weapon of extermination. As a science reporter for the *New York Times*, he had become a leading commentator on atomic energy in 1945. The Manhattan Project had given Laurence special access to information about the development of the atomic bomb that had allowed him to write the first newspaper stories about the weapon. With public attention on the hydrogen bomb, Laurence seized the opportunity again to shape discussion of atomic energy. He wrote a short book, *The Hell Bomb*, explaining the implications of the new super weapon. Despite the book's title, Laurence presented a rather benign and optimistic view, and he directly disputed the charges that the hydrogen bomb was an indiscriminate weapon of slaughter. Although he thought that the United States had no choice but to build the bomb in order to avoid emboldening the Soviet Union, he fervently believed that if the United States took the proper precautions and followed a wise policy, construction of the bomb could ensure security without endangering American values.

Laurence viewed the hydrogen bomb, if designed properly, as an ideal tactical weapon against the large armies of the Soviet Union. Laurence challenged the assumption that nuclear weapons could only be used against cities. The first uses of the atomic bomb against Japanese cities had misled people in their thinking about nuclear arms. Laurence claimed, "Since industrial centers, particularly in the United States, are densely populated areas, and since, conversely, all large cities are also important industrial centers, it has become almost axiomatic that the A-bomb and the H-bomb could be used only in strategic bombing of large centers of population, which, of course, means the wholesale slaughter of millions of civilians...." However, the hydrogen bomb might render strategic bombing obsolete. Laurence estimated that the blast effects of the H-bomb would destroy everything within 300 square miles and its fireball would incinerate everything within 1,200 square miles. This destructive power could annihilate armies in the field, which eliminated the need to prevent resupply of these armies from industrial centers. "It is thus the tactical weapon par excellence," claimed Laurence. Since large armies constituted the Soviet Union's greatest military asset, Laurence held out the hope that the hydrogen bomb could deter the Soviets from ever starting a war. In proposing the hydrogen bomb as a means to defeat an enemy's armed forces instead of as means to destroy an enemy's society, Laurence adopted many of the arguments that the disgruntled admirals had advanced in the October 1949 hearings and offered a way around the apparent conflict between an adherence to the norm of noncombatant immunity and the current practice of warfare.

Laurence's view of the hydrogen bomb led him to the conclusion that the United States should renounce the first use of the new weapon against civilian populations as well as renounce city bombing of any kind. Americans could seize a moral victory from the Russians in the Cold War because Laurence assumed that the Soviet Union would not make a similar declaration: "She would stand before the world as a nation bent on wholesale slaughter of civilian populations." With such a declaration, the United States would occupy a much more comfortable moral position. The country still might have to fight wars because it had a right and duty to defend itself against aggressors. However, the aggressor would be responsible for the evil of the deaths of soldiers on both sides, and the United States would not add to this evil of war by slaughtering noncombatants. Laurence urged, "Let us admit that the mass bombing of large populated cities (which, by the way, was started by the Nazis) is wholly inexcusable with any kind of weapons, and that we should never resort to such strategic bombing again. That does not mean that we should renounce our right to use A-bombs to destroy an enemy's armies, navies, and airfields, his transportation facilities and his oil wells — in a word, his capacity to make war against us." Radiation had given the new weapons an evil image, but bombs properly built and employed would not unleash this frightening and deadly force. For Laurence, attention to technique in the use of nuclear weapons and in their construction could remove any moral reservations about the new implements of destruction.[43]

Nowhere in his book did Laurence consider the possibility that nuclear weapons targeted solely at the military forces of an enemy would unavoidably kill noncombatants. Instead, The Hell Bomb presented a comfortable vision of future warfare. The hydrogen bomb would most likely prevent a war involving the United States from ever breaking out, but even if one did, Americans could use their most powerful weapons without the fear of unleashing deadly radioactive clouds or causing widespread civilian casualties.

Laurence's optimism about the possibility of using the massively destructive hydrogen bomb in a discriminating manner was not common. His claims that the hydrogen bomb would constitute an important tactical weapon attracted some attention in the press.[44] Reviews of his book chose to emphasize this prediction as one of his major points, but none endorsed his view and some, including the review in his own New York Times, were openly skeptical about the possibility of using the hydrogen bomb against enemy armed forces without killing civilians. Another book on atomic energy and the hydrogen bomb published just before Laurence's The Hell Bomb also disagreed with the science reporter. The author Gerald Wendt, a chemist and science writer, concluded that the bomb's "prime effect is to kill civilians" and that it "abandons the civilized rules of war which in recent times have protected women and children, the aged, non-combatants and prisoners of war."[45]

Although far from generally accepted, Laurence's opinions did coincide with a nascent belief about weapons of mass destruction. By the end of 1950, the idea was spreading that even nuclear, biological, and chemical weapons could be used against military targets in such a way as to spare noncombatants. Although few came to accept Laurence's claim that thermonuclear weapons would be used for military purposes other than city-busting, many came to believe that atomic fission weapons and to a lesser degree biological and chemical weapons could be reconciled with the tradition of noncombatant immunity.

A moral theologian at Catholic University, whose thinking on nuclear weapons began to emerge in the press during the discussion of the hydrogen bomb, had much in common with Laurence's perspective. Francis J. Connell argued that nuclear weapons were not necessarily evil in their effects. Their use could be moral if used in a proper manner. In the Jesuit magazine *America*, the editorials of which had stressed the importance of the moral issues surrounding the hydrogen bomb,[46] Father Connell received a sympathetic hearing on the morality of the new weapon. Father Edward A. Conway authored an editorial that closely compared the moral reasoning of Hans Bethe in his *Scientific American* article with that of Connell in a recent article in the Catholic periodical *Sign*. Conway praised Connell's reasoning over Bethe's because Connell argued that the hydrogen bomb, like the atomic bomb, was not intrinsically immoral but that the use to which it was put determined its morality. Connell argued that a hydrogen bomb used against a "military target, such as a fleet at sea, a body of troops, a railroad center, a road used by the enemy's supply trucks, or an ammunition dump" was completely legitimate. Like Laurence, Connell believed that the hydrogen bomb could be used tactically against military forces and that this use was morally justified. Unlike Bethe, Connell denied that the hydrogen bomb was inevitably a weapon of mass slaughter. The theologian did condemn the purposeful mass killing of populations and addressed the difficult question of bombing military targets in or near cities with their civilian residents. Refusing to accept the theory that modern total war rendered all civilians combatants, Connell argued that the hydrogen bomb could only be used against targets in cities if the target was "one of supreme importance, such as the only factory in which the enemy is making his own superbombs, or the building in which all the war lords of the enemy are assembled." Since the hydrogen bomb could conceivably be used in a legitimate manner, Connell concluded that Truman's decision to develop the weapon and the United States' possession of it could be reconciled with morality.

Father Conway had one suggestion for Connell. He proposed that the United States enter into agreement with the Soviet Union to outlaw the use of the hydrogen bomb against cities, but mostly Conway praised Connell's conclusions. In a later issue of *America*, Conway defended Connell against a reader who wrote a letter to charge Connell with being impractical. The letter said, "It is all very well for him to insist on the principle that one *could* use the H-bomb legitimately, and to distinguish between the *tactical* and *strategic* uses of the bomb, but does not the *practical* fact remain that in case of war our military would almost certainly pay no attention to these distinctions?" Conway replied that the moralist should be concerned with what ought to be done not with what might actually happen. He also charged that the reader was implying that the United States should not build the hydrogen bomb, which would leave the country vulnerable to Soviet threats once they had built the superior weapon.[47]

Connell rejected the charge that thermonuclear weapons were inherently immoral, and a stance like his encouraged the quieting of moral concerns. Although Connell suggested strict conditions that had to be met for its justified employment, he did sanction use of the weapon. Other more prominent public voices took a position similar to Connell's without detailing what constituted a moral use of the bomb. Dwight Eisenhower, Lewis Strauss, and columnist Holmes Alexander each commented publicly that the potential evil of the hydrogen bomb depended on how humankind employed it, but did not specify what the nature of the evil might be or how one would avoid it.[48]

Concerns over the destructiveness of the hydrogen bomb had propelled a small group of politicians, scientists, writers, and professors into contemplating how to avoid devastation against civilians in a world that would have thermonuclear weapons. Some placed hope in international control of the weapons, others in the avoidance of their use, and still others in their use against purely military targets. They had begun a process that would develop over the years to come of attempting to reconcile the preservation of some form of noncombatant immunity with a dependence on massively destructive methods of warfare.

3.4 Public Sensitivity, Secret Neglect

The hydrogen bomb decision and the discussion surrounding it illustrated the continued sensitivity to the idea of noncombatant immunity but also the limits of that concern. Truman's decision to accelerate the thermonuclear program was not appreciably influenced by the concerns over noncombatant immunity. The extent of the impact of those concerns on the Truman administration was a sensitivity to public statements about the new weapons that might associate the arms with harm to noncombatants. For example, this sensitivity led to the modification of the Department of Defense's semiannual report published in early 1950. The report was to contain a short statement on "unconventional weapons." A draft of this statement submitted to the State Department and previously approved by the Department of Defense and the AEC, included the sentence: "A military decision to attack, or fail to attack, a city or other 'civilian' target depends on many factors." Paul Nitze did not like the draft's choice of words. He proposed "that for 'a city or other civilian target', there be substituted 'major elements of the enemy's economy supporting his military effort'; or words to this effect which would not draw attention to the possibility of mass destruction of urban populations, especially at a time when our overall strategy may be under review." The new wording was used in the public report.[49]

The administration also refused to make any further statements on the hydrogen bomb after Truman's initial announcement. When Sumner T. Pike, the acting chairperson of the AEC, proposed to Truman in late May a more detailed public statement on the hydrogen bomb project, the military and the State Department objected. The military feared that another statement would prompt further public discussion and disclosure of "vital information." The State Department worried that a statement would assist Soviet propaganda and heighten fears in Europe. A position paper approved by Nitze said: "The feeling of terror among the Europeans at the prospect of annihilation through atomic warfare is beginning to recede somewhat in the face of announcements from this side of the water that we may develop small atomic weapons for tactical use. Statements stressing the development of the hydrogen bomb, which is generally thought to be usable only for purposes of obliteration bombing, may well cause a new wave of anxiety among Western Europeans." The State Department had already implemented measures to avoid scaring peoples abroad with news of the hydrogen bomb. When Truman delivered his statement on the new weapon, guidance went out to the State Department's international information programs such as Voice of America to not use the phrase "weapons of mass destruction" to refer to hydrogen bombs, and subsequent guidance encouraged reporting that minimized the importance of the hydrogen bomb as a news story.[50]

While concerns over noncombatant immunity influenced the Truman administration's public relations policy, they had little impact on military planning. The secret war plans of the JCS of the late 1940s clearly illustrated this. The U.S. planning showed that American sensitivity to harm to noncombatants bestowed very little protection on civilians in a future war. The studies and plans for war with the Soviet Union that the various committees of the Joint Staff created after World War II did not explicitly advocate attacks on the general Soviet population. The strategic air offensive, which became a fixture of American war plans, would launch atomic weapons as well as conventional bombs against the Soviet Union early in a war. The offensive's stated goal was the destruction of Soviet "war-making capacity and will." The plans and studies made it clear that the physical destruction of industrial facilities supporting the Soviet war effort was the major undertaking in fulfilling this goal. However, the documents did refer to using atomic weapons against "cities," "urban areas," and "population centers" and the names of Soviet cities were listed in the earliest studies and plans as the targets for attack based on the assumption that the devastation of these areas would include the destruction of industry. The 1948 emergency war plan code-named "Broiler" included a discussion of how urban areas were "inseparable" from industry as a target. A later report said, "Although aiming points are selected primarily to focus the damage on specific industries and industrial concentrations, it is inevitable that actual damage will be indiscriminate as to types and functions of other installations within the target areas." The study admitted that many of these "other installations" were houses and that their destruction in large numbers would impose "lasting hardship" on the urban population.[51]

In part, urban areas became the targets because the United States lacked adequate intelligence on the location of Soviet industry, but the Joint Staff documents also revealed another motivation for using the scarce atomic bombs against cities. Planners were reluctant to see any of the bomb's destructive potential unutilized. As one study of the effects of an atomic attack against the Soviet Union put it, "Significant is the fact that the atomic bomb is a weapon particularly effective against built-up, populated areas such as cities, that if used against isolated targets of limited size, although it might be effective against the target itself, much of its destructive effect may be unused." In other words, the general devastation of urban areas would contribute to the disruption of industry even if to an unknown and perhaps marginal degree.[52]

The plans and studies came close to proposing attacks on the general civilian population in their discussion of the "psychological effects" of the atomic attack. The planners did not specify how they believed atomic attack would undermine the morale of the Soviet people. Conceivably this lowered morale could have resulted from a fear that the war was lost with Soviet industry in disarray instead of from the suffering of the civilian population. However, several studies linked the psychological effects to general casualties, and one study made the connection directly with the phrase "the psychological shock effect of more than one million casualties."[53]

A study also noted that the total casualties for atomic attacks on urban areas would include a number of technicians and workers vital to industry. Those making a contribution to industrial production may have been the ultimate target, but killing of the general population had been made a means to that end. The study even mentioned the harm that the families of the industrial workers would suffer as if to suggest that industrial production could be slowed by hurting workers' families. The planners were not blind to the issue of protection of noncombatants in all cases. The war plans incorporated the assumption that atomic weapons would not be used against the Soviet Union's Eastern European allies except in extreme circumstances because of the desire not to alienate the potentially friendly populations of those countries.[54]

Another demonstration of the limits of Americans' and their government's concern over noncombatant immunity was the rejection of an appeal by the ICRC to ban all "blind" weapons including atomic bombs. In April 1950, the ICRC called on the nations who had signed the Geneva Conventions on war victims of 1949 to take steps to reach an agreement to prohibit all weapons whose effects could not be directed precisely by the user, such as atomic weapons. The appeal argued that protection of war victims under the new Geneva Conventions would be impossible in wars in which atomic weapons inflicted their "total" destruction. In contrast to the Soviet Union, which approved of the ban on atomic weapons, the U.S. government did not respond positively to the overture.[55] The significance of noncombatant immunity could not outweigh the importance of nuclear weapons to American military policy.

Concern over the preservation of noncombatant immunity in the face of the increasing destructive power of nuclear weapons infused the public and internal government discussions of the hydrogen bomb in early 1950. However, the discussions demonstrated that those who favored abandoning modern war's most destructive weapons, or even war itself, in order to preserve noncombatant immunity were a small minority just as the unification and strategy hearings had revealed sentiment to abandon noncombatant immunity to be marginal. The United States would not surrender the freedom to use its atomic weapons nor its most destructive techniques of warfare, but many Americans clung to the ideal of wars that could avoid the slaughter of innocents. Thus, Americans were left confronting an acute dilemma. Although the outlines of how Americans would attempt to reconcile these conflicting desires were apparent in the discussions surrounding the 1949 hearings and the hydrogen bomb, the strategies for reconciliation emerged more clearly when Americans again engaged in war in Korea.

4

A "Limited" War in Korea

When President Truman committed the U.S. military to expelling North Korean forces from the southern half of the Korean peninsula in June 1950, the dilemma of indiscriminate destruction ceased to concern simply a theoretical future war. In Korea, Americans confronted a real test of their conflicting commitments to massively destructive methods of warfare and to the norm of noncombatant immunity. During this war, public commentary revealed that an older approach to the problem still held much power. As if reviving views from the Second World War, most Americans discussed the Korean War as if a contradiction did not exist between U.S. war-fighting methods and noncombatant immunity. From the start of the fighting, American officials promoted the optimistic notion that, despite the much greater destructive potential of current weapons, the U.S. military could still apply violence in a discriminate manner against military targets while avoiding harm to civilians. The mainstream press mirrored back this notion, and much of the American public appeared to accept it.

The actions of the American military in the early months of the war initially made this optimistic idea seem reasonable. The course of the war appeared to contradict the notion that 1945 had been a harbinger of future American warfare. The Korean War did not develop into the atomic World War III that many Americans feared, and the war did not begin, as World War II had ended, with the obliteration of cities. Despite support among SAC generals for immediate fire raids intended to level entire North Korean cities, American forces restricted their attacks to a narrower range of military targets in the opening months of the war.

Ultimately, though, American forces would inflict great destruction on Korean civil society. By the fifth month of the war, most restrictions on the use of air power had disappeared, and the U.S. Air Force commenced burning and demolishing entire Korean towns and cities. American ground and naval operations gradually contributed to the widespread destruction as well. In addition, from the earliest weeks of the war, the U.S. military had difficulty managing the flow of refugees that the fighting created, and its refugee control policies, at times, proved deadly for these homeless civilians. Contrary to expectations, the war's devastation came in increments instead of from a sudden atomic or incendiary blitz from the air.

In the face of this destruction, the optimism about the discriminate use of violence persisted throughout the war. It survived in part because of the elasticity of American definitions of what constituted a "military target." During the war, American military and civilian officials stretched the term "military target" to include virtually all human-made structures, capitalizing on the vague distinction between the military and civilian segments of an enemy society. They came to apply the logic of total war to the destruction of the civil infrastructure of North Korea. Because almost any building could serve a military purpose, even if a minor one, nearly the entire physical infrastructure behind enemy lines was deemed a military target and open to attack. This expansive definition, along with the optimism about sparing civilians that it reinforced, worked to obscure in American awareness the suffering of Korean civilians to which U.S. firepower was contributing. The Korean War demonstrated both the limits that Americans could place on the means they employed in battle and the limits of the protection for vulnerable civilians that American concern over noncombatant immunity offered.

4.1 Initial Restraints on the Use of Force

On June 25, 1950, the North Korean People's Army swept across the thirty-eighth parallel into the southern half of the Korean peninsula. Supported by tanks and artillery that South Korean forces lacked, the North Koreans made quick gains. Within two days, President Truman, concerned with halting what he believed to be Soviet-inspired aggression, had ordered General Douglas A. MacArthur to use American air and naval forces in the western Pacific against the North Korean invaders.

The war escalated gradually, never igniting the tinder of global war and nuclear holocaust. American leaders restrained the force of their intervention initially. MacArthur's instructions from Washington restricted the use of American air and naval power to south of the thirty-eighth parallel and specified that the North Korean military forces should be the object of attack. The instructions read, "All North Korean tanks, guns, military columns and other military targets south of the 38th Parallel are cleared for attack."[1] With American strikes restricted to the territory of South Korea, it was understandable that the focus of attack would be North Korean armed forces and not industrial, transportation, or supply facilities that they might have captured in the south. The North Korean military posed an immediate threat and devastation of South Korean infrastructure would be wasteful if the tide of battle could quickly be reversed.

After four days, American air and naval power had not stemmed the advance of the North Koreans. The JCS sent a second set of instructions to

MacArthur permitting the extension of air and naval operations into North Korea. These again specified a narrow range of targets for attack: "You are authorized to extend your operations into Northern Korea against air bases, depots, tank farms, troop columns and other such purely military targets, if and when, in your judgment, this becomes essential for the performance of your missions ... or to avoid unnecessary casualties to our forces." The instructions also directed operations in North Korea to "stay well clear of the frontiers of Manchuria or the Soviet Union."[2] The initial sets of instructions to MacArthur functioned under two assumptions: one, that there were military targets, specifically enemy armed forces and their supplies, and nonmilitary targets, presumably everything else, and, two, that American commanders understood this common sense definition of "military targets."

In the meeting of the NSC that had agreed on the wording of MacArthur's June 29 instructions, both President Truman and Secretary of State Dean Acheson supported the limitations on operations apparently out of a desire to avoid provoking the Soviet Union into a general war. When Secretary of Defense Louis Johnson read a JCS draft of the instructions that had been written in consultation with the State Department, Truman interjected his concern about a possible war with the Soviet Union. When Secretary of the Army Frank Pace, Jr., offered his reservations about putting any limitations into the directive for MacArthur, the president responded that some restrictions were necessary. Truman said he only wanted to destroy air bases, gasoline supplies, ammunition dumps, and such places north of the thirty-eighth parallel. He was concerned with restoring order below the thirty-eighth parallel and did not want to do anything north of the line except that which would "keep the North Koreans from killing the people we are trying to save." Agreeing with the president, Secretary Acheson said he had no objections to attacks on North Korean airfields and army units but believed no action should be taken outside of North Korea. Acheson had already received an indication of Soviet opposition to a liberal use of American force. The Soviet representative to the United Nations Yakov A. Malik had expressed Soviet displeasure over American planes bombing Korean cities. Apparently, Truman and Acheson believed that attacks on targets other than "purely military" ones, as well as strikes against targets outside of Korea, held a greater risk of provoking the Soviet Union.[3]

The top generals of SAC had a different plan for how the opening phase of the new war should be fought. The SAC generals wanted to incinerate the five North Korean cities that contained much of the countries' industries. In early July, the JCS dispatched two groups of SAC B-29 bombers, under the command of Major General Emmett "Rosy" O'Donnell, to support MacArthur's forces in East Asia. When O'Donnell first met with MacArthur in Tokyo, he told the U.N. commander that he would like to do a "fire job" on the five industrial centers of northern Korea. O'Donnell argued that proper use of his bombers required heavy blows at the "sources of substance" for enemy frontline soldiers. His B-29s were "heavy-handed, clumsy, but powerful," and they were no good at "playing with tanks, bridges, and Koreans on bicycles." O'Donnell proposed that MacArthur announce to the world that as U.N. commander he was going to employ, against his wishes, the means that"brought Japan to its knees." The North Korean refusal to restore peace left him no alternative, the general could say. The announcement could ease concerns over harming civilians by serving as a warning, as O'Donnell put it, "to get women and children and other noncombatants the hell out." Deliberate and systematic operations could then start anytime after twenty-four or forty-eight hours. According to O'Donnell, MacArthur listened to the entire proposal and then said, "No, Rosy, I'm not prepared to go that far yet. My instructions are very explicit; however, I want you to know that I have no compunction whatever to your bombing bona fide military objectives, with high explosives, in those five industrial centers. If you miss your target and kill people or destroy other parts of the city, I accept that as a part of war." MacArthur interpreted his instructions from Washington as prohibiting fire raids. He was not yet ready to destroy entire enemy-held cities.[4]

MacArthur's discussion with O'Donnell was followed by a directive on bombing from Lieutenant General George E. Stratemeyer, commander of the Far East Air Forces (FEAF) under MacArthur. The directive forbade O'Donnell from attacking "urban areas" as targets but authorized strikes against "specific military targets" within urban areas. Two days earlier, Stratemeyer's director of operations had written a memorandum, approved by the FEAF commander, which had said that "reasonable care" should be exercised in air operations "to avoid providing a basis for claims of 'illegal' attack against population centers." In July, MacArthur placed other restrictions on air operations to prevent unwanted damage to Korean cities. He prohibited bombing attacks on the Seoul railyards, when they had to rely on radar to find targets, because he wanted no damage done to the city. Bombing by radar was more prone to error than visual targeting.[5]

For the first few months of the war, the United States did refrain from attacks on urban areas, and these restrictions did provide greater protection for Korean civilians. There is little evidence that American leaders were motivated primarily by humanitarian concern for sparing civilians. Instead, the limitation of attacks on cities was part of a strategy to avoid provoking a war with the Soviet Union. American leaders continued to place significance on the distinction between military and civilian elements of an enemy's society because they believed the Soviets did. In their minds, a "military target" could still be distinguished from a larger enemy society. What precisely constituted a "military target" and how much of the enemy's society would be left immune from attack would undergo a transformation as the war continued, but the division between combatant and noncombatant elements would remain, and a persistent stigma against harm to civilian society lingered. O'Donnell and

LeMay would later publicly claim that the United States had missed an opportunity to end the war quickly and at a cheaper cost in American and Korean lives,[6] yet the Korean War would witness few Americans publicly advocating as a legitimate tactic in war the destruction of the civil society and noncombatant population of America's enemies. Instead, American officials, the mainstream press, and other citizens who spoke publicly on the issue seemed primarily concerned with emphasizing that the American military was applying violence in a discriminate manner.

4.2 The Vision of a Discriminate and Controlled War

Public protests against "barbarous" American attacks on civilians emanating from North Korea and its supporters put Americans on the defensive from the very start of the war. *Pravda* reported that a June 29 attack on railyards in the North Korean capitol of Pyongyang destroyed many houses and left a "considerable number" of victims among the civilian population of the city. The London *Daily Worker* charged the United States with the "indiscriminate bombing of the civilian population of Pyongyang." Several days after the Pyongyang raid, the foreign minister of North Korea sent a letter of protest to the United Nations that accused the United States of imperialistic aggression and complained of "barbarous bombardments of Korean towns and villages" and "the inhuman slaughter of peaceful citizens." The North Korean, Soviet, and Communist Chinese media continued to charge throughout July that Americans were bombing civilians and nonmilitary buildings like houses and hospitals in North Korea. Similarly, the New York *Daily Worker* charged that U.S. planes were bombing civilians, killing women and children, and perpetrating genocide against the Korean people. Fifteen issues in the month of July alone contained some mention of attacks against civilians. On August 8, the Soviet representative Yakov Malik introduced a draft resolution to the Security Council, which called upon the United States to halt the bombing of towns and populated areas and the shooting of the peaceful population of Korea from the air. The resolution claimed that "the bombing by the United States armed forces of Korean towns and villages, involving the destruction and mass annihilation of the peaceful civilian population, is a gross violation of the universally accepted rules of international law."[7]

After initial efforts to demonstrate American concern for Korean civilians through support for relief aid,[8] U.S. officials began in August to organize a more vigorous response to Communist charges. With U.S. ground forces committed to the fight and MacArthur appointed commander for U.N. forces in Korea, MacArthur's headquarters took the accusations seriously. A telegram from MacArthur's U.N. Command to the Department of the Army called the propaganda about American bombing "extremely important" and the "most immediately dangerous" of enemy psychological warfare efforts. In a report to General Stratemeyer, General O'Donnell defended the operations of his

Bomber Command against the charges. O'Donnell dismissed as "completely erroneous" the claim that his B-29s were indiscriminately bombing peaceful towns and civilians. He said that every bomb was "aimed at a specific aiming point located within the area of a bona fide military objective." He praised the accuracy of his units' bombing even though he admitted that the planes had often been forced to employ less accurate radar bombing techniques, instead of bombing visually, because of weather. When the JCS sent a new list of strategic bombing targets to the U.N. Command on August 15, it specified that because the targets were within urban areas, warnings to the population of these areas were necessary. Three days later, American planes dropped two million leaflets over North Korea warning civilians to leave cities containing military targets and expressing the U.N. forces' wish to avoid harming civilians.[9]

By mid-August, Communist propaganda was not the only overseas reaction to American bombing worrying U.S. officials. A broad coalition of nations had aligned themselves with the United States to fight the North Koreans, and this coalition provided the largely American war with the mantle of a U.N. effort to restore the peace. Concerns over protecting civilians began in August to emanate from the United Kingdom and India, two important members of the U.N. coalition. British officials became worried that the dropping of warning leaflets to Korean civilians indicated that the FEAF intended to commence saturation bombing with the object of leveling entire cities. A British embassy official informed the State Department that his government believed that such action would have serious political effects in alienating Asian and especially Indian opinion and would allow the Soviets an opportunity for further antics in the Security Council. The British wanted approval of the United Nations for saturation bombing if the tactic had to be resorted to. General Bradley had to reassure the British that the United States was only bombing purely military targets like marshalling yards, warehouses, and industrial plants. The British press mirrored their government's concern over American air attacks. The London *Times* and the liberal newspaper the *News Chronicle* warned that American bombing could generate negative reactions internationally and among Koreans.

On August 24, Prime Minister Jawaharlal Nehru of India added his reservations to the welter of worries. In a press conference, he expressed concern that innocent persons might be killed and unnecessary damage done in the U.N. bombing. He argued against the tactic of heavy bombing, which he believed created problems for the future. He also claimed that the experience of the last war had demonstrated that heavy bombing was unable to produce the military results sought. However, since he did not know the specific circumstances in Korea, Nehru said he could not judge the issue. The American embassy in New Delhi alerted the State Department in the last days of August to the emergence of an "alarming" racial theme in the Indian press. Indian newspapers argued that the United States was bombing in Korea without concern for

civilian lives and that Americans during the last war had showed special solicitude for the European enemy but treated Asians differently. Because of this
sentiment, the United States selected Japanese cities as the targets for the first
atomic bomb, the argument ran. This Indian criticism was worrisome to U.S.
officials because India occupied a special position in the American strategy to
maintain a U.N. coalition to fight the North Koreans. India had significant
influence in the United Nations among the Arab-Asian bloc, which sought to
steer a neutral course in the competition between the western and Soviet
groups. The American officials had been grateful for Indian support for the
initial U.N. resolution condemning North Korean aggression and so feared the
diplomatic setback of alienating India.[10]

With concern over world opinion mounting, American leaders gave clear
assurances that the United States was using violence discriminately in Korea.
General MacArthur attempted to counter the charges of indiscriminate bombing in his public reports to the United Nations. "The problem of avoiding the
killing of innocent civilians and damages to the civilian economy is continu-
ally present and given my personal attention," MacArthur reassured.[11] At a
September 6 news conference, the secretary of state also denied the accusation
that U.N. forces were "bombing and killing defenseless civilians." Acheson said
that U.N. air strikes in Korea had been "directed solely at military targets of
the invader" and that these targets were "enemy troop concentrations, supply
dumps, war plants, and communication lines." The secretary accused the
North Koreans of compelling civilians to labor at military sites, using peaceful
villages to hide tanks, and disguising their soldiers in civilian clothes. He concluded by placing the blame for the calamities that war had brought to Korea
on North Korean aggression. State Department guidance directed its diplomatic officers around the world to stress the secretary's points as well as American concern for the Korean population as demonstrated through the leaflet
warnings to civilians and the plans for relief and reconstruction. The guidance
also instructed the officers to do everything they could to place the onus of
Korean suffering on the Soviet Union because it was helping to prolong the
conflict. The State Department sent similar guidance to its international information media outlets like the Voice of America.[12]

Press releases from MacArthur's U.N. Command played a crucial role in
presenting to the world a picture of a careful and discriminating use of force in
Korea. The releases that described daily air strikes and naval shelling meticu-
lously noted that the targets attacked by U.N. forces were "military targets"
and often identified the target as a war-supporting facility like a chemical factory, railroad yard, or warehouse. One release of just over 400 words concerning a U.N. attack against the port city of Chongjin mentioned six times that
the installations destroyed were "military targets."[13] Often the press releases
would emphasize the accuracy and precision with which U.N. forces would
destroy their targets and the care they would take to avoid residential areas

within towns and cities.[14] One airman was quoted in a release as saying of a
B-26 strike at Yechon, "We were very careful with this job, because the
[supply] dump is in a city. All of our bombs were well within the target area."[15]

Only rarely did the U.N. Command press releases fail to specify the military
nature of targets attacked and instead use vague references to attacks on
"towns" or "villages." When the releases acknowledged that U.N. forces had
destroyed villages, they often explained that enemy soldiers were hiding in the
villages and occasionally speculated that the civilian population had abandoned the village under attack.[16] The releases also explained how the North
Koreans used women and children to discourage American planes from
attacking them. One reported, "Guided by spotters to villages where enemy
forces were known to be assembling, the flyers found the streets thronged with
women and children and no men or troops to be seen, all presumably con-
cealed in the houses of the hamlets. The airmen refrained from bombing for
fear of causing maximum casualties among the noncombatants."[17] Because
Communist propaganda specifically charged that American forces were targeting school houses, a number of press releases noted that the North Koreans
were using the buildings to shelter their troops.[18] In the late summer, U.N.
Command press releases and State Department publicity guidance sought to
contrast humane American actions, such as the dropping of warning leaflets
and the provision of relief aid to Koreans, with atrocious North Korean behavior like the shooting of prisoners of war.[19]

The American press mirrored the official emphasis on the care that U.S.
forces in Korea were taking to apply violence discriminately. The press
depicted a fight in which the American military targeted only enemy soldiers
and war-related facilities for destruction; "precision bombing" was the norm;
and American soldiers took precautions to avoid harming noncombatants.
For example, a *Saturday Evening Post* article on the early American bombardment of North Korea reassured its readers that rather than bombing blindly
on days when the weather was poor and taking the chance of killing innocent
people, the B-29s salvoed their bombs into the sea. The *New York Times*
reported that most "officials" at FEAF headquarters rejected the possibility
that American bombers would be used for "out-and-out raids on residential
areas." A column by Walter Sullivan briefly gave the impression that less discriminate destruction was occurring in Korea. He reported that American carrier planes had set fire to twenty-three villages in two days. He named three
towns that had been half burned or mostly demolished. However, the column
quickly moved on to discussing the industries and transportation targets that
American forces had destroyed.[20]

The first two months of coverage of the Korean War in the pages of
Time and *Newsweek* magazines clearly demonstrated the press' emphasis
on the discriminate use of force. In the coverage, American firepower
almost always destroyed specific targets that it was difficult for one to deny

were war-supporting. Air strikes hit enemy soldiers, tanks, bridges, railroads, and oil refineries.[21] Occasionally, the coverage used vaguer terms like "sources of North Korean power" or "supply center" to describe the objects of attack, but these terms still suggested that American force was being applied to the military potential of the enemy.[22] Only twice did the coverage suggest more general destruction. Once at the very start of the war, *Time* referred to a bombing attack of Pyongyang without mentioning a specific military target and *Newsweek* once reported that the little town of Yongdok had been "destroyed" by naval gunfire after North Korean soldiers had driven U.N. forces out of it.[23] *Newsweek*'s coverage in reaction to Malik's accusations about bombing civilians included an explicit denial that the American air forces were conducting mass bombing in Korea. Although the article admitted that "under the best of circumstances the civilian population is bound to suffer," it reported that strategic attacks in Korea had been "carefully directed at industrial targets" and almost half of the bombs dropped by B-29s had been on tactical objectives. It also explained that "mass bombing" had been a British and not an American doctrine in World War II.[24]

A few American voices, besides the *Daily Worker*, questioned the extent to which the U.S. military was applying force discriminately in Korea, and others urged the military to take greater precautions to protect civilians. A citizen opposed to U.S. involvement in Korea wrote to Secretary Acheson expressing his distress at what he saw as "the bombing of helpless women and children." An American Jesuit then in Germany wrote a letter to the editor of *America* magazine to say that he could not see how the past bombing in Germany and the current destruction in Korea of strategic targets which killed friend and foe alike were necessary or unavoidable. A letter to the editor of *Air Force* magazine said sarcastically, "It must feel good to the South Koreans to see their cities demolished by their 'Friends.'"[25]

Doubts were not restricted to those of a liberal political bent. Several right-wing writers questioned the use of force in Korea. Henry Beston writing in the conservative newsletter *Human Events* condemned the "barbarities of aerial warfare" which the fight in Korea was once again showcasing. The reactionary columnist Henry H. Klein viewed the destruction of Korea and the human slaughter there as wasteful.[26]

Some in the mainstream press were not convinced that all that could be done to prevent indiscriminate destruction was being done. In one of his columns, Walter Lippmann cautioned that the United States had to convince its allies that America could defend a friendly nation without destroying it. He believed that a year of bombing Korea could only result in a "pyrrhic" victory: "We shall not have proved that we can contain aggression but only that we can wreck a country while the aggressor is trying to enslave it." A *Washington Post* editorial urged "extraordinary precautions" to avoid any unnecessary suffering and losses among Korean civilians. Just because Koreans might be behind enemy lines did not make them enemies, it prodded.[27] With the official depiction of a controlled use of force in Korea, which supposedly avoided general destruction and harm to civilians and which much of the press reflected in its coverage, most Americans could be reassured that the war was not requiring their country to abandon the norm of noncombatant immunity. Only a minority of skeptics publicly worried about the contribution of American firepower to the suffering of Korean civilians.

Official sensitivity to harming civilians translated into more than just attention to maintaining a scrupulous public image. In addition to the restrictions that caution over provoking the Soviet Union had placed against firebombing cities early in the war, concern for sparing civilians generated individual actions and general policies which provided some real protection for Korean noncombatants. The B-29s of Bomber Command did conduct precision strikes against industrial targets. One classified Air Force report describing an attack on the main industrial complex at Chinnampo said virtually all bombs struck target areas or open spaces and that negligible damage was inflicted on nearby housing. The FEAF implemented regulations to reduce civilian casualties. Seventeen Air Force veterans, who served in Korea, recalled in interviews fifty years after the war stern verbal policies to prevent attacks on noncombatants although none of them could recall any written policies on this subject. The American press during the war also reported that U.S. pilots were under orders not to strafe anyone on the roads unless they were positively identified as military. Pilots sometimes refrained from attacking apparently military targets because of the presence of civilians. When FEAF headquarters issued an order to the Fifth Air Force to destroy all vehicles around Seoul, it included the stipulation: "If there is reason to believe civilians are utilizing carts, disperse civilians on a low warning pass and then destroy the carts." A Fifth Air Force public relations officer described for the press the procedures that pilots were supposed to use to avoid strafing refugees: "To separate refugees from soldiers we have certain criteria. For instance, if they carry things on their heads, they are women. If they are in white and we haven't seen them change clothes, they are refugees. But if the Army reports they are troops in disguise, we strafe them."[28]

4.3 The Difficulties of Protecting Civilians

In practice, distinguishing enemy soldiers from civilians was much more difficult. During the North Korean retreat after the Inchon landing, a Navy pilot complained to intelligence officers about the problem of identifying civilians. "Commie soldiers may turn around and walk south as soon as they hear us coming," he said. "Hell, how can we tell a real refugee from a disguised soldier when they're all moving south?" An internal evaluation of Air Force operations in Korea, conducted during the war, related the experience of one pilot that it claimed was not unique. On a mission, the pilot had encountered a group of people in a village clad in the traditional white dress of Korean peasants. The presence of women and children in the streets and the friendly waves he received from the crowd made him hesitant to fire. An air controller assured the pilot that there were known to be enemy troops among the individuals and instructed him to attack. When the pilot did so, he received fairly heavy fire in return from the "peaceful civilians." The presence of women and children was not enough to prevent an attack in this particular case. Another interviewed pilot said that many of the reconnaissance missions that he had flown had not been as effective as they might have been because of the problem of enemy identification. He related that it was possible to tell that enemy troops had been in a town or a group of buildings, but it was guesswork in choosing which specific target to hit. He said that approximately 50 percent of the time, "I think we put our load on something that should have been left alone but we can't see through the buildings."[29]

Early in the war, the difficulties of identifying civilians from the air resulted in attacks on Koreans who were most likely refugees or farmers and led to the belief among at least a few American officers that pilots were under orders to strafe civilians. A July 31, 1950, mission report from the Thirty-fifth Fighter Bomber Squadron recorded a strafing of a sand bar in a river where people and fox holes were sighted. Pilots reported that the "people appeared to be evacuees." An operations report summary from the aircraft carrier the USS Valley Forge the same month described a similar attack. A Navy plane strafed a group of fifteen to twenty people dressed in white. After the first pass, the pilots decided that the people seemed to be civilians and investigated similar groups they encountered later on without firing. All of the groups appeared to be peasants working in their fields. The Valley Forge operations report explained that the attack on the civilians had resulted from information from the Army that "groups of more than eight to ten people were to be considered troops, and were to be attacked."

An Air Force colonel who had recently arrived in Korea quickly came to believe that the Fifth Air Force had a policy of strafing civilian refugees. In a memorandum to Brigadier General Edward L. Timberlake with the subject line "Policy on Strafing Civilian Refugees," the colonel wrote that because of concerns about enemy soldiers infiltrating American lines disguised as refugees, the "army has requested that we strafe all civilian refugee parties that are noted approaching our positions." He continued, "To date, we have complied with the army request in this respect." It is not clear how widely the policy was implemented and the purpose of the colonel's memorandum was to recommend that this policy be discontinued because of potentially embarrassing publicity, but at least he was convinced that American pilots were expected to strafe Korean civilians.[30]

The problem of identification led a few in the military to view attacks on civilians as justified. A pilot of the Thirty-fifth Fighter Group said in an interview for the wartime Air Force internal review that identification was very difficult because the Communist soldiers lacked the multitude of vehicles which made U.N. forces easy to distinguish. This pilot also believed that enemy soldiers were mixing in with civilian refugees and wearing civilian clothes. Therefore, he concluded, "It is my personal opinion that if the fighters would strafe these so-called civilians, and the ground forces would tell the civilians if they come through the lines, that they would be shot, the problem of infiltration could be stopped." A history of the first six months of the Korean War commissioned by the Department of the Navy argued that the strafing of civilians and the burning of Korean villages by U.N. planes was "wholly abhorrent" but "wholly defensible." It claimed that "warring against civilians" was forced upon the airmen by the practice of North Korean troops hiding themselves among civilians. These views were unusual in their willingness to accept explicitly the killing of civilians as a legitimate military method, but frustration with distinguishing noncombatant from enemy drove them to this extreme position.[31]

While the identification of civilians for American soldiers was difficult from the air, it was also a problem on the ground and this had terrible consequences for Korean noncombatants. During the first summer of the war, as American forces retreated before the North Korean onslaught, the intense fighting created a refugee crisis that became a serious concern for American commanders and soldiers. Tens of thousands of civilians moved southward along with the retreating American units. Some civilians had been told to evacuate their villages by the South Korean government; others were fleeing the violence of battle; and still others had been directed south by the North Korean soldiers hoping to hinder the U.N. forces. These refugees clogged roads and interfered with military transportation.

American soldiers also came to believe that the flow of refugees constituted a more direct military threat to them. Fear of attacks from the rear grew as the North Koreans used a double envelopment tactic which sent infantry around the flanks of American positions while other units supported by tanks and artillery would attack frontally to distract the defenders. American soldiers developed a strong belief that the refugee movements were increasing the effectiveness of this North Korean tactic by allowing North Korean soldiers to slip across the front lines to spy and to attack the Americans from behind. The Americans had caught North Korean soldiers on patrol in civilian clothes. Other North Korean troops dressed in civilian clothes were captured while trying to cross U.N. lines carrying uniforms and small arms in bundles. Two Army reports said that Koreans dressed as civilians actually fired upon American positions from the rear.[32]

Although it appears unlikely that large numbers of North Korean soldiers were using infiltration tactics to attack U.S. forces from behind,[33] American commanders treated the infiltration of the enemy disguised as civilians as a problem of major proportions. These leaders' concerns helped to ensure that their troops shared their fears, creating a climate of distrust of all Korean civilians. A State Department advisor to the South Korean government on the refugee problem told the *New York Times* that during the summer, American soldiers had developed a tendency to regard all Korean civilians near the battle zone as the enemy. In August, the Department of the Army issued a pamphlet to help prepare American troops going to Korea. In one section, the pamphlet told the story of Charlie Company which had learned about Korean guerrillas the hard way. One day a group of Korean "civilians" approached one of the company's quiet outposts. A Korean, who spoke English, offered to sell the soldiers a chicken, but when he reached into his coat, he pulled out a gun. In the firefight that followed, the company lost several men. The anecdote concluded: "At the risk of offending their South Korean friends, Charlie Company learned to be cautious of all Koreans whose identity and loyalty were not definitely known." However, the climate of fear posed more of a threat to Korean civilians than merely the risk of having their feelings hurt.[34]

To rectify the problems that refugees posed for their forces, U.S. commanders established in late July a strict policy to control the movements of civilians. The First Cavalry Division restricted the movement of civilians and refugees in their area to the two hours before noon. The highways were closed to ox carts, trucks, and civilian cars. No work was allowed in the fields, and schools, shops, or industries were closed unless they were essential to the war effort. The division expected the South Korean National Police and local authorities to enforce these rules, and the National Police were also to gather all refugees from the countryside and highways and transport them to screening points. The First Cavalry dropped leaflets on small villages in the area, telling the inhabitants to move north because American forces would treat them as the enemy if they remained in the combat area.

At a meeting on July 25, representatives of the South Korean government, the American embassy, the National Police, and the Eighth Army decided upon a more comprehensive policy to control refugee movements. The policy was sent to American units the following day. It said that no refugees would be permitted to cross battle lines at any time, and the movement of all Koreans in groups was to cease immediately. Each division would be assigned National Police liaison officers to assist in clearing any area of civilians that would interfere with operations. Evacuations of civilians were to be ordered only by division commanders and supervised by the police. All movement of civilians after dark was forbidden, and the Korean police were directed to enforce this prohibition rigidly. To disseminate information about the new policy to civilians, leaflets would be dropped in front and behind the battle lines, and the National Police would undertake further efforts to spread the word.[35]

4.4 No Gun Ri

What happened near the village of No Gun Ri in late July 1950 demonstrated the danger that the strict refugee control policy posed for Korean civilians. Revelations in 1999 from a team of Associated Press (AP) journalists about the shooting of refugees near No Gun Ri by American soldiers, unknown to the American public during the war, sparked an extensive Department of Defense investigation fifty years after the events.[36] Press coverage surrounding the investigation suggested that the killings at No Gun Ri could have been the Korean War's equivalent of the My Lai massacre, in which American soldiers during the Vietnam War killed more than 500 Vietnamese villagers including some whom, huddling in a ditch, were sprayed with machine gun fire at the orders of an officer. The killings at No Gun Ri were not an earlier version of the My Lai massacre. There were important differences, but in some ways, the terrible incident at No Gun Ri was as disturbing.

Korean survivors of the ordeal and the Department of Defense investigation offered different versions of the events at No Gun Ri in July 1950 although they agreed on several crucial points. According to Korean witnesses, U.S. soldiers evacuated 500–600 villagers from their homes in Im Gae Ri and Joo Gok Ri on July 25, 1950. Heading south, the villagers reached an American road block on the morning of July 26 where they were stopped by U.S. troops and ordered onto railroad tracks above the road. Tired and hungry, the refugees sat and ate while American soldiers inspected their belongings. Shortly afterward, planes appeared overhead and strafed and bombed the villagers on the tracks killing 50–150 of them. Many of the survivors scrambled for cover into twin tunnels running beneath the railroad tracks. There they crouched to avoid periodic gunfire that riddled the tunnel entrances for at least a day. This small arms fire killed another 60–300 villagers, according to the Korean witnesses.[37]

The Pentagon's No Gun Ri review spent a year examining over a million documents and the interview statements from approximately 275 American and Korean witnesses and issued its findings in early 2001. Despite the thorough investigation, many questions remain about what precisely happened at No Gun Ri. The Pentagon's report offered a different version of events than provided by the Korean witnesses, but did conclude that as a result of U.S. actions, Korean civilians were killed and injured in the vicinity of No Gun Ri in the last week of July. According to the evidence it gathered, the review could not rule out that American planes attacked refugees, but it determined that any air strike on civilians was not deliberate. The investigation could not determine an estimate of civilian casualties but believed the number to be less than the 248 dead, wounded, and missing that a separate South Korean government investigation of the No Gun Ri killings reported. The American Second Battalion, Seventh Cavalry Regiment of the First Cavalry Division was in the vicinity of No Gun Ri in late July. Some soldiers from the battalion interviewed for the investigation reported shooting in the direction of refugees either as a warning to keep them from moving or because they believed gunfire was coming from the direction of the refugees.[38]

Despite uncertainties on details, the Pentagon report was adamant that American soldiers had not harmed Korean civilians intentionally. Crucial to this claim was the finding that U.S. officers did not issue written or oral orders to shoot and kill Korean civilians in the last week of July 1950 in the vicinity of No Gun Ri. The refugee control policy issued by Eighth Army headquarters on July 26 did not explicitly authorize the shooting of civilians. No other written record of an order to fire on civilians was uncovered by the investigation, and none of the servicemen in their interviews with Pentagon investigators said that they had issued or received such orders. The report explained away other circumstantial evidence of a policy to fire upon civilians. The major piece of evidence, which the report dismissed, was a communications log entry for July 24 from another regiment of the First Cavalry Division, the Eighth Cavalry Regiment. The entry read: "No refugees to cross the frontline. Fire everyone trying to cross the lines. Use discretion in case of women and children." The September 1999 AP story, which had prompted the Pentagon investigation, had claimed that this entry demonstrated that an order from high-level U.S. commanders existed to shoot refugees.

The Department of Defense review had a different interpretation. It said that the source of the entry was a telephone call to the Eighth Cavalry's headquarters from a liaison officer working in the operations section at the First Cavalry Division headquarters. The Pentagon report surmised that the entry was not an order but more likely the liaison officer's misinterpretation of the soon-to-be-published Eighth Army's refugee control policy which forbade refugees from crossing battle lines. This misunderstanding was resolved, the report claimed, when the division received the detailed Eighth Army refugee control policy, "which clarified and superceded" the liaison officer's initial misinterpretation. The report also concluded that interviewed servicemen, who insisted that there had been orders to shoot refugees, had likewise misinterpreted the civilian control policy. Some American soldiers might have believed their commanders expected them to use lethal force to halt the movements of refugees, but, according to the No Gun Ri review, this assumption was mistaken and limited to a few isolated individuals on the frontlines.[39]

The Pentagon investigation, however, missed an important piece of evidence, a letter between the U.S. Ambassador to Korea and the State Department. This letter substantiates a dramatically different interpretation of the question of the existence of American orders to shoot civilians. A formal written order authorizing the use of lethal force to control refugees may not have existed precisely because harming civilians was a sensitive subject. Instead, a widespread understanding that firing on civilians might be required to enforce the explicit refugee control policy stretched from frontline soldiers and officers to the highest levels of the Eighth Army. The Pentagon report's claim that this understanding was wrongheaded and did not reflect the thinking of top Eighth Army officers rests on its interpretation of the meeting of Eighth Army staff and South Korean officials on the evening of July 25. It takes this meeting as the occasion at which refugee control policy was "clarified," and the shooting of civilians was not authorized. As the Pentagon report pointed out, the written formal policy sent to American units the next morning did not explicitly authorize them to fire on refugees. It only forbade refugees from crossing battle lines. Having a better idea of what was discussed at the July 25 meeting could reveal if there had been a general unwritten understanding, even among the top American officers formulating the refugee control policy, that lethal force might be used as a last resort against civilians to control their movements. The Department of Defense report offered few details about this meeting beyond which organizations participated and the formal guidance that was drafted because of the meeting.

But there exists an account of the meeting that the Pentagon investigation missed. On July 26, the American Ambassador to Korea John Muccio sent a letter to Dean Rusk, the Assistant Secretary of State for Far Eastern Affairs, about the refugee problem in Korea. The letter described the problem as having developed "a serious and even critical military nature." The letter told Rusk that the ambassador was writing because the military was "necessarily" making decisions about the problem, and the implementation of these decisions had the possibility of repercussions in the United States. The letter described the military problems of clogged roads and infiltration that the movements of refugees caused. It then reported to Rusk that a meeting had been arranged by request of Eighth Army headquarters at the office of the South Korean Home Minister on the evening of July 25 to address this problem. The letter said that the administration and personnel section (G-1), the intelligence section (G-2), the Provost Marshall, and the Counter-Intelligence Corps of the Eighth Army staff were represented at the meeting along with the American embassy, the South Korean Home and Social Affairs Ministries, and the Director of the National Police.

Muccio reported to Rusk his impression of the decisions made at the meeting, the same meeting that the Pentagon report claimed had clarified that refugees would not be shot. Muccio's letter listed the meeting's decisions, and the first read: "Leaflet drops will be made north of U.S. lines warning the people not to proceed south, that they risk being fired upon if they do so. If refugees do appear from north of U.S. lines they will receive warning shots, and if they then persist in advancing they will be shot." The letter also reported that refugees would be warned that no group could move south unless so ordered and then only under police control. All movement of Korean civilians had to end at sunset or those moving would "risk being shot when dark comes." Muccio's impression of the meeting may have been mistaken, and it is not clear from the letter whether Muccio himself attended the meeting or if he had received a report from another embassy officer, but obviously the meeting did not clarify for the American embassy that refugees were not to be shot. Something was said at the meeting that suggested to the embassy representative that there existed an understanding that civilians who approached American frontline positions would be shot.[40]

With this additional piece of evidence the Pentagon report's interpretation becomes difficult to sustain. Instead of isolated misunderstandings, the communications entry of the Eighth Cavalry and the claims by interviewed veterans that "orders" to shoot advancing refugees existed appear to be evidence that the understanding on shooting refugees was widespread across units and resided all the way up and down the chain of command from Eighth Army headquarters to the soldiers on the frontlines. Other evidence, which the Pentagon investigation uncovered, lends support to the interpretation that this understanding was widespread across units. The Twenty-fifth Infantry Division's war diary for July 24 addressing the problem of infiltration said, "Native personnel in the combat zone must be considered hostile until proven friendly." A directive dated July 27 from the division's headquarters to its units' commanders and staff sections stated that the South Korean police had removed all civilians from an area in front of the division's lines. As a consequence, it directed, "All civilians seen in this area are to be considered as enemy and action taken accordingly." The division's war diary for the same day said that the division commander General William B. Kean had ordered commanders at all levels to take drastic action to prevent the movement of any Korean civilians into their areas. Soldiers were to consider all individuals in civilian clothing moving within the combat zone as enemy. What treatment as an enemy entailed was obvious to observers. The AP reported on July 27: "All Korean civilians have been ordered out of the fighting zone southeast of Taejon. In an area once cleared of civilians, anyone in civilian clothing may be shot." According to the division's daily journal for 26 July, General Kean directed his staff to notify the local police that "all civilians moving around in combat zone will be considered as unfriendly and shot."[41]

Reports also exist of the commanding generals of the two other Army divisions fighting in Korea ordering their soldiers to shoot civilians during the summer retreat. O. H. P. King, a journalist for the AP who had covered the Korean War, recalled in his memoirs that the commander of the First Cavalry Division, General Hobert Gay, had resorted to drastic measures to stop infiltration during the summer retreat. Writing ten years after the war, King remembered the general ordering that after a specified period, any Koreans discovered in the area between U.N. lines and the enemy would be considered hostile and shot on sight. The warning to civilians was widely circulated, King claimed. The official Army history of the Korean War recorded that General

John H. Church of the Twenty-fourth Infantry Division gave similar orders in his area of operations. He demanded that all civilians evacuate a zone five miles deep in front of the division. He warned the civilians that if they failed to do so, his troops might shoot them on sight as enemies.[42]

Another piece of evidence, which the Pentagon report did not utilize and which supports the notion of a widespread understanding in the Army that refugees could be shot in order to control their movements, comes from a book published by the Department of the Army. In 1952, the Army's Office of the Chief of Military History put together a short volume describing the first six months of the Korean War. The book explained how American soldiers dealt with the problem of infiltration in the summer of 1950. It noted that the "passage of civilian hordes through combat areas troubled the Americans, who shrank from shooting at them but who knew that their appearance often implied that the enemy was lurking in the vicinity." The official history continued, "Eventually, it was decided to shoot anyone who moved at night." Refugee movements, it concluded, were allowed during the day when screening the Koreans was easier.[43] This description may not have been an entirely accurate depiction of the refugee control policy in Korea, but it did demonstrate that even the Office of the Chief of Military History in Washington believed lethal force had been authorized to control the movements of civilians. Any servicemen, who made the decision to fire on Korean refugees, were hardly isolated exceptions in believing that Army policy expected them to take such extreme measures.

This widespread acceptance of these harsh tactics appears less surprising when one considers the limited means that American soldiers possessed for enforcing the order to halt civilian movements. The Eighth Army policy charged South Korean police with ensuring that civilians did not cross American battle lines, but when refugees did approach American positions unaccompanied by police — as apparently they did at least in the case of the No Gun Ri killings — the frontline soldiers had limited options. The soldiers were few in number, and they were not equipped to control crowds with tear gas or batons. They could shout or wave off approaching civilians; they could fire warning shots; and they could fire into the refugees.

A number of circumstances can explain why the Department of Defense investigation did not unearth further evidence of a formal written policy to shoot refugees as a last resort in controlling their movements. For one, a crucial document is missing. The Pentagon review could not find the July communications log for the Seventh Cavalry, one of the most likely places that an order to fire on refugees would have been recorded. It is also possible an order to fire upon refugees was never written down and instead passed by word of mouth. Lawrence Levine, who was at No Gun Ri as the chief of radios in the headquarters company of the Second Battalion of the Seventh Cavalry, told reporters after the Pentagon investigation that orders and instructions were often not written down. Levine was convinced that his battalion received orders to shoot civilians.

The sensitive nature of any instruction to shoot refugees may have created for American officers and soldiers an added incentive to neglect record keeping concerning it. American servicemen in Korea realized that such a policy was a harsh and repulsive tactic. Plenty of evidence reflected their disquiet over the notion. Ambassador Muccio understood the sensitivity of the subject and its "possibility of repercussions." The Eighth Cavalry's log entry also displayed some ambivalence toward firing upon civilians with its reference to using discretion in the case of women and children. An entry in the First Cavalry Division's war diary for July 24 reflected the reluctance to shoot refugees. It read: "The control of refugees presented a difficult problem. No one desired to shoot innocent people, but many of the innocent looking refugees dressed in the traditional white clothes of the Koreans turned out to be North Korean soldiers transporting ammunition and heavy weapons in farm wagons and carrying military equipment in packs on their backs. They were observed many times changing from uniforms to civilian clothing and back into uniform. There were so many refugees that it was impossible to screen and search them all."[44]

Taken in view of the sensitivity of the issue, it is rather startling that the 8th Cavalry headquarters recorded the understanding in their communications log and unsurprising that more written records of it do not remain. It is also less than surprising that more veterans interviewed for the Pentagon's investigation did not attest to an understanding about shooting civilians as a last resort nor to an explicit order to do so. Not only had fifty years elapsed in which unpleasant memories could have faded, but the initial AP report of the No Gun Ri killings set the stakes rather high when it claimed that experts in international law considered orders to shoot civilians a war crime. Some veterans might have been concerned about smearing the Army or making themselves or other veterans vulnerable to prosecution or stigmatization due to their testimony.[45]

A 1950 story from John Osborne, the senior *Time-Life* correspondent in the Pacific during the Korean War, reinforced many aspects of this interpretation that a general understanding existed among American soldiers to control refugee movements with gunfire as a last resort. The August 21 issues of *Time* and *Life* printed versions of Osborne's report which he called an "ugly story of an ugly war." Osborne argued in his article that the fighting was pushing American soldiers into "acts and attitudes of the utmost savagery."

He described a vivid example of this that occurred at an unnamed regimental command tent on a recent evening while the enemy was gathering in the hills for an attack. The command post received a call that three or four hundred refugees were approaching B Company, but members of the staff urged the colonel in charge not to let the refugees through because they feared the refugees were covering an enemy attack. "All right, don't let them through," the colonel finally agreed. "But try to talk to them, try to tell them to go back."

"Yeah," said one of the staff, "but what if they don't go back?"

"Well, then," the colonel reluctantly replied, "then fire over their heads."

"O.K.," an officer said, "we fire over their heads. Then what?"

The colonel, seeming to brace himself, concluded, "Well, then, fire into them if you have to. *If you have to*, I said." An officer then turned to the telephone and sent the order out to the frontline.

In the *Life* version of Osborne's report, the anecdote continued, relating that the following afternoon riflemen reported to the command post that they had had to fire into another party of refugees who marched at them, against shouted warnings and waving. Osborne quoted an officer in the command post saying over a field telephone: "My God, John, it's gone too far when we are shooting children....Watch it, John, watch it! But don't take any chances." The anecdote lent credence to the claim that American soldiers out of concerns for their own safety shot Korean refugees in the summer of 1950 and not only at No Gun Ri. Osborne's story offered another piece of evidence of a widespread understanding, even among commanders, that these harsh tactics were necessary. Instructions to shoot civilians were given orally and the soldiers were reluctant, and at times ashamed, to carry them out.[46]

Further investigation by the AP reporters who broke the No Gun Ri story has uncovered evidence that American commanders gave direct orders to fire upon refugees later in the summer of 1950 as the U.N. forces fought along the Naktong River in southeastern Korea. A communications log from a battalion of the First Cavalry Division recorded an officer's August 9 order to "shoot all refugees coming across the river." In late August, the division commander General Gay ordered his artillery to fire on all refugees, according to unit journals. Also during the fighting at the Naktong, the journal of the Thirty-fifth Regiment of the Twenty-fifth Infantry Division stated, "Any refugees approaching our defensive position will be considered to be En[emy] and will be disperwde[sic] by all availlabe[sic] fires including Art[illery]."[47] By August, recording orders to shoot refugees was becoming routine.

The sad incident at No Gun Ri was not the younger twin of the My Lai massacre in Vietnam. American soldiers killed civilians at No Gun Ri under a general understanding that this was necessary to control their movements as a last resort. The soldiers at No Gun Ri did not execute captured civilians completely under their power at the direct orders of an officer as would later happen at My Lai.

Although the killings at No Gun Ri were less calculated, in some ways they were as disturbing as those at My Lai. The events at No Gun Ri appear to be part of a larger pattern, though we will never know how many innocent Koreans were harmed as a result of the strict American refugee control policy in the summer of 1950. American soldiers in a desperate military situation fearing for their own lives used at times potentially deadly violence to enforce a policy that officers high up the chain of command understood might require such lethal action. Individual American soldiers were troubled by the harsh policy, and the formal orders did seek to evacuate and protect the refugees. Nevertheless, circumstances — and the decisions that Americans made — conspired to curtail severely the protections that refugees received. Americans may have wanted to protect innocent noncombatants from the war's violence, but the events of the summer of 1950 demonstrated the practical limits of noncombatant immunity given the priorities under which American soldiers functioned.

4.5 The End of Restraints

While some of the treatment of Korean refugees grossly contradicted the picture of a humanely discriminate American war effort that predominated in official sources and the American press, greater contradictions between the fighting in Korea and the goal of a controlled application of force emerged as the war took a dramatic turn in late 1950. In October after the successful counterattack at Inchon, U.N. forces marched steadily into North Korea behind the retreating North Korean army. Americans believed that the war would soon end. However, during that month thousands of Chinese soldiers began crossing the Manchurian frontier, at first unbeknownst to the U.N. Command. Chinese intervention in the Korean War delivered a smashing defeat to the U.N. forces, compelling them to withdraw behind the thirty-eighth parallel. In response, General MacArthur and his commanders resorted to methods that are more destructive and accelerated a human catastrophe that the war would inflict on Koreans.

Early November, when U.N. soldiers first fought with Chinese units, marked the end of American restraint on the destruction of enemy cities. Although U.N. forces had already damaged many villages and towns in the process of battling the North Koreans,[48] the U.N. Command adopted a policy of the purposeful destruction of cities in enemy hands after the intervention of the Chinese. The FEAF began incendiary raids against urban areas reminiscent of World War II, and MacArthur spoke of making the remaining territory held by the North Koreans a "desert."

The perception of the war from the United States, though, changed little. Military officers and the press continued to discuss the violence in Korea as if its application continued to be discriminate and as if risks to noncombatants had not increased. The objects of attack were still "military targets," but the implicit definition of the term "military target" had grown to include virtually every human-made structure in enemy-occupied territory. The protection of noncombatants was not rendered meaningless by this definition since Americans never came to the point of arguing that the noncombatant population itself was a "military target" and, therefore, a legitimate object of attack, but the expanded definition of the term and the acceptance of the destruction it entailed offered meager protection for Korean noncombatants.

The "fire job," which the SAC generals had advocated in July, but Washington had forbidden as too provocative, commenced in early November. In the middle of October, General Stratemeyer had recommended to MacArthur an attack on the city of Sinuiju, a provincial capital with a population estimated at over 60,000 across the Yalu river from the Manchurian city of Antung. Stratemeyer's first choice for the type of attack on the city was one "over the widest area of the city, without warning, by burning and high explosive," but he was willing to settle for an attack only against "military targets in the city, with high explosive, with warning." The FEAF commander offered no direct military justification for the attack but instead argued Sinuiju could be used as the capital of North Korea once Pyongyang was evacuated, which would provide more legitimacy to the Communist government than if it were a refugee government on foreign soil. He also believed the psychological effect of a "mass attack" would be "salutary" to the Chinese across the Yalu. The closest Stratemeyer came to a military justification for the attack was his observations that the city served as a rail exchange point between Korea and Manchuria and that the city had considerable industrial capacity which could provide "some means" of supporting a North Korean government, but he did not tie either of these points to the fighting then occurring. MacArthur's headquarters returned a reply to Stratemeyer's suggestion the next day which read: "The general policy enunciated from Washington negates such an attack unless the military situation clearly requires it. Under present circumstances this is not the case."[49]

On November 3, Stratemeyer again asked MacArthur for permission to destroy Sinuiju. That day Stratemeyer forwarded the request of General Earle E. Patridge, commander of the Fifth Air Force, for clearance to "burn Sinuiju" because of heavy antiaircraft fire from the city and from Antung. Later in the afternoon, Stratemeyer met with MacArthur to discuss the request. Their conversation demonstrated the subjectivity that went into defining what constituted a "military target" for the U.N. forces. General MacArthur told Stratemeyer that he did not want to burn Sinuiju because he planned on using the town's facilities once the Twenty-fourth Division seized it. MacArthur did grant permission to send fighters to attack the antiaircraft positions in Sinuiju with any weapon desired, including napalm. Stratemeyer then raised the subject of the marshalling yards near the bridge between Sinuiju and Antung, and MacArthur told him to bomb the yards if Stratemeyer considered them a military target.

At the meeting, Sinuiju was spared from burning, but other North Korean cities were not so lucky. MacArthur desired an increase in the use of the B-29s which had run short of targets to bomb and so he was sympathetic to Stratemeyer's further recommendation to attack the town of Kanggye. The Air Force commander suggested the FEAF could burn some towns in North Korea as a lesson and indicated that Kanggye was a communications center for both rail and road and, he believed, was occupied by enemy troops. MacArthur answered: "Burn it if you so desire. Not only that, Strat, but burn and destroy as a lesson any other of those towns that you consider of military value to the enemy." MacArthur left the decision to his air commander. Apparently, MacArthur did not feel the towns to be so vitally important to the enemy's war effort that it was obvious to him that they should be burned, but Stratemeyer's idea about teaching the Communists a lesson did appeal to him. After the meeting, Stratemeyer informed Partridge of MacArthur's decision not to burn Sinuiju but instead only to authorize strikes against the antiaircraft batteries in and around the city.[50]

MacArthur's prohibition on burning Sinuiju lasted only a few hours. The general may have changed his mind because of the intelligence he was then receiving that more than 850,000 Chinese soldiers had gathered in Manchuria. By the evening, MacArthur's chief of staff told Stratemeyer that the burning of Sinuiju had been approved. On November 5, MacArthur conveyed his new instructions to his air commander. Stratemeyer wrote in his diary that the "gist" of these instructions was "Every installation, facility, and village in North Korea now becomes a military and tactical target." The only exceptions were to be hydroelectric power plants, the destruction of which might provoke further Chinese intervention, and the city of Rashin, which was close to the Soviet border. MacArthur later told Ambassador Muccio that the attacks he was ordering would leave the area between U.N. lines and the Chinese border a "desert."

Stratemeyer demonstrated a single-mindedness in carrying out MacArthur's wishes even at the risk of unwanted destruction. Stratemeyer's staff pointed out to him how reported sites of prisoner of war (POW) camps, hospitals, and prisons would be vulnerable to incendiary attack. The Air Force commander later wrote in his diary about the danger to these sites, "Whether vulnerable or not, our target was to take out lines of communication and towns." Stratemeyer sent orders to the Fifth Air Force and Bomber Command "to destroy every means of communications and every installation, factory, city, and village." In reviewing Stratemeyer's orders, MacArthur had him add a sentence that explained the rationale for the escalation. Inserted immediately after the phrase about destroying all communications and settlements, the sentence read, "Under present circumstances all such have marked military potential and can only be regarded as military installations."[51]

Stratemeyer also evidenced some concern over justifying the new attacks. He was troubled to learn that ten media correspondents would accompany the B-29 raid on Kanggye. After consulting with his vice commanders and his public information officer, he decided on a general statement on the bombing if asked: "That wherever we find hostile troops and equipment that are being utilized to kill U.N. troops, we intend to use every means and weapon at our disposal to destroy them, that facility, or town. This will be the answer to the use of the incendiary-cluster type of bombs." Stratemeyer included a similar rationale in his cable to the Air Force Chief of Staff on the attack: "Entire city of Kanggye was virtual arsenal and tremendously important communications center, hence decision to employ incendiaries for first time in Korea."[52]

Twenty one B-29s struck Kanggye with 170 tons of incendiary bombs on November 5. Sixty-five percent of the town's built-up area was destroyed. On November 8, seventy bombers dropped over 500 tons of incendiaries on Sinuiju, destroying 60 percent of the city, more than a square mile area of buildings. In General O'Donnell's report on the work of his bombers over Sinuiju, he declared that "the town was gone." Other towns were to follow. By November 28, Bomber Command reported that 95 percent of the town of Manpojin's built up area was destroyed, for Hoeryong 90 percent, Namsi 90 percent, Chosan 85 percent, Sakchu 75 percent, Huichon 75 percent, Koindong 90 percent, and Uiju 20 percent. One B-29 bombardier said that with the switch to the use of incendiaries in November, the bombers had "completely wiped out innumerable cities in North Korea." The fighter-bombers of the Fifth Air Force also conducted fire raids against North Korean towns.[53]

The destruction continued into the winter as Chinese forces compelled the U.N. soldiers to retreat south. As U.N. units withdrew from the major North Korean cities, those cities too became targets. On December 30, Stratemeyer informed Partridge that the FEAF had the authority to "destroy" Pyongyang, Wonsan, Hamhung, and Hungnam, four of North Korea's largest cities. The attacks were to be conducted without warning or publicity. Stratemeyer cabled O'Donnell that "no publicity whatsoever" was desired on these strikes and that no reporters or even observers from Bomber Command were to be permitted to accompany these missions. In incendiary attacks on January 3 and 5, U.N. air forces burned out 35 percent of Pyongyang.[54]

The fire bombing of North Korean towns that commenced in November made meaningless the earlier claims by the FEAF that their bombing operations avoided the destruction of residential areas. While avoiding direct acknowledgment that U.N. forces were systematically burning North Korean cities, the U.N. Command did admit that it had escalated the air war. The U.N. Command offered new justifications for the expanded destruction which clung to the notion that its planes were attacking military targets. The justifications were far distant from the Air Force's primary vision of how a strategic air offensive should be conducted. As Air Force leaders had been claiming from before World War II and had reiterated during the Revolt of the Admirals in 1949, the purpose of strategic air power was to destroy war-supporting industries in order to deprive the enemy's forces in the field of weapons, ammunition, and supplies. Shortly before he left his post as head of Bomber Command, General Emmett O'Donnell said in an interview that his bombers had been prevented from destroying the enemy's true sources of supply in China and the Soviet Union and, therefore, had been prevented from doing the job that they were made to do.[55]

Instead, the Air Force viewed its escalated bombing in Korea as part of a campaign to interdict the flow of weapons, supplies, and additional men to the Communist army in Korea and explained it to the public as such. But the campaign went beyond precise attacks against transportation and communication systems in North Korea with bridges, railroad yards, docks, and vehicles as targets. U.N. forces undertook the destruction of entire towns, particularly those along major transportation routes from Manchuria and the Soviet Union, in order to deprive the Communists of shelter in which to conceal their supplies and soldiers from the U.N. planes. The destruction also stripped the enemy soldiers of protection from the elements. Although the U.S. military still described these methods as attacks on "military targets," they had greatly expanded the notion of what constituted a military target past the American military's common definition of the term from early in the war.[56]

Public communiques from the U.N. Command rarely discussed or justified the destruction of Korean towns and villages directly. Instead, the press releases named "buildings," often identified as enemy-occupied or storage for supplies, as the usual target of U.N. planes, disaggregating the Korean communities into their constituent structures. Besides being regularly mentioned in the daily releases on air operations, the destruction of buildings became part of the public and internal measure of progress of the air campaign. In September 1950, the Navy introduced the category of "buildings destroyed" to its periodic public tallies of targets eliminated by naval aircraft. On January 2, 1951, a release, labeled the six-month "box score," placed the Navy total for buildings destroyed at 3,905. These buildings were presumably not ammunition dumps, command posts, fuel dumps, observation positions, radio stations, roundhouses, power plants, or factories because the tallies listed these categories separately. The Air Force introduced the category of "enemy-held buildings" into their press release target tallies in the fall of 1951 and by that time they were advertising the destruction of more than 4,000 buildings a month and over 145,000 since the beginning of the war. Within the Air Force, the square footage of buildings destroyed eventually became a semiofficial measure of progress in the air campaign. Communities divided up into their constituent "buildings" by official press releases proved a much less controversial target for demolition than the blatant admission that American air power was leveling much of the Korean peninsula.[57]

The press releases of the U.N. Command also avoided directly acknowledging attacks on entire villages and towns by the use of the term "supply center" and similar phrases such as "communications center," "military area," and "build-up area." MacArthur's public report to the United Nations on military operations during the first half of November described the escalation in the air war this way: "Command, communication and supply centers of North Korea will be obliterated in order to offset tactically the handicap we have imposed upon ourselves strategically by refraining from attack of Manchurian bases."[58] With the fall escalation, the daily press releases began to make vague references to strikes against supply centers. Sometimes the wording of the releases would use a Korean town name interchangeably with the phrase supply center implying that they were one and the same. More often, the releases would report attacks against supply centers "at," "in," or "of," a Korean town or city: "the supply center of Hamhung," for example. These prepositional phrases could imply either that the entire town was considered by the U.N. forces a supply center or that the town contained within it a supply center. Only rarely would the releases explicitly identify the Korean place names referred to as villages, towns, or cities. With "supply center" identified as a military target, use of the term and similar phrases helped to maintain the perception that U.S. forces were only attacking military targets.[59]

However, the press releases' reliance on describing operations as attacks on "buildings" and "supply centers" was not always enough to quiet the U.N. Command's fears about the American image in Korea. In August 1951, the U.N. Command's Office of the Chief of Information wrote a memorandum for the Public Information Office of the FEAF. The memo said that General Ridgway had suggested that in news releases of targets destroyed by air attacks, the Air Force publicists might "specify more definite military targets" such as tanks, antiaircraft guns, or armored vehicles. This would prevent anyone from pointing to the releases as evidence that American forces were "wantonly attacking mass objectives such as cities and towns" in North Korea. The U.N. Command, despite its expanded air attacks, continued to work to present an optimistic image of the war it was waging as a discriminate use of force directed solely against military targets.[60]

These efforts met with considerable success in the United States. Press coverage of the escalated air assault did not challenge the comforting picture the U.N. Command presented. Newspapers did note the U.N. forces had initiated some of the largest air strikes of the war in November and at times acknowledged the burning of entire cities, towns, and villages. Nevertheless, the reporting indicated the military usefulness of the physical infrastructure being destroyed and avoided discussing the impact of the destruction on civilians.

Briefly in the second week of November, the fire raids received attention in daily newspapers. The FEAF released to the press a long communique about the strike against Sinuiju and the attack was covered widely. The press release reported that planes had showered 85,000 incendiary bombs on two–and-a-half square miles of the built-up area of the Sinuiju making it clear that large portions of the city had been attacked. However, the release contained the assurance that the aiming points for the bombers were away from hospital areas. It also claimed, "All targets were of a military nature, with the principal objective being to eliminate Sinuiju as a future stronghold for supplies and communications needed by the Communists to continue war against the United Nations forces."[61]

Newspaper reports followed the official line closely. While they identified Sinuiju as a city of 100,000 and reported that 90 percent of it was destroyed in the incendiary raid, they also described Sinuiju as a supply base for the Communists. Some stories elaborated on the city's military importance by reporting that it was a mining, lumber, and chemical manufacturing center before the war and astride an important road and rail route from Manchuria, while others repeated the rationale from the FEAF release.[62]

Newspapers avoided mention of the fate of the 100,000 residents of Sinuiju except in one AP article run by a few newspapers. Hal Boyle wrote a dramatic story about the destruction of Sinuiju that opened with the line "Ever see a city die" and closed with the observation, "And the people died or fled." But a more detailed picture of the fate of Sinuiju's civilians was left to the imagination of the reader, and Boyle offered his own defense of the attack. Although he did not explicitly justify the killing of the city's population, he did describe the city as a "communist nest" and a "focus point for the enemy" and wrote that the attack was "very necessary."[63] After the attack on Sinuiju, the fire raids received brief and sporadic mentions in newspapers, and the coverage took to labeling the targets of attack military supply and communications centers, bases, or areas.[64]

Only isolated protests against the November escalation appeared in the press. The *National Guardian* of the Progressive Party, the party abandoned by Henry Wallace because it opposed U.S. intervention in Korea and which was moving rapidly to the left fringe of American politics, printed an article entitled "Press Drops Curtain on Korean Horrors." The article chided the mainstream press for its hypocritical silence on the destruction of communities in Korea. The story began with a quote from a May 10, 1940, editorial from the *New York Times* that condemned the Nazis for bombing private homes in defenseless Norwegian villages to gain a temporary military advantage. The story informed its readers that in Korea "hundreds of villages have been set to the torch and most of the cities leveled by U.S. bombing attacks," including Sinuiju and Hoeryong.[65] However, the *National Guardian* was a solitary voice of protest.

For an average reader of American newspapers in November 1950, it would have been easy to miss that U.S. air forces had changed their tactics to destroying entire cities and towns, thereby overturning their earlier assurances that they would not attack residential districts in Korea. However, the lack of public reaction to this development may have also been a result of many Americans accepting the notion that virtually all physical structures were military targets and, therefore, legitimate objects of attack. Official press releases and press coverage explained to Americans how any building could serve a military purpose by providing camouflage or shelter for supplies and soldiers. Only hospitals seemed to retain a protected status, a status explicitly codified in international law.

The destruction of buildings, which served as their homes, markets, shops, and schools, added to the suffering of Korean civilians, but American public discussion rarely touched upon this in late 1950. Americans were certainly distracted by the setbacks that their soldiers were facing against the new Chinese opponent, but they did not publicly use the desperate military situation to justify intentional attacks against North Korean civilians nor did Americans even clearly articulate that North Korea was being flattened in order to save U.N. forces. Except for a small minority, neither U.S. officials nor other Americans framed the escalation of air attacks as an intentional assault against the civilian population of North Korea to gain military advantage or any other benefit. Americans had not abandoned the tradition of noncombatant immunity, but they were in the process of severely narrowing the concept so that only the direct and intentional killing of noncombatants constituted an illegitimate tactic in warfare.

Actions of the U.N. naval and ground forces added to the civil destruction on the Korean peninsula during the winter. In February, the U.N. Command's navy began an interdiction campaign of coastal supply routes that included the naval shelling of North Korea's coastal towns and cities. At times, naval forces took special precautions to minimize damage to civilian buildings. One admiral prevented his men from shelling a railroad yard because he believed a stray shell might hit a school and hospital that were nearby, but later the admiral acceded to the bombardment when his gunners convinced him that they were accurate enough to hit only the railyard. An order from Admiral Arthur Struble, commander of the Seventh Fleet, advised against unnecessary destruction in the shelling of Inchon before the invasion.[66]

Nevertheless, the Navy's bombardment campaign contributed to the general devastation. The city of Wonsan on the east coast of the peninsula suffered heavily under naval shelling. Wonsan was an important transportation hub laying astride one of only two north-south railroads in North Korea and along an important coastal highway route in the narrow plain between the mountains of central Korea and the Sea of Japan. The U.N. forces sought to deny use of the city to the enemy. At the end of March after forty-one days of naval bombardment, Rear Admiral Allen E. Smith described the effect on the city: "In Wonsan you cannot walk on the streets. You cannot train troops in Wonsan. You cannot manufacture or store supplies in Wonsan. You cannot sleep in Wonsan today. Wonsan is a dead city." The bombardment of the city continued every day for more than a year. By December, U.N. Command press releases were admitting that naval forces were systematically destroying entire sections of the city.[67]

The ground fighting in Korea had also proved destructive. U.S. forces relied on extensive artillery and close air support in their combat operations, in part to minimize casualties among their soldiers, but this reliance increased the risks that Korean towns, villages, and noncombatants faced. The North Koreans, and later the Chinese, contributed to the destruction of towns both by their looting and sabotage and by their decisions to fight within settlements, but the liberal use of American firepower was an important ingredient in the damage. While the U.N. and North Korean forces had battled along the Pusan perimeter, the line of furthest retreat for U.N. forces in the summer of 1950, villages in a ten-mile strip along that front had been burned down. In late September, the FEAF had halted the strategic bombing deep behind enemy lines because the damage that it caused no longer appeared worthwhile in view of the progress U.N. forces were making. Only tactical bombing in support of ground units was to be undertaken, but American ground commanders had to be restrained in their requests for close air support to limit the damage to Korean cities. FEAF Headquarters cabled the Eighth Army about its requests for B-29 strikes that simply named South Korean cities. The FEAF said that such strikes were not politically desirable or of sufficient military value. The cable read, "It will be appreciated if your future requests for close support designate specific tgts or aiming points in cities concerned." In November, the Civil Assistance Section of the Eighth Army's I Corps, which was concerned about resettling refugees, reported, "Shelter situation north of 24th Division area will be critical as villages are being destroyed in path of advance."[68]

When the U.N. ground forces withdrew before the Chinese assault in late November, they sought to hamper the Chinese advance by destroying whatever supplies and structures might be useful to them. This practice further exacerbated the desperate situation for Korean civilians caught among the fighting. By early January, the *New York Times* was reporting that the U.N. forces were implementing a "scorched earth policy" and creating a "no man's land" for miles in front of their lines. Several soldiers recalled after the war that their units destroyed most of the houses and villages that they came across in their retreat south in order to deprive the Chinese of shelter. Shortly after General Matthew B. Ridgway became Eighth Army commander in late December, he issued an order to his forces that "the execution of demolitions and necessary military destruction in South Korea shall be such as to combine maximum hurt to the enemy with minimum harm to the civilian population." He would not condone anything approaching scorched earth tactics.

However, General Edward M. Almond, who commanded X Corps in eastern Korea, continued to use air and artillery to destroy all structures which were being used or suspected of being used by enemy personnel. His forces made extensive use of napalm to burn down villages in their rear areas that were "guerilla infested." Ridgway knew about Almond's tactics as the general had provided Ridgway an extensive explanation of them after one of X Corps' division commanders had complained to Almond that the burning of enemy villages in his sector where no enemy was apparent went "against the grain of

U.S. soldiers." Ridgway ordered no change in Almond's practices but did, at a subsequent commanders' meeting, warn against "the wanton destruction of towns and villages, by gun-fire or bomb, unless there is good reason to believe them occupied" by the enemy.[69]

The X Corps' napalm raids were not the only operations during this period of fighting that involved burning villages as part of antiguerrilla campaigns. A *New York Times Magazine* feature described a single soldier's experiences in the war and his involvement in such undertakings. One of Sergeant William A. Nedzweckas' most unpleasant memories was participating in operations to deprive Communist guerrillas of any support from villagers. Guerrillas, who hid in the hills by day, would persuade or force villagers to give them food and supplies during nocturnal visits. To hinder the guerrillas, Sergeant Nedzweckas was ordered to go into some of these villages with his squad and burn down all the houses. Since the houses were thatched-roofed huts, the soldiers would simply use their cigarette lighters. The soldiers would then enter the hut shouting "Okay, Sayonara! Sayonara!" at the startled Korean occupants who would hesitate in confusion until the flames started streaking through the roof. Hut after hut went up in black smoke, according to this grim procedure.[70]

Air support for the U.N. ground forces continued to take its toll on Korean villages and civilians as the war progressed. In the first four days of 1951 alone, the FEAF claimed to have "rendered unusable" 5,300 "enemy" buildings. Offering a counterpoint to the precise and accurate use of force that official press releases emphasized, a pilot of the Twenty-sixth Fighter Squadron after flying twenty missions, most of them close support for ground troops, described his targets as mostly "large areas such as villages and troop concentrations so a high degree of accuracy is not necessary." At one point during the winter, American bombs killed more than 100 children in a crowded Seoul orphanage run by the Christian Children's Fund. Long after the war, Moon Yun Seung recalled witnessing U.N. planes strafing refugee columns repeatedly during his flight south to escape the Communists in late 1950. One B-29 bombardier expressed his belief that greater destruction would have benefited U.N. ground forces. He said in an interview for an internal Air Force review, "My first opinion is that we lost possibly some of our potentials as strategic bombers in that we didn't go in ahead of the ground troops on targets, such as Pyongyang and Seoul, and sort of level the town to save a few more American lives, more equipment and time."[71]

By the end of the winter in March 1951, the war had created more than three million homeless Koreans by the estimate of U.N. officials, and many of these became refugees who attempted to reach the relative peace south of U.N. lines.[72] As happened during the previous summer, the refugees overwhelmed the U.N. Command's ability to handle them. Concerns reemerged that the flow of civilians through U.N. lines allowed enemy infiltration and that refugees would hamper U.N. troop and supply movements. Once again, American commanders placed restrictions on civilian movement exacerbating the refugees' ordeal in the bitterly cold Korean winter. General Ridgway issued a series of orders intended to manage the tide of refugees. With the Communist forces threatening to retake Seoul, Ridgway issued a January 2 order that refugees not be permitted to pass through forward positions nor along main roads and bridges. The orders again put American soldiers and the refugees into a terrible conflict of purposes. The soldiers wanted to ensure their own safety and effectiveness, while the refugees sought to flee south as quickly as possible.

This time the commander of the Eighth Army would explicitly authorize his troops to shoot refugees who violated the movement restrictions. Ridgway passed instructions to General Charles D. Palmer of the First Cavalry Division that his military police were first to fire over the heads of refugees who attempted to use Route 1, the main road out of Seoul, and as a last resort to fire at them. A day earlier the Eighth Army headquarters had issued an even more sweeping directive to "stop all civilian traffic in any direction." It instructed subordinate commands that "responsibility to place fire on them to include bombing rests with you." Apparently this order was difficult to implement because the First Cavalry Division resorted to threatening its officers with a $100 fine for allowing any civilians to pass through the front lines. On January 4, leaflets were dropped warning civilians that further crossing of the Han river south of Seoul was prohibited and anyone attempting to cross would be fired upon. The Army's official history of the Korean War said that no firing was necessary to enforce the ban on crossing the river. However, the directive to prevent civilians from crossing front lines by fire if necessary appears to have remained in effect into the spring of 1951. In June, intelligence officers from the Second Infantry Division were recommending a modification of this policy, in part "due to the hesitancy on the part of the younger officers to fire directly upon groups of old men, women, and children."[73]

How many, if any, Korean refugees were shot by U.S. troops during the winter fighting will probably never be known, but at least one American officer claimed after the war that his revulsion at harming innocent civilians led him to choose not to fire on refugees even though it put his men at greater risk. This infantry captain recalled refusing to give his soldiers an order to shoot civilians. The refugees were pressing in on a roadblock held by his company, and his troops were urgently requesting permission to fire on them. The captain understood that if disguised enemy soldiers were mingled among the civilians, they would be in the rear of his company in the morning. Despite this fear, the officer could not bring himself to order the shooting of the women and children who made up most of the group of refugees.[74]

4.6 The Persistence of the Optimistic Vision

By late 1950, U.S. forces had abandoned the restraints on the use of force they had adopted early in the war, and consequently American firepower took a greater and more indiscriminate toll on Korean civilians and their communities. However, the optimistic notion that the U.S. military was applying force in a discriminate manner in Korea persisted in the American imagination. Americans developed ways of rationalizing the evidence of the destruction that they could not deny, but until the end of the war many continued to reassure themselves with the idea that the U.S. military had not lost control of the violence that they were employing in East Asia. Noncombatant immunity retained its cultural status, discrimination remained a virtue, and few challenged either by advocating attacks on civilians as the path to victory.

The vision of a discriminate and controlled war survived in the pages of the Air War College's journal. Officers in their contributions continued to insist that the Air Force was successfully refraining from bombing civilians in Korea. In the spring 1951 issue, Colonel Raymond S. Sleeper writing about the strategic bombing of the B-29s in Korea argued that benefits had accrued from the great care taken to bomb only military targets, the precautions taken to avoid bombing civilian areas, and the efforts made to warn civilians to evacuate target areas. The article ignored entirely the firebombing of North Korean towns, and Sleeper concluded, "There is no question but that the U.S. Air Force made a largely successful effort to refrain from bombing Korean civilians." Optimism about the discriminate use of air power ran deep among Colonel Sleeper's comments.[75]

An exchange of letters between the American socialist leader Norman Thomas and the Truman administration in 1951 illustrated the continued life of the optimistic vision of a controlled use of force in Korea. The exchange demonstrated an attempt by officials to pacify a potential critic of the war with reassurances that the U.S. military was using force discriminately in Korea. Norman Thomas had long been a pacifist who had opposed American involvement in both World War I and World War II, but he had decided to support the U.N. intervention in Korea. In May, after a trip to Asia, Thomas wrote the president concerning Asian attitudes, and he noted their strong feelings about American bombing in Korea. Thomas gave the U.S. military the benefit of the doubt writing, "I assume that our air force in Korea is doing what can be done to minimize the bombing of towns and villages, except for imperative military reasons." However, he wondered whether some official statement of policy to this effect might not help to allay Asian feeling. Such a statement, Thomas believed, would also restate what he had always understood as the historic American position. In Truman's reply three days later, the president ignored Thomas' concerns about American bombing, commenting only on the other topics in Thomas' letter, but this would not be the end of the correspondence.[76]

In October, the shooting of two Korean boys by U.N. aircraft prompted Thomas to write the Secretary of Defense Robert Lovett and the president once again about American military policy in Korea. On October 15, General Ridgway admitted that an investigation into two attacks, which had violated the neutral zone surrounding the Kaesong area where armistice negotiations were being conducted, revealed that a strafing run by U.N. planes had killed a twelve-year-old Korean boy and wounded his two-year-old brother. A *New York Times* report explained the shooting as a result of the planes attempting to strafe three North Korean soldiers who were hiding in a ditch that the two boys were standing near. Ridgway ended his announcement with the claim that "it has heretofore been, and will continue to be, the prime objective of the United Nations Command to avoid loss of life and destruction of property of the noncombatant population. To this end the United Nations Command will continue its efforts to prevent any recurrence of incidents which may bring suffering to blameless individuals."

Thomas wrote to question the nature of the use of American air power. He said, "It is fantastic to believe that this kind of mistake could happen unless our airmen were under orders to strafe or bomb any miserable collection of huts or anything that might move in enemy occupied territory." Thomas saw this as a "ghastly way to liberate a country," and it reminded him of what Americans used to call "baby killing" when it was done by the Germans in the last war. Thomas requested that an investigation be undertaken to determine if the war in Korea was being conducted in such a way and informed the administration that he was sending a copy of his letter to the U.N. Secretary General. Thomas had also vented his concerns about the "baby-killing" by U.N. pilots in a *Denver Post* column.

Truman only acknowledged Thomas' letter with a thank you note. The job of answering Thomas' charge was delegated to R. L. Gilpatric, the Under Secretary of the Air Force. After evading Thomas' complaint about indiscriminate strafing in an initial letter, Gilpatric reassured Thomas in a second letter that the Air Force had issued orders against indiscriminate bombing and strafing. Writing back, Thomas expressed his appreciation for the reassurance although he still thought it odd that the shooting of the Korean boys had occurred under such orders. However, Thomas was more concerned that the Air Forces' orders be broadly publicized because he still worried about Asian opinion. He concluded his letter: "I do not think I need tell you that it isn't merely important that our orders should be correct but that the knowledge of correct orders should be widely diffused at a time when communist propaganda is so persuasive." To this end, Thomas quoted Gilpatric's reassurances in a *Denver Post* column, but Thomas was not fully satisfied with the Air Force's response. In his column, he wondered how the shootings of the boys could have occurred with such a policy and questioned why Gilpatric had delayed in answering his concerns if the policy against indiscriminate bombing had already been in place.[77]

Even as the war turned against the U.N. forces with Chinese intervention and then settled into a protracted and bloody stalemate as the two sides attempted to negotiate a cease fire, few Americans publicly challenged the ideal of providing Korean noncombatants with protections from the war's violence. Public sensitivity to harming civilians persisted despite discussions of options for escalating the war. One of the most discussed options was expanding U.N. bombing to China. Although some appeared insensitive to harming Chinese civilians in their advocacy of such attacks, many of the main supporters of this strategy were careful to specify that air strikes against China would be against military targets instead of cities. Similarly, those who opposed the bombing of China, at times, appealed to arguments that drew on the disadvantages of harming noncombatants.

Some vague statements about bombing the Chinese sounded as if they could be dismissals of noncombatant immunity. General Emmett O'Donnell in early 1951 on his return to the United States after finishing his service with the Far East Bomber Command said about the war in an interview, "Eventually we're going to have to cope with this realistically and courageously — not put the Marquis of Queensbury rules on it — and have to cope with a thug who's going to hit you in the back of the head with an ax." A *Green Bay Press-Gazette* editorial was more specific. It advocated the dropping of atomic bombs, if the United States had enough, "to reduce the Chinese cities to ruins and kill off 50 to 100 million of their teeming populations and therefore paralyze the Chinese Soviets." A *U.S. News and World Report* article reflected a similar insensitivity to the prospect of killing millions of Chinese in atomic attacks, but was less optimistic about the usefulness of the atomic bomb against China. The article declared that the atomic bomb's "most effective use is as a destroyer of civilians, concentrated in big cities." But China had only five cities with more than a million people and ten others with more than 500,000. Therefore, military men, the article said, believed that most of the targets for air attack in a war against China would be small targets like bridges, freight yards, and factories inappropriate for the atomic bomb.[78]

Those who spoke specifically of destroying Chinese cities and killing Chinese civilians were an exception, though. Many of the advocates of bombing China talked in terms of destroying targets more directly involved in the war effort. Senator William Knowland wanted the war plants supplying the Communist aggressors destroyed; Senator Robert Taft spoke of bombing Chinese airports, communications, and armies; and Senator John Bricker urged the bombing of Manchurian air bases. Carl Spaatz, the former Air Force chief of staff, writing for *Newsweek* said that if the U.S. was forced to fight China, it should use strategic bombing against the country's "industries, communications, and transportation."[79]

Concern over further American casualties motivated much of the sentiment to bomb China, but while emotions could run high on the subject, most refrained from advocating attacks on Chinese civilians. Eugene R. Guild, who organized a campaign to lobby his local congressman, showed this kind of restraint. Guild had lost a son in the fighting in Korea and had founded a group in December 1950 called "Fighting Homefolks of Fighting Men" in Glenwood Springs, Colorado. In an attempt to convince his congressman to support an end to what Guild characterized as tying the hands of American soldiers in Korea, Guild collected some 1,500 ballots in Glenwood Springs and another nearby town, Rifle, on a proposition to end the restrictions on the fighting. The proposition specified the restrictions to be lifted. In his bitterness and frustration, Guild did not advocate the destruction of Chinese cities or the killing of millions of enemy civilians. Instead, the proposition called for the bombing of the Korean dams "furnishing power to make munitions to kill" American soldiers, the bombing of "Red Chinese supply lines and bases," and the use of the atomic bomb, America's "best tactical weapon." Even a man whose support for an escalation of the war was deeply and tragically personal still argued in terms of a discriminate use of force.[80]

When administration officials discussed with allies the possibility of bombing China as a last resort, they were careful to clarify that strikes would be against military targets. General Bradley and Secretary Lovett had assured British Prime Minister Winston Churchill and his Foreign Minister Anthony Eden that if the United States escalated its bombing attacks as a result of armistice talks dragging on, they would not target population centers but military targets such as transportation and air concentrations.[81]

Those who opposed the bombing of China raised in support of their position the deleterious effects of destroying cities and harming noncombatants. Editorials from the *Nation* and *Christian Century* believed that bombing Chinese cities and communications would intensify Chinese nationalism and increase support for the Communist regime. *Life* magazine questioned in an editorial the prudence of bombing mainland China. It said, "There is little or no industry there, and bombings which just kill civilians — especially if the announced purpose is punitive and retaliatory — could have the reverse of their intended effect." Even the conservative radio commentator Dan Smoot agreed that destroying Chinese cities was unwise. Smoot wanted the U.S. government to assure China and the Soviets that Americans would "not incur the hatred of the Chinese people" by bombing their cities and villages. He also said, "To prove that we are moral and humane, we should positively assert that we have no intention of using our ghastly atomic energy weapons on the people of Asia." The sentiments among Americans against harming Chinese civilians were reinforced by voices from overseas. For example, John Strachey, Britain's War Secretary, condemned the strategy of an all-out assault on China. He said such attacks "would degenerate into bombardments of the great cities of China, with the slaughter of millions of Chinese people" but "without necessarily having any marked effect on the Chinese Government or its armies."[82]

The so-called MacArthur hearings in front of the Senate Committees on Foreign Relations and Armed Services in the spring of 1951 also reflected the continued sensitivity to the subject of harming enemy noncombatants. After his relief from command in East Asia, MacArthur sparked a heated controversy over the Truman administration's military and foreign policies with a speech before Congress. The general's suggestion that the United States was not doing everything it could to win the war in Korea created a political crisis for the president, embattled by Republican charges that he was soft on Communism. Members of Congress called hearings to question MacArthur and Truman's top military and foreign policy advisors about the conduct of the war in Korea.

During the hearings, participants on both sides of the controversy employed sympathy for noncombatants as an argument against the positions of their opponents much as the Navy's leadership had used the sentiment against the Air Force during the Revolt of the Admirals. MacArthur expressed his feelings of horror at the devastation that the war was inflicting on the Koreans, the worst he had ever seen, he said, in his long career as a soldier. The general presented his suggestions to escalate the war in order to bring it to a speedy conclusion as the most humane solution to the terrible situation. General George C. Marshall, who as Secretary of Defense defended the Truman administration's policies against MacArthur and his supporters at the hearings, also reassured the committee that the administration understood the importance of sparing noncombatants. Marshall testified that even if the United States was certain that the Soviet Union would not intervene in the event that the United Nations expanded its use of air and naval power in East Asia, the power would not be used entirely without restrictions. He said, "The restrictions would be, I would say, not to use those powers, if avoidable, in a way that claimed a great many innocent victims and left a bitterness that we would be 50 years in overcoming."

When Senator William F. Knowland challenged the Army Chief of Staff Lawton J. Collins to explain restrictions placed on the bombing of Pyongyang, Collins compared the situation to the German occupation of the Ukraine during World War II. The Army chief of staff believed that the destruction of Pyongyang would alienate the Korean population just as Nazi depravations had angered the Ukrainian people. Knowland agreed with the general that "there should not be a mass bombing of cities," but believed that Pyongyang with its rail yards and supply depots was a legitimate target for bombing. Even if participants in the hearings did not believe deeply or consistently in protecting noncombatants, they found appealing to the idea was a convenient ploy in arguing both for and against an escalation of the war in Korea.[83]

The politicians and generals in Washington were deferential to a norm of noncombatant immunity during the MacArthur hearings, but soldiers in Korea also acknowledged this standard, often in a backhanded way. Dark humor from American pilots in Korea acknowledged the taboo of harming the helpless. The Eighth Fighter-Bomber Wing had put together a song book which included a ditty titled "Ten Thousand Dollars Home to the Folks." The song was based on the tune "What Do You With a Drunken Sailor" but made a drunken flyer the protagonist of its rendition. After two verses, the Eighth Fighters' version diverged greatly from the traditional song. The third and fourth verses repeated the refrains "We're gonna bomb the sick and wounded" and "We're gonna bomb the old and decrepit." The ironic tone of the song was fully brought forward in the fifth and final verse, which referred to ten thousand dollars being sent home to the families of pilots who died in crashes from engine failure.[84]

Another example from a Korean veteran of grim and caustic humor, which played on the sensitivity to harming civilians, came from Lieutenant Colonel Melvin B. Voorhees. Voorhees, a former newspaper editor, had served as the chief censor for the Eighth Army in Korea before returning to the United States in May 1952. In a book he wrote shortly thereafter, a chapter entitled "The Clobber," which Voorhees called fiction but said it was "based upon actual happenings either in part or *in toto*," parodied an example of press reporting.

The story began with a press censor reading over a report from a rookie war correspondent who had just finished his first jet plane flight in Korea. The standard Air Force initiation had left the reporter tense and excited, and his article gushed with his enthusiasm. It described the jet's take off and its skimming of the Korean mountains and rivers. The report also related the action of the day which included an encounter with a lone man dressed in traditional white Korean garments walking down a road. The novice journalist had written that the pilot thought the man was "probably" a soldier because the enemy often disguised themselves that way. The pilot turned his machine guns on the man and made a second pass to ensure the man was dead.

When the censor was done reading the report, he leaned back, removed his glasses, and wearily rubbed his eyes. "Quite a story," he commented.

"Did I get the picture across, do you think?"

"You sure did."

"It was a big thrill," the reporter said.

"Yeah," the censor replied, "also maybe a war crime."

Voorhees had lampooned his archetypal irresponsible correspondent by highlighting the reporter's vacuous obsession with a thrilling jet ride and insensitivity to the graver issue of harm to civilians.[85]

American concerns over attacking noncombatants provided significant, if limited, protections for Korean civilians, but the way in which many Americans viewed the war obscured the contribution to Korean suffering for which U.S. firepower was responsible. American officials promoted, the mainstream press accepted, and few public voices challenged the optimistic notion that the

U.S. military could apply violence in a discriminate manner. Attacks restricted to military targets and an emphasis on precision and accuracy in bombing more accurately described the first four months of the war although there were exceptions even during this period as the problems with refugees demonstrated. Concern over preserving noncombatant immunity did play a role in limiting the war's initial violence, but it did so indirectly. Little evidence suggests that American leaders restrained the early bombing campaign out of humanitarian sentiments. Instead, they functioned under the presumption that destroying nonmilitary targets and harming civilians were provocations which the Soviet Union might consider atrocious outrages demanding retaliation. Adhering more closely to the international norm of noncombatant immunity early in the war was one way that American leaders attempted to communicate to the Soviets that they wanted to keep the conflict a limited one.

After U.N. air attacks escalated to destroying entire communities in November, the emphasis on discrimination between military and civilian targets lost much of its meaning. The stretching of the notion of "military targets" to include virtually all of the physical structures in enemy territory greatly increased the risks of harm to Korean civilians and led to a replication of the firebombing raids of World War II. Yet the emphasis on discrimination remained, and most Americans did not advocate the abandonment of a core notion of noncombatant immunity; they did not accept purposeful killing of noncombatants as a legitimate method of war. The optimism about discrimination allowed a reconciliation of American methods of war with some notion of noncombatant immunity but also allowed a form of denial that Americans might be to blame for some of the harm to the people of Korea.

The optimism was understandable if not always reasonable. Americans were concerned about their country's image as a humane nation, both to preserve their self-conception of national identity and to keep friends abroad; they desired to distance their practices from those of the Nazis; they believed in the power of their technology that was supposed to allow the precise use of force; they could provide themselves with plausible rationales for considering almost all of North Korea's civil infrastructure as a military target; and they wanted to avoid thinking about the awful human suffering in Korea. Possibly the most important factor in explaining the optimism was that the Korean War was a limited war from the American perspective and did not develop into a dreaded World War III. American leaders actively attempted to avoid a global conflict with the Soviet Union and its allies. By refraining from the immediate obliteration of North Korean cities, American leaders had sought to lessen the possibility of global war. For many Americans, in comparison to the Armageddon they had expected their country's next war to be, the destruction in Korea must have appeared very limited indeed, even though it was anything but limited for Koreans.

Regardless of its ultimate sources, the optimism about discrimination was a powerful attitude. As it was helping Americans to rationalize the situation in Korea, it also increasingly pervaded discussion of nuclear weapons. The paragon of massively destructive weapons was undergoing a reevaluation by some Americans, and they saw potential for a controlled use of force even with these unwieldy instruments of devastation.

5
Taming the Bomb

While the war in Korea was demonstrating that conventional warfare could be devastating for civilians, the destructive power of nuclear weapons remained the clearest threat to the norm of noncombatant immunity. Reliance on the potentially genocidal weapons fed criticism of American policies in the early 1950s and complicated American claims that they sought to fight wars that would spare civilians. The apparent contradiction between a nuclear arsenal and noncombatant immunity gave Communists a tool against the United States, fueled self-criticism as well as international anxiety when Americans twice considered using the atomic bomb early in the Korean War, and made western Europeans nervous over the defense of their countries. This tension gave Americans good reason to seek relief.

In 1951, an unusual shift in how Americans discussed nuclear weapons helped to provide some relief. In contrast to the discussion of early 1950 surrounding the hydrogen bomb, which stressed the almost limitless power of the weapon to destroy, more Americans began to consider the possibility that nuclear weapons could be used in a discriminating manner. Led by officials, many talked of the tactical use of atomic bombs or of new nuclear weapons specifically designed for use against an enemy's armed forces. A number explicitly proposed that tactical nuclear weapons would assist in solving the American dilemma over indiscriminate destruction in war. These weapons, used only against the military forces of an enemy, would be akin to any conventional weapon and, therefore, could not be stigmatized as uniquely inhumane, they argued. In this atmosphere of humanizing new weapons, some American officials also argued that chemical, biological, and radiological (CBR) weapons could be reconciled with noncombatant immunity. Although others, especially western Europeans, doubted these developments would alleviate the problem of harm to civilians and nuclear weapons never lost their old image as city-destroyers and population-killers, this new conception reduced the dissonance between the U.S. atomic arsenal and American espousal of noncombatant immunity.

This attempt to reconcile even the ultimate weapon of mass destruction with noncombatant immunity revealed the strength of the norm among Americans. As they optimistically assured themselves that conventional military force was being used discriminately in Korea, some took comfort in the even more fanciful notion that nuclear weapons could be employed solely against an enemy nation's military. New weapon technologies were not rendering older values obsolete. Instead, many Americans were shaping their thinking about the weapons to conform more closely to the norm of noncombatant immunity.

5.1 The Bomb's Stigma

As the tension between the United States and the Soviet Union grew in the early 1950s, the Soviet Union and its sympathizers escalated their campaign to stigmatize the atomic bomb, one weapon in which the United States possessed a marked superiority over the Soviets. In March 1950, the Soviet government joined with the delegates to the World Peace Congress in Stockholm in calling for the prohibition of the atomic bomb. The World Peace Congress, which the Communist Information Bureau (COMINFORM) helped to organize, brought together delegations from around the world to discuss peace issues, and at Stockholm adopted a resolution against the atomic bomb.[1]

The Soviet government quickly endorsed the resolution as well as a petition campaign to gather millions of signatures in support of it. The petition indicted the atomic bomb as an inhumane weapon that should be banned because it killed indiscriminately. The petition read, "We demand the absolute banning of the atom weapon, arm of terror, and mass extermination of populations … . We consider that any government which would be first to use the atom weapon against any country whatsoever would be committing a crime against humanity and should be dealt with as a war criminal." From the beginning of the campaign until early June, the Soviet Union devoted an average of 40 percent of its radio commentaries for foreign consumption to the petition campaign, the most sustained attention Soviet radio had given any special theme since the end of World War II. On May 31, it was announced that 100 million signatures worldwide had been collected in the campaign. At a press conference, Secretary Acheson told the American people that the petition was a Soviet propaganda trick, and he argued that the "real crime against humanity is aggression" and not the type of weapon used. The Soviet Union continued to push for the prohibition of the atomic bomb on humanitarian grounds at various forums including a meeting of the League of Red Cross Societies and at the United Nations in October.[2]

Unease over the stigma attached to the atomic bomb appeared among American officials and a wider public when they started to consider the weapon's potential use in Korea. With the military situation grim for U.N. forces in the summer of 1950, American policymakers began to deliberate over the bomb's role. Although many considerations weighed against the weapon's use such as its scarcity, the possibility that it would provoke the Soviet Union into war, and the lack of suitable targets, the concern that its use would harm civilians and that the American public would find this unacceptable figured in State and Defense Department discussions.[3]

Anxiety over the issue was more apparent outside the government. Concern for noncombatants appeared as a caveat in public calls for the bomb's use by Congressman Lloyd M. Bentsen, General Eisenhower, and the American Veterans (AMVETS) national executive committee.[4] Opinions in magazines, newspapers, and letters on editorial pages[5] provided further evidence that many Americans remained uneasy about inflicting harm on noncombatants. The editorial pages of the *Saturday Evening Post, Chicago Tribune, Detroit News, Boston Post,* and *Philadelphia Bulletin* each questioned the use of atomic weapons in Korea citing concern over adverse international reaction and indiscriminate harm of the innocent.[6] Only a few letters to newspapers took exception to these public expressions of concern for Koreans. They felt that saving American soldiers' lives was more important than sparing innocent Korean civilians.[7]

The atomic bomb talk and the Stockholm petition campaign stimulated discussion among Catholics over the morality of weapons of mass destruction. In the Catholic lay magazine *Commonweal,* discussion was split during the late summer over the atomic bomb. Although Catholic theology on the conduct of just wars made noncombatant immunity a central concern, the church was also anxious to protect Catholics from conquest by the atheistic Communists. Pope Pius XII in a July papal encyclical lamented the inhuman weapons that killed even innocent children with their mothers, the sick, and the undefended old, but he did not ask that the atomic bomb be outlawed.[8]

A series of pieces in *Commonweal* presented the poles of opinion on the contradiction between noncombatant immunity and nuclear weapons. It illustrated Catholic opinion but also presented a microcosm of the larger public debate. In August, Robert Barrat wrote an article about the French clergy's opposition to weapons of mass destruction because they inflicted harm on noncombatants. Barrat dismissed their concern over noncombatant immunity as naive. He denied the relevance of the notion because virtually all weapons that killed from a distance had the potential to harm noncombatants. In addition, Barrat argued the church no longer had the temporal power to influence the conduct of belligerents, and as for spiritual power, it was useless against heads of state who believed in neither God nor the Devil. Barrat was one of the small minority that rejected noncombatant immunity in the age of total war.[9]

The sociologist Gordon C. Zahn responded to Barrat's article initially in a letter to the editors of *Commonweal.* He criticized Barrat's amorality in rejecting noncombatant immunity, a central tenet of Catholic just war theory. Zahn elaborated on his stance in a September article. He claimed that the atomic bomb by its nature was an indiscriminate weapon. It obliterated areas, and its effects could not be controlled. It was not the same as any other weapon. Therefore, he argued that moral judgments should be revised to acknowledge that the weapon's use was illegitimate. Zahn represented the other minority that rejected nuclear weapons rather than abandon noncombatant immunity.[10]

Commonweal gave Francis Connell, the Catholic University theologian who had argued against the intrinsic immorality of nuclear weapons during the hydrogen bomb debate, the chance to respond to Zahn's article. Connell, as he had argued earlier, agreed with Zahn that the indiscriminate killing of non-combatants was wrong. Connell wrote that he had issued a public statement the day the atomic bomb was dropped on Hiroshima condemning its use because of the large number of noncombatants harmed. However, Connell disagreed that the atomic bomb was an inherently indiscriminate weapon or that any killing of noncombatants was unjustifiable. For example, the atomic bomb could be used against a fleet at sea killing no civilians. Appealing to a principle of proportionality, Connell argued that a limited killing of noncom-batants might be justified by the military advantage gained through the destruction of a crucial military target.

Connell represented a middle pole in the debate between Barrat and Zahn. He rejected neither the principle of noncombatant immunity nor the atomic bomb. Connell's focus on how nuclear weapons were to be used allowed him to reconcile them with noncombatant immunity, and this emphasis aligned squarely with the emerging discussion of tactical nuclear weapons and the mainstream of American commentary. Atomic arms used against enemy armed forces, which did not destroy cities and kill civilians indiscriminately, sufficed as a legitimate weapon for Connell. Barrat had written in his article that a French Dominican, concerned over noncombatant immunity, had admitted that his criticisms of nuclear weapons would not apply to "the use of a baby atom bomb made for tactical and properly military use."[11]

Father Connell went further than simply saying that weapons which avoided harming civilians were moral, though. He allowed for the legitimacy of the killing of some noncombatants in pursuit of a vitally important military goal. Without referring to it by name, Connell was using in his reasoning an idea developed by Catholic theologians called the principle of double effect. Derived from the teachings of Thomas Aquinas, the principle acknowledged that a given action could have multiple consequences, some of them good and some of them bad. As theologians and moral philosophers formulated the principle in the twentieth century, it held that as long as only the good conse-quences of an action were intended, the evil results were not a means to the good outcome, and the positive benefits outweighed the negative, such an action was morally justified.[12] For Connell, use of nuclear weapons was morally justified if their intended targets were objects of military significance and did not kill large numbers of civilians which would outweigh any military benefit achieved.

As U.N. forces gained the advantage in Korea, the summer talk of atomic attack died away, but when the Chinese entered the war in November, Americans again considered use of their nuclear arsenal. As during the summer, American officials raised possible harm to civilians as a liability of the atomic bomb. State Department officials considering its use against Chinese cities forecast significant negative political effects. A "repetition of Hiroshima and Nagasaki" would undermine the United States' moral position and harm relations with Asians in general, one concluded. Paul Nitze worried that atomic attacks on Manchurian cities would "result in the destruction of many civilians and would almost certainly bring the Soviet Union into the war."[13]

A public expression of concern by President Truman over atomic weapons harming innocent people created diplomatic turmoil in late November. At a news conference on November 30, a reporter asked Truman if the atomic bomb was under active consideration for use in the Korean War. The president replied that there had always been consideration of its use, but he followed this up with the qualification: "I don't want to see it used. It is a terrible weapon, and it should not be used on innocent men, women, and children who have nothing whatever to do with this military aggression. That happens when it is used." The statement was ambiguous. Was Truman saying that he would not let the atomic bomb be used against noncombatants or only that he was reluctant to see it employed because it harmed civilians when it was used? A reporter at the news conference tried to clarify and Truman's brusque response would lead to further misunderstanding. The reporter asked, "Does that mean, Mr. President, use against military objectives, or civilian —." The president interrupted the questioner: "It's a matter that the military people will have to decide. I'm not a military authority that passes on those things." A further question about whether U.N. authorization was necessary for the bomb's use led to the president's denial of this and a second reference to the military being responsible for the use of the weapons: "The military commander in field will have charge of the use of the weapons, as he always has." Laying responsibility on the military for how the atomic bomb would be employed allowed Truman to dodge the sensitive question of whether or not the weapon would be used against civilians, but this evasion contributed to a public misunderstanding over the possibility that the president had authorized MacArthur to use the atomic bomb when the general saw fit.[14]

Simply the president mentioning the possible use of the atomic bomb might have provoked public controversy, but the inference that MacArthur might determine whether the bomb was dropped or not ensured trouble for the president. Within hours of the president's comments, the White House had realized that Truman had made a mistake. It issued a clarification of the president's earlier comments. The press release said that only the president could authorize the use of the atomic bomb and he had not done so. If such an authorization was ever given, the military commander in the field would have "charge of the tactical delivery" of the weapon.[15] The clarification did not prevent extensive controversy in the American media and abroad. Concerns over unilateral American use led the British Prime Minister Clement Attlee to fly to Washington to consult with Truman.[16]

Some of the negative international reaction to President Truman's comments focused on the potential harm to noncombatants. Pope Pius XII offered an encyclical praying for an end to war. In an allusion to the atomic bomb, it lamented that the human mind had introduced "instruments of war of such power to raise horror in the souls of all honest persons, above all because they do not strike only the armies but often wipe out private citizens — children, women, the aged, and the sick…." A Djakarta newspaper editorialized that in an atomic bomb attack "hundreds of thousands of Chinese and Koreans, mostly civilians, would be sacrificed and Russia would have more propaganda material." The Canadian External Affairs Minister warned that the bombing of Chinese cities could destroy the cohesion and unity of purpose of the Atlantic community, and the *New York Times* reported that graffiti was appearing in Italian cities that called Truman a war criminal. Arab and South Asian leaders warned the American government that another use of atomic weapons against people of color would be disastrous for U.S. foreign relations. They argued that it would demonstrate that American leaders did not value Asian lives as much as those of white people.[17]

As with the previous summer, the talk among Americans of the atomic bomb's use stirred up by President Truman's comments contained expressions of concern over harm to civilians with only a few openly dismissive of the sentiment. Civic leaders like Harold Stassen, the prominent Republican and president of the University of Pennsylvania, and seventy-eight Protestant ministers from New York opposed the weapon's use because of the innocent civilians it would kill.[18] Similar arguments found expression in editorials from the *Washington Post* and *Chicago Tribune* as well as articles and letters in various newspapers and magazines.[19] Defenders of the bomb's use against the charge that it was immoral appeared less frequently and in less prominent venues such as letters to editors.[20]

Twice in 1950, discussion of U.S. use of the atomic bomb in Korea had generated self-criticism among Americans centered on the problem of harming civilians, but contemplation of the devastating effects of nuclear war outside Korea also could prove problematic for the United States. The American military's reliance on atomic weapons proved a liability for U.S. relations with western Europeans worried about a war that might be fought on their lands. Polls conducted for the U.S. government revealed that there was general agreement among western Europeans that the United States had not been justified in using the atomic bomb against Japan. Only Great Britain appeared to have opinion evenly divided on the issue. The West German respondents were asked to elaborate on the reasons for their judgment. The two major reasons, they selected, were that the bombing was inhumane and that it was unnecessary since victory had already been assured.[21] In early 1951, the State Department prepared an intelligence report on western European opinion on the immorality of the atomic bomb. It concluded that widespread opposition to the weapon existed in large part because of the fear that its destructive effects would be "general and indiscriminate."[22] One Italian responded when asked about the new weapons that the United States could use to defend Europe: "You think these will be used with such discretion? Atomic bombs, bacterial warfare — and only Russian soldiers will fall victim to them? Oh, you're right, the Americans won't give up. They're tenacious. I know them. Before they give up they'll transform the world into a desert."[23]

Western Europeans had good reason to be fearful of the destructiveness of the nuclear weapons in American hands. American politicians had begun to discuss the possibility of the United States dropping the atomic bomb on western European industry if the Soviets were to capture it. The "Great Debate" in early 1951 over the dispatch of additional American divisions to supplement North Atlantic Treaty Organization (NATO) ground forces in western Europe provided the forum for these unsettling comments. Senator Robert Taft in a speech before Congress argued that the United States would have to destroy vital western European industry such as its steel production, despite any danger to European civilians, if the Soviets carried out a successful invasion. Retired General Lucius D. Clay, former commander of American occupation forces in Germany, also raised the prospect of such destruction if NATO did not have sufficient ground forces to prevent a Soviet invasion.[24] European jitters about massive destruction in future wars gave Americans and their leaders an additional motivation to work for a better reconciliation of the modern techniques of warfare and noncombatant immunity.

5.2 "Tactical" Nuclear Weapons

In its capacity for indiscriminate destruction, the atomic bomb clearly possessed a liability that fed Communist propaganda, occupied American officials, roused self-criticism among Americans, and scared western Europeans and others overseas. However, in 1951 a new conception of atomic weapons gained prominence among Americans that promised to alleviate this liability. Americans began discussing the possibility of using atomic weapons against the armed forces of an enemy instead of solely against its industry and cities. This new option of tactical use, in theory, promised to reduce or even eliminate harm inflicted on noncombatants. The optimism about restraining the destruction of atomic weapons, which this new idea reflected, mirrored the optimism in which many Americans were indulging concerning the fighting in Korea.

Some discussion of the tactical use of atomic weapons occurred before 1951, but developments during that year made the notion a common one. In late 1949, military leaders began to discuss publicly the use of atomic arms on the battlefield. Besides comments by the admirals during the unification and strategy hearings in October, two Army generals broached the subject. General Jacob L. Devers, who retired as chief of the Army Field Forces in September, recommended in his "farewell" report that the atomic bomb be used as a tactical weapon to support ground forces, a suggestion that the *New York Times* called directly counter to the prevailing military view that atomic weapons were for use solely against cities and industrial centers. Several weeks later, Lawton Collins, the Army chief of staff, announced that his service was interested in developing atomic weapons for use on the battlefield.[25] Periodically during 1950, publications discussing military policy mentioned the possibility of tactical nuclear weapons offering an alternative to atomic city-destruction.[26] In the middle of 1950, the military editor of the *New York Times* Hanson Baldwin repeatedly took up the issue of tactical nuclear weapons in his commentaries.[27] By early 1951, Robert Oppenheimer was lecturing and writing about the possibility of the tactical use of atomic weapons against military targets instead of against population centers.[28] The idea that atomic weapons were only for city-busting was starting to change.

In early 1951, nuclear tests in Nevada, and the secrecy that veiled them, encouraged speculation that tactical nuclear weapons were becoming part of the American arsenal. Between January 27 and February 8, the Ranger series of nuclear tests detonated five fission bombs in the desert near Las Vegas. The smaller explosions of the Ranger tests gave rise to the idea that the AEC was experimenting with smaller nuclear weapons for battlefield use. An interview with General Collins encouraged the speculation. He told reporters that guided missiles and atomic artillery would soon be available for tactical use against troops in the field. The increased accuracy over the airplane that these delivery methods would provide meant that nuclear weapons would no longer be confined to use against cities, he said. Other comments by officials and former officials spread discussion of the new weapons, and the AEC refused to confirm or deny that tactical nuclear weapons were being developed.[29]

With the Nevada tests, the notion that the atomic bomb was no longer only a destroyer of an enemy's cities and industry appeared repeatedly in the press. One report by Cabell Philips in the *New York Times* elaborated on the theoretical appeal of tactical nuclear weapons over conventional atomic bombs in opposing a Soviet invasion of western Europe. The new weapons could be used against the invaders while avoiding atomic "saturation bombing — intolerable to contemplate and probably impossible of execution." The press had quickly adopted the notion that new tactical nuclear weapons could avoid some of the indiscriminate destruction of a future war.[30]

David Lilienthal, former chairperson of the AEC, moved beyond simply pointing out the possibility that the atomic bomb could be used against military forces instead of cities. In articles for *Collier's* magazine after the January tests, Lilienthal presented a moral vision of nuclear weapons that offered an explanation of how possession and use of the atomic bomb could be reconciled with American goals and values. He claimed that the U.S. potential to devastate Russian cities with atomic bombs was important to deter the Soviet Union from attacking the country and that this potential would be used if the Soviet Union did strike American cities first.

However, he criticized what he saw as Americans' fixation on a large and overly destructive atomic war to protect themselves from the Soviets. Lilienthal questioned the military value of the use of a hydrogen bomb against any except the largest targets because it would incidentally destroy many areas with no military significance. The preoccupation with a big atomic war, he said, also obscured the possibility of engineering atomic bombs so that they could be used to support American troops in the field or to destroy "particular military targets such as oil fields, marshalling yards, and ports of entry and supply." Lilienthal believed that American leaders should consider using the atomic bomb only for the destruction of clearly military objectives. They should not use the weapon "to create terror for terror's sake, or as an instrument of sheer annihilation." The general killing of population would cause little harm to populous countries, stiffen the survivors' resistance, and make a lasting peace more difficult to achieve. Lilienthal, therefore, asserted that the "primary targets in war, apart from direct combat, are things, not people — oil fields, power stations, steel centers, transportation centers and the other essential means of carrying on."

Lilienthal admitted that there was no way to wage war without killing people but believed a conscientiously fought war was quite different from "killing for the sake of killing." People, who dismissed criticism of the atomic bomb as immoral by arguing that war itself was immoral, did not actually mean that any means in war was justifiable. As an example, he pointed out that few would find sufficient justification for the shooting of prisoners of war. To Lilienthal, an ethical aspect to American actions in war remained. This vision of limited atomic war, warfare not directed at people behind the front lines, provided a less unsettling view of what the United States would do in a war against its Communist opponents.[31]

As the Nevada nuclear tests sparked optimistic discussion of tactical nuclear weapons, a report from the Federal Council of Churches prompted exchanges among Protestants about the legitimate use of nuclear weapons. Similar to the discussion among Catholics in the pages of *Commonweal*, the report and reactions to it illustrated the prevailing attempt to reconcile nuclear weapons with noncombatant immunity, but also reflected the dissenting poles of opinion, which on one end rejected nuclear weapons and on the other rejected noncombatant immunity. In December 1950, a special commission of nineteen theologians and laymen led by the Episcopal Bishop of Washington Angus Dun released its report on "The Christian Conscience and Weapons of Mass Destruction." Searching for middle ground, the report strained toward a reconciliation of nuclear weapons with Christian morality, the stress apparent in the report's convoluted structure and many qualifications. It sanctioned American possession and potential use of nuclear weapons but identified immoral purposes that the weapons could be put to. Like Father Connell and other Catholic theologians, the report claimed that only intentions and not particular weapons could be declared immoral in warfare. The report conceded to what it saw as the widespread acceptance of the bombing of cities as an "inescapable" part of modern war. Cities contained the industrial and technical potential that made them the arsenals of nations. Total warfare involved the whole nation and made distinguishing the guilty from the innocent practically impossible.

However, for the authors of the report this did not mean that all moral restraints should be abandoned and military expediency left to govern conduct in wars. Restraints should still be placed on killing, and some forms of violence were worse than others. That some weapons, like the atomic bomb, were more indiscriminate in their effects made their use more morally suspect than precise weapons, but their prohibition would not eliminate the potential for mass destruction from war. Conventional weapons could also be used for indiscriminate harm. The report asserted that "the real moral line between what may be done and what may not be done by the Christian lies not in the realm of distinction between weapons but in the realm of the motives for using and the consequences of using all kinds of weapons."

The report disdained "legalistic" prescriptions that could apply to all situations. Instead, it settled for pointing out that "the destruction of life clearly incidental to the destruction of decisive military objectives, for example, is radically different from mass destruction which is aimed primarily at the lives of civilians, their morale, or the sources of their livelihood." The report also offered the general guidance: "In the event of war, Christian conscience guides us to restraint from destruction not essential to our total objectives, to a continual weighing of the human values that may be won against those lost in the fighting, and to the avoidance of needless human suffering." Wanton destruction and devastation disproportionate to the good won from it constituted immoral conduct in war. With atomic weapons not intrinsically immoral, the report concluded that it could not recommend their prohibition when other nations possessed them. Such a ban would leave the United States inadequately defended. The destructiveness of the weapons did place a special burden of responsibility on those who would use them first, but "even more fundamental" was the immorality of those who would initiate a major war through aggression, which could lead to an atomic conflagration.

Two members of the commission appended short statements of dissent to the end of the report. Robert L. Calhoun of the Yale Divinity School challenged the adequacy of the report's guidance on the moral conduct of war. Beyond condemning wanton destruction, he saw the report as simply advising Christians to do reluctantly what military necessity required. Georgia Harkness of the Pacific School of Religion disputed the idea that atomic weapons could ever be used legitimately. She wrote, "To say that our government might justifiably use atomic weapons in retaliation 'with all possible restraint' seems a contradiction in terms."[32]

The reconciliation of nuclear weapons with noncombatant immunity, which the Dun commission offered, received criticism from both those who felt this stance did not preserve noncombatant immunity adequately and from those who believed it was too generous to enemy civilians. Religious pacifists were the most common critics who could not accept the report's sanction of nuclear weapons. Several expressed their opinions in the *Christian Century*. George M. Houser shared his concern that the doctrine of necessity could justify any use of weapons in war, and this in turn would undermine the difference between American democracy and totalitarianism. Stewart Meacham asserted that it was a patent absurdity that Christians would not kill more than was necessary and that distinctions could be maintained between industrial and population targets in use of the atomic bomb. The National Council of the Fellowship of Reconciliation issued a statement expressing its disappointment in the Dun report. It felt that the moral sanction provided by the commission made the use of atomic weapons by American leaders more likely. It warned, "The entire concept of a just war is challenged when the nature of the force employed is such as to undermine justice and destroy social order." The statement also reminded the Dun commission that the earlier Calhoun commission of the Federal Council of Churches in 1946 had declared that both the use of atomic bombs and the obliteration bombing which preceded it had constituted a sin against God and the Japanese people. True security, the earlier commission had assured the council, would not be found in continued resort to the weapon.[33]

The archconservative Executive Committee of the American Council of Christian Churches criticized the Dun report for reasons virtually opposite to the pacifists. The American Council, organized by a small cadre of fundamentalists who felt that the Federal Council of Churches was too liberal, believed that the report restricted American first use of atomic weapons too severely and was too protective of enemy civilians. It adopted the unusual stance that the threat of Soviet attack on American cities justified the preemptive killing of the Russian population. The Executive Committee's statement ended: "Instead of the peoples of a free land being thus annihilated, it is better and just that people committed to an anti-God system of the darkest tyranny be the victims of their own folly."[34]

Although the American Council's position was rare among Americans, it was not alone among conservative Christians. A sermon in early 1951 by a Baptist minister from Colorado also argued that killing civilians was a legitimate method of warfare and that noncombatant immunity had become meaningless. Reverend Sam Bradford's sermon "Should the United States Use the Atomic Bomb?" was sent to President Truman by the chairperson of the board of deacons of the Denver Beth Eden Baptist Church. The sermon was an argument for the use of the atomic bomb and against the "confused thinking" of some religious leaders. The first bit of confusion to which Bradford addressed himself was the notion of innocent noncombatants. He denied that there remained any "innocent populations" in modern war. All contemporary war was either "total war" or not war at all. He argued that there was no more guilt waging war against those behind the battle lines who produced the food, supplies, and arms for frontline troops than against the combatants themselves. Bradford portrayed virtually everyone as a contributor in war. He reminded his audience of how American children during World War II saved toothpaste tubes to contribute tin for the building of bombers and gathered scrap metal and paper for the war effort. Housewives had gathered used fats and conserved critical materials. Denying that anyone would remain innocent in a war, Bradford asserted modern wars meant victory and survival or defeat and doom for the nations involved and denied the atomic bomb was any more inhumane in how it killed than any other weapon of war.

The rest of the sermon appealed to the Bible to claim that war had been an instrument of God and that God himself wrought judgment through "mass annihilation" with the great flood and the destruction of Sodom and Gomorrah. Bradford concluded that the nuclear eradication of the Soviet Union, which he called the "evil, God-denying, God-defying octopus" and the "unholy scourge of hate and slavery," might be the will of God.[35] Reverend Bradford's rejection of noncombatant immunity did not appear to satisfy many, though. The Dun report's effort to delineate the legitimate use of nuclear weapons reflected the larger struggle to reconcile the new weapons with older values, which the emerging talk of tactical nuclear weapons also reflected.

The discussion of battlefield nuclear weapons progressed through the spring and summer, but the fall of 1951 witnessed growing attention to the issue and further suggestions that the new weapons could help to alleviate the dilemma over indiscriminate destruction. The Greenhouse nuclear test series in the Bikini islands during April and May fueled further speculation about the development of tactical nuclear weapons.[36] In August and September, statements by top military officials, such as the secretary of the Air Force, the Air Force chief of staff, and the commander in chief of the U.S. Atlantic fleet, appeared to confirm the U.S. military was developing a capability to use atomic weapons tactically despite the AEC's persistent refusal to confirm or deny that that was the case.[37]

The attention to tactical nuclear weapons generated further suggestions in the press that these new weapons might assist in resolving the dilemma over indiscriminate destruction. A *Life* magazine article observed that the tactical use of atomic weapons "provides a partial alternative to the strategic air bombing technique hitherto aimed almost exclusively at Soviet industrial centers, with all the heavy moral responsibilities that form of indirect attack involves." *Newsweek* wrote that when nuclear weapons could be used tactically as well as strategically the nature of war would change. Instead of destroying Soviet "industrial and transportation centers," tactical nuclear weapons could destroy the Communist armies in the field leaving Russian cities reasonably intact. This would relieve American forces of "occupying chaos" and of "the moral problem inherent in the bombing of enemy cities and civilian population." Anthony Leviero of the *New York Times* also saw new smaller tactical nuclear weapons as an alternative to the destruction of cities. The new arms "would mean atomic weapons would not be limited to large strategic targets like cities, in which many thousands of civilians are wiped out, but could be used also against enemy troops on the battlefield." The *Times'* military editor Hanson Baldwin saw the interest in the weapons as a reflection of a move away in American strategy from city and industry destruction, "so-called 'population bombing,'" since the October 1949 unification and strategy hearings.[38]

In the middle of 1951, the speculation about tactical nuclear weapons was mostly talk. The military was still months away from deploying a nuclear weapon system designed for the battlefield. Lighter bombs which fighter-bombers could carry and atomic artillery would not come until 1952 and even then in limited numbers.[39] It would be years before the United States possessed a significant capability to use nuclear weapons on or near the battlefield. Much of the official comments concerning tactical nuclear weapons in 1951 simply amounted to thinking ahead. However, those officials familiar with the country's atomic energy program had reason to believe that an era of atomic plenty was around the corner. American facilities for producing the nuclear materials for weapons had expanded production. President Truman had approved increases in plutonium and uranium-235 production in the fall of 1949 and in October 1950.[40] With the weapons materials no longer quite so rare, some envisioned a variety of nuclear weapons which could serve a multiplicity of strategic and tactical purposes.

In publicly advocating a further expansion of nuclear production, Senator Brien McMahon saw tactical nuclear weapons as one of the major benefits. On September 18, he gave a speech on the floor of the Senate arguing that the United States could reduce its spending on defense by relying more heavily on nuclear weapons. He asserted that plentiful nuclear arms could be used against both the war industry of an enemy and its armed forces. In another speech in Washington a week later, McMahon suggested how tactical nuclear weapons could alleviate the political and moral dilemma of atomic energy. McMahon acknowledged that the Soviet Union had had a measure of success convincing the world through its propaganda that the atomic bomb was immoral. The success was due in part to the "belief that the atomic weapon must inevitably destroy the guilty and the innocent alike." The senator challenged this belief with a number of arguments. He claimed that "actually our military men have always regarded the bomb as a precision weapon to be used only against specific targets vital to the enemy war machine," and the proof of this, he said, was that the military spent as much as $250,000 on each bombsight for its planes to ensure precision bombing. McMahon also speculated that Soviet citizens would abandon their jobs in war industries if their leaders ever embarked on an aggressive war, making the United States' destruction of the industries less morally objectionable. However, an accelerated program to produce tactical nuclear weapons would also reduce the "phony appeal of Stalin's propaganda to the effect that atomic weapons are only good against civilians."[41]

In October, Gordon Dean, the chairperson of the AEC, drew even greater attention to the possibility that tactical nuclear weapons offered a way out of America's dilemma of massive destruction. Earlier, Dean had testified before Congress about a revolution in thought on nuclear weapons, but in a speech at the University of Southern California on October 5, Dean explained his ideas to a wider public. Stressing the importance of American moral leadership in the world, Dean laid out the problem that possession of the atomic bomb posed for the United States. He admitted that many people feared the weapon and questioned whether the United States was pursuing the right course. He said, "They have no difficulty in imagining the suffering and desolation among innocent civilians that would follow in the wake of an all-out, global atomic war." Dean argued that the United States was pursuing the right course in resisting Communist aggression, and he praised American moral sensitivities. However, the sensitivities, he believed, had been exploited by the Communists.

To Dean, a solution presented itself in the "revolutionary change" in atomic warfare that the expansion of the atomic energy program and recent technological developments had stimulated. The whole truth of atomic warfare, Dean argued, was no longer the enormous destruction epitomized by the attacks on Hiroshima and Nagasaki in which long-range bombers struck at the large cities and industrial centers of an enemy nation. With the era of atomic scarcity coming to a close, a "new, quite different kind" of atomic warfare could be envisioned, warfare that would be "much less fearsome as far as non-combatants are concerned, and much more promising as a means of halting aggressors without the risk of destroying large parts of the world in the process." Dean concluded, "It means ... an era when we can use atomic weapons tactically as well as strategically." Dean believed that this change in atomic warfare resolved some of America's moral dilemma. The "tactical atom" could be treated as any other weapon, no more destructive than necessary to meet any situation.[42]

Dean's speech attracted attention in the national press[43] and his comments on the morality of tactical nuclear weapons figured in some of the coverage. *Life* magazine printed an editorial praising Dean's moral reasoning calling it a "wonderfully encouraging outlook." Anthony Leviero of the *New York Times* wrote an article proclaiming the importance of Dean's speech, and he placed the commissioner's claim that tactical nuclear weapons eliminated the moral issue from considerations of the use of atomic arms as the speech's most significant revelation. Father Edward A. Conway, associate editor of *America* magazine, believed that Dean's speech represented an attempt to gauge public reaction to new policy by the Truman administration.[44]

Conway's surmise was wrong. Dean's speech was not part of a coordinated information campaign by the administration,[45] but it did motivate a number of official efforts to capitalize on his theme. The speech excited some State Department officers responsible for overseas information programs. One officer, who believed that Dean's speech meant that the United States now had "weapons that will kill lots of troops without endangering innocent civilian populations" and that this would take the United States "off the Hiroshima-Nagasaki moral guilt hook for good," went so far as to claim that the commissioner's speech was "the most important announcement relating to the Cold War" since General Marshall proposed his plan for the reconstruction of Europe. The Voice of America broadcast the speech around the world in forty-five languages.[46]

Congressman Henry M. Jackson quickly joined Dean in praising the virtues of tactical nuclear weapons. Jackson, a member of the Joint Congressional Committee on Atomic Energy, was from Washington state, which contained the Hanford nuclear reactors that produced the country's plutonium for atomic bombs. Not surprisingly, he was a strong supporter of the expansion of the atomic energy program. In an October 9 speech on the House floor, Jackson touted the "revolution" in military thinking. Not only would tactical nuclear weapons help the United States defeat the Soviet Union's mass armies and allow the country to end little wars, they would answer Stalin's propaganda claims that American weapons were immoral. Jackson entreated his colleagues, "I would like to emphasize strongly to the Members of the House my very firm belief that one of the worst things that has happened to the United States and the free world is that the atomic bomb has been held up to the free world as a weapon that could be used only against women and children." On the CBS television program "Man of the Week" five days later, Jackson complained, "the Russians very cleverly have associated the use of atomic bombs with the killing of women and children and they have, in effect, through clever propaganda sterilized our stockpile." Emphasis on the tactical use of atomic weapons against troops in the field rather than their strategic uses, Jackson felt, would solve this problem.[47]

Senator Henry Cabot Lodge, Jr. believed that the development of tactical nuclear weapons removed the moral objection to the atomic bomb's use in

Korea. In a Senate speech on October 11, he claimed, "The use of atomic weapons for purely military purposes and solely against military personnel could not possibly justify any moral disapproval of us on the grounds that we are using the atomic weapon against civilians." He even suggested that the use of atomic weapons to create a line of "atomic craters" across the Korean peninsula would be justified if civilians were given ample time to evacuate the areas of attack. For Lodge, the idea of tactical nuclear weapons free from the stigma of indiscriminate civilian destruction simplified the question of the use of America's most powerful weapons in the Korean War. A number of other senators called for the use of tactical nuclear weapons in Korea in the wake of Dean's speech.[48]

Another set of seven nuclear tests in Nevada in October and November, one of which included military units moving into the test zone after the explosion, convinced much of the media that the AEC had in fact developed new battlefield nuclear weapons. William Laurence reported that the tests were the "debut" of "baby" atomic bombs of much smaller explosive yields than the weapons used against Japan and marked the beginning of the revolutionary new era of which Commissioner Dean had spoken. A senator also announced that the U.S. military possessed atomic bombs tailored for battlefield use. Although some of the tests in this series, code named Buster-Jangle, involved weapon designs promising for tactical use, deployment of atomic weapons for the battlefield was still in the future. Nevertheless, because of the secrecy surrounding nuclear weapons development, Americans were left with the impression that these new weapons were a practical reality. This erroneous thinking was hardly surprising given that the president himself had mistakenly believed in the summer of 1951 that the military already possessed atomic artillery.[49]

During the month that the Buster-Jangle tests were convincing people that the United States already possessed the tactical nuclear weapons that Commissioner Dean had promoted, *Collier's* magazine published a special issue on nuclear war. The issue offered one of the clearest examples of the prevailing optimism about a controlled use of violence even in a nuclear war. The October 27 special issue was devoted to discussion of what a third world war might be like, and the issue of inflicting civilian casualties was prominent. This special edition used the unusual and sensational device of having its contributing authors write their pieces as if it were 1960 and they were looking back on World War III that had occurred from 1952 to 1955. Robert E. Sherwood, playwrite and author, wrote a fictional narrative of the war, and other articles offered analyses of various aspects of the imagined conflict. Although the entire issue was fictional, *Collier's* had gathered a number of prominent and respected journalists and politicians to contribute to the magazine including the military editor of the *New York Times* Hanson Baldwin, the columnist Walter Winchell, the editor of the *Christian Science Monitor* Erwin D. Canham, and Senator Margaret Chase Smith.

The World War III that *Collier's* envisioned was a war in which Americans had largely been able to avoid massive harm to Soviet civilians despite the extensive use of nuclear weapons. Sherwood's narrative described a war in which the United States for more than a year had refrained from deliberate attacks on Russian population centers. As Sherwood described it, "The U.N. grand strategy had been firmly fixed; we were not making war on the Russian people, our limitless destructive powers were to be directed at the centers and the instruments of Soviet militaristic aggression and not against the humble, simple, peace-loving Russian peasants and workers whom we wanted eternally to be our friends." The Air Force did eventually destroy twenty square miles of Moscow with atomic bombs, but this occurred only after the Soviets atomized several American cities and American leaders could not resist public pressure to retaliate. Even then, Sherwood wrote, the United States provided ample warning to the civilian population to evacuate the city, broadcasting the warning every hour for the four days before the attack on the Voice of America, Radio Free Europe, the British Broadcasting Corporation, and every other available United Nations facility. The leaders in the Kremlin, however, did not allow the city to be evacuated. Amazingly, Moscow was the sole population center destroyed in the Soviet Union. Instead of an atomic blitz on Soviet cities, U.S. forces attacked specific military targets such as oil, steel and atomic bomb plants, and the turning point in the war came when the United States and its allies repelled a Soviet invasion of Europe with atomic artillery.

Other pieces in the issue underlined the importance placed on avoiding indiscriminate attacks on civilian populations. Praising their wisdom, Hanson Baldwin wrote that American leaders had deliberately chosen to fight a limited war for limited ends, avoiding an atomic holocaust, and instead had waged a war primarily against Communism and its leaders and not against the Russian people. The editorial, which began the special issue and the only piece that did not adopt the fictional tone, made its advocacy of this type of warfare explicit. The editors wrote, "The free world has no quarrel with the oppressed Russian people, but only with their Soviet masters. Those masters would probably attack the civilians of this and other free countries in a campaign of atomic extermination. But we hope and trust that the atomic bombs of those free, humane countries would be used not for retaliation, but for the destruction of strategic targets, and only after advance warnings to civilians to evacuate the areas."[50]

Despite failing to explain how the United States could have attacked with atomic bombs Soviet industries like steel and oil production which were mostly located near cities without killing multitudes of civilians, the publishers of *Collier's* believed they had created a reasonable vision of World War III. The magazine believed that the U.S. government might find the special issue useful for its information programs overseas. They offered the State Department discount copies for distribution abroad. The State Department turned them down.[51]

The notion of a general war without indiscriminate destruction that the *Collier's* special issue peddled was reinforced by other articles in national publications which stressed the precision with which American strategic bombing could inflict damage on an enemy. The *Saturday Evening Post* had printed an article on the Strategic Air Command that noted the organization's concern for avoiding indiscriminate destruction. The article related, "SAC's stern insistence on bull's-eye accuracy is a little surprising to a layman, who is prone to think of atomic bombing in terms of indiscriminate mass destruction." But the bomber command had both military and humanitarian reasons for its emphasis on precision, the article claimed. Not only was it a waste when bombs destroyed residential areas and left factories standing, SAC did not want to be accused of "irresponsible slaughter of civilians" if war should come. Despite this purported humanitarian concern, the article observed that the SAC was not looking for "overly quiet and introspective types" to fly its bombers because they "might, after searching their souls, find out in the final moments of a bombing run that they could not carry out their jobs for humanitarian reasons." Francis V. Drake in the *Reader's Digest* sought to lay out what he saw as the facts of strategic bombing. He distinguished strategic bombing that sought to destroy only critical war supplies from area bombing, which he dismissed as "useless savagery."[52]

The optimism about the discriminate use of destructive power even extended for a few to the hydrogen bomb. The thermonuclear weapon, predicted to be 100 to 1,000 times more powerful than the atomic bomb and, therefore, well suited for destroying an entire city, some believed held great potential for use against enemy forces. After the appearance of his book *The Hell Bomb*, William Laurence continued to promote the idea that the hydrogen bomb would be an important tactical weapon.[53] When testing of a prototype thermonuclear device appeared imminent in mid-1952, others joined Laurence in touting the battlefield uses of the enormously powerful bomb. Writing about the top secret, government-sponsored Cal Tech study of the application of firepower on the battlefield Project Vista,[54] Hanson Baldwin reported that some in the Air Force foresaw significant uses for the hydrogen bomb in support of ground forces. Senator McMahon in a speech before the Connecticut Democratic State Convention contended that the tactical hydrogen bomb would prove devastating against invading Soviet soldiers, enemy ships in port, and other military targets like ammunition depots.[55]

Those in the military actively worked to spread the idea that U.S. armed forces applied force discriminately and avoided harm to civilians. In military journals, Air Force officers continued to insist that strategic bombing did not necessarily lead to the annihilation of civilian populations, and Navy and Marine officers continued to assert that force should be focused on the destruction of enemy armed forces instead of against industry and population.[56] The secretary of the Air Force in a Washington speech reiterated: "Any idea that [Strategic Air Command's] purpose is to bring mass destruction to civilians is completely wrong. Where military targets are in populated areas, civilians will suffer, but so they do in case of invasion."[57]

The Army had been working on a public information campaign that would stress the humane qualities of tactical nuclear weapons. In March, the Office of the Assistant Chief of Staff for Operations had initiated a staff study that sought to devise a public information policy concerning the tactical employment of atomic weapons. The study sought to correct the situation that "no coordinated action has been taken by the U.S. government to educate citizens of the free world on the fact that atomic weapons can be used with great effectiveness on strictly military targets without directly affecting the cities or civilian populations." In July, Assistant Secretary of the Army Karl R. Bendetsen and Gordon Dean agreed that a real obstacle to using atomic weapons was the widespread idea that the weapons could only be used against cities in which civilians rather than military personnel would be the victims. On October 16, the Army Policy Council heard the operations staff's proposal for an information campaign to counter this notion. The campaign would educate the public on three points: atomic weapons were an essential part of the U.S. arsenal, the weapons were not intrinsically different "in respect to humanitary considerations" from conventional weapons, and atomic weapons could be used "tactically without inhumane destruction of powerless civilians." At the same time, the campaign was supposed to avoid deemphasizing strategic employment. This extensive campaign, which included a press conference by the secretary of the Army, was not implemented, but the Army chief of staff continued to make public statements along the lines suggested by the operations staff. At Fort Bliss in November, General Collins said that the Army was developing atomic artillery that could be used "with great accuracy on a definite military target."[58]

Nuclear war certainly did not lose its image among Americans as a massively destructive endeavor despite the optimism generated by the emerging ideas concerning tactical nuclear weapons. The destruction of cities and the deaths of millions remained a central element of most visions of a future world war.[59] In particular, a common assumption in discussions of civil defense was that the Soviet Union would destroy American cities with atomic weapons if a war were to start, although this talk did not usually give rise to expressions of the necessity and legitimacy of destroying Soviet cities and civilian population in retaliation.[60] Some like Stewart Alsop rejected the notion that nuclear weapons could be used in an entirely discriminate manner against enemy armed forces or special isolated targets. He believed that the weapons would not be decisive unless they were used against the massed populations of great cities.[61] However, tactical nuclear weapons provided others with hope that the destruction in such a war could be limited and would allow a greater degree of immunity for noncombatants.

U.S. war planning in the early 1950s reflected in small measure the new attention that use of atomic weapons against an enemy's armed forces was receiving. In August 1950, the JCS approved a new targeting scheme for the strategic nuclear attack planned for a war against the Soviet Union. The scheme differentiated between "disruption," "blunting," and "retardation" missions. The disruption mission targeted industries in urban areas which earlier war plans had singled out for atomic attack. The change in the targeting scheme came from the introduction of blunting and retardation targets that were theoretically to receive priority over the disruption operations. Blunting targets were those which hindered the Soviet Union's ability to deliver atomic bombs, and retardation targets were ones that hampered Soviet advances into western Europe. Natural marks for such targeting priorities would be Soviet bombers or concentrations of enemy forces or military supplies.

However, despite the new priorities, the blunting and retardation missions were not quickly incorporated into operational plans or target lists. Many of the new targets would be ones of opportunity difficult to plan for and highly dependent on intelligence that was hard to come by, and General LeMay at SAC complained about this in early 1951. LeMay also objected to using scarce atomic bombs on targets that might not utilize the full destructive power of the weapons. He argued against selecting any target system that "failed to reap the benefits derived from urban area bombing." If a bomb were to miss an isolated target, it might do no more than plow up fields and scorch grass, but if the bomb's target was industry located within an urban area, an errant bomb would still achieve a "bonus" effect by destroying surrounding structures. With this argument, LeMay had won a dispute inside the Air Force against making the Soviet electrical power system a targeting priority. Because of the remote location of many Soviet power plants, targeting of the industry failed to offer this destructive "bonus." Bernard Brodie, a political scientist who worked as a consultant to the Air Force, described SAC's targeting priorities to the Air Force chief of staff in 1951. "SAC desires to place primary emphasis on cities as such ...," he wrote. SAC views predominated in war planning as that organization came to hold greater responsibility for writing the detailed operational plans that would govern the actual implementation of a strategic air offensive.[62]

Despite the formal targeting priorities, most American nuclear weapons remained targeted against industry in Soviet cities with the purpose of maximizing destruction. Many Americans may have believed that the United States was moving toward taming the destructiveness of its nuclear arsenal with new weapons and ideas, but the country's highly secret plans for war reflected little of this. American leaders still believed that the nation's security rested upon its ability to devastate the Soviet Union with nuclear arms.

This strategic dependence on nuclear mass destruction placed some constraints on what American officials were willing to say in order to reassure the public that the country did not intend to harm civilians if compelled to fight. The production of a NSC paper concerning official publicity on "novel" weapons, which included nuclear, chemical, and biological weapons as well as guided missiles, illustrated this obstacle in late 1951 and early 1952. The drafting process, which resulted in the policy paper NSC 126, evidenced officials' desires to counter public perceptions that the government might use new weapons recklessly. Earlier drafts of the guidance included instructions to promote the idea "we are … against the principle of city-bombing" and "don't highlight the mass-destruction aspect" of novel weapons.[63]

However, the final NSC paper was vague because of the desire to avoid public commitments on how the weapons might be used. Some officials had raised objections to specific instructions encouraging officials to state publicly that the United States would not attack cities or only strike military targets. "To tell the world that we are against city bombing in principle would be virtually meaningless inasmuch as no one doubts that we would engage in it under the pressure of exigency," one State Department officer wrote. "The statement would probably cause much raising of eyebrows in Tokyo, Hiroshima, Frankfurt, and dozens of other places where people still remember the terror of American bombing." The Soviet expert Charles Bohlen questioned whether public statements could imply that the United States would only bomb military targets without committing the government to follow this practice strictly in a war. The closest the NSC 126 guidance in the end came to the subject of noncombatant immunity was encouraging officials to consider whether a particular public statement might bolster the fear that the United States might act recklessly in the use of novel weapons.[64] Balancing U.S. plans for war and the norm of noncombatant immunity was a tricky act for American officials even with Americans' optimism about restraining the destruction of nuclear war.

5.3 Humanizing Chemical and Biological Warfare

While the prospect of tactical nuclear weapons was quieting fears about the inhumanity of atomic energy, other new and exotic weapons were undergoing a similar humanizing process. Chemical, biological, and radiological weapons acquired a frightful, if somewhat fanciful, reputation for deadliness in the late 1940s and early 1950s. To rehabilitate these new technologies in the public's estimation, American officials attempted to deny that they were weapons of "mass destruction." CBR weapons shared certain qualities and were, therefore, often lumped together in policy discussions. These invisible killers harmed only living things and gave little or no warning of their attack. They also shared with nuclear weapons the controversial moniker "weapons of mass destruction" in the popular mind. Many Americans considered them different from and more terrible than conventional guns, explosives, and incendiaries. Poison gas had gained the stigma of an unusually horrible weapon during its use on the battlefields in World War I. Chemical and biological warfare was outlawed as a method of war by international convention in 1925. The mysterious nature of radiation, about which many Americans understood little more than its potentially lethal effects, enhanced the frightfulness of radiological weapons, which in theory would distribute large amounts of radioactive material, exposing the enemy to harmful levels of radiation.

In the late 1940s and early 1950s, exaggerated reports of their deadliness compounded the fear and revulsion toward CBR weapons. One retired admiral claimed that new chemical and biological weapons were "capable of exterminating the last vestige of human, animal and even vegetable life from the face of the earth." The director general of the World Health Organization made several statements about the extreme danger that biological warfare posed for the human race including the claim that "mankind can be wiped out by seven ounces of a known biologic if spread widely enough." In the summer of 1950, reports of radioactive "death sands," which could kill the entire population of a city without warning, added to the fearful image of these weapons. Some objected to these weapons specifically because they believed their effects would be indiscriminate. A University of Chicago biologist was appalled at the prospect of biological weapons because many of the men, women, and children that they would kill or maim would have no responsibility for the threats to American national security.[65] CBR weapons had a controversial image to overcome if the American public were to accept them as legitimate weapons of war.

Ironically, some American officials came to laud these "weapons of mass destruction" for their nondestructive and nonlethal properties. That CBR weapons did not destroy urban infrastructure and were not necessarily lethal in their effects became virtues which officials, who wanted the weapons more fully integrated into American military operations, used to counter objections to the controversial weapons. To these advocates, CBR arms were not horrible weapons of mass destruction, but instead uniquely humane instruments of war.

Claims about the humane nature of CBR arms surfaced in the confidential discussions of several government committees established to examine policy on CBR warfare. In 1947, the report of the Research and Development Board's Committee on Biological Warfare asserted that biological weapons could not be considered weapons of mass destruction that had the capability of indiscriminately killing large numbers of civilians. No biological agent capable of starting an epidemic had yet been developed by the American biological weapons research program. The report also argued that biological agents might be "more humane and less objectionable" than the use of even conventional incendiaries and explosives because property and production facilities would not be destroyed and because a debilitating but nonlethal disease could be used against an enemy. The report concluded that biological weapons should be considered simply another weapon of war, no more morally objectionable or inhumane than any other. The following year Ernest O. Lawrence, a distinguished physicist intimately involved in the government's nuclear program, tried to convince the Secretary of Defense James Forrestal of the humane virtues of radiological weapons. As Forrestal wrote in his diary, this new use for atomic energy, Lawrence claimed, could deny the use of large areas such as cities and industrial centers "to massed population, but do it in a way that would not expose such populations to extermination."[66]

A six month study by the Secretary of Defense's Ad Hoc Committee on Chemical, Biological, and Radiological Warfare in 1950 considered similar arguments in its deliberations. The Ad Hoc Committee, chaired by the businessperson Earl P. Stevenson, brought together officials from the Defense Department and State Department with civilian experts to consider U.S. policy on these new forms of warfare. Colonel William M. Creasy, the Chemical Corps' chief of research and engineering, gave two presentations to the committee which praised CBR weapons for their ability to incapacitate enemies with a minimum of death and physical destruction. The committee's final report agreed with the earlier Research and Development Board report that CBR weapons could not be realistically classified as weapons of mass destruction in their current state of development.

However, in discussing the morality of the weapons, the 1950 report offered different arguments to defend the weapons against the charges that their use was immoral. As a top secret document, the report could adopt, without fear of public outcry, the unusual and unpopular stance that wars had become total conflicts between peoples instead of limited fights between professional armies. It concluded that no restrictions should be placed on the use of weapons out of fallacious considerations of morality. The report said, "Restricting ourselves in the weapons we use merely means that we offer our enemy a better chance to kill our soldiers and civilians than we need to, out of deference to a habit of thought based on conditions of former times." The report did not completely banish, though, the idea of immorality from warfare, but it placed moral opprobrium only on those who started wars. Its discussion of war morality concluded: "Immorality attaches to those who initiate a war of aggression. Once the immorality of aggression has been committed, one cannot usefully dwell on the morality or immorality of specific weapons."

A third study on biological warfare in 1952, approved by the JCS, demonstrated that the views of the Secretary of Defense's committee about the irrelevance of noncombatant immunity for modern war were not in the mainstream of thought, even among American military advisors. The report by the Joint Advanced Study Committee included a number of statements that demonstrated the continued salience of the problem of indiscriminate destruction for military planners. The study pointed out that biological warfare was a distinctive weapon that would not destroy structures and property thereby simplifying postwar economic rehabilitation problems. It concluded that the decision to use biological weapons against Soviet crops and livestock "must be carefully weighed" in part because the tactic "would be essentially nonselective and would affect men, women, and children throughout the Soviet Union." In discussing the morality of biological weapons, the study argued: "There is no valid reason to consider any one weapon more immoral than another; more properly, IMMORALITY SHOULD BE ATTACHED TO THE METHOD OF EMPLOYMENT OF WEAPONS [emphasis in the original]. For example, the indiscriminate use of conventional weapons against civilian population not in furtherance of a military objective is considered to be immoral." The JCS study argued for the same conclusion that biological weapons were not immoral as the Secretary of Defense's committee had, but offered a different rationale, one closer to the mainstream of public sentiment, which continued to place importance on providing civilians some protections.[67]

Government officials began to praise publicly the humane qualities of CBR weapons in the early 1950s. Two chiefs of the Army Chemical Corps gave public speeches which presented gas warfare as a way to restrain the destruction of modern war. General Anthony C. McAuliffe in 1950 told the American Chemical Society that use of the newly developed nerve gases could obtain victory without extensive destruction of an enemy's economy. Nerve gas was a valuable weapon because, McAuliffe argued, "We have no quarrel with the peoples of a nation; we have no desire to destroy their national life, or their economy...." Two years later, McAuliffe's successor at the head of the Chemical Corps, General E. F. Bullene, made similar public comments. He argued that experience from World War II demonstrated that the use of weapons like gas which did not destroy physical property could avoid destroying an enemy's economy and bringing a "pyrrhic victory."[68]

Other officials made similar claims about radiological and biological weapons. In 1950, the chief scientist for the Air Force Louis N. Ridenour wrote an article about radiological warfare that praised the method's humane qualities. Ridenour conceded that radiological weapons could be regarded as a "horrid and insidious" weapon because they harmed people without the victims being able to perceive the assault, but he argued that, on the other hand, the weapon could be viewed as a "remarkably humane one." The weapons gave a target population a choice to live or die. Soldiers and civilians could flee a contaminated area quickly and enjoy an excellent chance of survival unlike high-explosive and incendiary bombs which gave the enemy's population no such choice. Several military officers also wrote articles that suggested radiological weapons could bring war without death or destruction. To the Austrian scientist Hans Thirring, radiological warfare provided a humane answer to the dilemma of defending Europe against an invader. By contaminating all the big cities of Europe with radioactive dust, the United States could force an aggressor into defeat without destroying a single building or killing a single civilian or enemy soldier. A Navy scientist argued that since biological weapons could incapacitate an enemy population without being lethal, the arms might be the most humane way ever employed to wage war.[69]

Beyond the public statements praising the humane attributes of CBR weapons, the U.S. military made several attempts to shape the public discussion of the weapons and counter their stigmatization as immoral implements of mass destruction. In late 1951, the Department of Defense issued a directive on public information policy for CBR weapons. The directive instructed that official information and statements should express no moral implications concerning these weapons and that the terms "weapons of mass destruction" and "unconventional weapons" should be avoided when discussing them. Along these lines, the Air Force staff and the State Department attempted to coordinate the drafting of resolutions for the United Nations on disarmament so that, inasmuch as possible, the resolutions avoided connecting the term "weapons adaptable to mass destruction" specifically with biological warfare. When the Army Chemical Corps in 1954 was preparing a script for a television special on its contribution to national defense, the Office of the Chief of Psychological Warfare suggested changes. While it passed over the script's introductory comment that World War II had demonstrated modern war to be total war that "spares neither man, woman, or child," the office proposed a change in wording that would clarify that U.S. military operations would be conducted against military targets, as prescribed by national policies, and not against civilian targets. It also suggested eliminating a reference to the number of civilians killed in an incendiary attack against a Japanese city because this was the type of information that Communist propaganda used against the United States.[70]

Official efforts to humanize CBR weapons continued through late 1955 when the Army released to the press the conclusions of a civilian advisory committee studying the weapons. A UP story quoted the advisory committee's comments about the valuable nondestructive and nonlethal qualities of CBR weapons. The committee said that recognition had to be given to the unique potential of these weapons to be effective in warfare without the attendant destruction of facilities and consequent problems of rehabilitation. The committee also pointed out the weapons' abilities to weaken the will of enemy's armed forces and civilian population without loss of lives or permanent injury.[71]

In the early 1950s, U.S. officials struggled to envision CBR weapons as humane tools of war reconcilable with the norm of noncombatant immunity, and they worked to convince American and world opinion that this was so. The idea did not spread much beyond official circles although it would reemerge during the Vietnam War amid controversy over the use of incapacitating gas by the U.S. military. Nevertheless, the attempt to humanize CBR weapons, like the more widespread effort to tame the bomb, demonstrated the strength of many Americans' optimistic faith that modern weapons could be reconciled with noncombatant immunity. Even the most exotic and potentially deadly weapons could be humanized for some.

The emergence of thinking about tactical nuclear weapons demonstrated that nuclear and other new weapons were not revolutionary in the sphere of norms. Values did not change to conform to the novel destructive technologies. Instead, conceptions of the new technologies adjusted to conform to traditional values. Noncombatant immunity shaped ideas about the atomic bomb instead of the bomb ending the tradition of seeking protections for civilians. As they had in their views of the Korean War, many Americans adopted the optimistic view that force could still be used in a manner that avoided massive harm to noncombatants. Even the devastating nuclear technologies, along with biological and chemical weapons, could be tamed to conform to the notion of noncombatant immunity. Historians have argued that opposition to nuclear weapons died down in the early 1950s because of the growing tensions between the United States and the Soviet Union and because of the acceptance of the comforting notions that nuclear deterrence might prevent wars and atomic energy had peaceful applications.[72] The changing idea of how nuclear weapons were to be used in war should also be added to the reasons for American complacency with the nuclear status quo.

Although the power of optimistic denial was strong, it had limits. Nuclear weapons still remained potential city-destroyers even if they were no longer exclusively viewed in this way. Most Americans could not completely deny that the United States might find itself in a war where its nuclear weapons would inflict massive devastation on civilians, and the war in Korea was providing ample evidence of the destruction that conventional American weapons could inflict. The problem of reconciling undenied harm to noncombatants with the taboo against killing innocent civilians remained.

6
Korean Refugees and Warnings

Pannam, a village north of the thirty-eighth parallel, had been a typical fishing settlement on Korea's east coast before the war. By June 1951, only a few solitary, straw-roofed huts standing amid rubble remained to mark where the village had been. Naval shelling and air attacks from the U.N. forces had left the village in ruin. As early as the previous December, the villagers had begun scratching out caves in the red clay hills near the town to escape the barrages. With the war intensifying along the coast, entire families were forced to move into the caves. There they fashioned a crude underground city. Most of the holes could only be dug large enough to shelter five or six people. Thin straw mats, hung at the entrances, served as doors and provided some insulation. A few of the burrows had roof supports to prevent cave-ins from the bombardment, but shells occasionally penetrated the caves and new holes had to be dug. The villagers, mostly women and children, came out of their underground shelters at night to do what farming they could. During the winter, some villagers returned to their ruined homes to dig up hidden caches of rice, potatoes, and vegetables buried for protection against Communist seizures. When South Korean soldiers arrived in the town, they found that some of the villagers suffered from typhus. One village resident, a twenty-four-year-old mother with seven children to feed, was a refugee from further north whose family had tried to reach South Korea but could not make it past Pannam. Her husband decided to leave her and the children in this "safe, out-of-the-way" fishing village while he joined the army. She lived in one of the largest caves in the cliff city, a circular dwelling about ten feet across, and her fingernails were raw and ugly from repeated digging in the clay. She said that most of the time the villagers were too afraid to go outside to wash. One sixty-year-old man refused to come out of his dark and damp cave. The man was ridden with typhus, too sick even to brush away the hundreds of flies that swarmed around him. "I am not afraid of anything any more," he said softly. "I want to die — I would rather die than live like this." Pannam served as a stark example of what the war could inflict on Korean civilians, and Americans and their leaders had a difficult time avoiding such knowledge completely. The story of Pannam had been front-page news in the *New York Times*.[1]

The optimism that the United States could apply force discriminately, so prominent early in the war and which molded evolving American views toward nuclear weapons, persisted throughout the Korean War. However, as the story of Pannam illustrated, the devastation from the fighting on the peninsula became more difficult to deny as more information about the impact of the war on Korean civilians became available to Americans. The visibility of the devastation increased as the war moved beyond its early phase of serial crises and triumphs, which had monopolized the attention of the American media.

Despite continual official reassurances that U.S. force was being applied discriminately, the civil destruction in Korea and massive flows of refugees raised the question of what role the liberal use of American firepower had in subjecting Koreans to this suffering. Communist governments continued to hammer at the theme of American barbarism, but some Americans, who rejected the dominant optimism about the controlled use of force, also suggested that a portion of the blame for the harm to Korean civilians lay with the American war effort. Concern among Americans for the suffering of Korean refugees did foster both government and private relief efforts that ameliorated some of the terrible consequences of the war's devastation. However, this concern rarely translated into an acceptance of responsibility for the contribution to the destruction that U.S. military tactics made. Whether discussing the creation of refugees, escalated air attacks, or the use of napalm, Americans admitted that their weapons caused much of the physical destruction in Korea, but they developed arguments that shifted the blame to others and emphasized American good intentions. These arguments stressed the unintended nature of the harm to Korean noncombatants that came from American weapons. They laid the blame for all of the war's destruction at the feet of Communist aggression and contrasted calculated Communist cruelty with American efforts to provide warnings and evacuations for civilians caught in the war's violence. Many conceded that optimistic intentions to control and limit violence against Korean civilians often went unrealized, but they came to view the failure not as a moral indictment of American behavior demanding drastic reform, but as a tragedy, the responsibility for which was diffuse.

6.1 The Devastation of Korea

The war devastated Korea. By the summer of 1951 when the fighting had stabilized around the thirty-eighth parallel, the hostilities had ruined large areas of the Korean peninsula both north and south, and the human toll was terrible. Quantification of the suffering of Korean civilians is a poor reflection of what the war put them through, but some numbers can give an idea of the scale. In the summer of 1951, the U.N. Command estimated that five million

Koreans had left their homes and become refugees. The Statistics Bureau of the Republic of Korea's Office of Public Information reported in August 1952 that $954,659,023 in civilian property damage, including the complete destruction of over 400,000 civilian houses and 8,700 primary schools, had occurred in the war. The U.N. agent general for reconstruction in Korea reported that in the capitol Seoul, which had been fought over four times, 85 percent of its industrial facilities, 75 percent of its office space, and 50 to 60 percent of its living space had been destroyed. Estimates of the number of civilians killed in the entire war range from 244,000 to 990,000 for South Korea.

North Korea would continue to suffer from U.N. air attacks and naval bombardment until the end of the war, but by 1951, the country was already devastated. U.N. bombardment had destroyed or forced underground virtually all of the north's heavy industry. By the end of the war, eighteen of twenty-two major cities in North Korea had been at least half obliterated according to damage assessments by the U.S. Air Force. The North Korean government has never published estimates of civilian deaths in the war, but more than one million killed has been an estimate common among historians who have studied the Korean War. Charles R. Joy, the head of the Cooperative Association for Remittances to Europe (CARE) mission in Korea, summarized his impression of the destruction left by the war. He wrote, "In twelve successive years of relief work in different parts of the world I have never seen such destitution and such wider spread misery as I have seen here."[2]

The vast scale of destruction in Korea, which increasingly became a story for American journalists[3] and around the world, disturbed American claims that they were using violence discriminately. Knowledge of the civil destruction raised the questions of responsibility and blame. Officials from the Soviet Union, China, and North Korea had an unequivocal answer for the international community: with brutal methods of warfare, the United States and its puppet government in South Korea had intentionally destroyed Korean society in pursuit of their imperialist aims. As they had from the beginning of the war, Communist leaders continued to condemn what they saw as an indiscriminate use of force by the U.S. military.

In June, the Soviet ambassador to the United Nations Yakov Malik submitted an inflammatory report to the Security Council. The Women's International Democratic Federation, which claimed to represent 91 million women around the world and which American officials called a Communist front, had completed an investigation of atrocities by American troops in Korea. The forty-page report offered detailed descriptions of the results of the bombing of Sinuiju, Pyongyang, Kanggye, and several smaller towns mixed with numerous accounts of brutal killings, torture, and rape by American soldiers. According to the report, the November bombing of Sinuiju destroyed 6,800 out of 11,000 dwellings in the city and killed over 5,000 inhabitants, 4,000 of them women and children. A letter from the League to the Security Council pleaded for the "immediate cessation of the bombing of Korean towns and villages and of the civilian population." The conclusion of the report accused the United States of conducting a "merciless and methodical campaign of extermination" in violation of the rules of warfare laid down in the Hague and Geneva conventions, a campaign which surpassed the atrocities of the Nazis in occupied Europe. The North Korean Foreign Minister followed up this report with a letter to the United Nations demanding that the American perpetrators of atrocities be tried as war criminals. The U.S. ambassador to the United Nations Warren Austin dismissed the report as malicious propaganda. Austin assured the United Nations that U.S. forces in Korea were under orders to obey the Geneva and Hague conventions and suggested that the North Koreans' refusal to allow the ICRC into their territory to observe whether these conventions were being followed demonstrated that the Communists only sought to generate propaganda.[4] The armistice negotiations, which began in July, also provided a forum for Communist accusations that the United States was killing noncombatants with its bombing. During negotiations over the cease-fire line, the North Korean negotiators repeatedly charged that the United States was conducting inhumane and indiscriminate bombing of civilians and cities in Korea.[5]

The Communist charges placed the blame for the civil destruction in Korea on the United States, but some Americans also suggested that the massive use of U.S. firepower contributed to the harm of Korean civilians. These skeptics questioned the U.S. military's ability to sufficiently control the violence it was employing, and their questioning helped to make the American contribution to the destruction of Korea difficult to avoid or deny completely for other Americans. Peace activists challenged the tactics of American soldiers in Korea as too destructive. The National Council for the Prevention of War's newsletter *Peace Action* criticized the American method of "liberating" the Korean people. It condemned the killing of large numbers of Koreans and the obliteration of their homes with "reckless and irresponsible" population bombings, which promised to sour Asian sympathies for the United States. The Fellowship of Reconciliation's journal *Fellowship* printed several articles accusing the United States of destroying towns and villages and contributing to the suffering of Korean civilians. Alfred Hassler, the editor of *Fellowship*, denied the war could be a necessary police action since it victimized innocent noncombatants. In one article, he wrote that the war could only punish North Korea "by visiting death and destruction on the individuals, innocent and guilty alike, who happen to inhabit it." Hassler continued, "The infant in arms, the rebellious citizen in the concentration camp, the bewildered, the ignorant, the helpless, all are as certain targets for the bombs and machine-gun bullets of the world police force as are the government officials and military officers who have instigated whatever 'aggression' is being opposed."[6]

Some religious periodicals acknowledged the role the U.S. military played in the devastation of Korea. Editorials in the *Christian Century* saw the police action in Korea as creating a desert and calling it peace. The United States had helped to pulverize "the whole apparatus of a society." A long letter to the editor by a Canadian, which *Commonweal* printed, equated the United Nation's effort to repel aggression with the destruction of the enemy's country. Condemning the devastation and arguing for peace, the author believed that modern war had become calculated savagery where "everything, literally everything, behind [a] frontier is to be destroyed." Modern war had a terrible new meaning: "to slaughter indiscriminately men, women, and children, soldiers and civilians, to render useless [an enemy's] natural resources, to smash his industries, his public utilities, his dams, bridges and reservoirs, to pound his cities to rubble, to smash, to destroy, to kill, unconditionally and completely." S. D. Newberry's poem "Delectable Slaughter" in *Catholic World* compared American war through the air with its firebombs and blockbusters to humankind's extermination of animal species and to Stalinist atrocities. The poem alluded to the war in Asia as only giving further opportunities for this new form of killing.[7]

Two books written during the war criticized excessive American use of firepower in Korea. One of several charges that I. F. Stone in his work *The Hidden History of the Korean War* leveled against the United States was that the U.N. Command had demonstrated a complete indifference to the welfare of noncombatants through its policies of bombing and village destruction. Stone argued that American bombing had ignored Truman's instructions to strike only specific military targets when necessary. The author condemned the scorched earth policy that U.N. forces had implemented in their retreat from the Chinese. He asserted that the military's press releases substantiated these charges of indiscriminate destruction. Stone pointed to the Air Force's claimed destruction of Sinuiju and the Navy's extensive shelling of Wonsan.[8]

Reginald Thompson, a British correspondent who visited Korea, criticized American overreliance on their deadly machines. According to Thompson, Americans made excessive use of the firepower available to them. He viewed the city of Seoul as a victim of this massively destructive American way of war. Automatic weapons in the hands of trigger-happy soldiers led to unnecessary and wild fire, he asserted. One American tactic that he singled out for particular criticism was how American soldiers would respond to receiving fire from a nearby village. Instead of sending a patrol to investigate and assess the size of the enemy force in the village, the Americans would call in an air or artillery strike on the settlement. Not only would it destroy another village, but it could allow a few enemy soldiers to hold up an entire regiment. Thompson was skeptical that these tactics saved soldiers' lives, but he wrote, "It is certain that it kills civilian men, women, and children, indiscriminately and in great numbers, and destroys all that they have."[9] Neither book had wide audiences in the

United States during the war, but they made a small contribution to placing the war's destruction before the American public.[10]

The mainstream press occasionally attributed some responsibility for the suffering of the Korean people to the United States. Liberal magazines like the *Nation* and the *New Republic* repeated the theme that the United States had destroyed Korea in order to save it. The editor of the *Nation* Freda Kirchwey labeled American policy "liberation by death." She argued that the aggression of the Communists did not excuse the "terrible shambles" American force had made of the peninsula and the accompanying "civilian horrors." The U.S. military had conducted "vast slaughter of civilians, the burning of whole villages because a few Communist guerrillas were suspected to be hiding there, the systematic destruction of factories and water systems and transportation facilities — down, almost to the last ox-cart." The destruction had made a mockery of any notion of freeing Korea or strengthening collective security. The U.S. military, to Kirchwey, was on the verge of becoming an enemy in itself, because its subordination of everything to the cause of killing Communists was turning Koreans against the United States and transforming the cause into a hateful one. Kirchwey believed that when Americans learned more of the facts of the destruction in Korea that they would rise up in horror against their government's policy.[11]

Harold L. Ickes, in one of his columns for the *New Republic,* called the war in Korea worse than hell. A third of the column was devoted to quoting a UP report which described dead refugees along the road to Osan that U.N. planes had strafed because of reports of Chinese soldiers mingling with refugee columns. The UP reporter saw women and children among the dead but not soldiers. Ickes observed that the United States was not only bringing aid to the Koreans but also "wounds and dismemberment and death." U.N. bombs and bullets from the air could not "distinguish between the sexes or between the aged and infants." Ickes wanted the public to know the true costs of the war in Korea as a caution against expanding the war. Ickes received a supportive letter from a reader of his column, who wrote, "I earnestly hope that you will persist in pricking the conscience of a people who feel so righteous in burning South Korean towns and villages so that the 'Reds won't have places to hide;' in machine gunning crowds of civilian refugees who 'get in the way….'"[12]

Newspaper editorial pages showed occasional glimpses of criticism over excessively destructive American methods. A *Washington Post* editorial argued that the United States needed clearer war aims. It said, "Without war aims showing an outline of what we would settle for, villages are blotted out, civilians killed indiscriminately with soldiers, and the prospect is that all that will remain of Korea is a mass of rubble." The editorial feared that this situation was a legacy of the saturation bombing and policy of unconditional surrender of the last war. It questioned, "Are we all becoming hardened to the degeneration of warfare into barbarism?" The *New York Times* printed a letter from a woman under the title "Korea's Holocaust." The author compared American killing in Korea to Nazi atrocities and wondered, "what this is doing to our boys and young men who are forced to carry on this holocaust of human suffering."[13]

A few conservatives and strong anti-Communists criticized American methods of warfare in Korea as too destructive. Senator Robert Taft in arguing before Congress against an American commitment of ground forces to Europe worried about the precedent that Korea appeared to be setting. "We saved Korea at the expense of the destruction of every city in Korea and the killing of an infinite number of Korean civilians," he said. "I do not believe that we are so welcome in Korea today." Taft later made criticism of the Korean War a prominent issue in his campaign to capture the Republican nomination for president in 1952, denouncing the casualties among American soldiers, the deaths of Koreans, and the destruction of the peninsula. On his radio show, Upton Sinclair, who by the early 1950s had become a strident anti-Communist, worried that American methods in Korea were playing into the Soviets' hands. He believed that the Soviet Union was trying to "make us destroy so many Korean cities, villages, fields and people that any other nation will be afraid to have us come in to *save* them, and to make all Asiatics hate us as invading destroyers." The United States had to devise a way to free itself from having to destroy Asian villages and farms in order to achieve anything constructive in Asia, Sinclair believed.[14]

The sheer level of destruction, which critics from the left and from the right helped to keep in the public eye, was difficult for Americans and their leaders to deny or ignore completely. Contemplation of the devastation, and the human suffering that it caused, forced Americans to confront their country's responsibility in creating the terrible situation. Some relief for feelings of guilt or remorse must have come from the repeated pronouncements that emanated from South Korean leaders, which declared that Koreans did not resent the destruction inflicted on their country through the U.N. war effort in its fight to keep Korea free.[15] However, American justification of the destruction in Korea went beyond faith in these reassurances.

6.2 Confronting the Refugee Crisis

Public discussion of the refugee crisis in Korea revealed the ways in which Americans rationalized the destruction of war. The five million refugees in South Korea and the piteous images that they presented attracted a significant amount of attention in the United States. In July 1951, *Newsweek* placed a picture of a Korean child in the street on its cover with the caption "Korean Kids: Peace or War, They Lose."[16] Numerous articles and photographs brought the plight of Koreans displaced by the war into American homes. Attention in the press to the refugees both reflected and helped to spread concern about the suffering in Korea. The concern for the refugees translated into real help for homeless and destitute Koreans through the relief programs that the U.N.

Command established to aid refugees and through the work of nongovernmental relief organizations, but the aid served other purposes as well. The relief programs helped to rationalize the destruction in Korea and helped Americans demonstrate to themselves and to the world that they did not intend harm to Korean civilians and were not insensitive to their suffering. The image that Americans relieved suffering and did not seek to cause it was prominent in the American press, and the U.S. government actively promoted this perception. In the discussion of the refugee tragedy, many avoided acknowledging any American contribution to the terrible situation, instead blaming the malevolence of the Communists for all of the suffering. Even with the significant relief that Americans did provide Korean refugees, the aid had severe limits and the U.N. Command neglected some of its responsibilities under international law for the care and management of displaced civilians.

Relief aid that the U.N. Command, the U.S. government, and American charitable organizations provided to Korean refugees saved countless lives and prevented the human tragedy in Korea from becoming much worse. The American armed forces had learned during World War II the importance of managing local civilian populations to prevent them from interfering with military operations. In Korea, this meant providing for the basic needs of hundreds of thousands of uprooted civilians to minimize confusion and disruption behind U.N. lines. During the war's first two desperate months, the U.N. Command left the management and relief of the multitude of refugees who packed themselves into the Pusan perimeter to the South Korean government. On September 5, the first personnel from the U.N. Command's Public Health and Welfare section arrived in Korea, and they had already requested procurement from Washington of three months' emergency medical and sanitation supplies for the entire population under the South Korean government's control, along with blankets, clothing, tents, soap, and powdered whole milk for 300,000 refugees. The Eighth Army established a Civil Assistance Command in November, which later became the United Nations Civil Assistance Command, Korea (UNCACK), to handle aid to the civilian population. By the summer of 1951, the command had 345 officers, enlisted personnel, and civilians on its roles. To fight the spread of disease, the Civil Assistance Command implemented a series of public health programs, which had some dramatic successes. The number of deaths from typhoid, typhus, and smallpox, diseases commonly associated with the turmoil of war, dropped from over twenty-four thousand in 1951 to fewer than six hundred the following year. In July 1951, a U.N. official noted other accomplishments of the relief efforts. Food distribution had prevented widespread famine. The United Nations had shipped 245,000 metric tons of grain as well as other foodstuffs. The average Korean was supposed to receive about one pound of rice a day and a small cash allowance to buy fish and other foods. Blankets and clothing saved many from dying of cold during the winter. U.N. shipments included 1,000,000 blankets and 1,800,000 undergarments. By October 1952, the U.S. government had contributed over $328 million in relief supplies to Korea, and a majority of Americans approved of their government's efforts to help Koreans. An opinion poll from April 1952 showed that 59 percent approved of "our government spending money to help the South Koreans repair the damage caused by the war," whereas 35 percent disapproved.[17]

U.N. forces also tried to assist civilians by conducting several large operations to evacuate them out of harm's way during the winter retreat. In December 1950, as the Navy was evacuating X Corps from its beachhead around the North Korean port of Hungnam in the face of the Chinese advance, the Navy made room on its ships for 91,000 refugees. One Navy transport crowded 14,000 Koreans on board and despite the difficult conditions caused by the overcrowding, the Navy reported that everyone survived. The X Corps justified the civilian evacuation to the U.N. Command headquarters in part because of "humanitarian" concerns. The U.N. Command also relocated thousands of refugees to the numerous islands off South Korea's coast during the winter. These relocation operations included the airlift of 989 orphans to the island of Cheju.[18]

Supplementing the efforts of the U.N. Command in Korea were a number of American relief organizations. One of the most active was American Relief for Korea (ARK), a product of cooperation between the government and private charitable organizations. In November 1950, the State Department's Advisory Committee on Voluntary Foreign Aid established a working committee to organize ARK, which would channel voluntary aid to meet the needs of Korea as specified by the U.N. Command. By April 1951, ARK had taken on a more definite form. The Hollywood star Douglas Fairbanks, Jr., agreed to serve as the organization's national chairperson and announced that ten private relief agencies, members of the American Council of Voluntary Agencies for Foreign Service, would participate. The ten agencies were the American Friends Service Committee, Brethren Service Committee, Church World Service, American Federation of Labor's Labor League of Human Rights, Lutheran World Relief, Mennonite Central Committee, Save the Children Federation, National Catholic Welfare Conference's War Relief Services, Young Women's Christian Association's World Emergency Fund, and World Student Service Fund.

In ARK's initial "Clothing for Korea" drive in 1951, the relief agencies would help to collect clothing for destitute Korean refugees. The cost of the processing, baling, and delivery of the clothing from ARK warehouses to shipside would be met from funds raised by the United Defense Fund through the nation's Community Chests. The clothing would then be transported to Korea by the Department of the Army and delivered under the direction of General Ridgway for distribution by the U.N. Civil Assistance Command. The House and Senate passed a resolution of support for ARK and President Truman declared September a month for a special effort to gather clothing for Korea. The governor of New Jersey had proclaimed August "American Relief for Korea Month" and urged the state to fill a ship with clothing for Korean war victims. The mayor of New York City launched a two-week clothing drive in November to collect a million pounds of apparel. All police precincts, fire houses, and schools served as collection sites and the police along with local Girl Scouts and Boy Scouts distributed posters for the campaign. The Junior Chamber of Commerce in Buffalo collected fifty tons of clothing for ARK. ARK opened one warehouse in New York, one in California, and one in Missouri to gather clothing donations. By June 1952, ARK had delivered over $2 million in relief to Korean refugees.[19]

A number of relief organizations ran campaigns for Korean aid independent of the ARK program. Two of the larger operations were conducted by War Relief Services of the National Catholic Welfare Conference and by CARE. War Relief Services established the Korea Adopt-a-Family Program through which Americans could buy food packages for refugee families. It also ran a Thanksgiving clothing drive in 1952, which gathered more than $1 million worth of apparel and footwear from parishes around the country. CARE, which had expanded from an organization focused on providing assistance to Europeans after World War II into a general relief agency, organized a CARE-for-Korea program early in the war. In November 1950, President Truman called on Americans to contribute to the campaign in order to provide gift packages of food, clothing, and other needed goods. In 1951, CARE packages provided 373 tons of food, 75 tons of cotton sheeting, 27 tons of clothing, and 7 tons of blankets for Koreans.

Charles R. Joy, who served as the head of the CARE mission in Korea, wrote of the spirit behind ordinary Americans' donations and the good that they did for Korea. Joy noted the group of young people in Caldwell, Ohio, members of the local 4-H Club, who planted several acres of corn and cultivated them until it was possible to sell the grain. They donated the money to CARE, requesting two plows and three CARE food packages to be sent to Greece with the rest of the money to be used for food packages for Korea. A farmer in Kansas sold a cow and sent the proceeds of $147 to CARE that it might help war victims in Korea and elsewhere. A small boy in Iowa, ten years old and dying of cancer, asked his father to take $10 from his savings and send it to some poor Korean child. As an example of the good that CARE packages could do, Joy quoted Kang Chung Ae, the superintendent of the Taegu City Children's Home. "Every morning I go to the gate and listen for a baby's cry for in the night as some poor mother may have been forced to desert her infant on the steps. I have found them there often. I always take them in for I cannot find it in my heart to close the gate on them. But I could not take them in if it were not for the CARE packages I receive...." Joy also described how other Koreans were using CARE donations to help themselves. In early 1952, CARE sent

15 cartoons of knitting wool to the women's section of the Seoul city government. Sixty women and girls volunteered for a knitting class to turn the wool into warm clothing for orphans. After six weeks, one hundred and fifty articles of clothing had already been distributed to orphanages.[20]

Encouraged by regular appeals for donations from periodicals like the *Christian Century* and the *New York Times*,[21] Americans donated large amounts of used clothing and money to private relief organizations. Some appeals for relief argued explicitly that aid to Korea was the proper compensation for its people's sacrifice in the fight against international Communist aggression. Edward S. Skillin in *Commonweal* urged that extensive reconstruction of Korea be carried out in order to eradicate the doubt among people of the east and west about the wisdom of accepting the challenge of resisting aggression. The Korean Foreign Minister Pyun Yung Tai echoed these sentiments at a CARE-sponsored conference. He said, "Whether Korea was wise in putting up a heroic fight against communism, or the now Soviet satellites were comparatively wiser in succumbing to communism, will be decided eventually by the part played by the free world in the wartime relief as well as in the postwar rehabilitation of Korea." By June 1952, U.S. voluntary agencies including ARK had contributed an estimated $8.6 million for relief programs. The National Catholic Welfare Conference's War Relief Services' share of this total was over $3.6 million and CARE's was almost $900,000.[22]

Although Americans and their government made extensive efforts to help relieve the suffering of Korean refugees, expressions of concern for the refugees and the aid itself served purposes beyond the welfare of Koreans. Proclaimed sentiments and proffered aid served to maintain an image of the United States, a moral identity for Americans, as a humane nation. American officials had worked to project a public image that accentuated the humane aspects of U.N. actions and obscured the brutal. The U.N. Command provided material for the media that emphasized the U.S. military's solicitude for the refugees, and the State Department helped to spread the information through its media outlets around the world. Censorship, which at first was voluntary and then formally imposed in December 1950, discouraged the reporting of brutal acts by U.N. soldiers. Press censorship criteria used by U.N. Command censors prevented the publication of material that would embarrass, place in disrepute, or harm the morale of American or allied soldiers. The regulations specified that photos "of enemy dead in such a position as to indicate wholesale killing or mass execution" or "of U.N. troops and POWs dead or alive which suggest or hint actual or possible atrocious acts, or other violations of the Geneva Convention by U.N. forces" would not be passed.[23]

The press in the United States mirrored the humane ideal that Americans wanted to believe their efforts in Korea to be. Stories about American soldiers helping Korean children orphaned or crippled by the war, the military's efforts to remove civilians from harm's way, and the more general efforts to relieve refugee's suffering were commonplace.[24] Nora Waln wrote an article for the *Saturday Evening Post* entitled "Our Softhearted Warriors in Korea." She acknowledged that American bombing had taken a heavy toll in housing and lives but explained how the Communists had used the community buildings of every village they captured. To get at the enemy, American planes hit the villages, she explained. The focus of the article, however, was on how American soldiers were helping to care for orphaned Korean children. The article expressed the reassuring theme: "For all the killing they have done, our warriors still have dreams and ideals. They don't want orphans to be hungry or cold or sick." A *New York Times* editorial commented explicitly on the important role that aid to Korea had in maintaining America's reputation. It declared that generous relief and reconstruction in Korea would show that accusations impugning the United States with dark and sinister motives to be false. Striking a noble note, the editorial said that Americans need not consider this "reputational advantage," but instead urged that the aid be undertaken out of humanity and generosity.[25]

When Americans' humane self-perception collided with harsh actions in the war that journalists were unwilling or unable to deny, articles attempted to reconcile the two. The explanation often took the form of admitting the injury that American soldiers were inflicting on Korean civilians and refugees while insisting that Americans had nothing but the best intentions toward the Korean people. An article, thoroughly conflicted over the humanitarian values but cruel actions of Americans in Korea, appeared in the *Saturday Evening Post* in February 1951. William L. Worden in his story "The Cruelest Weapon in Korea" rationalized U.N. treatment of refugees during the desperate winter fighting with the Chinese. He condemned the Communists as brutal for using helpless civilians as a weapon against American forces but then explained how American soldiers had become desperate enough to use this weapon as well. The leader to the story said that "we" could not use refugees as a weapon because "we" were not brutal enough. The leader was misleading because most of the article was devoted to explaining how Americans had come to use this weapon, but the leader was effective in conveying a second message contained in the article that Americans were not "brutal." This negative and judgmental term was reserved for the Communists.

To Worden, the Communists were brutal because they used refugees and civilians in a calculating manner to clog roads, disrupt U.N. lines and communications, and screen their own forces from attack. They would spread rumors or threats to send refugees flooding toward U.N. lines and would mingle with women and children in villages to inhibit U.N. air strikes. The Communists were using Americans' humanitarian sentiments against them, Worden claimed. These humane values had made the U.N. Command reluctant to turn the tables on the enemy and adopt a policy of forcing refugees back north to burden the Communists instead, but in the desperate winter of 1951 with

Chinese forces pressing down the peninsula, the U.N. forces had no choice according to Worden. "At long last," Americans had become "merciless" and had come to use refugees as a weapon by preventing any more of them from crossing through U.N. lines. However, he insisted that this was an act of desperation and not brutality. He inaccurately claimed that such a policy had not been adopted during the U.N. force's 1950 retreat. Worden alleged that U.N. forces had not used this merciless tactic out of humanitarianism and because of the difficulty of enforcing the order. American and British troops "dislike shooting unarmed civilians and, except in the most desperate circumstances, will not do it, regardless of orders," he wrote. During the second U.N. retreat down the peninsula after the Chinese intervention, Worden deemed the situation desperate, but he also offered other reasons, which had little to do with desperation, for why it was easier to exploit the refugee weapon this second time. The refugees now were North Koreans who had not fled the Communists earlier and, therefore, were not friends. Worden wrote, "Nobody felt any necessity to leave bridges for them to cross rivers, or food or shelter." Still, Worden reserved the appellation "brutal" for the Communists. Worden ended his story: "It isn't a pretty thing, this employment of helpless people as a weapon. But this is how wars are fought here, and how we must fight them."[26]

An article in the *New Yorker* also tried to explain how brutal acts in Korea could be committed by compassionate Americans. Christopher Rand thought he observed the "etherialization" of American pilots in Korea. Rand believed that pilots flying high above the people they were harming on the ground became emotionally detached as if they were in a "shooting gallery." He described a flight controller in an observation plane asking some fighter-bombers to drop napalm on a village. The controller had not been told that the village contained enemy soldiers and as it turned out an officer over the radio intervened to prevent the burning of the village. Rand wrote that the pilot "was simply following an abstract rule of thumb: Chinese hide in villages, so villages must be attacked." His discussion of etherialization closed with the "probably superfluous" observation that the American pilots he had met were the "warmest human beings imaginable."[27]

The desire to maintain the image of a humane American effort in Korea produced depictions of the preservation of moral values in the face of the hard realities of killing. Americans wanted to view their military forces as deadly and powerful but also as moral and humane. A *Saturday Evening Post* article by Harold H. Martin entitled "The Pious Killer of Korea" was an example of this uneasy combination of sentiments. The protagonist of the article was Dean Elmer Hess, an Air Force fighter pilot in Korea, whom to Martin embodied this seeming contradiction. Martin fully acknowledged that Hess represented a type of paradox. The story introduced Hess as "one of the deadliest killers of the Korean war" and detailed how he experimented with new ways to kill the enemy such as with napalm, the jellied-gasoline incendiary. Yet the story was primarily concerned with showing that Hess was a deeply moral man. He was devoutly religious and read the Bible every night, Martin reported. Not only did Hess suffer "considerable anguish of spirit" when he strafed enemy soldiers, he also had "a deep fear of killing noncombatants — an old man, woman, or a child — and his aerial attacks are therefore never made in haste." The article described Hess' rule of thumb for distinguishing soldiers from civilians on the ground. He would make a low pass over people on the ground and if they ran, he would open fire reasoning that civilians would stand paralyzed by fear while trained soldiers would dive for cover. Martin also described Hess as sad over destroying villages and careful to firebomb only buildings that he was positive enemy soldiers were using.

Beyond these sensibilities, the article suggested that the greatest demonstration of Hess' humanity was his efforts on behalf of orphaned Korean children left homeless by the war. Hess was instrumental in organizing the winter airlift of almost 1,000 orphans out of harm's way to Cheju island off the South Korean coast and then helped to establish an orphanage for them. The article said, "By the help he gives the children he feels he compensates a little for the enormous suffering caused the innocent in this war." The story concluded by relating that the Air Force "which at heart is about as soft as Hess where little children are concerned" awarded the pilot the Legion of Merit award. According to Martin, the Air Force, and not Hess alone, embodied these humane values.[28]

6.3 The Question of Responsibility

Although Americans touted their relief efforts and concern for Korean refugees, they tended to avoid acknowledging any American responsibility for the dislocation of refugees in the first place. Koreans left their homes during the war for many reasons. They fled nearby fighting; they were instructed to leave by officials or soldiers; they feared or were loyal to one side or the other; or their means of livelihood had been disrupted. The destruction caused by American action, particularly the heavy shelling and bombing that the U.N. forces undertook against any building that might shelter an enemy, was only one reason that Koreans were displaced from their homes. Nevertheless, American discussion of refugees largely ignored this contributing factor and instead chose to view the movements of refugees as a flight from communism and a confirmation of the righteousness of the U.N. cause. For many Americans, the Communist aggressors and not U.S. forces were responsible for the suffering of Korean refugees.

Most in the American press avoided placing any responsibility for the suffering of the refugees on the United States. A few acknowledged the contribution that American firepower was making to the physical destruction that produced so many refugees and viewed aid to the refugees as a necessary rectification of this tragedy.[29] Many ignored the question of where the refugees came from. Relief organizations like ARK and CARE usually circumvented the question of who or what specifically was responsible for displacing the refugees. An article in the American Red Cross' monthly magazine treated the devastation and the millions of refugees as a terrible fact and simply ignored how the situation came to be beyond a vague attribution to it being a result of "war." A common way that journalists and commentators avoided the question of responsibility was through the use of the passive voice in writing about the war's destruction. Homes were destroyed and refugees made to flee but the causes of these events were obscured by the language describing them.[30]

Articles also refrained from placing much blame on American action by depicting the destruction in Korea as a result of the fighting that both sides conducted. An article by Michael Rougier in *Life* magazine about orphaned children in Korea described how artillery fire and patrols from both sides had destroyed one boy's village which in turn led to the starvation of his family. Another orphaned girl in Rougier's piece believed that bombs from an airplane had killed her family. Rougier did not point out that if planes had killed her family, it would have almost undoubtedly been a result of U.N. action because U.N. planes dominated the skies over Korea. Instead, Rougier offered a comment that suggested the likelihood that planes had not killed her family. He wrote, "Her word for bomb could also mean a bullet or shell, and because they all bring death there was not much difference in her mind." Whether intentionally or not, Rougier had shifted the reader's attention from a weapon used almost exclusively by Americans and their allies to weapons that both sides employed.[31]

Instead of ignoring the question of responsibility or dividing the responsibility equally between the two sides, much of the press discussion of Korean refugees blamed the Communists for the refugees' terrible plight. According to these accounts, North Korean and Chinese aggression had started and prolonged the war. Koreans where fleeing Communist oppression and brutality and not American bombs or the devastation the weapons left in areas controlled by the Communists. John Denson in *Collier's* described the migration in stark terms. "They had taken the only course they could in this massive Korean tragedy," he wrote. "When the Korean Communists are coming, it is a case of run or die." Denson claimed that the Communists executed all who did not fully submit to their domination. Denson also discredited the idea that the refugees ran from the fighting and its destruction. He quoted a Canadian observer for the United Nations who said that some military men thought the refugees were running from battle areas, but the observer had found that civilians were fleeing areas in which there was no fighting. A *Time* magazine article admitted that U.N. aerial bombardment contributed to the ravaging of the land as did the exactions of the hard-pressed Communist armies, but attributed the refugees' movement south largely to one factor. "Amid death, destruction and hopelessness, millions of Koreans held on to a simple fact," the article said. "They would rather live where the Americans are than where the Communists are. To the bulk of Koreans, it still makes a great difference whether or not their country — or half their country — is run by Communists." Editorials in the *St. Louis Post-Dispatch* and the *New York Times* provided similar explanations for the torrent of refugees.[32]

In a special report, George Barrett, a correspondent in Korea for the *New York Times*, examined the story of one refugee family that revealed a much more complicated set of circumstances that put the family to flight than either the humane policies of U.N. forces or the fear of Communist terror. Following the common trend of blaming the Communists, the *Times* editors bestowed the subtitle "Fleeing their farm in fear of the Communists, they have known tragedy, face a dark future" on Barrett's report, but the article provided a rather more nuanced picture of the origins of the family's suffering. The report told the story of the Pak family during the first half year of the war. Pak Sung Won lived with his wife, three children, mother, a brother, a sister, and a cousin on a farm outside the city of Suwon before the war. The Paks did not flee the first invasion by the North Koreans. The idea of North Koreans moving into South Korea struck them as a political matter that did not vitally concern them. They had heard that the Communists in the north were supposed to be evil and that the invading soldiers would kill, rape, and pillage, but the Paks reassured themselves that after all only other Koreans were coming down across the border. When the Communists arrived, whatever fears the Paks and their neighbors had had quickly vanished. The North Korean soldiers were disciplined. There were no rapes or killings. They paid for the rice they needed. The Communists did impose some unwanted burdens such as higher taxes, intimidating visits from political officers who stressed the need for loyalty, and the risky task of delivering rice to North Korean troops amid the bombings and strafing of U.N. planes, but nothing so onerous as to compel them to flee their homes.

When the Chinese-led forces returned in late 1950, the Paks were more concerned. Again they heard that the soldiers would rape and kill, and this time the family could not reassure itself that the invading troops were fellow Koreans. The Paks were also concerned that the Communists might return angry since Syngman Rhee had ordered executions of their compatriots. However, the final circumstance that convinced the Paks to abandon their home was that ROK officials told all loyal citizens to flee south. The trip was a difficult one for the Paks. A ROK police officer sold them a truck for an extortionate price and their baby son died on the journey south. Once in Taegu, the family was supposed to receive a small rice ration from the government, but they like many of their neighbors had not received their allotment in two months. Barrett concluded the story with the observation that the experiences of the Paks had not done much to clarify for the family the differences between the North Korean and South Korean authorities. Sung Won said that he felt less afraid in the south than under the Communists, but the South Korean police still pushed people around. Under the Communists, the men would suddenly find themselves hauled from their houses to repair roads without pay, but the South Korean authorities did the same thing. Whether or not the Pak's experiences were representative of Korean refugees in general, the complicated picture that Barrett provided of the displacement of a family was uncommon in the wider American discussion of the refugee problem, a discourse preoccupied with blaming the Communists.[33]

Not surprisingly, the American government promoted the explanation that Communist aggression was responsible for the refugee crisis, destruction, and human suffering that had resulted from the war. Besides the Korean victims themselves, American officials occupied the best vantage point from which to understand the contribution that American firepower made to the problems. After a trip to Korea in January 1951, General Collins and General Vandenberg reported that the refugees feared the Chinese but were equally afraid of the bombing that they expected the United States to commence once U.N. forces withdrew. Nonetheless, when General Ridgway added his name to the ARK national committee in August 1951, he urged clothing donations for "the children of war-torn Korea who suffer as the result of the ruthless aggression forced upon them." President Truman made a number of public statements that blamed the destruction in Korea on Communist aggression and reassured the world that Americans were deeply aware of the horrors of war. At one luncheon for the press, Truman described America's Communist opponents as the "inheritors of the program of Genghis Khan and Tamerlane, who were the greatest murderers in the history of the world." Public information policy guidance from the State Department told its officers and media outlets to attribute suffering in Korea to Communist aggression and their neglect of the people's welfare, to "play" the refugees' flight south as the strongest possible evidence of their "detestation" of the rigors of Communist rule, and to avoid the implication that the human suffering was the result of U.N. military action. U.N. resolutions on economic aid to Korea, which the United States supported, included a direct attribution of blame to the North Koreans. Resolutions adopted in November and December of 1950 contained the phrase: "Mindful that the aggression by North Korean forces and their warfare against the United Nations seeking to restore peace in the area has resulted in great devastation and destruction which the Korean people cannot themselves repair."[34] The abdication of responsibility for exacerbating the Korean refugee problem, which American leaders promoted and the press largely accepted, deflected public questioning of U.S. methods in Korea. Americans, when concerned, focused on the amelioration of the refugees' suffering and not on preventing their dislocation in the first place.

6.4 The Limits of Aid to Refugees

Despite their role in rationalizing the destruction in Korea, American concern over the refugee situation and the relief to assist with it had severe limits. Aiding Korean civilians came second to fighting the war, conditions in refugee camps were appalling, and the U.N. Command refused to carry out its full responsibilities under international law to care for civilian war victims. Despite professing a commitment to noncombatant immunity and making efforts at providing relief, the United States ultimately provided Korean civilians with little protection from the violence of the war.

For American officials, the war effort came before aid to Korean refugees. This sense of priorities was acknowledged in the press. As a *Saturday Evening Post* article put it, the UNCACK axiom was "the war must be won, above all other considerations, and anything done for the people of Korea must come second to that necessity."[35] Because of military priorities, the U.N. Command required that all donations from the private relief agencies be distributed by UNCACK in conjunction with the South Korean government. It could, therefore, coordinate the handling and transportation of aid supplies and ensure that they did not interfere with the support of military operations. Several of the relief agencies believed that the UNCACK monopoly on the distribution of aid hindered them from making their maximum contribution to assisting the refugees.[36]

Edgar S. Kennedy, a British civil affairs officer who worked for UNCACK, described some of the shortcomings in the food distribution system. In early 1951, Kennedy reported starvation in certain areas of Chung Chong Namdo province and pressed his UNCACK superiors for immediate distribution of rice to avoid famine. UNCACK headquarters designated a shipload of rice for the province, but five weeks later the rice still had not arrived and Kennedy had lost hope it ever would. Instead of rice, Kennedy received a lecture from a superior to never again use the word "starvation" in one of his reports because UNCACK's primary purpose was to prevent starvation and to say Koreans were starving was to admit that the organization had failed.[37]

Congressional appropriations also reflected the low priority that the U.S. government attached to relief aid in the war effort. The Senate slashed an early congressional appropriation for civilian relief in Korea after the Chinese intervened despite Secretary of Defense George Marshall's military justification for the relief. The Army believed that $100 million was the minimum needed to prevent disease, starvation, and unrest. However, the senators, in an ungenerous mood with the Chinese advancing down the peninsula, cut the appropriation in half. One Republican senator said, "We ought to be more concerned now with shooting the Communists instead of feeding them." In the summer of 1951, Congress voted to cut the U.S. contribution to the United Nations Korea Reconstruction Agency from $162 million to $62 million.[38]

While the United States government poured soldiers, weapons, and money into Korea to prevent the North Koreans and the Chinese from expelling the United Nations from the peninsula, it did not provide sufficient resources to avoid atrocious conditions at the refugees camps in which homeless Koreans found shelter. Chinese intervention created a refugee crisis for the U.N. Command that surpassed the one at the outbreak of the war. Ensuring the health and welfare of these hundreds of thousands of fleeing Koreans would have been extremely difficult during the winter months of 1950 and 1951 when U.N. forces were scrambling to halt the Chinese advance. It is difficult to see how deplorable conditions in refugee camps thrown up to accommodate this human flood could have been avoided initially. One *New York Times* reporter in December found a refugee camp near Seoul of 1,600 people living with such poor sanitary facilities that it reminded him of the conditions in Naples after World War II that had led to a typhus epidemic.[39]

However, terrible conditions in refugee camps persisted for more than a year after the initial crisis of the Chinese invasion had ended. The South Korean government was directly responsible for the management of the refugee camps, but the U.N. Command and U.S. government did not do everything they could have to ameliorate the suffering they had helped to create. Greg MacGregor of the *New York Times* in late July filed a dramatic story about the conditions in the Koochon refugee camp near Seoul which he called "a blot on the United Nations' record in Korea." The camp overflowed with 37,000 refugees. Some were North Koreans forced out of their homes and into the camp by U.N. forces concerned about espionage and enemy exploitation of the civilian population, and some were South Koreans trying to move north back to their former homes in the Seoul area. In the camp, army tents designed to house four soldiers were crowed with as many as forty men, women, and children. Some of the less fortunate had to camp in the open and huddle under the remains of a ruined bridge during the summer downpours because there was no more room in the huts and tents of the camp. The camp hospital was staffed by five doctors and eighteen nurses with facilities for about 120 patients. On the day MacGregor visited, the hospital contained 817 patients with many lying on grass mats on the floor. MacGregor wrote that the people "are forced to live worse than any animal kept by an American farmer." The U.N. public welfare officer responsible for the area had tried to do what he could to rectify the situation. Recently he had ordered 200 more tents, but he complained that official red tape delayed his requests and hindered his efforts. Within a week of MacGregor's story, the U.N. Command had undertaken greater efforts to relieve the situation at Koochon. Tents were delivered, and half the camp's population was forced south to other better equipped refugee camps, despite the refugees' reluctance to move further from their former homes.[40]

Other camps had problems, though. E. J. Kahn reported in the *New Yorker* about poor conditions in a refugee camp near Pusan and noted that U.N. camps for prisoners of war maintained much better living conditions. William Worden writing in the *Saturday Evening Post* conceded that the camps were "horrible, by Western standards," but, professing his detestation of what he thought Communist rule to be, he claimed that the camps were "a thousand times better than the real horror from which North Koreans in particular have fled."[41]

The continuing poor conditions in South Korean refugee camps prompted the U.N. Command to avoid its full responsibilities under the four Geneva Conventions of 1949. The Geneva Conventions were an expansion of the international laws of war updated after World War II. The first two conventions revised the Red Cross treaties dating from the nineteenth century on the treatment of the sick and wounded on land and in the sea. The third convention replaced an older convention on the treatment of prisoners of war and the fourth convention introduced new rules for the treatment of civilian populations during times of war. The ICRC based in Switzerland served as an advocate for these laws and provided its services as a neutral observer to help ensure that the laws were properly implemented. The U.S. government had been an active participant in the drafting of the new Geneva Conventions and had signed them along with forty-four other governments in 1949. The Senate had not ratified the conventions by the time of the outbreak of the Korean War, but MacArthur had announced that U.N. forces would adhere to the conventions in their conduct of the war, a promise the South and North Korean governments had also made.[42]

Early in the war, U.N. Secretary General Trygve Lie, responding to pointed questioning from a reporter of the New York *Daily Worker,* said, "Don't you know that the United States Army has always adhered to the Geneva Convention — always when they have been in action?"[43] However, the war would lead to exceptions to American fastidiousness over the Geneva laws. The implementation of the conventions particularly the civilian convention ran into difficulties in Korea. In February 1951, representatives of the ICRC complained that the U.N. Command was not fully applying the conventions. They did not charge that the U.N. Command was violating the conventions, but that the command was not providing transportation and authorization to visit areas such as refugee camps and hospitals so that the ICRC could carry out its full responsibilities under the conventions. The U.N. Command was only cooperating with the Red Cross representatives in the application of the third convention on prisoners of war. The State Department entered into a prolonged dialogue with the U.N. Command and the Defense Department in an attempt to obtain the military's full cooperation with the ICRC. After the State Department had made several unsuccessful attempts to instruct the U.N. Command to cooperate on all four conventions, Assistant Secretary of State John D. Hickerson wrote to the Secretary of Defense. Hickerson argued that the State

Department considered it "essential that this Government obtain from the International Committee a clean bill of health with respect to the treatment of civilians as well as prisoners of war." Ridgway's headquarters had to allow Red Cross representatives to fulfill their role as neutral observers to do this.

The U.N. Command and the Department of Defense refused to accredit ICRC representatives except under the POW convention. Military leaders feared that the ICRC would not give a clean bill of health on the treatment of civilians. In early 1952, Secretary of the Army Frank Pace, Jr. wrote to the Secretary of Defense that if the U.N. Command allowed ICRC inspections under the fourth convention, they would reveal the deplorable conditions existing in civilian hospitals and refugee camps managed by the South Korean government. Published reports of these conditions would cause worldwide criticism and condemnation of the U.N. Command, the United States, and the United Nations, he believed.

Attached to Pace's memorandum was an extract from a report by the chief physician of the hospital ship *Jutlandia*, a Danish vessel dispatched to assist the U.N. effort in Korea. The extract described the terrible conditions in one refugee camp that an ICRC investigation might uncover. The camp, one of several just south of the Han river, contained between 50,000 and 70,000 refugees who had been left to their own initiative to procure shelter against the elements on a bare patch of ground. The camp "hospital" consisted of a structure resembling an open shed under which 600 to 700 lay and sat. Some rested on bare earth while others lay on rush mats soaked with urine and feces.

The doctor described the scene at the hospital as an "inconceivable sight." In one corner lay cases of small pox, most of them children whose faces were almost unrecognizable because of large festering wounds. Scattered elsewhere he noted patients with typhoid fever, dysentery, typhus, tetanus, or leprosy. Many of the patients had puss-filled swellings on their bodies from hunger, and on one patient the puss had burst the skin. However, what affected him the most was the silence of the hospital, a silence of the apathetic and the dying. He concluded, "I shall never forget the hopelessness I see in the eyes of a mother who is sitting with her little dying child at her flabby, hollow breast."

The *Jutlandia's* chief physician called the hospital "a disgrace for the U.N." He credited the Korean doctors at the camp with heroic efforts, but they could neither obtain sufficient food nor medicine for these suffering people. Despite the difficulties of war, the doctor felt that thousands of people should not be dying in Korea because they did not have access to modern medicines, and he believed that poor administration and the lack of cooperation among the different U.N. relief organizations was an essential cause of the misery.

Because of concerns that such conditions would be exposed to public scrutiny, the U.N. Command and the Department of Defense refused to accredit ICRC representatives except under the POW convention. As a compromise, the Department of Defense suggested that ICRC delegates not be "accredited" or "recognized" but instead "invited" to join a guided inspection tour "prescribed by" the U.N. Command. The delegates would then be required to make their reports to the U.N. Command which would have the opportunity to comment on them before they were forwarded to the United Nations. The State Department refused the proposals because it did not believe they would be acceptable to the ICRC "since they are inconsistent with its necessary freedom of action as an impartial humanitarian organization." Unable to reach a compromise, the situation remained unresolved. ICRC representatives were not accredited under three of the four Geneva Conventions, and this lack of accreditation deprived them of the necessary access to transportation and relevant areas.

Despite the U.N. Command hampering the Red Cross inspections into such conditions, the International Committee never publicized the command's obstructionism. A confidential ICRC report in July 1952 continued to protest the failure to provide adequately for three to four million refugees who were "slowly dying." However, the Defense Department's conscious suppression of information about miserable conditions at refugee camps and the United States' failure to apply fully three of the four Geneva Conventions in the Korean War went unchallenged.[44]

The American government also rejected an additional proposal from the ICRC intended to protect Korean civilians. The fourth Geneva Convention on the protection of civilians contained a section that suggested but did not require belligerents to establish safety zones where noncombatants could take shelter. In April 1951, Paul Ruegger, president of the ICRC, urged the creation of safety zones in Korea to protect women, children, and old people from the ravages of the war. The following year, the idea of safety zones was raised in both the United Nations and the Consultative Assembly of the Council of Europe. An Air Force letter to the Secretary of State explained some of the American objections to the safety zones. It said that Communist guerrillas in South Korea might use the zones to provide themselves with immunity, and the United Nations would require a guarantee through neutral supervision that safety zones in North Korea were not contributing to the war effort. Since the North Korean and Chinese governments, suspicious of the International Committee's neutrality, refused to allow ICRC observers into their countries, the proposal for safety zones was not acceptable to the U.S. government.[45]

6.5 Warning Civilians

The millions of refugees were only the most dramatic development in the war that compelled Americans to confront the question of responsibility for the vast destruction inflicted on Korea. An escalation of the U.N. air war against North Korea in 1952 contributed to the difficulties of denying harm to Korean noncombatants from American arms. The public response to the escalation included further claims that Americans did not intend to hurt civilians even though the U.S. military did harm them. The armistice negotiations had dead-locked over the issue of voluntary repatriation of prisoners of war, and this prolonged stalemate encouraged American leaders to look for ways to increase the pressure on North Korean negotiators to concede to U.N. demands at the conference table. An "air pressure" campaign of escalated bombing was one of the methods that the U.S. government pursued to this end. The initial opera-tions of the air pressure campaign were relatively unproblematic for the U.S. humanitarian image. They provoked few challenges to the claim that Ameri-can force was being used solely against military targets. In June 1952, Fifth Air Force, Marine, and Navy planes attacked hydroelectric power plants across North Korea including the Suiho power complex on the Korean side of the Yalu River. The operations against the power plants generated some contro-versy because since early in the war, the plants had been considered politically sensitive. In the fall of 1950, American officials had worried that protection of hydroelectric facilities on the Yalu, which provided a substantial amount of electricity to Manchuria, might motivate China to intervene in the war. An attack on the Suiho complex also risked violating Chinese air space because it was so close to the Chinese frontier. After the June air strikes, a number of European and Asian countries complained that the attacks could hamper peace negotiations, and the British protested because they had not been given prior notification of the operation. The North Koreans challenged the strikes as attacks on nonmilitary targets that could only contribute to the suffering of civilians. Nevertheless, public commentary in the United States and around the world generally accepted the U.S. government's claim that the attack was made against a legitimate military target out of solely military considerations. American officials argued that the hydroelectric plants were supplying increas-ing amounts of power to war industries in North Korea and China and that, therefore, the attacks did not constitute any basic change in policy.[46]

As the air pressure campaign accelerated, the American claim that opera-tions were only damaging military targets became more difficult to defend. Like with the discussion of refugees, emphasis in the summer of 1952 began to shift from denying that American use of force harmed noncombatants to asserting that the harm U.S. military operations inflicted on civilians was unintended. The idea of providing warning to civilians of their potential danger from American firepower became the evidence that was supposed to demon-strate that the United States did not intend to harm noncombatants. However, civilian warnings constituted more a comforting notion to Americans than ever an extensive or realistic undertaking to save the lives of noncombatants in enemy territory.

The idea of civilian warnings as an answer to the American dilemma over indiscriminate destruction had been gaining strength since World War II. During that war, Curtis LeMay's Twentieth Air Force implemented a limited program of warning Japanese civilians. In the summer of 1945, after LeMay's bombers had begun to burn large urban areas, American B-29s flew several missions over Japanese cities in which they dropped leaflets appealing to civilians to evacuate the area in order to save themselves. The operations were designed to hasten Japanese surrender by demoralizing the population with a stark demonstration of the Japanese government's inability to defend its citizens, but General LeMay also believed that the warnings were helpful in lessening the stigma attached to the firebombings.[47]

After World War II ended, the idea of warnings came to help a wider public rationalize the past and potential future use of nuclear weapons. The MGM feature film *The Beginning or the End*, which premiered in Washington, D.C. in February 1947, presented its version of the first American use of the atomic bomb. Ostensibly a documentary, the film implied that the United States had issued warnings to the population of Hiroshima prior to the city's destruction. "We've been dropping warning leaflets on them for ten days now," commented an Enola Gay crew member in one scene. "That's ten days' more warning then they gave us before Pearl Harbor." General LeMay's bombers had been dropping warning leaflets on Japanese cities in the ten days before the destruction of Hiroshima, but the scene was misleading in that these leaflets were not dropped on Hiroshima or Nagasaki and the warnings made no mention of a new, more devastating atomic bomb. The scene used the idea of warnings to add an undeserved moral dimension to the American use of the bomb.[48]

American warnings to civilians also became a feature of imagining a third world war with nuclear weapons. A book by a retired Army general envisioned leaflet and radio warnings for European civilians if the United States was forced to bomb industries captured through a Soviet invasion. A *U.S. News and World Report* article on the possibility of war with the Soviet Union during the tense month of August 1950 believed that U.S. bombers if called to strike the Soviet Union might delay their attack for several days in order to provide warning to Russian civilians.[49] Besides repeatedly appearing in the discussions of 1950 concerning American use of the atomic bomb in Korea, warning to civilians was a prominent element in the October 1951 *Collier's* special edition that envisioned World War III.[50]

During the Korean War, the U.S. military became increasingly interested in the issuing of air attack warnings to civilian populations. The interest stemmed from two sources. Some believed that by lowering the civilian population's morale and by convincing civilians to abandon their war-related jobs, warnings might maximize the effectiveness of air power in suppressing an enemy nation's ability to wage war. The warnings also supplied a defense against the charge that Americans were callous to harm noncombatants, a rationalization that the military could use abroad against Communist propaganda as well as to reassure the American public and themselves. The FEAF had conducted a few leaflet operations to warn civilians early in the Korean War and the U.N. forces had frequently broadcast general warnings to North Koreans to avoid military installations, but the program was sporadic. The irregularity of the program did not prevent the U.S. Ambassador to the United Nations Ernest Gross from highlighting the civilian warnings in the Security Council when Soviets first condemned American bombing practices in the summer of 1950.[51]

In 1951, signs of the military's growing interest in civilian warnings were evident. The Psychological Warfare Section of the U.N. Command issued a policy directive to all American psychological warfare units in East Asia. The directive was concerned with countering Communist propaganda aimed at Koreans that propagated the beliefs that U.N. attacks deliberately failed to discriminate between civilian and military targets and resulted in the needless and inhumane death of civilians. The directive instructed psychological warfare specialists always to indicate that attacks were directed only at military targets and to describe in detail what was meant by military target, for example, specifying the targets as military supply depots or key bridges. However, the directive admitted that "it is obvious — both to us and to the North Koreans — that civilian casualties have occurred and will continue to occur." Therefore, warnings to civilians offered a way to "maintain the propaganda initiative." The directive instructed its readers to "publicize the fact that U.N. leaflets and broadcasts are giving constant warnings to civilians so that loss of life can be held to a minimum." It also said that psychological warfare operations should claim that the Communists were to blame for civilian casualties because they prevented Koreans from receiving the warnings, used civilians for war work, and disguised soldiers as civilians. Ridgway's reports to the United Nations for August and September noted that his command had dropped warning leaflets to minimize the harm to North Korean civilians.[52]

In September 1951, the RAND Corporation, a research institution contracted to work for the Air Force, submitted a study to the Air Force staff on psychological warfare which built on earlier work conducted at the think tank. One of the primary recommendations of the study was to implement a comprehensive program for warning Korean civilians to counter Communist propaganda that, the study said, had achieved alarming success in Korea and around the world in persuading people that American bombing was "completely ineffective militarily while at the same time vastly destructive to civilian life and welfare." The Air Force Association was also proclaiming the importance that the Air Force attached to civilian warnings. In a special report on the Korean War, the organization's president clarified the Air Force's concern over harming noncombatants. "It is important to understand that our potential enemy is a government and its war-making machine," he wrote. "Our enemy does not include enslaved civilian populations who have suffered much under the heel of Communistic oppression." This was the fundamental reason, he claimed, for the Air Force's insistence on bombing precision. In addition, he said the Air Force was sponsoring research of "great importance" into warning civilian populations in target areas without endangering American flyers.[53]

By mid-1952, the U.N. Command implemented two extensive warning campaigns. Plan Blast accompanied a July attack against targets in Pyongyang and Plan Strike provided warnings to the residents of seventy-eight towns targeted for attack because the settlements lay along North Korean supply routes. These two psychological warfare operations included both the dropping of warning leaflets and radio broadcasts. A typical warning leaflet contained illustrations of bombs falling on trucks, repair shops, and buildings housing soldiers. The text said that the U.N. forces had to destroy Communist military supplies and installations and they knew where they were. It told civilians to leave the area of these military targets because the United Nations did not want to make them suffer. The planners who developed both operations emphasized the importance of the warnings for the neutralization of enemy propaganda and the demonstration of the U.N. Command's regard for humanitarian considerations. Warning operations by leaflet, radio broadcast, and loudspeaker-equipped airplane continued sporadically for the rest of the war.[54]

As the FEAF launched some of its largest attacks of the war in July, its press releases specified that the targets had been showered with warning leaflets and that extensive measures had been taken to avoid harming civilians. After a massive strike against Pyongyang in which almost 600 tons of bombs fell on the city, General Otto Weyland, Stratemeyer's successor as FEAF commander, stated that the U.N. air targets in the city had been carefully chosen to avoid as far as possible damage to civilian installations. In an attack on an aluminum plant at Yangsi, Air Force spokesmen said that the main buildings, boiler houses, electric transformer yards, warehouses were the principal targets, but more than 300 barracks, presumably used to house workmen, were spared.[55]

On August 5, General Glen O. Barcus, commander of the Fifth Air Force, announced the leaflet warnings of Plan Strike to the press. The headquarters statement said, "In an effort to save the lives of North Korean civilians, an audacious program of prior warnings of bombing attacks is in effect." The statement announced that FEAF planes had been dropping warning leaflets on seventy-eight North Korean cities and towns known to house Communist "military installations or supplies" with the leaflets advising civilians to remove themselves from these areas of danger. The announcement resulted in some exaggerated media coverage, which was evidence itself of lingering sensitivity to the destruction of cities. Both the AP and UP wire stories decided to label the seventy-eight cities and towns as "doomed." The editorial page of the *Washington Post* felt that the exaggerated stories had depicted the new bombing plan as a "saturation terror bombing campaign."[56]

The sensational talk about the air attacks compelled the Air Force to attempt to clarify Barcus' announcement. The following day, an Air Force spokesman said that there was no truth in reports that North Koreans had been warned that their cities were to be destroyed. He said, "The Air Force will strike and destroy military targets in these areas, but our aim is to get the civilians out before the bombs fall." On August 7, Secretary of the Air Force Thomas K. Finletter issued a public clarification of the warning policy. He explained that the Communists had built up large stores of military supplies in populated areas that the U.N. forces needed to destroy. However, he insisted that they "want to do so with a minimum of damage to the civilian economy and, above all if it is possible, without any civilian casualties." He pointed out that the warnings were especially targeted at the women and children in the areas that would be attacked. In a statement of less than 500 words, he repeated three times that the warnings were intended to avoid harm to civilians. Finletter's statement issued to the press at the Pentagon was accompanied by similar assurances from General Weyland. The *New York Times* reported that defense authorities had been concerned lest the Barcus statement about the bombings be misinterpreted, especially by Communist propagandists. General Weyland later in an interview for *U.S. News and World Report* explained the rationale for the new bombings and the accompanying warnings: "The primary and long-term objective of our operations is to destroy the enemy's military machine in being and to create the maximum military effect with minimum casualties to the hapless and innocent civilians in Communist-held territory.[57]

Because of the sensation surrounding Barcus' announcement, a number of other officials regretted that he had raised the subject. The warnings helped to defray blame for harming civilians in the bombing of populated areas, but they interfered with the optimistic view that American force was being applied discriminately. The discussion of warnings acknowledged that the U.S. bombing could put civilians at risk if they remained in their towns. It admitted that American air power was not so precise as to be able to excise the intended military targets that the U.N. Command claimed were the objective without endangering the surrounding populated areas. The State Department in particular preferred that the government do what it could to avoid any mention of harm to noncombatants at American hands. They worried that the Communists would exploit to their advantage the attention given the warnings and air attacks.

The State Department sent a circular to its embassies in Europe and Asia cautioning about Communist exploitation of the bomb warnings in Korea. It said that the massive use of air power was reminiscent to Asians of Japanese methods in World War II and to Europe of Nazi terror bombing and, therefore, made these peoples vulnerable to Communist propaganda on the subject. The circular admitted, "However handled in output subject [of] massive bombing MIL targets in or near heavily populated areas cannot RPT be useful [to] our purposes." It advised that the best approach was to give the topic no more emphasis than necessary but to avoid the appearance of playing it down. The heaviest stress was to be placed on the "strictly military" purpose of the operations and the "strictly military" character of the targets selected. The circular suggested emphasis on the theme that the air action was "emphatically" not aimed at the civilian population whom U.N. flyers risked their safety to warn. The State Department did believe that Finletter's statement on the warnings was excellent and should be used as guidance on the topic.[58]

An earlier proposal to warn civilians in Pyongyang prior to a large air attack had been dismissed precisely because of the potential for attracting the kind of unwanted attention that Barcus' announcement did. In the summer of 1951, General Ridgway had proposed to the JCS an air strike against military targets in Pyongyang. In his cable he included precautions his command would take to avoid harm to noncombatants: "Elaborate prior planning for this atk to include pinpointing mil tgt and warning of civil populace by leaflet drops to be accomplished at least 36 hours prior to the atk, will constitute practicable guarantee against unnecessary killing of non-combatants." The cable included the full text of the warning leaflet Ridgway proposed dropping. After initially hesitating because of concern that singling out Pyongyang for an all-out attack might appear "in the eyes of the world" to constitute an attempt to break off armistice negotiations, the JCS approved the attack. However, it required that no warning be given and no publicity concerning the "mass" nature of the attack be allowed. The U.N. Command portrayed the operation against Pyongyang as a normal strike against an enemy buildup. In this case, avoiding unwanted attention won out over providing Korean civilians with the assistance of a prior warning.[59]

As the State Department feared, the Communist press did attempt to exploit the 1952 warnings and the bombings in populated areas. Beijing radio broadcast that the threatened attacks were aimed at civilians and that the American war "is becoming a war against Korean women and children and the old people in the rear." After a strike against targets in Pyongyang, the Chinese claimed that more than 500 bombs fell in residential areas killing or wounding more than 1,000 civilians and destroying 676 houses. North Korean officials protested against indiscriminate American bombing, and Moscow radio depicted the new attacks as the mass bombing of civilians, mostly women and children. American embassies in Europe reported that local Communist media was equating the action against the seventy-eight marked towns with atrocities against civilians. A State Department analysis of the response to increased U.N. air attacks in countries around the world concluded that the attacks would strengthen neutralism among South Asians in part because the bombings would "bring misery to defenseless civilians." The New York *Daily Worker* dismissed the warnings as a cloak to conceal "the merciless carrying of saturation bombing to the civilian population," and one of its editorials called the threatened bombings a "program of extermination." The Communist protests were so loud that Secretary of Defense Robert Lovett made a public statement refuting the charges in which he pointed to the warnings that American forces were issuing as evidence of concern for the protection of civilians.[60]

Even though the State Department was uncomfortable discussing possible harm to noncombatants from U.S. action and Communist media did use such discussion as a bludgeon against American methods in Korea, the American media gave significant attention to the civilian warnings and incorporated them into rationalizations for the increasingly destructive air campaign. *Time*, *U.S. News and World Report*, and NBC commented on the warnings in their coverage of the escalated bombing. *Time* quoted from one of the warning leaflets that directly addressed the question of responsibility for civilian harm. The quote said, "United Nations forces cannot be responsible for your death if you ignore this warning." Carl Spaatz, retired Air Force chief of staff, writing for *Newsweek* devoted one of his columns to the question of the value and humanity of bombing military targets in North Korean cities. Spaatz answered the rhetorical question, "Why visit the terrors of bombing upon North Korean civilians, many of whom are innocent and unwilling victims of Communism?" He argued that the bombing was an important way to continue to apply pressure to the Communist forces and to prevent the Chinese from building up sufficient stockpiles of supplies to win the war. As for "humanitarian considerations," Spaatz wrote, the U.N. could do no more than it was doing by warning civilians with leaflets and radio broadcasts and by taking every possible precaution to confine the area of attack to military objectives. He admitted that the warnings might do little good because the Communists used Korean civilians to handle supplies and exercised ruthless control over them. "Nevertheless," he wrote, "the warnings are a bold gesture, made in good faith, and are the best the U.N. command can do in the circumstances to prevent needless bloodshed."[61]

American newspapers also were attracted to the way in which the warnings provided legitimacy for the increased air attacks on North Korea. The AP and UP wire stories of Barcus' announcement made the front page of many papers. The AP story emphasized the humanitarian aspects of the warnings saying they were intended to spare noncombatants' lives and were aimed in part at countering Communist charges of the wanton bombing of women and children.[62] Besides giving prominent coverage to Barcus' announcement and Finletter's clarification, the *New York Times* continued to mention the civilian warnings in its coverage of U.N. air strikes into October.[63] The editorial pages of the *Washington Post* and *New York Times* viewed the warnings as an important factor legitimizing the escalated bombings. In an editorial entitled "No Wanton Bombing," the *Washington Post* complained about the flamboyant reports that implied the new bombings were a "saturation terror bombing campaign designed to destroy 78 cities and towns." The editorial rejected this depiction and insisted that the attacks were against specific military targets such as transportation facilities, supply dumps, and small munitions industries within the targeted cities. "There is, of course, a vast difference between attacks on legitimate military targets and the bombing of cities for terroristic purposes," it said. The editorial saw the warnings serving a dual purpose of helping to spare civilian lives and of causing absenteeism from industrial production. However, the editorial did admit that "inevitably a campaign against military targets in and near cities will result in civilian casualties and the destruction of homes." The editorial ended with the question of whether the military value of the targets marked for destruction was great enough to justify the other damage the raids would cause. In two editorials, the *New York Times,* likewise, praised the policy of warnings and acknowledged that harm to civilians was unavoidable, but offered an additional defense of American action. One editorial claimed that the risk of killing civilians had been minimized as far as possible by the warnings and that this was "humane and wise." It concluded, though, "If this war, like all wars, is cruel, let the world remember who started it." A second editorial expanded on this theme of blaming the aggressor for the negative consequences of the war to which American actions had led. The editorial claimed that it was unhappily true that changes in the character of warfare had exposed civilians to danger. Wars were no longer fought by small professional armies but by entire populations. However, this meant that wars had become an even greater evil and, therefore, an even greater transgression when a nation decided to start one. "The suffering brought on innocent people was inevitable when the Communists made their decision to strike," it said. Both papers acknowledged that American force would harm civilians, but they attached no moral opprobrium to this. The harm was unintended. Warnings had been given. While the *Washington Post* offered a proportionate military gain as a justification for any civilian harm, the *New York Times* placed the ultimate responsibility for the consequences of the war's violence with the Communists who had started the conflict.[64]

Those who implemented the warning program also believed it had served a useful role in insulating the escalated air campaign from criticism. An Air Force report on psychological warfare operations concluded that the 1952 warning program was successful in demonstrating the "humanitarian consideration" of the U.N. Command. The warnings, the report asserted, allowed the command "to meet and to subjugate" criticism in the non-Communist press against the bombing of the seventy-eight target cities and also enabled the U.N. forces to channel resentment of the North Korea workers against the Communists who forced them to remain in the danger areas. From July until October, General Mark W. Clark's reports to the United Nations regularly noted that American forces were warning civilians of impending air attacks.[65]

Although the warning program did help Americans demonstrate to themselves and the world that they did not intend to harm noncombatants in Korea, it did not offer much practical protection for Korean civilians. Leaflet operations were few and far between. Two large operations were conducted in August 1950 and July 1952 and a smaller operation in September 1950. Illiteracy among Koreans interfered with the leaflets' ability to convey clear messages. Radio warnings were more consistently delivered, but a lack of radios made access to the warnings for Koreans more difficult. All of the warnings were predicated on the problematic assumption that Korean civilians could properly identify "military targets" when the U.S. military had expanded its definition of a military target to any structure that could shelter enemy troops or supplies. On top of the problems communicating the warnings, becoming refugees or living in caves could be worse options than risking American bombs. One U.S. intelligence report illustrated how warnings could prove ineffective in clearing civilians from targeted towns. The report estimated that 35% of the population of Yonan read the warning leaflets dropped on the city prior to a raid on August 4, 1952. Some people evacuated the city, but many could not because they were serving as compulsory labor. As a result, "many civilians" were killed by the U.N. raid. Because of a lack of radios, broadcast warnings of the impending attack were ineffective in the city. With warnings that civilians often times did not receive or could not heed, the warning program did more to soothe American consciences than to shelter innocent Koreans from harm.[66]

6.6 Napalm

Beyond the attention that Americans paid to the refugee crisis and the idea of warning civilians, the controversy surrounding the U.S. military's use of one of its more unusual weapons in Korea further demonstrated the difficulty for Americans of completely ignoring their contribution to civilian suffering and illustrated the trend of stressing their lack of intent to harm noncombatants when the injury occurred. Extensive use of napalm provided a challenge for Americans and their leaders who wanted to promote the image of the United States as a nation that waged humane wars. Although napalm provoked much greater controversy during the Vietnam War, the exotic weapon began to gather a tarnished image during the war in Korea. Napalm was a mixture of gasoline and aluminum soaps that combined to make an incendiary gel resembling brown Jello. Dropped from planes, napalm bombs would shower an area with flaming globules of jellied gasoline that would stick to surfaces and burn for several minutes, often igniting other flammable materials in the area. If napalm landed on a person's clothes or skin, it was difficult to brush off or extinguish and could cause severe burns. A group of scientists at Harvard University and the Massachusetts Institute of Technology invented napalm during World War II, testing it on the athletic fields near Harvard Stadium. Napalm filled the firebombs that burned Tokyo and other Japanese cities, and the U.S. military used it widely as a tactical weapon in support of ground forces during World War II. In the campaign to recapture the island of Luzon in the Philippines, American planes dropped more than one million gallons of napalm in support of ground forces. The weapon attracted little attention during World War II in part because the name "napalm" was classified.[67]

During the Korean War, napalm achieved a greater notoriety. The U.S. Air Force dropped more than 30,000 tons of napalm on Korea.[68] In the first two years of the war, the U.S. military came close to bragging about the destructive qualities of napalm. Security concerns about using the name "napalm" to describe the incendiary disappeared. The name "napalm" as it turned out had the virtue from a counterintelligence perspective of being misleading. The term "napalm" was derived from aluminum naphthenate and aluminum palmitate the ingredients that the Harvard team, which invented the incendiary, thought they had used to thicken gasoline into a suitable weapon. Upon further investigation, the researchers discovered that the aluminum soap supplied to them by a chemical company under the name of "aluminum palmitate" and which had performed so well in their experiments was not aluminum palmitate at all but another aluminum soap derived from coconut oil. But the name napalm stuck and when the term was released for public use anyone hoping to puzzle the formula for the incendiary from its name would be partially misled.[69]

Throughout the Korean War, the U.N. Command's press releases frequently mentioned the use of the weapon by name. Since the dropping of napalm was spectacular visually, the weapon became a regular feature of photographs and film footage released to the press. Between February and July 1951, the Department of Defense nine times released footage for television newsreels of napalm in action in Korea. However, the military's attention to napalm stressed the weapon's virtue on the battlefield against enemy armed forces instead of its ability to incinerate cities and villages. Napalm's usefulness against the North Korean tanks, which repeatedly broke through South Korean and U.N. lines early in the war, attracted particular attention in the press.[70]

A few stories appeared in the media that acknowledged that the U.N. forces used napalm to burn buildings and villages. For example, a *Collier's* article in the fall of 1950 noted the burning of a village with napalm by Navy planes. In February 1951, a smattering of articles addressed the harm that napalm used against villages could have on Korean civilians. In one of his reports from Korea, George Barrett writing for the *New York Times* offered this description of a village struck by napalm as American forces advanced toward Seoul. "The inhabitants throughout the village and in the fields were caught and killed and kept the exact postures they had held when the napalm struck — a man about to get on his bicycle, fifty boys and girls playing in an orphanage, a housewife strangely unmarked, holding in her hand a page torn from a Sears-Roebuck catalogue...," Barrett related. "There must be almost 200 dead in the tiny hamlet." A *Washington Post* editorial reiterated Barrett's grisly description as an example of the war's awful cost for Koreans. *U.S. News and World Report* ran a piece about the air war which highlighted the role of napalm in countering guerilla tactics. Showering napalm on "whole areas" of villages and towns, it said, destroyed the buildings that enemy soldiers used for cover and sheltered in against the winter's cold. Although the articles on napalm often explained how enemy soldiers were using the villages burned, they included hints at the danger napalm posed for noncombatants. However, since the vast majority of the news coverage of napalm depicted the weapon as one used against enemy soldiers and their equipment, the use of napalm generated little public controversy among Americans.[71]

By 1952, napalm had stimulated opposition to its use, but the locus of controversy was centered in Britain, not the United States. In March, the *Manchester Guardian* printed an editorial about the horrible injuries inflicted by napalm as reported by Rene Cutforth, a BBC correspondent. Late the following month, Dr. Cyril Garbett, the Archbishop of York, called for the outlawing of the jellied gasoline bomb used by the United Nations in Korea. "It is a weapon which inflicts terrible and indiscriminate loss and suffering," he wrote in a diocesan leaflet. "It burns up all life and buildings over a wide area; and there is little possibility of escape for man or animals." Sparked by the Archbishop's plea, several members of Parliament asked Foreign Secretary Anthony Eden some pointed questions about napalm. One member asked if Eden was aware "that many Christian church folk in this country regard with profound disquiet the continued use of the napalm bomb, in view of the atrocious suffering it inflicts upon innocent civilian people?" Unsatisfied with Eden's answers, the concerned members raised the issue twice with the Parliamentary Secretary to the Minister of Defense Nigel Birch and once with Prime Minister Churchill. When confronted with the charges that the U.N. forces were using napalm indiscriminately against villages and women and children, Birch replied that the members were misinformed. Napalm, Birch assured, was only being used against military targets and was not directed against civilian populations. He argued that napalm was a tactical weapon dropped from low altitudes and was, therefore, more discriminate than ordinary high explosive bombs. He also made the fallacious claim that napalm was "not effective against towns and villages." Birch did not deny that napalm had harmed civilians but said that this mainly occurred in 1950 and 1951 during a period of mobile operations when it was much more difficult to use air power precisely. The secretary said much greater care was being taken now that the forces occupied static positions. Although he conceded that, as with any bombs, one could not guarantee that civilians would not be killed, he believed that those who start wars should be the ones to consider this terrible consequence.

The government's reassurances did not quiet the opposition to napalm, though. The United Free Church of Scotland appealed to the United Nations to ban the use of napalm and have it outlawed under international law. A group of prominent British citizens including seven members of Parliament sent a letter to the U.N. Secretary General and to the *London Times* pleading for an end to the indiscriminate use of napalm. The British peace organization the National Peace Council also began printing pamphlets that compared the horrors of the use of napalm against innocent civilians and soldiers with the Belsen and Buchenwald concentration camps.[72]

Naturally, Communist countries and their sympathizers capitalized on the controversy surrounding napalm. Communist media had first categorized napalm as an "atrocity weapon" in early January 1951. As the FEAF began its campaign of civilian warnings, Communist charges about napalm escalated in August 1952. Alan Winnington, the leftist reporter from Australia, wrote about the U.N. force's napalm "atrocities." Criticism of the use of napalm also appeared in the New York *Daily Worker* including a grisly poem describing the weapon's victims: "Their eyeballs bulged, like wide, red sores;/Scars of purple, red and blue/Were stamped upon their faces, too,/Like bright flowers of pain."[73]

In response to British concerns and Communist propaganda, American military officials scrambled to formulate a public position on the use of napalm. The resulting defense of the weapon relied heavily on the newly implemented civilian warning campaign. By early August, the Air Force Deputy Chief of Staff for Operations approved a draft of an official Air Force stance. The position stated that napalm was an effective and accepted weapon of war which the United States and Britain had used against military targets in World War II. The Communist propaganda campaign against napalm, the statement claimed, was a direct result of the effectiveness of the weapon and the inability of the Communists to provide air protection to their forces in Korea. The statement insisted that the U.N. forces in Korea had endeavored to employ napalm only against military targets. It pointed out that U.N. planes were warning civilians in "military target areas" by leaflets and radio to evacuate those places. JCS Chairman Omar Bradley, likewise, used arguments about napalm's effectiveness and the FEAF warning precautions in a letter to a RAF liaison in Washington. The Air Force Deputy Chief of Staff for Operations had passed these arguments along to the general.

The Air Force also supplied Austin Stevens of the *New York Times* with its position on napalm for an article Stevens was writing on the Communist propaganda campaign against the weapon. The Air Force Public Information Office provided, and Stevens used in his article, a quote from General Nathan F. Twining, the acting Air Force Chief of Staff, on the care the U.N. forces were taking to avoid harm to noncombatants. The long quote included Twining's assurance that the "United Nations Air Forces in Korea have never employed napalm against civilians" and the American and allied air forces in Korea "have from the beginning conducted their war operations with a regard for safety of non-combatants perhaps never before surpassed in history." Twining contrasted American efforts to warn civilians of air attacks that might put them at risk with the enemy's treacherous ploy of hiding their military facilities and supplies within civilian areas.

The official American stance on napalm stressed that the weapon was not intentionally used against civilians as evidenced by the warnings that U.S. forces provided. Of course, this statement failed to mention that the United States had not dropped warning leaflets on Sinuiju and most of the other cities which U.N. air forces had burned with napalm-filled firebombs or on the many villages that American planes had destroyed with napalm. After the Air Force's attempt at managing the issue, the State Department sent a circular to a number of its embassies and overseas media outlets instructing them to avoid giving any more publicity to Communist charges about napalm as the United States derived "no benefit from publicity regarding its use."[74]

The use of napalm could generate feelings of ambivalence among American pilots concerned about the possibility of harming innocent civilians, but plenty of rationales offered themselves to reassure a troubled soldier. One jet pilot in Korea expressed this mix of concern and rationalization to a writer for the *New Yorker*. He said that the first few times he participated in a napalm strike he had an empty feeling and wondered whether he should have done it. "Maybe those people I set afire were innocent civilians," he thought. However, the pilot developed a number of ways of thinking that helped him cope with any lingering feelings of guilt. He decided that many of the civilians were not the innocents they appeared to be. Some of those who appeared to be civilians lit up "like a Roman candle" when he hit them with napalm, a sure sign to his mind that they had been carrying ammunition. Not seeing his victims also allowed him to avoid thinking about who he might have killed. Fulfilling his role as a military pilot provided him compensation in the form of feelings of competence and accomplishment and made his actions seem selfless and inevitable.[75]

The napalm issue did not make a big splash in the American press. Besides the Stevens article and a few reports on the British controversy, only a few voices protested the American use of napalm. After reading reports of the U.N. bombing of Suan in which 12,000 gallons of napalm burned out a two-square-mile area of the town, a doctor wrote the *New York Times* of his revulsion at this act. He lamented, "There is no doubt that many thousands of aged, sick and infirm people, patients in hospitals, women and children were killed, mangled or indescribably burned." In one day, he said, the American-led U.N. air force had killed and maimed more people than he could cure in his entire life as a doctor. The bombing reminded him of the dreadful tactics of the Italian Fascists and the Nazis. The *Christian Century* printed two editorials that questioned the American policy of napalm use. One told of the petition of the National Christian Council of Korea to Eisenhower during his visit to Korea in late 1952. One of the Council's requests was that more attention be paid to protecting the lives of civilians and, as a means to that end, that the United States reconsider the policy of dropping napalm. The editorial noted that this request was in line with some British church leaders, but said "the implications are more disturbing when the condemnation comes from Christians among the very people the napalm bombs are supposedly protecting." The *National Guardian* also contained unsympathetic reports on napalm use in late August.[76] Napalm had begun to gain a stigma during the Korean War, but the official reassurances that the weapon was used against military targets, the rationalization that civilians had been warned and any harm to them was unintended, and the association that the questioning of napalm had with Communist propaganda helped to limit the controversy in the United States over the weapon.

The spectacle of destruction in Korea undermined the optimistic notion that the U.S. military could employ its massive destructive potential discriminately. Many Americans had to acknowledge that the liberal use of firepower by their armed forces contributed to the suffering of Korean civilians. However, this acknowledgment did not lead to widespread calls for reigning in the American arsenal or for more effective government efforts to prevent the devastation. Instead, individuals working through relief organizations and American officials focused their attention on mitigating the aftereffects of the destruction by assisting Korean refugees, although even this help often came as a secondary priority to the war effort. This aid saved lives and reduced suffering, but constituted an anemic form of civilian protection, hardly constituting an immunity from war's violence. Nevertheless, the aid to refugees such as American efforts to warn civilians of air attacks helped Americans convince themselves as well as others abroad that the United States was a humane nation that did not intend to harm innocent civilians in its wars.

The issue of intention, and not the question of whose weapons literally killed civilians or destroyed their homes, became the morally significant one for many Americans. If soldiers and officials did not intend the harm inflicted on noncombatants, Americans decided that their country's methods conformed to the humanitarian notions that undergirded the norm of noncombatant immunity. Americans proclaimed this lack of intention on two levels, more broadly, as reluctant belligerents forced to fight because of Communist aggression and, more specifically, as protectors of civilians who did not wish to bring harm to innocents. In this way, American warfare was understood to be humane and Americans' self-identification as humanitarians remained protected despite the harm that American weapons inflicted on Korean civilians. Lack of intention was taking its place as a key element in the popular reinterpretation of noncombatant immunity emerging after World War II. Although the distinction over intention had important cultural meaning for Americans, it went a long way toward undercutting any practical protection that civilians might have hoped to retain under the refashioned version of noncombatant immunity. The importance of absent intention in rationalizing war's violence took on greater importance as the hydrogen bomb moved from the realm of scientific theory to military reality.

7

The Thermonuclear Challenge

Shortly before Dwight Eisenhower took office as president in 1953, the United States detonated its first thermonuclear weapon. The tests, codenamed IVY, were conducted on a small atoll in the Pacific Ocean and demonstrated that American scientists had devised a method for combining hydrogen atoms to produce helium through thermonuclear fusion. The byproduct of this fusion was an explosion vastly more powerful then those produced by the atom-splitting fission bombs that had destroyed Hiroshima and Nagasaki. One of the IVY tests generated an explosion equivalent to ten million tons of trinitrotoluene (TNT), five hundred times the magnitude of the Nagasaki bomb. In theory, a thermonuclear explosion could be made as large as desired.

The arrival of the hydrogen bomb coincided with an extensive reevaluation of American military policy under President Eisenhower. The "New Look" that Eisenhower and his advisors proposed for the U.S. armed forces increased the country's dependence on nuclear weapons, including the new hydrogen bomb, and ushered in what scholars have called a thermonuclear revolution for which the Truman administration had laid the foundations. These changes did not spell the end of popular support for noncombatant immunity anymore than the developments of World War II had. Americans approached this further expansion of their military's destructive capacity as they had in their early discussions of the protection of noncombatants in the late 1940s and early 1950s. Americans would retain their massively destructive ways of war but would reconcile them with the norm of noncombatant immunity. They remained optimistic that the new methods of warfare could still allow for the sparing of civilians. They rationalized civilian damage that American weapons did inflict as an unintended side effect of the legitimate conduct of war.

7.1 Unease Over the New Look

The arrival of the hydrogen bomb did not occasion the widespread discussion and soul-searching that the appearance of the atomic bomb had. Two years of media attention to the projected fusion weapon had denuded the bomb of its novelty. The American government was slow to acknowledge that the test on

November 1, 1952, had demonstrated the feasibility of a hydrogen bomb. This first thermonuclear explosion also had no obvious victims like the attacks on Hiroshima and Nagasaki that had introduced the world public to fission weapons.

The successful test did revive anxieties about a thermonuclear weapon's potential for excessive destruction. Americans continued to associate the hydrogen bomb with the destruction of cities, and some worried that such indiscriminate devastation in a war would be a liability to the United States. Following the Soviet announcement in August 1953 that they had developed their own thermonuclear weapons, the press adopted the vivid practice of superimposing onto maps of American cities, like Chicago, circles representing the radii of the different levels of destruction that a hydrogen bomb could inflict. These illustrations further strengthened the association of fusion bombs with city destruction.[1]

As the hydrogen bomb was becoming a new military reality, a reevaluation of U.S. military policy under Eisenhower helped to raise further anxieties over indiscriminate destruction. Concerned about the harmful effects of excessive military spending on the American economy and unconvinced that the Cold War would end any time soon, Eisenhower led a restructuring of U.S. military posture that he believed would provide the country with adequate security at a price that the nation could bear for the long term. Announced at the end of 1953, this New Look for the American armed forces cut the country's ground forces and increased its reliance on air power and nuclear weapons. With the hydrogen bomb as the new pinnacle of nuclear weaponry, the administration gave the impression that the United States would become increasingly dependent on massively destructive weapons to ensure its security. In January 1954, Eisenhower's Secretary of State John Foster Dulles strengthened this impression when he delivered a nationally broadcast policy speech to the Council on Foreign Relations. The speech attempted to explain how the military's New Look would further U.S. foreign policy, economic, and security goals, but Dulles' references to nuclear weapons attracted the most attention in the media. Dulles had incorporated into the speech a comment suggested by Eisenhower, which the president believed succinctly summarized the administration's new policy. The sentence read: "The basic decision was to depend primarily upon a capacity to retaliate, instantly, by means and at places of our choosing." Journalists interpreted the speech to mean that the administration intended to rely on a policy of "massive retaliation" with nuclear weapons to forestall and fight both limited and general wars.[2]

Many Americans believed Dulles' statement signaled that the country would depend on the hydrogen bomb and the capacity for massive destruction to protect its interests. The former ambassador to India Chester Bowles worried that the new policy threatened to violate American moral and religious values and erode the distinction between the American way of life and the Communist system. He feared that Dulles' proposed policy might require the United States to bomb cities devoid of "legitimate military or industrial targets" and wipe out millions of "helpless" men, women, and children. A *New Republic* editorial concluded that the administration had decided that the next war would be a "war of annihilation." One author in *Commonweal* asked, "But can any church reconcile itself to the deliberate concentration of our military defense on the use of weapons which involve a holocaust of civilians, if any alternative exists?" The writer believed that the administration planned to concentrate American defense "almost exclusively on the use of the most inhumane weapons not from necessity but from selfishness" in order to avoid greater sacrifices in dollars and manpower. A retired naval officer wrote the Secretary of State urging an international treaty to ban the use of nuclear weapons against cities. He worried that the New Look meant that the United States had adopted a strategy of "indiscriminate bombing of the enemy population." He feared that the country was abandoning the "longtime principle of observing the distinction between combatants and noncombatants."[3]

With the stigma attached to mass killing, the Eisenhower administration quickly realized its mistake and began work to counter the impression that the United States would rely on indiscriminately destructive methods of warfare to ensure American security. Since the administration was not about to rule out the use of nuclear weapons, its approach followed the two paths which public discussion had laid out since the Korean War. On the one hand, officials stressed that nuclear weapons could be used in a discriminate manner against enemy armed forces. On the other, when the hydrogen bomb made it difficult to deny that cities and civilians would be obliterated, officials emphasized in a number of ways that the U.S. government and its citizens did not intend to harm noncombatants even when it used or threatened to use weapons of mass destruction.

Even before Dulles' massive retaliation speech, the Eisenhower administration sought to combat the perception that nuclear weapons were solely city-destroyers. Its attention to destigmatizing nuclear weapons only intensified after the realization that Dulles' speech had created something of a public relations dilemma. Eisenhower's advisors built on the efforts of the Truman administration, its supporters, and military leaders who had continued to insist that nuclear arms no longer had to be used solely against cities and their populations after the first widespread discussions of tactical nuclear weapons in 1951.[4]

In addition to promoting talk of tactical nuclear weapons as an alternative to the atomization of cities,[5] the Eisenhower administration encouraged the notion that nuclear arms had become "conventional" weapons, no different from any other weapon. When Eisenhower announced his Atoms for Peace plan to the United Nations in December 1953, he observed that, with the remarkable developments in size and variety, atomic weapons "have virtually achieved conventional status within our armed services." The new chairman of the JCS, Admiral Arthur Radford repeated Eisenhower's suggestion several days later. Sterling Cole, the Republican chairman of the Joint Congressional Committee on Atomic Energy, echoed the administration's remarks. He said it would be foolish to outlaw the use of atomic weapons because he saw them as no different than any other weapon of war. Several weeks after Dulles' massive retaliation speech, Secretary of Defense Charles E. Wilson reiterated the administration's message that nuclear weapons were no different from other arms. At a press conference, Wilson said the problem with public thinking about nuclear weapons was people believing them only to be big bombs. He claimed on the contrary that the arms came in different sizes and were becoming tactical weapons.[6]

7.2 Castle Bravo

The Eisenhower administration's problem of disassociating nuclear weapons from indiscriminate destruction became even more difficult when the military tested another thermonuclear device in the spring of 1954. On March 1, 1954, the detonation of a redesigned hydrogen bomb did not go as planned. The scientists and soldiers observing the test, code named Castle Bravo, did not anticipate the blast would measure ten megatons, five hundred times larger than the fission bomb dropped on Nagasaki. The experiment's managers also did not expect the vast cloud of radioactive fallout which formed from the explosion. Winds carried the dangerously radioactive fallout beyond the testing grounds on an isolated Pacific atoll. Twenty-eight Americans from a weather and observation station and 236 Marshall Islanders from four nearby islands were hospitalized, and nearly all of the Marshallese suffered from radiation burns and loss of hair. A Japanese fishing boat with twenty-three crew were also caught by the fallout and one later died.[7]

Throughout March, information about the secret test slowly leaked to the American public and abroad. As some began to discuss the innocent victims of the explosion and complained that the U.S. government had lost control of the test, the Chairman of the AEC Lewis Strauss inadvertently added to the anxieties about the new thermonuclear weapon. At a press conference on March 31 held by the president to discuss the Bravo test, Strauss found himself grasping to describe the magnitude of the new bomb's explosive power. In response to a reporter's question, Strauss replied that the hydrogen bomb "can be made to be as large as you wish, as large as the military requirement demands, that is to say, an H-bomb can be made as — large enough to take out a city." Strauss repeated, "To take out a city, to destroy a city."

"How big a city," another journalist asked.

"Any city," Strauss replied.

"Any city, New York?"

"The metropolitan area, yes."

Strauss later clarified that he meant that a hydrogen bomb could destroy the heart of Manhattan and not the entire 3,000 square mile New York metropolitan area, but the chairman had already fanned fears about city destruction. His comments were the first official American statement that the world now faced an implement of war capable of threatening any city no matter how large. The public speculation about the increasing destructive power of nuclear weapons now had official confirmation, and the hydrogen bomb again appeared in the guise of a destroyer of cities. Eisenhower's public relations advisor C. D. Jackson lamented to Dulles in early April that the "curse was almost off the a-bomb — which was just about to be accepted as the newest conventional weapon," when the hydrogen bomb again made Americans look for alternatives to nuclear weapons.[8]

The Bravo test provoked reactions abroad that condemned the hydrogen bomb as a barbarous and indiscriminate weapon of war. Indian Prime Minister Nehru said the test was new evidence of the hydrogen bomb's horror and called on the United Nations for new efforts to eliminate weapons of mass destruction. The Egyptian Minister of Foreign Affairs, when asked about his country's attitude toward the use of the hydrogen bomb, answered, "Egypt is against any trends to revert to barbarism and the destruction of humanity." In May, the French representative to the U.N. Disarmament Commission called for a ban on the hydrogen bomb. The same month, the Church of England adopted a resolution condemning the hydrogen bomb as "a grievous enlargement of the evils inherent in all war and a threat to the basic obligations of humanity and civilization." The Dean of Winchester E. G. Selwyn, who seconded the resolution, argued that the new weapon appeared to be exclusively a weapon of indiscriminate destruction and slaughter. Several months later, Pope Pius XII said the use of atomic, biological, and chemical weapons would be illegitimate if they annihilated populations indiscriminately. The controversy surrounding the Bravo test added to American concern that Europeans objected to the U.S. nuclear arsenal, and this worry manifested itself in articles about this European sentiment.[9]

In the wake of the Bravo test, more American voices spoke out against the hydrogen bomb and the policy of massive retaliation out of concerns over indiscriminate destruction. In an article for *Commonweal*, Chester Bowles reiterated his arguments against the policy of massive retaliation. Following the Bravo test, Bowles observed that "we are now, almost casually, proposing to immolate millions of noncombatant men, women, and children, in retaliation for an aggression launched by leaders over whom they have admittedly little control." The social critic Lewis Mumford wrote a letter to the *New York Times* condemning the hydrogen bomb and the administration's military policy. He labeled the bomb a weapon of "extermination" and pleaded for an alternative to "our accepting total extermination as a method of war." Mumford elaborated on his criticism in a book the same year in which he repeatedly equated modern warfare with genocide. Other letters to the *New York Times* voiced continuing concerns over indiscriminate destruction given current American military policies.[10]

Peace activists stepped up their criticism of U.S. policies following the Bravo test. Two peace organizations — the Women's International League for Peace and Freedom (WILPF) and the Fellowship of Reconciliation — condemned the hydrogen bomb as an implement of war too indiscriminately destructive to use. Gertrude C. Bussey as Policy Committee chair of the U.S. section of the WILPF, wrote the *Nation*, "In the face of the realities of war in the hydrogen world, the threat of massive retaliation seems insanely reckless." Bussey worried that "despite the President's assurance, we may once more be guilty of using a weapon that will lead to a war of annihilation." The Fellowship of Reconciliation issued a public statement calling on President Eisenhower to halt the further testing of "weapons of extermination." It also sent to the president a letter and petition to stop the testing that contained almost 5,000 signatures. The two documents intermingled concern about the radioactive fallout from the tests harming innocents with revulsion that the use of the weapon would indiscriminately kill. The letter expressed its "horror at the kind of indiscriminate slaughter that this government is prepared to contemplate," while the petition stated, "No nation has the right for purposes of military experimentation to inflict this horror upon innocent and defenseless multitudes who are not consulted as to whether they shall thus be exposed to the risk of starvation or poisoning." In July, the organization devoted an entire issue of their journal *Fellowship* to the problem of the hydrogen bomb, and many of the articles in the special issue criticized the weapon for the harm it would inflict on civilians.[11]

After the Bravo test, condemnation against harming innocents became a notably more prominent theme in the Fellowship's antiwar efforts. The executive committee of the organization encouraged chapters to sponsor an advertisement in their local newspapers along these lines. Under the boldface heading "Modern armies make war on babies!," the advertisement graphically described the suffering of a young woman and her two babies who had been burned by the Nagasaki bomb. The organization also produced an antiwar pamphlet, the major theme of which was that modern warfare required the killing of innocent women and children. The pamphlet presented a satirical tale about Arthur, a young man who wanted to fight for his country, but Arthur lived in a make-believe nation whose selective service laws were opposite to those of the United States. In order to be allowed to fight, Arthur had to convince a board that he was a conscientious combatant. Just as American selective service boards vigorously tested the commitment of conscientious objectors to pacifism, the board that Arthur faced tested the young man's commitment to war.

After Arthur explained his devotion to the use of violence under certain circumstances, the board asked Arthur how he would deal with a man who attacked his mother. If he had a machine gun, would he be willing to kill his attacker's "wife and little children, his mother and father, and in fact everyone who lives on the same street with him" and be willing to "poison their drinking water, burn their houses, and spread disease germs among them?" While at first appalled by the thought of murdering innocent people, Arthur eventually offered a half-hearted acceptance of the killing of noncombatants that modern war required. As the committee repeatedly reminded Arthur of the ways in which his military service might require him to kill civilians, he pleaded, "Why do you keep harping on women and children? Don't soldiers fight soldiers any more?"

"Yes," the chairman replied, "they do. Sometimes. Mostly, though, they fight civilians now — noncombatants. They destroy and ravage across the face of the earth with instruments of destruction capable of slaughtering half the human race — and designed, perhaps, to do just that. Didn't you know?"

"Well," said Arthur, "I guess I did, but I haven't been thinking about it exactly that way."[12] The Bravo test and its innocent victims had reinvigorated the vocal minority of Americans who objected to nuclear weapons because they killed indiscriminately.

7.3 The Domestication of Nuclear Warfare

Throughout the controversy in 1954 surrounding Dulles' massive retaliation speech and the Bravo test, the Air Force did its best to fight the special stigma attached to the use of nuclear weapons. Being the service primarily responsible for delivering a nuclear attack, the Air Force was particularly sensitive to the problem. Its leaders spoke out on the issue following the massive retaliation speech. The Air Force Chief of Staff Nathan Twining explained that all the talk of "retaliation" should not be confused with a policy of indiscriminate destruction. "It makes a great difference whether victory is sought by the depopulation of a nation or by the disarming of a nation," he affirmed, and the Air Force, he claimed, could now aim directly to disarm an enemy nation and, therefore, would be able to avoid inflicting wanton destruction. General James Doolittle argued along the same lines as his chief. He believed the Air Force should limit its attacks to military targets so that the responsibility for "atomic slaughter" would clearly be on the Soviets if it occurred. The generals had returned to the optimistic theme that even wars fought with nuclear weapons could largely spare civilian populations.

The editors of *Commonweal* were among those reassured by the two generals' statements. Quoting Twining and Doolittle extensively, an editorial argued that tactical nuclear weapons could avert the "unimaginable horror" of a war of "strategic population bombings." They admitted that modern wars could not be fought without civilian casualties, but insisted that the use of tactical nuclear weapons could "materially reduce" the numbers of civilians killed.

The editors suggested that a promise by the U.S. government to warn civilians in enemy countries prior to any nuclear bombing of populated areas, a promise that Great Britain supposedly planned to make, would further alleviate concern over nuclear weapons. The editorial stated its disappointment over the United States' failure to make such a pledge.[13]

Proposals in 1954 to employ U.S. air power and possibly nuclear weapons to assist the French in Indochina gave other Air Force representatives the opportunity to express their support for narrowly targeted uses of force. General Otto P. Weyland, the former Air Force commander in the Korean War, shared his hope that air strikes would be against military targets. In an interview, Weyland said he wanted attacks not on Indochinese "hamlets, towns, and villages" but against "the main communications and supply centers, beyond Indo-China, used by the aggressors."[14]

Despite the sensitivity to the norm of noncombatant immunity at the Air Force's highest levels, a diversity of views on harming civilians remained among airmen. Brigadier General Dale O. Smith came close to declaring attacks on civilians a legitimate method in war in his article "The Morality of Retaliation," which he wrote for the *Air University Quarterly Review*. He argued that the Soviet leaders were dedicated to the destruction of the United States by any means and had proved their ruthlessness in their treatment of the Soviet population. Therefore, to Smith it was "perfectly moral" to employ "any conceivable weapon" against the Soviet Union in self-defense. "Those who speak of massive retaliation as being 'purposeless destruction, wasteful militarily, and indefensible morally,' are putting out the welcome mat for international desperados," he wrote. Although General Smith did not justify attacks on civilians explicitly, his arguments implied the legitimacy of such methods and certainly displayed less concern over harming civilians than did much of the Air Force leadership.[15]

During the summer of 1954 while controversy over the Bravo test still simmered, the U.S. military released a report that offered somewhat reassuring predictions about a nuclear war in Europe and that suggested the conventional nature of nuclear weapons. The Supreme Allied Command in Europe under General Alfred Gruenther released the study which examined how a war in Europe would be fought. The report concluded that any war in Europe would be a nuclear war but asserted that centers of population, capital cities, industrial centers, and ports would not be the first targets in an atomic war. The report contradicted the thinking of some top British strategic thinkers. It offered comfort to Europeans flirting with neutralism in the Cold War because of their concerns that they would be the first ones sacrificed in a third world war. The study's conclusion also proclaimed nuclear weapons integral to the American strategy to fight for Europe, while implying that this dependence would not necessarily result in massive destruction.

That same summer, the popular press began offering another round of articles on tactical nuclear weapons similar to the attention the arms received in 1951. These articles purported to clarify or offer an alternative to the policy of massive retaliation. They shared the view that tactical nuclear weapons would allow the United States to avoid city-destruction and the killing of civilians in its wars. *Fortune* magazine printed a piece by their Washington bureau chief Charles J. V. Murphy that criticized opponents of the massive retaliation policy like Adlai Stevenson and Chester Bowles. He argued that they had missed the "atomic alternative" to the destruction of cities that the use of tactical nuclear weapons against military targets provided. He wrote, "The real new meaning of 'massive retaliation' is that it can be dealt out in varying degrees, in a wide variety of military situations, and that it does not mean unconditional war upon cities alone."[16]

Several military officers wrote articles offering the tactical use of nuclear weapons as a substitute for city destruction. Colonel Richard S. Leghorn's contribution entitled "No Need to Bomb Cities to Win Wars" was featured on the front cover of *U.S. News and World Report* and had seventeen pages devoted to it. The former Air Force planner went further than most of the other tactical nuclear weapon enthusiasts in advocating that the United States unilaterally renounce nuclear attack on enemy cities unless friendly cities were attacked first. Colonel Leghorn believed that an enemy's armed forces could be defeated by striking them with nuclear weapons in a zone 100 miles deep from an aggressor's border and that industry, cities, and agriculture deeper in the hostile country's interior did not need to be attacked. If the enemy proved recalcitrant, the colonel speculated that a threat to "pulverize" production and cultural centers might be needed, but only after "appropriate warnings to the population to evacuate in keeping with our promise not to bomb population centers unless ours were first attacked." Indeed, Leghorn forecast disadvantages from American attacks on noncombatants. "As World War II demonstrated," he wrote, "to carry out wanton massacre of largely guiltless peoples would solidly unite any survivors in firm opposition to us and drive them into the hands of their regime." The colonel equated nuclear obliteration of innocent populations with genocide and maintained that fears of this destruction haunted world opinion and stimulated neutralism in Europe and Asia.[17]

All of the articles promoting tactical nuclear weapons were concerned with more than the problem of harm to noncombatants. They worried that unlimited nuclear war, now that the Soviet Union possessed thermonuclear weapons as well, would lead to the destruction of American cities and mutual suicide. They sought to make nuclear weapons interchangeable with conventional arms so that the United States and NATO could avoid a costly buildup in conventional forces to oppose Soviet might. Nevertheless, these articles also recognized that reconciling American methods of warfare with concerns about mass killing was a desirable objective, and they were optimistic that this could be done even in a nuclear war.

This second round of popular enthusiasm for tactical nuclear weapons coincided with increasing tensions between the United States and China over Taiwan. The first Taiwan straits crisis provided additional motivation for Eisenhower and his advisors to clarify that the United States would not depend on massively destructive methods to protect American interests abroad. The Eisenhower administration would not refrain from making nuclear threats against China, but they would work hard to convince American and world opinion that any nuclear attacks against China would be against purely military targets.

During late 1954 and early 1955, the United States and China again approached the brink of war. In September 1954, the armed forces of the People's Republic of China had begun shelling the Nationalist Chinese-occupied islands of Quemoy, Matsu, and the Tachens, which lay just a few miles off the Chinese coast between the mainland and Taiwan. U.S. allies in Europe, especially Britain, became uneasy over ambiguous American expressions of determination to defend Taiwan. Official U.S. statements left unclear whether the country would go to war over the offshore islands and what means the United States would use to respond to Chinese attacks.

As the tensions increased in early 1955, the Eisenhower administration responded in March with nuclear threats against the Chinese. The threats, however, carefully specified that the United States did not intend to use nuclear bombs indiscriminately against Chinese cities but instead would use tactical nuclear weapons against military targets. The previous month had brought several indications of public unease over the idea of obliterating enemy cities if a war were to come. In an NBC television interview, Senator Clinton Anderson, the chairman of the Joint Congressional Committee on Atomic Energy, warned about the international ramifications of threatening to use the atomic bomb indiscriminately. "I do feel there's a psychological danger if we just pitched in and said, we're going to blow everybody off the map," he commented. "I think that's a completely wrong approach." A few days later the branch of the State Department that monitored public opinion compiled a memorandum on the latest opinion polls on the hydrogen bomb from the National Opinion Research Center. Unlike earlier surveys that had shown predominant approval for bombing Russian cities in the case of a Soviet attack against Europe, the new polls revealed that 47 percent would oppose dropping the hydrogen bomb on Russian cities, while 41 percent would support it. More Americans also opposed striking Chinese cities with the hydrogen bomb in retaliation for attacks against Formosa than favored it according to the surveys. Four percent of those polled volunteered the thought that the United States should never use the hydrogen bomb.[18]

After the Secretary of State had returned from a trip to Asia, he and the president had two meetings in early March to discuss the Taiwan crisis and a speech that the secretary was preparing on the Asian situation. According to Dulles, they agreed that the use of nuclear weapons would be necessary to defend the offshore islands and that further efforts were needed to educate the public on the nature of nuclear weapons and to combat the taboo against their use. Eisenhower proposed that Dulles include a paragraph in his speech indicating that the United States would use atomic weapons interchangeably with conventional weapons. Dulles wrote in his memorandum of the conversation that this "did not, of course, mean weapons of mass destruction." Eisenhower was considering using nuclear weapons against Chinese airfields and gun emplacements because of the limited forces that the United States had in the western Pacific. In their second meeting, they again discussed the importance of educating the public on the distinction between "atomic missiles for tactical purposes and the big bomb with huge radioactive fall-outs."[19]

This education campaign, which echoed the attempts in 1951 to sanitize the image of nuclear weapons, became a widespread effort across the highest levels of the Eisenhower administration with Dulles serving as its leading voice. In the secretary's speech on Asia, he said the United States might respond to Chinese attacks with greater force. To back up his threat, he referred to American sea and air forces "now equipped with new and powerful weapons of precision, which can utterly destroy military targets without endangering unrelated civilian centers." The press immediately inferred that the "new" weapons that Dulles had mentioned were tactical nuclear weapons rather than "city-destroying" hydrogen bombs.

On March 10, Dulles brought up the need to shape public thinking on nuclear weapons during a NSC meeting. Since the military insisted that nuclear weapons would have to be used in a fight to defend the offshore islands, Dulles expressed his concern that American leaders might wake up one day and find that they were inhibited in using these weapons because of negative public opinion. The secretary said that the military people on the spot in Taiwan were greatly worried over this prospect. Dulles believed the solution could be found in reassuring the public that tactical nuclear weapons were no different from conventional weapons, that they were not necessarily implements of mass destruction. He wanted to convince world opinion that the arms could be used against solely military targets without destroying cities and killing civilians. At the NSC meeting, the secretary insisted that it was of vital importance that the administration urgently educate American and international opinion about tactical nuclear weapons. He believed much more needed to be done beyond the comments in his recent speech to mold public perceptions. He feared that Asian opinion was not attuned at all to the possibility of using tactical nuclear weapons in the straits of Taiwan.[20]

Dulles, the president, and the vice president each made comments about tactical nuclear weapons in the week following. At a press conference, the secretary of state elaborated on his previous comments about "new" weapons. He clarified that he had indeed been referring to tactical nuclear weapons, which he claimed were "weapons of precision" and were becoming "conventional" in the U.S. armed forces. Prompted by a reporter who asked if these weapons were "for military targets," Dulles assured that they were and shared his belief that the likelihood of the use of weapons of mass destruction might actually decrease as tactical nuclear weapons became more plentiful. Dulles explained, "To a very considerable extent in the last World War it proved necessary, or judged necessary, to have bombing on cities and population centers because it was not possible otherwise to put the actual military works out of business. If you can put the military works definitely out of business, I don't think you're going to need to kill civilians on the scale that was done, unhappily, during the last World War."

The following day the president at his own press conference reinforced his secretary's comments. Eisenhower explained that he saw no valid objection to using tactical nuclear weapons against military objectives. He said: "Now, in any combat where these things can be used on strictly military targets and for strictly military purposes, I see no reason why they shouldn't be used just exactly as you would use a bullet or anything else. I believe the great question about these things comes when you begin to get into those areas where you cannot make sure that you are operating merely against military targets. But with that one qualification, I would say, yes, of course, they would be used." The president's statement made the destruction of civilian communities and harm to noncombatants the single consideration impinging on the use of nuclear weapons in war, and Eisenhower endorsed this view again in another press conference a week later. Several days later, Vice President Nixon, after consulting with Dulles, wrote into one of his speeches a reiteration of the line that tactical nuclear weapons were now "conventional."[21]

Dulles and Eisenhower were not using the expanded definition of "military target" that Americans had utilized during the Korea War which included virtually all physical structures. They seemed to be promising that American use of tactical nuclear weapons would not destroy cities or slaughter civilians. By promoting the supremely optimistic view that the effects of nuclear weapons could be restricted entirely to military targets narrowly defined, America's top leaders sought to strip away what they saw as the primary liability of nuclear weapons: that they were weapons of mass destruction which harmed civilians.

To plan for future efforts to mold public opinion concerning nuclear weapons, the NSC staff organized a working group effort on "courses of action to achieve better public understanding of the varying effects of sizes and types of nuclear weapons." A paper from the group identified the sources of "misunderstanding" among Americans and peoples abroad. For one, questioning of

U.S. official statements that had "depicted employment of small nuclear weapons as without significant hazard to unrelated civilian areas" contributed to the problem. The Communist press also exploited concerns over the radiation hazard from nuclear testing in order to convince the world that all nuclear weapons, small or large, were "horror weapons." The working group sought to convince world opinion that the United States possessed a varied "family" of nuclear weapons adaptable for use in a variety of military situations and that not all detonations of nuclear weapons produced great amounts of radioactive fallout.[22]

The press latched onto the March 1955 statements by Dulles, Eisenhower, and Nixon and declared that the administration had modified its policy of massive retaliation. The administration's comments about the discriminate use of nuclear weapons were a regular feature of New York Times coverage during the month of March. The newspaper's writers labeled the new policy "less-than-massive retaliation" or "measured retaliation." They elaborated on the official statements turning them into even greater promises of protection for noncombatants than the comments stated explicitly. One article depicted the Secretary of State as suggesting that the new tactical nuclear weapons offered "a chance for victory on the battlefield without harming civilians." Ernest K. Lindley, a Newsweek columnist, believed that Dulles had ruled out the use of the hydrogen bomb with its "far-roaming deadly fallouts" against the Chinese and predicted that Hiroshima would not be repeated. Lindley admitted that the line between tactical and other uses of nuclear and conventional weapons might be difficult to define, but he believed it was an important distinction to make. He wrote, "But there is a difference between precise attacks on selected military targets with bombs of strictly limited power and the bombing of whole cities or depopulation of whole areas with weapons of other magnitudes. It is a difference which, if there has to be war, may be important to establish." An issue of Life ran an editorial and a photo essay highlighting the administration's message that tactical nuclear weapons could limit the risk to civilian populations. The editorial referred to this process as the "domestication" of atomic warfare.[23]

Secretary Dulles was a prime example of an American who worried about modern war's potential for indiscriminate destruction, but came to believe that the United States could tame its nuclear weapons and use them discriminately in war. Not fully understanding the American discourse on noncombatant immunity, historians have had a difficult time making sense of Dulles' ambivalent attitudes toward nuclear weapons.[24] Indeed, Dulles vacillated on the questions of international control and the value of the weapons as a deterrent, but his thinking on nuclear weapons possessed a coherence held together by his confrontation with the dilemma of indiscriminate destruction. Dulles demonstrated a consistent concern over indiscriminate destruction in war throughout his public career, but he changed his mind when he was Secretary of State about the nature of nuclear weapons. Shedding an earlier skepticism, he came to believe that nuclear weapons were not inherently implements of mass destruction.

From the first appearance of the atomic bomb, Dulles demonstrated his penchant for anxiety over indiscriminate destruction. When confronted with the devastation wrought by World War II, Dulles had expressed this concern. As chair of the Federal Council of Churches' Commission on a Just and Durable Peace, Dulles authored a press release that had called for the slowing of the atomic bombing campaign to give the Japanese people a chance to surrender. In the release, Dulles argued that continuing to wreak "mass destruction" on Japan would "inevitably obliterate men and women, young and aged, innocent and guilty alike" and would set a disturbing precedent for the use of atomic weapons which could threaten the annihilation of humankind. His 1950 book *War or Peace*, likewise, observed that after World War II the moral condemnation of war had become nearly universal. "There is no longer any glorification of war, and the religious conception of a 'just war' is undergoing modification now that wars carry with them mass and indiscriminate destruction of non-belligerents." Following Truman's decision to proceed with the construction of the hydrogen bomb in early 1950, Dulles concluded a Chicago speech with his thoughts on the matter. He again acknowledged the importance of the "moral issue about the nature of modern war and its mass and indiscriminate destruction," but he expressed his puzzlement over what he called the "hysteria" over nuclear weapons because conventional weapons such as fire bombs could cause mass destruction as well. Dulles was starting to frame the central issue as indiscriminate destruction and not the particular weapon that delivered it.[25]

Before his appointment as Secretary of State, Dulles had opposed the idea that nuclear weapons should be thought of and used as if they were conventional weapons.[26] Although it is only speculation, he may have taken this stance in part because he still believed that nuclear arms were unavoidably weapons of mass destruction. However, once in office, Dulles became progressively more optimistic that nuclear arms could be used as discriminate weapons of war. Before the administration began its efforts in late 1953 to foster the acceptance of nuclear arms as conventional and precise weapons, Dulles began expressing in private meetings the need to dispel the taboo against using nuclear weapons and to eliminate the stigma of immorality attached to them.[27] Dulles' change of heart might have been influenced by information that he was being fed from the JCS Chairman Admiral Arthur Radford, another committed optimist. During the Taiwan Straits Crisis, Robert Bowie, the head of the State Department's Policy Planning Staff commissioned a Central Intelligence Agency (CIA) study to estimate the number of civilian casualties that a nuclear attack on Chinese military targets would entail. Bowie feared that Radford was providing Dulles with overoptimistic assurances.

The CIA report estimated that millions of civilians would be killed.[28] Dulles' new attitude was also probably fueled by wishful thinking. He found indiscriminate destruction contrary to his moral beliefs but believed nuclear weapons to be important for the defense of the United States against the Soviet Union, a deterrent to indiscriminate nuclear war but also a useful weapon in more limited forms of conflict. Dulles' hope, which lingered until the end of his tenure as secretary of state, that the United States could develop smaller "clean" nuclear weapons that would cause very little radioactive fallout and less destruction, was a sign of his wishful thinking.[29]

7.4 The Importance of Intention

As the Taiwan Straits Crisis and the continued attention to tactical nuclear weapons demonstrated, American optimism that force could still be used discriminately, even in a nuclear war, remained vigorous despite the arrival of the hydrogen bomb. However, this persistent faith was not the only way that Americans attempted to preserve a notion of noncombatant immunity in the face of the thermonuclear challenge. As it had during the Korean War, the importance of intentions became central to American thinking about its massively destructive nuclear arsenal.

The evolution of President Eisenhower's thinking about nuclear weapons reflected this growing significance of intentions. Eisenhower followed a different path in his attitudes toward nuclear weapons than his secretary of state. Eisenhower shared Dulles' concern over indiscriminate civilian destruction and believed, especially early in his administration, that nuclear weapons in the abstract did not differ from conventional weapons in that both could be used discriminately against an enemy's armed forces or liberally against noncombatant populations. However, unlike Dulles who grew more optimistic that nuclear weapons could realistically serve as a precisely controlled form of violence, Eisenhower became less convinced that nuclear weapons could be employed in war without massive civilian death. The general-turned-president instead came to hope that the threat of the terrible devastation that a general war with the Soviet Union would bring would make such a dreadful war less likely.

Recent scholarship has forcefully argued that Eisenhower's views toward nuclear war changed with the advent of thermonuclear weapons. Toward the end of his first term as president, Eisenhower became convinced that the growing American and Soviet arsenal of hydrogen bombs had made a war between them senseless. He abandoned the idea that a general war, like World War II, could be won in any meaningful sense and that tactical nuclear weapons could be used as conventional weapons without sparking a thermonuclear conflagration.[30] "There is a distinct difference now between the present and the past in so far as in past wars there had always been a victor — now there would be none as all parties engaged in the war and a large segment of humanity not engaged would be destroyed," Eisenhower said in a 1960 conversation.[31] A better understanding of Eisenhower's thinking about harm to civilians helps to illuminate this transformation, both his changed attitudes toward nuclear arms as conventional weapons and his apparently contradictory statements and actions concerning nuclear war.

From Eisenhower's public and private statements, there is good reason to believe that he was disturbed by the idea of indiscriminate harm to civilians in war and particularly the potential of nuclear weapons to inflict such harm, an attitude that earlier studies of Eisenhower have missed. Although he never articulated his unease as concerns for the protection of innocent civilians, he made a number of comments about the horror of nuclear weapons and his desire to see the arms used only against military targets. In his memoirs of World War II, Eisenhower recalled when the Secretary of War first informed him of the atomic bomb's existence. He remembered disliking the prospect that the United States would introduce into war something as "horrible and destructive" as the bomb.[32] When Americans were discussing the possible use of atomic weapons early in the Korean War, Eisenhower said publicly, "I would avoid using anything that our own people or other peoples might consider inhuman. It is imperative that we stand before the world as champions of decency." He believed the atomic bomb should not be used "against personnel" but said he did not object to its employment against a material target of great value to the enemy such as a vast warehouse area.[33] Likewise, while historians often quote Eisenhower's comment during the first Taiwan Straits Crisis about using nuclear weapons like a "bullet," they have neglected his qualification that the weapons be exclusively used against military targets. Early in 1956, Eisenhower directed the JCS to review SAC war plans to ensure that thermonuclear weapons were only used when necessary. He feared that the current plans might be overly reliant on the weapons and could produce unnecessary population losses.[34] These pieces of evidence suggest that Eisenhower was consistently concerned with avoiding civilian casualties in war.

Eisenhower's sensitivity to indiscriminate destruction helps to explain the change in his beliefs about tactical nuclear weapons. Until his change of heart about nuclear war, Eisenhower talked about tactical nuclear weapons as if they could be used like conventional weapons in a discriminate manner against enemy armed forces. In addition to his public statements in 1955, he had discussed with the JCS, the possibility of using tactical nuclear weapons against "military targets" to bring to a close the Korean War, and he made other private comments to the effect that tactical nuclear arms should be considered conventional weapons.[35] Like other Americans, Eisenhower could abstractly conceive of ways in which nuclear weapons might be used without causing massive and indiscriminate destruction. However, with growing Soviet nuclear strength, he lost his faith that nuclear weapons could be used in a limited manner without escalating to all-out thermonuclear war.

Other historians have suggested that Eisenhower changed his thinking about nuclear weapons because he came to believe that modern war required the use of means unfettered by humanitarian sentiments.[36] However, there is evidence that his shift in attitudes came about not because of what he thought about modern war in general but because of what he thought of the Soviets in particular. He came to believe he faced an enemy in the Soviets who did not value the humanitarian sentiments that Americans did. In Eisenhower's thinking, the amorality of the Soviets, and not the logic of war itself, would lead to uncontrollable escalation.

For example, in May of 1956, Eisenhower argued with the new Army Chief of Staff Maxwell Taylor that the United States should plan to use nuclear weapons in every kind of war. Eisenhower's staff secretary, Colonel Andrew J. Goodpaster, wrote that the president thought Taylor's position against this mandatory use of nuclear weapons was based on a flawed assumption. Eisenhower criticized Taylor for assuming "that we are opposed by people who would think as we do with regard to the value of human life. But they do not, as shown in many incidents from the last war. We have no basis for thinking that they abhor destruction as we do." Goodpaster's memo went on to explain that the president believed that should the Soviets decide to go to war against the United States they would be under "extremely great" pressure to use atomic weapons in a sudden blow. Therefore, the United States had to plan for the use of nuclear weapons in any war with the Soviets.[37] Although Eisenhower may have thought that the United States could use nuclear weapons in a discriminate manner, he came to believe that a Soviet retaliation would not. The Soviets, therefore, would force America into a suicidal cycle of massive destruction.

Believing that war with the Soviets would become a thermonuclear holocaust, Eisenhower sought to shape American policy to reflect this belief. Paradoxically, out of a concern over indiscriminate devastation, he worked to ensure any war with the Soviet Union would be massively and indiscriminately destructive. His counterintuitive approach was based on the hope that the threat of this devastation would prevent the dreaded war. As historian Campbell Craig has argued, Eisenhower from 1955 to 1957 worked to remove the idea of limited war against the Soviet Union from American war plans. Eisenhower had as his goal the strengthening of deterrence. When the basic national security policy for 1957 came under review, Eisenhower insisted that it be rewritten to emphasize greater reliance on nuclear weapons, to restrict the notion of limited war to wars in the developing world, and to eliminate reference to the need for the flexible and selective use of force.[38] Eisenhower's repulsion at massive and indiscriminate destruction strengthened his conviction that nuclear war must be avoided, but to do so, he believed, required preparations for an irrational, genocidal war he never intended to wage. Eisenhower's nuclear policies in his second term, which might superficially appear to reject any notion of noncombatant immunity, ironically stemmed in part from the president's concerns over indiscriminate devastation. They also aligned with the American reinterpretation of noncombatant immunity that accepted the possibility of harm to civilians in war but only if it was unintentional.

Others outside the government came more quickly to skepticism about the possibility of using nuclear weapons without massive civilian destruction than had Eisenhower. During the Taiwan Straits Crisis, the broadcast commentator Edward Murrow questioned the administration's claim that nuclear weapons could be used to defend the offshore islands without destroying cities and slaughtering civilians. Murrow feared that any use of nuclear arms, particularly because of the danger of radioactive fallout, would harm large numbers of civilians and spur the Soviet Union to retaliate against the American civilian population. The military editor of the *New York Times* Hanson Baldwin voiced similar views. He argued that while the accuracy of bomb delivery had improved, no dramatic methods for ensuring that a nuclear weapon would be placed exactly on target had emerged. Delivery remained subject to the whims of weather and human error. Many military targets such as air fields were close to cities which the large explosions of nuclear bombs could threaten. A joint maneuver by the Army and Air Force in late 1955 that simulated a war with tactical nuclear weapons reinforced Baldwin's impressions. The exercise postulated the use of 275 nuclear weapons by both sides ranging in explosive power from between the equivalent of two kilotons of TNT to forty kilotons, which was twice the power of the bomb that destroyed Hiroshima. To Baldwin, the maneuver demonstrated that a so-called tactical nuclear war would cause vast devastation. He claimed that if the exercise had been a real war, the southern United States, where the simulation took place, would have suffered far more death and destruction than the Union forces had inflicted on the region during the entire Civil War.[39]

Having difficulties maintaining his optimism over discriminate nuclear weapons, Hanson Baldwin was one of a number of Americans who had embraced more fully than Eisenhower a mode of rationalizing the possession of nuclear weapons that characterized the United States as a reluctant possessor of the arms intent on avoiding their use. Like some during the discussion of the hydrogen bomb in early 1950, Baldwin perceived a need for nuclear weapons, but at the same time believed their actual use in war would be a disaster. With both sides armed with thermonuclear bombs, Baldwin equated nuclear war with indiscriminate destruction. He believed that the weapons' large areas of effect would spread death and destruction widely to cities and entire populations and that the use of tactical nuclear weapons would likely escalate to an unlimited holocaust. The mutual devastation that an atomic war would bring, Baldwin argued, could serve no political objective, would not establish a more stable peace, and would deliver only a Pyrrhic victory to the winner. As he put it, "The wholesale and indiscriminate nuclear bombardment of cities is not war; it is suicide." Even though nuclear war would be a catastrophe for all involved, Baldwin still saw a use for nuclear weapons. "We must maintain the power to wipe out Moscow in order to deter the enemy from wiping out New York," he wrote. Baldwin's position accepted the need for nuclear weapons to deter unlimited war at the same time that it expressed revulsion at their use. This thinking conveniently acknowledged the horrors of indiscriminate destruction and stressed the lack of intention on the part of Americans to use the massively destructive weapons. It would be insane to Baldwin's way of thinking to intend the consequences of a nuclear war as he foresaw them.[40]

However, if use of the weapons was so irrational, the question remained whether a potential enemy had anything to fear from this unusable arsenal. Ideas, such as Baldwin's, differed dramatically from conventional thinking about deterrence, so much so that they constituted a new paradoxical form of the concept. Deterrence whether in wars or penal systems had traditionally been based on the notion that punishment would be meted out to those who violated an injunction. Others would learn to uphold the injunction both from the threat of punishment and the example of those punished. However, if the punishment itself created a situation disastrous to all concerned, as many argued nuclear war would, how could the sanction ever be imposed? The certainty that a violator would be punished — the basis for the intimidation that would restrain potential miscreants — could not exist. Baldwin's nuclear deterrence could only threaten in the hope of never having to punish. This paradoxical idea of nuclear deterrence allowed many Americans to reconcile the possession of terrible weapons and a theoretical willingness to use them with an abhorrence at their use and the indiscriminate destruction that they caused. The stance may not have been strictly logical, but it did serve as a useful mechanism for some to combine in their thinking two contradictory values, the belief that nuclear weapons enhanced American security and the norm of noncombatant immunity.

Thomas Finletter, who served as secretary of the Air Force under Truman but continued to write about military policy after he left office, was another prominent example of this way of thinking. As secretary of the Air Force, Finletter revealed in public and confidential remarks his beliefs about modern war and the balance of terror. Finletter believed that the escalation in destructive firepower, which nuclear weapons introduced, changed the fundamental nature of war. War had always been destructive, but with the new weapons it would be cataclysmic for both sides. The secretary believed that banning certain methods of war would not eliminate the moral concerns that exercised Americans. War was unlimited and terrible, and the only way to avoid its horror was to prevent it from occurring by thoroughly preparing for it. In a widely discussed book published in 1954 after he left public service, Finletter marshaled his cataclysmic views of nuclear war to support his arguments for a great expansion in U.S. capability to deliver a devastating nuclear blow against the Soviet Union. Finletter admitted that actually fighting a nuclear war would be a catastrophe for the United States, which would leave its cities in ruins. Such a war could not be won in the traditional sense. It could only be won "by seeing to it that the Russians dare not start the war." They would refrain from doing so, according to Finletter, if the United States had the capacity to devastate their nation. Finletter was not simply reluctant to use nuclear weapons in war when necessary. He believed it would be an unmitigated disaster. To use nuclear weapons would be a catastrophe, but to live without them would eliminate America's best chance for peace.[41]

Thinking like Baldwin's and Finletter's laid a foundation for the peculiar policy of "mutually assured destruction" that many American leaders in later years claimed enhanced U.S. security. Understanding Americans' struggle over the contradiction between massively destructive methods of war and noncombatant immunity helps to explain the apparent contradiction that historians have observed that some of the country's noted liberals, especially by the early 1960s, most strongly supported plans to enhance U.S. potential for indiscriminate destruction. It was those most sensitive to concerns about harm to noncombatants, but who could not remain optimistic that a nuclear war would spare cities and civilians, who sought reassurance from the balance of terror that would supposedly prevent their worst fears from coming true.

In confronting public concerns about the potential holocaust of a World War III, various officials emphasized that the United States desired to avoid a horrible war implying that the country never intended to harm civilians. In early 1954, the chairwoman of United Church Women of the National Council of the Churches of Christ wrote Secretary Dulles to question whether the shift in defense policy toward a greater dependence on nuclear weapons, which could result in the "dreadful" weapons' use against Moscow or Beijing, was morally defensible. The State Department's response assured the organization that President Eisenhower fully understood the terrible consequences of an atomic war and that, therefore, U.S. policy sought "to achieve peace and avoid war," while arming against the Communist threat. The newly organized U.S. Information Agency (USIA) issued guidance to its officers overseas on how to present U.S. policies on nuclear weapons in the wake of the concern over the Castle Bravo test. The guidance said that the USIA must demonstrate that a "responsible, humane, calm, and rational attitude" characterized American policies. One of its specific recommendations was to make clear that U.S. nuclear weapon development was designed to deter aggression. The instructions suggested giving prominent place to President Eisenhower's April 5 statement that the hydrogen bomb would never "be used by our initiative."[42] Government publicists worked to convey the impression of a humane American people reluctant to use weapons of mass destruction.

This image of an American people reluctant to kill civilians posed a tricky problem for the Air Force's SAC. SAC commanders and publicists had to strike a balance between toughness and sensitivity in their efforts to depict the organization's contribution to national security. Since SAC's primary mission was to deter war through the threat of nuclear devastation that its bombers could deliver, the organization could not appear to be constrained from carrying out this threat by moral qualms over harming civilians. SAC Commander Curtis LeMay, therefore, cooperated with journalists on articles that emphasized his and his forces' toughness and professional certitude. A *Life* magazine piece called General LeMay, the "Toughest Cop of the Western World." It assured its readers that LeMay had not been deterred from firebombing the cities of Japan — operations that he commanded during World War II — despite the numerous "innocent and hapless men, women, and babies" that were killed, and he would not hesitate to use nuclear-armed SAC against any enemy of the United States in a war.

Yet SAC and General LeMay sought to temper their tough image so as not to appear callous to harm to civilians. In the press, SAC fought the impression that they would ever intentionally conduct indiscriminate bombing or that they sought to fight a war against civilians. The military editor of the *New York Times* assured that the SAC training program was not based on "promiscuous devastation" but instead stressed accuracy in bombing. In an interview for *U.S. News and World Report*, General LeMay explicitly denied that wars could be won by killing or terrorizing civilian populations. "I don't think it is humane or effective to attack a people or a population as such," he stated. The interviewer responded, "There has been an impression, I think, in the country that the purpose of these nuclear weapons was to terrorize the other people and hence bring a war to a successful end. What is your view on that?" LeMay said, "No, I don't believe that. You don't win wars by terrorizing people." SAC did not want to appear hampered by moral norms, but neither did it want to be smeared as a force that waged calculated wars against civilians.[43]

Even away from the public eye, those most familiar with how the U.S. military planned to fight a war with the Soviet Union asserted that American armed forces did not intend to kill civilians. Like in U.S. war plans from the late 1940s and early 1950s, other confidential documents show military officers unwilling to depict their proposals for how to conduct war against the Soviet Union as intentional targeting of civilian populations. In April 1954, Major General R. C. Lindsey, director of Plans for the Air Force, delivered a top secret briefing to Defense Department officials on the strategic air offensive. In discussing the effects of a massive nuclear attack on the Soviet Union, Lindsey admitted that the Air Force could not readily calculate how the damage would effect the enemy's will to continue hostilities. To produce the maximum shock effect on the Soviet population and government, air attacks, the general explained, would be completed in as few days as possible, but by this

he did not mean that civilians would be intentionally targeted. Lindsey continued, "While it is not our purpose deliberately to cause civilian casualties, the
large number of casualties that would necessarily occur, plus widespread
urban damage and difficult living conditions, will have a serious if not decisive
effect on the enemy's desire to prolong the war." The Air Force predicted heavy
civilian casualties from American weapons; it hoped to gain an advantage in
the war through noncombatant suffering and death; yet its director of Plans
believed it necessary to add the qualification that the Air Force did not intend
to harm civilians. Whether Lindsey qualified his remarks because it made
thoughts of the terrible consequences of the strategic air offensive easier for
him and his colleagues to bear or out of concern that those outside his service
would again attack the Air Force for planning to kill civilians like the Navy did
in 1949, the briefing suggested that intention to kill noncombatants was
becoming the core of what Americans believed the norm of noncombatant
immunity forbid. Lindsey could not deny that the Air Force would kill civilians, but he could insist that was not their deliberate purpose. When Americans could no longer deny that their massively destructive weapons would kill
noncombatants, they clung to a remnant of the tradition of noncombatant
immunity by claiming that harm to civilians was an unintended consequence
of the way Americans had chosen to prepare for war.[44]

Outside the government, the idea of warning civilian populations of
nuclear attack remained a popular way of demonstrating American good
intentions. Richard Leghorn's prominent article on tactical nuclear weapons
advocated warnings to civilians if the United States had to resort to destroying
industry. The pages of *Commonweal* repeatedly expressed support for warnings and affirmed the moral significance of intention. The editors explained
that the traditional Christian principles of just warfare held that the destruction of noncombatants could not be directly intended in a military action.
Harm to civilians was justified only if it occurred as an unavoidable consequence of an attack against a legitimate military target and only if the importance of the target outweighed the evil of the injury. A reprinted editorial from
the Indiana diocesan newspaper believed the country's moral integrity was
secure because Americans did not "intend" to use nuclear weapons and would
only do so if attacked.[45]

7.5 The Revolt of the Generals

The public equation of massive retaliation with indiscriminate destruction,
which the Eisenhower administration worked to dispel but could not always
elide, allowed noncombatant immunity again to become a weapon in the bud-
getary duels of the U.S. military as it had in 1949. A less dramatic but more
persistent "Revolt of the Generals" played itself out from 1954 to 1956 as Army
generals stood in for the earlier Navy provocateurs and clubbed administration policy with the blunt instrument of professed concern for enemy

civilians. Central to Eisenhower's New Look for the armed forces were budget cuts and force reductions that struck the Army the hardest. When the Army Chief of Staff Matthew Ridgway failed to stem these cuts through wrangling within the administration, he and his fellow Army officers took their case to the public. They argued that cuts in conventional ground forces would leave the country unwisely dependent on massive retaliation with nuclear weapons. One of their primary charges against massive retaliation was that it inflicted massive harm on noncombatants.

The generals did not have so dramatic a venue for their complaints as the public congressional hearings that had captured national attention for the Navy in 1949, but the Army leadership made use of the outlets they had open to them to broadcast their message. In late 1954, the Army issued a new basic field manual on operations that included choice words against waging war on civilians. The manual declared that "indiscriminate destruction" against an enemy was militarily unjustifiable. It suggested that, except "in the prosecution of war in furtherance of a policy of ruthless annihilation," the Army, of all the services, most closely conformed to the requirements of national policy since its forces were "designed to apply power directly against military power, with minimum damage to civilian populations and economies." The manual conceded that "damage to civilian economies and enemy centers of population is an incident to military operations that may be unavoidable," but assured readers that "Army forces do not deliberately make or invite war upon civilian populations." In January 1955, the *New York Times* noticed the inflammatory additions to the field manual and printed an article about them, quoting the passages that condemned war against civilians and those that declared minimizing civilian casualties a requirement of national policy.

The *Army Combat Forces Journal* published an article the same month written under the pseudonym "Colonel Shillelagh" that laced its criticism of the New Look's dependence on air power with references to civilian destruction. The author was most likely the three-star general James M. Gavin, the deputy chief of staff for Research and Development, who had started organizing in 1953 Army officers disgruntled over the implications of American reliance on strategic bombing. The article argued that the New Look had distorted military thinking in a number of ways. Military leaders had "accepted civil destruction as an object of war and a means of war where formerly it was an incident of war," and they had "rejected the precept that indecisive brutality and destruction which advantages neither side will be outlawed by mutual consent or forbearance." These misguided beliefs had obscured, according to the author, that wars had political objectives and that defeating an enemy's armed forces was a surer way to these objectives than attempts to extinguish an enemy's intangible "will to resist," which led to "brutalization of war" and "a preoccupation with mass destruction." Trying to sound hardheaded, the article insisted that it was raising not a question "of humanity but of reality," but the piece clearly smeared current military policy as unnecessarily brutal.

When General Ridgway retired as Army chief of staff in June 1955 largely because of his conflicts with Eisenhower's advisors over military policy, he made several more public criticisms. A letter he had written to Secretary of Defense Charles Wilson leaked to the press and in the subsequent long-simmering controversy, Ridgway elaborated his criticisms through a series of *Saturday Evening Post* articles and the publication of his memoirs in 1956. A professed concern over indiscriminate destruction pervaded this criticism. Ridgway said he opposed mass bombing and the destruction of enemy industry because he believed that wars were won by defeating enemy armed forces. "Furthermore," he wrote, "such mass destruction, to my mind, is repugnant to the ideals of a Christian nation, and incompatible with the basic aim of the free world in war, which is to win a just and lasting peace." Although Army criticisms did not attract the public attention that the earlier Navy protests had, noncombatant immunity remained a sentiment that military officers could use to appeal for public support of their favored policies.[46]

7.6 Ratification of the Geneva Conventions on War Victims

The same year that Ridgway retired, the U.S. Senate finally ratified the four Geneva Conventions on war victims. In 1949, the U.S. government had signed the conventions, which concerned the treatment of the sick and wounded, prisoners of war, and civilians in war time, but the State Department had asked the Senate to postpone ratification of the conventions during the Korean War. The treaty's ratification in 1955 was ironic but understandable. The United States became a full party to an international agreement for the protection of noncombatants just as it was incorporating into its arsenal the hydrogen bomb, the largest threat to civilian populations that military technology had ever introduced into warfare. Nevertheless, since 1949, so many U.S. officials and other American citizens speaking out on the issue had expressed their continued support for noncombatant immunity it is not surprising that policymakers in 1955 decided it was necessary to enshrine in law protections for noncombatants. Soviet ratification of the Geneva Conventions in May 1954 provided the final nudge that revived American interest in the agreement.

Almost immediately after the Soviet ratification, the Department of Defense sent a letter to the Department of State requesting that it end its objection to the ratification of the four Geneva Conventions. Besides pointing out that ratification of the conventions could simplify military planning, the letter raised the political disadvantage that the country would face if it remained the sole great power not a party to the Geneva Conventions of 1949. France had ratified them; Britain was in the process of ratifying them; and the Soviet Union had recently become a party to them. State Department officials initially hesitated to move on the treaty because they feared that U.S. action during the Korean War had not been entirely consistent with the conventions. Once they studied this issue more closely, they uncovered the U.N. Command's lack of compliance with the convention on civilians during the war. Yet concerns over the propaganda advantage that the Soviet Union would reap if the United States did not follow their lead pushed aside the liability that the U.S. military had refused to implement the civilian convention in the only American war since the agreement had been drafted. The Senate Foreign Relations Committee held hearings on the conventions in June 1955 and the full Senate ratified the treaty the following month.[47]

Given the American military's past record on implementing the civilian convention, its passage served more as another official expression of optimism about the country's ability to fight a war that spared civilians from excessive suffering than as a practical solution to the terrible problem of harm to noncombatants. Hopes, aspirations, and good intentions governed American thinking about mass killing and wartime civilian suffering after World War II. Optimism for reconciling noncombatant immunity with modern warfare remained strong even after the United States had incorporated into its arsenal the most destructive weapon humankind had ever invented. When Americans could not deny that their way of war would kill immense numbers of civilians, they created rationales that reinforced the idea that Americans never intended injury to noncombatants. These ways of thinking made American warfare appear more humane to many in the United States and others overseas, but they provided little guarantee that American soldiers and their weapons would not kill civilians by the thousands or conceivably millions.

8
An Uneasy Reconciliation

The confused ambivalence toward noncombatant immunity apparent among Americans in 1945 had given way by the middle of the 1950s to a widely accepted, if uneasy, reconciliation. Dissenters at the poles of opinion continued to advocate abandoning all protections for civilians or giving up massively destructive methods of warfare, but most Americans appeared weary of the costs of these parsimonious solutions. Forsaking the norm of noncombatant immunity promised international condemnation and distrust. It also threatened Americans' conceptions of themselves as a humane people. Giving up massively destructive war threatened to heighten Americans' sense of vulnerability and insecurity. Instead, Americans kept their devastating weapons and adapted the international tradition of noncombatant immunity to their circumstances and purposes.

As they had before 1945, Americans persisted in optimistically denying a conflict between their methods of warfare and the protection of noncombatants despite the phenomenal burgeoning of U.S. firepower. Many still believed that the American military could control the violence it unleashed and avoid harming civilians. Faith in American ingenuity and technological wizardry helped to bolster this optimism. However, the reinterpretation of noncombatant immunity that emerged during this period also made the optimism easier to maintain. The protections that Americans offered to the civilian segment of an enemy's society shrunk with the Korean War and the expansion of the U.S. nuclear arsenal. In war, virtually any physical structure that made the slimmest and most indirect contribution to an enemy's war efforts could become a "military target," and attacking cities as such became less controversial among the public, but few Americans came to accept direct attacks on civilians as a legitimate means for waging war. Even more significantly, the American adaptation of noncombatant immunity identified intent as the vital distinction between war and atrocity. The importance of intention manifested itself in Americans' provision of relief aid to suffering civilian populations, preoccupation with the impractical notion of warning civilians of impending attacks, tendency to place blame for civilian suffering on an enemy aggressor, and invention of a form of unenforceable deterrence. Other attempts at reconciliation — technical fixes guaranteeing reliably precise uses of force, elaboration of international law, or the international control of atomic energy — were unfeasible or inadequate on their own in easing the post war dilemma.

8.1 The Enduring Legacy

Although this reconciliation formed in the decade after World War II, its legacy lasted through the Cold War and beyond. Optimistic denial, elastic definitions of military targets, and the significance of intention continued to dominate public discussions of American mass killing. The three themes infused controversies over nuclear strategy, the Vietnam War, the Persian Gulf War, and the interventions in Afghanistan and Iraq. Although the full story of Americans and noncombatant immunity from 1955 to the early twenty-first century cannot be told here, the following survey argues for the pervasive legacy of the uneasy reconciliation forged in the aftermath of World War II.

After the introduction of thermonuclear weapons, noncombatant immunity continued to complicate discussions of nuclear strategy. Debate over nuclear strategy reached a climax in the early 1960s when John F. Kennedy entered the White House. Having criticized the inflexibility of the New Look, Kennedy selected Robert S. McNamara to serve as his Secretary of Defense and to review the country's military policies. McNamara's forays into nuclear policy brought greater public attention to two competing schools of thought on nuclear strategy: counterforce and assured destruction. These doctrines dominated discussions of nuclear war for the rest of the Cold War and each partially conformed to the uneasy reconciliation of massive destruction and noncombatant immunity.

Early in the Kennedy administration, counterforce doctrine gained McNamara's favor. The strategy targeted American nuclear weapons against enemy armed forces such as missile silos, air bases, and submarine pens. Civilian analysts from the RAND Corporation, several of whom came to work for McNamara in the Defense Department, had promoted a version of counterforce strategy that not only targeted armed forces but intentionally avoided the destruction of cities and their populations. McNamara briefly adopted this no-cities idea as the basis for nuclear war planning and announced this policy to the public in a June 1962 commencement address at the University of Michigan. In the speech, McNamara said that nuclear war should be approached in much the same way as conventional warfare. This meant that the primary military objectives in a nuclear war should be the "destruction of the enemy's military forces, not of his civilian population." The United States, he said, had the ability to maintain a reserve of nuclear weapons even after suffering a massive surprise attack, which would allow the country to "destroy an enemy society if driven to it." This ability to survive a surprise attack would give an opponent strong incentive to refrain from hitting American cities in the first place.

McNamara had primarily been drawn to this idea because he sought to provide the president with more options in a nuclear war and because the strategy promised to limit damage to American cities. However, the secretary, like the RAND analysts who had developed the no-cities strategy, had also been disturbed by the indiscriminate destruction that existing war plans envisioned. In one instance, McNamara learned that Albania, despite its break with Soviet policies, would be almost entirely destroyed if the existing war plan against the Soviet Union was implemented because the little country contained a large Soviet air-defense radar. When the SAC Commander General Thomas Power, who briefed the secretary on this point, joked, "Well, Mr. Secretary, I hope you don't have any friends or relations in Albania, because we're just going to have to wipe it out," McNamara was shocked.[1]

The no-cities strategy conformed comfortably with the American reinterpretation of noncombatant immunity and reflected the continued optimism that even nuclear wars could be fought in a discriminate manner. Some outside the Kennedy administration explicitly linked the counterforce strategy to the protection of civilians. Thomas E. Murray in his 1960 book on nuclear policy sought to reconcile morality and security for a United States armed with nuclear weapons. Murray, who had served on the AEC in the 1950s, praised the tradition of noncombatant immunity. He wrote, "Indeed, one of the noblest features of the Western military tradition was the protective wall which was erected around civilian populations and peaceful activities...." He argued that the answer to the balance between morality and security was a large stockpile of small, less destructive nuclear weapons "which lend themselves to discriminating use." Murray was a devoted optimist and advocate of the counterforce strategy.[2]

Counterforce strategy also encountered its skeptics who, for one, doubted that targeting military bases and forces would greatly reduce civilian casualties since often these targets were close to urban populations. Many Americans simply had a difficult time believing that nuclear weapons were anything but mass killers. In the mid-1960s, optimism about the discriminate use of nuclear weapons appeared to have left the mainstream as Barry Goldwater, running for president in 1964, faced extensive criticism for advocating the use of small tactical nuclear weapons in wars against Communism. However, this optimism persisted in official circles and reemerged as a national issue in the 1970s with the military's and eventually President Jimmy Carter's interest in a neutron bomb. The new nuclear weapon was designed to produce a relatively small explosion, but to release a large amount of instantaneously lethal radiation. Its promoters, like physicist S. T. Cohen, promised the neutron bomb would be a less destructive weapon because it would leave cities intact.[3] In contrast to thinking about nuclear weapons, optimism about the discriminate use of conventional force remained strong as American public discussions of the Vietnam War and Persian Gulf War would illustrate.

With McNamara, counterforce strategy did not remain in favor for long. He was disturbed that some thought a counterforce strategy could win a nuclear war for the United States. The Air Force also believed a counterforce strategy required greater spending on nuclear weapons, which McNamara opposed. After all, there were many more counterforce targets in the Soviet Union than cities. By January 1963, McNamara informed the Air Force that they were no longer to use the no-cities doctrine as a basis for strategic planning.[4] Instead, McNamara encouraged a nuclear posture that threatened to inflict unacceptable damage on Soviet cities, population, and industry, a strategy that came to be known as assured destruction. Superficially, assured destruction appears to be the antithesis of noncombatant immunity with nuclear weapons targeted at enemy cities and their civilian populations. However, assured destruction doctrine followed lines of reasoning similar to the paradoxical ideas about nuclear deterrence that Eisenhower, Hanson Baldwin, Thomas Finletter, and others had acted upon and expressed in the 1950s. According to this thinking, the consequences of war would be made to appear so awful that deterrence would be strengthened and war avoided. Planning to kill civilians would prevent their deaths. Like Eisenhower, McNamara argued that the United States had to prepare for a thermonuclear war and maintain the readiness of nuclear forces to bolster deterrence, but that the initiation of such a war "would not be a rational act."[5] Assured destruction's focus on the avoidance of war distanced its supporters from the intentional killing of civilians. Believers in assured destruction could reassure themselves that a threat of indiscriminate devastation was intended to evade that calamity. The doctrine, although a gamble in actually protecting civilians, was not irreconcilable with the version of noncombatant immunity that Americans had forged after World War II.

8.2 The Vietnam War

The Vietnam War appears not to have marked a dramatic departure from the way in which Americans had struggled with the dilemma over noncombatant immunity since World War II. Although the war brought an intensification of controversy surrounding harm to civilians, the controversy owed much to the earlier discussions of noncombatant immunity in the 1950s. The Vietnam War did introduce some new elements into Americans' engagement with the norm. The military doctrine for fighting counterinsurgency wars in the developing world, which emerged in the early 1960s and which was applied in Vietnam, provided new rationales that reinforced noncombatant immunity. Counterinsurgency doctrine sought to mix the use of force against revolutionary guerrillas with inducements to local populations to end their support for the rebels. In the early years of American intervention in Vietnam, American counterinsurgency advisors and officers pointed out that the United States was making its job of winning over local peoples more difficult by indiscriminate uses of force. Bombing villages would not make the hearts and minds of villagers any easier to capture.[6]

The Vietnam War introduced other elements into the discussion of non-combatant immunity that heightened the controversy surrounding the issue. The international media provided extensive coverage of the violence of the conflict that made harm to Vietnamese civilians more visible to Americans. Although television's influence on American attitudes should not be exaggerated,[7] the medium did bring to the American public numerous images of the war's violence including the destruction of villages and wounded villagers.[8] Visits to North Vietnam by journalists and other Americans, such as Harrison Salisbury and Jane Fonda, also brought more information about the suffering of enemy civilians to the attention of Americans. However, media reporting had provided Americans with a fair amount of information about civilian suffering during the Korean War, which had helped stimulate support for relief aid to Koreans. The difference in media coverage of the two wars was one of degree, not kind.

Even more than the greater media coverage, opposition to the war in southeast Asia intensified the controversy over noncombatant immunity. Concern over the killing of innocent civilians was a primary reason to protest the war for some, especially since the revolutionaries' guerrilla tactics made it difficult for American soldiers to distinguish between combatants and noncombatants. Others opposed the war for a variety of reasons including doubts about the prudence, necessity, or morality of the intervention in the first place. For them, broader public sensitivity to the protection of noncombatants became a useful rhetorical tool against the war. Protests against a war that killed and maimed women and children could gain wider sympathy among Americans than denouncements of the war as imperialistic or futile.

The vulnerable civilian became a centerpiece of the protests of many antiwar organizations. For example, antinapalm protests, which accelerated in 1966, often featured the image of burned children. In organizing a boycott of the Dow Chemical Company, the leading American producer of napalm, activists handed out leaflets and carried signs with graphic pictures of napalm's young civilian victims. One speaker from the peace organization Women's Strike for Peace cried, "Robert McNamara would not go out in the street and pour acid on a little child…. He would be horrified at the very thought of it. And yet he can let his airplanes go out there and pour it on these Vietnamese children!" In a 1967 New York protest, marchers carried signs that said, "Children are not born to burn." The memorable chant "Hey, hey, LBJ, how many kids did you kill today?" evoked the deaths of young American soldiers as well as Vietnamese children.[9] The norm of noncombatant immunity, which reemerged after World War II, provided antiwar protesters with an important cultural sanction.

The Vietnam War controversy over harm to civilians, although more intense, reflected the attitudes toward noncombatant immunity that had come to predominate in the 1950s. The U.S. government and military demonstrated a pronounced concern over how the American public and the international community perceived the fighting in Vietnam. Harm to civilians was a significant vulnerability. Officials did not deny completely that American forces caused civilian casualties and suffering, but they did work to establish the optimistic expectation that civilian casualties would be kept to a minimum and that the war's violence could be controlled. Within four months of the arrival of American ground forces in South Vietnam in 1965, General William Westmoreland's command began to set up a system of rules to direct the American use of force in order to minimize civilian casualties and the destruction of property. This system of rules was extraordinary in its scope and included suggestions to commanders to consider the cautious use of firepower when fighting in populated areas.[10] The Air Force, likewise, adopted rules of engagement that sought to avoid civilian casualties.[11]

American officials struggled to convey to the media that the U.S. military sought to fight a discriminate war, and they fought to suppress information contrary to this message. For example, President Johnson in August 1965 woke the president of CBS early in the morning to berate him for allowing the airing of a news story that included footage of U.S. Marines burning down a Vietnamese village. The Department of Defense also tried to restrict the flow of photographs to the press that would reveal the use of napalm or antipersonnel cluster bombs or would demonstrate that pilots had mistakenly attacked a nonmilitary target.[12]

Their attempts to impart an image of a discriminate war was made a little easier by the continued flexibility of American definitions of a military target. Similar to practices from the Korean War, the U.S. armed forces deemed large parcels of the South Vietnamese countryside to be "enemy base areas" or "enemy supply areas." The American embassy and the South Vietnamese government, not military leaders, were the ones who designated these areas unlike in Korea. These supply areas in South Vietnam were also not simply enemy-controlled towns and villages. Often they were heavily forested countryside in which enemy forces could hide, but these designated enemy domains could contain the sites of villages and hamlets. These areas were called "free fire zones" and later "specified strike zones" or "special operating areas." Within this territory, which the embassy and the South Vietnamese government declared free of civilians and friendly personnel, any building, vehicle, or person could be targeted. The U.S. Air Force subjected these enemy areas to attacks with incendiaries, cluster bombs, and pattern bombing intended to strike the widest possible area. B-52 bombers would repeatedly hit these zones, laying carpets of bombs over a few square miles at a time. The strict rules of engagement designed to protect civilians that guided most employment of

American firepower in Vietnam did not apply here, even though those harmed might be peasant supporters of the rebels or simply residents who did not want to leave their homes. Because these entire areas came to be defined as military targets, the calculated uses of indiscriminate firepower within their boundaries could still be depicted as part of a discriminate use of force that spared noncombatants.

Despite the continued role that elastic definitions of military targets played in facilitating Americans' optimism, the Vietnam War, even more than the Korean War, revealed the limits of Americans' confidence in their military's ability to conduct a war that would spare civilians. Again, the significance of intentions became crucial for rationalizing the harm to noncombatants that Americans were unable to ignore. Since the U.S. military's rules of engagement in Vietnam did not deny completely that American firepower would cause civilian casualties, they suggested ways to establish that harm to civilians was unintentional. A September 1965 directive proposed several measures designed to lessen the "psychological" impact of civilian casualties. It suggested that Vietnamese forces be included in operations "so that the war does not appear to be a U.S. action against the Vietnamese people," and the directive urged demonstrations of the U.S. forces' "concern for the safety of non-combatants — their compassion for the injured — their willingness to aid and assist the sick, the hungry and the dispossessed." Like in the Korean War, warnings to civilians of air attacks also became a feature of military policy.[13]

The highest American authorities publicly proclaimed that civilian casualties were an inadvertent and tragic consequence of U.S. military operations in Vietnam. For example, General William Westmoreland said to reporters in 1966: "Regrettably, there are wounded because from time to time accidents on the battlefield hurt innocent parties despite the fact that we have gone to great extremes to try to minimize such accidents. We have minimized them, but through mechanical and human error we still have accidents." In a 1967 speech to the Tennessee legislature, President Johnson commented on the bombing of North Vietnam. He said, "Now as to bombing civilians, I would simply say that we are making an effort that is unprecedented in the history of warfare to be sure that we do not." The president insisted that it was U.S. policy to bomb only military targets. He denied that the U.S. had ever "deliberately bombed cities" or "attacked any target with the purpose of inflicting civilian casualties." Johnson acknowledged that U.S. bombing had killed some people working or living near military targets in North Vietnam, but also noted that "men and machines are not infallible and that some mistakes do occur." He pointed out that the United States had warned the people of North Vietnam to stay away from military targets. Finally, he contrasted American policy with that of the National Liberation Front in South Vietnam. He said, "Any civilian casualties that result from our operations are inadvertent, in stark contrast to the calculated Vietcong policy of systematic terror."[14]

As in the Korean War, this American sensitivity to noncombatant harm provided only limited protections for civilians. A conservative estimate of civilian deaths from a semiofficial American history of the war placed the toll at 65,000 North Vietnamese killed by bombing and 250,000 South Vietnamese killed by military operations, some unknown portion of whom were killed by Communist forces.[15] Even if losses were this low, and some estimates of civilian deaths reached three million, the civilian toll was heavy.

The most notorious failure of American policy to protect civilians was the carnage in the hamlet of My Lai. On the morning of March 16, 1968, army helicopters dropped a company of American soldiers outside the small settlement in central Vietnam. The soldiers expected to encounter an enemy battalion in the village, but apparently the guerrillas had slipped away before the Americans arrived. It is unlikely that the company was ever fired upon during its operation in My Lai. The unit never called for artillery or air support, suffered only one casualty from a self-inflicted wound, and recovered only three weapons in the village. However, the morning's mission was far from peaceful. Over the course of four hours, the soldiers killed approximately 500 villagers, most of them women, children, and old men. A few might have died from the brief artillery and helicopter gunship barrage that preceded the ground assault and targeted the western edge of the hamlet. Some were shot while they fled or were gunned down from a distance before they could be identified or surrender. Others probably died as the Americans shot or lobbed grenades into dark huts or into the underground shelters that the villagers had dug to protect themselves. Many, though, were killed when they were under the control of the American soldiers and virtually helpless. Soldiers rounded up dozens of villagers at gunpoint. Lieutenant William Calley, a platoon leader, had some of his men gather over 100 villagers in a drainage ditch. He later ordered his men to fire on the group and then participated in the killing himself. Other soldiers carried out several smaller executions as well. The violence against the villagers also included several rapes, the slaughter of all their livestock, and the demolition of their entire hamlet.[16]

Reaction to the My Lai massacre demonstrated widespread agreement on the definition of atrocity within the American military establishment. Their eventual response drew a sharp line demarcating the intentional killing of noncombatants as an unjustifiable crime. Some officers went through an initial phase of denial and cover up. The Army failed to conduct a full-scale investigation into the massacre for a year until prompted by a veteran's letter to Congress, and the massacre still did not become public knowledge for another six months. After a formal inquiry substantiated allegations against Calley and his unit and the massacre could no longer be denied, the military leadership and a series of courts-martial distinctly defined for themselves what crime had been committed at My Lai. Amid the varieties of violence and destruction inflicted on the villagers, Calley was ultimately the only one convicted of a crime. He was held accountable only for the intentional shooting of helpless civilians. Calley was charged with 109 counts of premeditated murder, which included the execution of the villagers gathered in the drainage ditch as well as an old man and a child elsewhere. During his court-martial in front of a jury of six officers, the lieutenant did not deny killing civilians. Instead, he defended himself by arguing that he believed the villagers to be the enemy. In effect, Calley tried to deny that any of the village's women, children, or old men were innocent noncombatants, but this was going too far for his fellow officers. Calley had entered the limited confines of unacceptable behavior in war. Although for these officers the idea of noncombatant immunity had shrunk to the simple prohibition against executing helpless civilians, they would not abandon this taboo even in such a brutal and confusing war as the one in Vietnam. The jury convicted Calley of twenty-two murders and sentenced him to life at hard labor.

To the military establishment, Calley became an aberration, the one who had strayed from accepted norms. Inadvertent killings were acceptable; intentional killings were not. In his memoirs, General William Westmoreland put it this way: "That some civilians, even many, died by accident or inevitably in the course of essential military operations dictated by the enemy's presence among the people was no justification or rationale for the conscious massacre of defenseless babies, children, mothers, and old men in a kind of diabolical slow-motion nightmare that went on for the better part of a day...."[17] The military would punish Calley for his execution of villagers. In contrast, the rest of the violence perpetrated at My Lai inhabited a moral gray area. Americans may have found this other violence disturbing and regrettable, but not enough so to hold a fellow citizen accountable for it. No one else was convicted for the rapes, the destruction of homes, or the shootings of Vietnamese who were not at the complete mercy of American soldiers.

The public reaction to Calley's conviction surprised some contemporary observers. Many Americans condemned the verdict and supported Calley. To them, Calley was not a monster, but a martyr. However, how much this response can be understood as a public challenge to the military establishment's condemnation of intentional killing of noncombatants is questionable. A few of Calley's supporters appeared to be rejecting the notion of noncombatant immunity as Calley had in his trial. A federal judge unsuccessfully tried to overturn Calley's conviction, arguing that killing innocent civilians was a common feature of war. He pointed to Joshua's destruction of Jericho and General Sherman's march through Georgia as illustrative.[18] Nevertheless, it appears that many of Calley's sympathizers were misinformed about what had occurred at My Lai and what Calley had been convicted of. A high-level Army memorandum that the Secretary of Defense sent to the White House expressed the concern that much of the public believed that the My Lai killings had occurred in the heat of combat.[19] Indeed, some of Calley's supporters denied the killings had occurred at all. One claimed at a rally that "no American would ever kill 109 people like that."[20] Tension over antiwar protests made many sensitive to any criticism of the military or the country, and many veterans felt that Calley had been made a scapegoat.[21] Support for Calley did not necessarily equal endorsement of what he had done.

The Vietnam War reinforced the norm of noncombatant immunity among Americans but did not create it. The Vietnam controversy over civilian casualties followed the reinterpretation and rejuvenation of the norm that had taken place during the 1950s. The Vietnam War experience alone does not explain American sensitivity to harm to noncombatants in the second half of the twentieth century.

8.3 The Coining of "Collateral Damage"

Even though the Cold War had played an important role in reinvigorating the norm of noncombatant immunity because it made Americans more attentive to their country's reputation abroad, Americans continued to discuss harm to civilians after the end of the Cold War in ways similar to those that had emerged in the 1950s. Optimistic denial and the importance of intention infused American, especially official, discussion of the use of force in the Persian Gulf War and the interventions in Afghanistan and Iraq. During the Gulf War, the term "collateral damage" emerged from its obscurity as a technical term used by soldiers and military specialists and became a stock media phrase. The term encapsulated much of the post-World War II reinterpretation of noncombatant immunity. It acknowledged the lack of control that U.S. armed forces had over the violence they employed, but implied that the violence they inflicted on civilians was unintentional, literally beside the point.

When Iraq invaded Kuwait in the summer of 1990, the United States led an international coalition to end the Iraqi occupation. The short ground campaign against Iraqi forces was preceded by a month-long assault by an air armada of more than 2,000 planes.[22] U.S. officials worked to create the understanding among the American public and international community that the destruction the bombing inflicted against Iraqis was highly controlled and directed against military targets. Like many Americans since World War II, they implicitly denied a conflict between the massive use of firepower and noncombatant immunity. An optimistic faith in high technology provided the supposed solution. With the help of government public relations specialists, stories of "precision guided munitions," "smart bombs," and other marvels of the technological control of destruction pervaded the media. The military fed journalists video that showed Tomahawk cruise missiles turning corners, smart bombs entering bunkers by front doors, and precision weapons dropping down chimneys to destroy factories.[23] Although many Americans publicly questioned this vision of a discriminate war, noting, for example, that most of the bombs dropped in the war were not "smart" bombs,[24] government representatives and those they had convinced spent most of their time talking as if harm to Iraqi civilians would not occur.

When American officials did not deny the killing of civilians, they rationalized the violence by emphasizing its inadvertence. From the beginning of the war, Pentagon officials assured the press that U.S. forces were under orders to try to avoid civilian casualties.[25] The U.S. military did not give warnings to Iraqi civilians before its first air attacks, but it started reassuring the American public that it would consider warnings after the destruction of a Baghdad building produced lurid television footage of civilian casualties. The U.S. military said it believed the building to be a command center, but the attack killed about 300 civilians because it was then being used as an air-raid shelter.[26]

During the Persian Gulf War, this notion of lack of intent was encapsulated in the phrase "collateral damage," which became a common term in media coverage. The expression most likely originated in the late 1950s or early 1960s as a technical military term referring to the destruction that nuclear weapons caused beyond the target against which they were directed.[27] By the early 1960s, the term had migrated into the scholarly literature on limited war in which it was used to refer to concomitant damage from both nuclear and conventional weapons and was often associated with harm to civilians.[28] The phrase was making occasional appearances in the mainstream press by the mid-1970s.[29]

The Persian Gulf War, and the military spokespeople and media commentators who used the term, not only made collateral damage a common phrase but also imbued it with the strong connotation that collateral damage was unintentional. Before the Gulf War, a dictionary of military terms written in the mid-1980s defined collateral damage as "damage to nonmilitary structures and facilities resulting from a strike on a nearby military target." This definition only vaguely implied a lack of intent, if it did at all. After the Gulf War, the term collateral damage appeared in standard English dictionaries in addition to specialized military dictionaries, and these common dictionary definitions had come to include explicit reference to the "unintended" or "inadvertent" nature of the destruction that the phrase described.[30]

With the U.S. attacks on Afghanistan and Iraq following the destruction of the World Trade Center in 2001, official expressions of optimism about the discriminate use of force and denials of intentional attacks on civilians became standard. During these operations, the American government again paraded the military's high technology before the press, emphasizing that high-tech guided missiles could help avoid civilian casualties. As the United States began its bombardment of Baghdad in the opening days of the Iraq War, Secretary of Defense Donald H. Rumsfeld assured reporters that the "weapons that are being used today have a degree of precision that no one ever dreamt of in a prior conflict."[31] American officials also insisted that the United States had no desire to harm noncombatants and any civilian casualties were an unintended consequence of the military operations to fight terrorism. In announcing his decision to attack Iraq, President George W. Bush said, "I want Americans and all the world to know that coalition forces will make every effort to spare innocent civilians from harm."[32] The legacy of Americans' struggle with noncombatant immunity after World War II lasted through the end of the twenty century and beyond.

8.4 Revival of the Just War Tradition

Another aspect of this legacy manifested itself in a revived scholarly interest in the just war tradition. In the first half of the twentieth century, only a few Catholic theologians had published studies in the United States which considered in any depth the problem of morality and warfare.[33] By the late 1950s, the just war tradition was undergoing a scholarly rebirth. The result was a burgeoning of specialized writing on the legitimate initiation and conduct of warfare in which the problem of noncombatant immunity figured prominently. Catholic writers were in the forefront of the revival,[34] but Protestant scholars also contributed, writing some of the most influential works.[35] Those outside the study of religion and ethics but interested in the relationship of just war to American policy made contributions to the growing field as well.[36] Since the Vietnam War, the literature on just war has become extensive.[37] Engagement with the dilemma over noncombatant immunity in the wake of World War II on the part of officials and a broader public preceded and helped to stimulate scholarly work on the just war tradition.

In this revived scholarly discourse, the importance of right intention became central to the understanding of noncombatant immunity. A prohibition against the intentional killing of civilians emerged as the consensus view in the literature. Writers disagreed over whether unintended killing of noncombatants was moral. As Father Connell had in the early 1950s, some continued to argue that the principle of double effect allowed for such killing. They maintained that individuals were not accountable for the evil consequences of their actions if those results were neither intended nor outweighed the good brought by those deeds. Critics argued that the principle of double effect did not provide adequate justification for the killing of noncombatants in war and these criticisms had started as early as Connell's defense of the idea. For example, a British theologian F. H. Drinkwater argued in 1951 in the pages of *Commonweal* that use of an atomic bomb against a city without a warning to the population was certain to kill tens of thousands of civilians. Since this evil was certain, he asserted it was hypocrisy to claim that it was not intended.[38] The principle of double effect, as well as controversy over it, has remained important to this reanimated area of study. Like broader public discussion, academic literature on the just war tradition has reflected the growing cultural significance of intention for noncombatant immunity.

International humanitarian law has also reflected the expanding significance of intention, suggesting that this aspect of the American reinterpretation of noncombatant immunity was not unique to the United States. In the 1960s and 1970s, the prohibition on intentional killing of noncombatants was written more clearly into international conventions and U.S. military regulations. In 1968, the U.N. General Assembly affirmed a resolution of the ICRC that banned attacks against civilian populations as such. In 1976, the U.S. Army amended its twenty-year-old manual on the law of land warfare to state explicitly this prohibition. The following year, an international conference completed drafting two additional protocols to the Geneva Conventions of 1949. The first and second protocols, relating to the protection of victims of international and noninternational armed conflicts respectively, each included the provision: "The civilian population as such, as well as individual civilians, shall not be the object of attack. Acts or threats of violence the primary purpose of which is to spread terror among the civilian population are prohibited."[39] Focus on intention may have helped Americans reconcile noncombatant immunity with massively destructive methods of war, but its significance resonated enough with other countries to be incorporated into international law.

Among Americans, the significance intention attained for protecting noncombatants also shaped their notions of terrorism in the late twentieth century. Terrorism gained an added connotation that policymakers commonly emphasized. Instead of denoting simply any political violence deemed illegitimate, terrorism in the rhetoric of Americans became associated specifically with intentional attacks against civilians. Whether discussing the Viet Cong or Al Qaeda, harm that terrorists inflicted on civilians, which Americans were convinced was deliberate, became the special mark of their depravity in American eyes. Americans applied their reinterpretation of noncombatant immunity with its attention to intention to the new forms of political violence they increasingly faced as the Cold War wound down. The application was self-righteous and self-serving, but also self-limiting. By making calculated attacks on civilians, a badge of the terrorism they opposed, Americans reinforced the expectation that they would abstain from similar methods.

8.5 Soldiers versus Civilians?

The legacy of Americans' uneasy reconciliation of noncombatant immunity with massively destructive warfare had an additional aspect, one which was a primary source of unease. Americans' optimistic faith that even the most destructive weapons could be used in a discriminate manner and their preoccupation with intent supplanted an agonizing question in public discussion. In the second half of the twentieth century, Americans avoided openly considering the potential conflict between saving the lives of soldiers fighting for the United States and preserving noncombatants from harm. The world had reasons to believe that such a conflict existed. The broad trends of the world wars suggested as much. World War II had avoided slaughter in the trenches, but a much higher proportion of the dead in that war was civilian.[40] After World War II, a small minority of Americans, many of them believing that warfare had become a total struggle between entire nations, did think that modern war demanded a tradeoff between the lives of combatants and noncombatants. As Congressman Charles Elston had during the 1949 Revolt of the Admirals, they argued that it was legitimate to kill civilians to save American soldiers' lives.

Yet most Americans avoided discussing noncombatant immunity in terms that weighed the safety of soldiers against the protection of civilians and understandably so. The moral calculus of such balancing is torturous. Not many have attempted to answer such questions as how many babies of another nation can be justifiably killed in order to preserve the life of one young American soldier. Indeed, Americans after World War II eschewed various forms of justifying harm to civilians by judging it a lesser evil in pursuit of a greater good. Only rarely did Americans publicly argue that the death of noncombatants was the acceptable cost for the achievement of a greater good, even the saving of American soldiers' lives.

This type of reasoning has been more common in academic writing on just war, but even there it has not been used to justify the intentional killing of noncombatants. Drawing on utilitarian moral philosophy, some scholars of just war theory introduced a principle of proportionality into their reasoning about unintentional harm to noncombatants. They argued that benefits from attacks against targets of military value can outweigh the incidental harm the attacks inflict on noncombatants. However, such arguments justifying a lesser evil by achieving a greater good were rare in broader public discussions.

Although one can only speculate on why this way of reasoning was not more common among the American public, it is not difficult to suggest explanations. One can imagine that Americans had enough trouble balancing the concrete death and suffering of the innocent against abstractions like "security" or "democracy" or "freedom." When the balancing act suggested setting the stark loss of American lives against harm to foreign noncombatants, the question could be even more agonizing. Arguing in terms of proportionality required at least a rough fixing of commensurability, and the possible relationships each had their liabilities. If Americans judged noncombatant lives more valuable or even of equal value to those of their soldiers, this could embitter those in military service and make them more reluctant to risk their lives for their country. If Americans judged the lives of innocent noncombatants as less valuable than their soldiers, they risked distrust and hostility from the international community and made their self-conception as a humane people more difficult to maintain. These considerations weighed on top of more visceral feelings driven by the fact that the soldiers might be family or friends or that individuals had deep personal convictions that killing the helpless was wrong. Instead, Americans avoided openly discussing such unappealing judgments.

The general rule that Americans have refrained from discussing the calculus of noncombatants' versus soldiers' lives has had one major exception. The contested memory of the atomic bombing of Japan has repeatedly raised this issue. The claim that the atomic bombings saved American lives became a crucial element of the dominant public justification of the weapon's use. Although Americans largely avoided justifying future killing of civilians with nuclear weapons by arguing that it would save American lives, many did defend the bombing of Hiroshima and Nagasaki in this way. However, this form of rationalization has sparked so much controversy that it helps to demonstrate how unsettling Americans have found weighing the lives of soldiers against noncombatants and, therefore, why they avoided the problem when they could.

The death of Japanese civilians remained a stain on what many Americans wanted to see as the triumphant first use of nuclear weapons. Quickly, Americans came to acknowledge that tens of thousands of Japanese civilians had been killed in Hiroshima and Nagasaki. Truman's initial statements that described Hiroshima as an army base and assured that the atomic bombs had been used against purely military targets in Japan receded from public discussion. In their place emerged from officials a new defense against the charge that the bombings had killed civilians indiscriminately, one that would gain a widespread public following.

Even though only a small minority in 1945 were voicing challenges to the use of the weapons, the dissent worried several of Truman's advisors. One of these men was Harvard president James Conant, who had served as an advisor on the Manhattan project and would later show himself to be sensitive to the problem of indiscriminate destruction during the deliberations over the hydrogen bomb. To combat the criticism, Conant urged former Secretary of War Henry Stimson to compose a public explanation of the decision to use the bomb. In a 1947 *Harper's Magazine* article, Stimson provided his explanation that would anchor the dominant narrative of the atomic bomb's first use. Stimson defended the use as the "least abhorrent" choice. He asserted that Truman and his advisors had closely considered the alternatives for ending the war with utmost speed. After dismissing other options, the article depicted the decision as a choice between the atomic bomb and an invasion of the Japanese home islands that would cause "over one million" American casualties, dead and wounded. Implicitly, Stimson balanced Japanese civilian deaths against those of American soldiers. Other prominent figures such as Winston Churchill, George Marshall, Leslie Groves, and James Byrnes claimed that the atomic bomb had saved hundreds of thousands of American lives. In his 1955 memoir, Truman claimed that the army had estimated half a million would have been killed in an invasion of Japan.

These high figures made the weighing of lives easier for Americans. Compared to the rough estimate of 100,000 Japanese civilian deaths from the atomic bombings, Truman's estimate put the ratio at five to one, *hundreds* of thousands of Americans would have died as opposed to the *tens* of thousands of Japanese. Even if one were to value the prevention of noncombatant over combatant deaths, the calculus could be easily seen as favoring the bomb's use in light of such high invasion casualty estimates. Nevertheless, any comfort that Americans could derive from this argument depended upon high counterfactual estimates of American deaths in a war prolonged by abstention from the atomic bomb's use.

Motivated in part by concerns over the killing of civilians, other Americans would challenge these high estimates and precipitate a heated controversy fifty years after the end of the war. By the mid-1980s, historians were questioning the origins of the high casualty estimates for the invasion of Japan. Stimson's 1947 estimate did not have a clear source, and JCS's estimates from 1945 and 1946 claimed that less than 50,000 American soldiers would die in the planned assault on the Japanese home islands. This obscure historical detail, but one fraught with meaning, became a hotly contested issue among scholars.[41]

The casualty estimate took on greater significance with the fifty year anniversary of the atomic bombings and the Smithsonian's Air and Space Museum's plans for a commemorative display of the *Enola Gay*, the B-29 bomber that dropped the first atomic bomb on Hiroshima. Veterans organizations objected to the script for the exhibition that they saw as too sympathetic to the Japanese. As the museum's officials attempted to forge a compromise to satisfy the veterans and the historians who had written and approved the script, the deal came apart when the museum director tried to include the low invasion casualty estimates alongside Stimson's claim of one million. The dispute ignited a national controversy that drew the attention of Congress, the president, and the press. The script was purged and the *Enola Gay* was displayed with little historical commentary accompanying it in the museum. The dispute demonstrated how important the high casualty estimate was and how explosive the balancing act of soldiers' and civilians' lives could become.[42]

The controversial memory of the atomic attacks against Japan has been an exception that proves the rule. Americans embarked on this unusual foray into considerations of proportionality because in contemplating the destruction of Hiroshima and Nagasaki, they could not easily deny the harm to civilians nor construct a strong case for a lack of intent. The bombs had been dropped on the center of cities not aimed at specific military targets, tens of thousands of civilians had been killed, and no explicit warning had been given to the Japanese. However, when the possibility that a national museum would enshrine in a commemorative exhibit a challenge to the conventional wisdom that many more American soldiers were saved than Japanese civilians killed by the atomic bombings, controversy muted discussion. Denied a detailed script, the exhibit became silent on the issue of noncombatant immunity and Americans again retreated from the tortuous calculus. Finding optimistic denial and disavowal of intention more comfortable approaches for addressing the problem of noncombatant immunity in modern warfare, Americans have never had sustained public discussions over the potential conflict between the lives of soldiers and the lives of noncombatants.

Another form of reasoning was largely absent from the American public discourse on noncombatant immunity after World War II. Americans rarely deployed claims of military necessity to justify harm to noncombatants. They have avoided arguing publicly that requirements for victory must displace limitations on warfare although this has been a more commonly voiced opinion among military professionals in private discussions.[43] The idea of military necessity has figured prominently in academic moral and legal discussions of warfare, but its meaning has been ambiguous and contested.[44] The term has begged the question of "necessary" to achieve what ends in victory and at what costs. This ambiguity might help to account for why the concept has not been used often in public discussion of noncombatant immunity. This mode of reasoning had an additional liability. Appeals to military necessity had long been associated with German militarism, the tradition that Americans believed the Nazis had piloted out of control in their atrocities of World War II and from which Americans desired to distinguish themselves and their actions.

8.6 The Limits of Good Intentions

In avoiding discussions of saving American soldiers' lives and military necessity, Americans have shunned justifications of their way of war that might have appeared nationalistic and selfish. This has allowed them to conserve their humane reputation despite their actions in war. Americans have tried to project a magnanimous universalism in their continued adherence to the international norm of noncombatant immunity while reinterpreting the norm to align more closely with their interests and parochial concerns. It is fatuous to say that Americans abandoned the norm of noncombatant immunity after World War II. Pressures on Americans to conform to the international custom helped to prevent this. Fears that their country's massively destructive methods of warfare resembled Nazi atrocities complicated Cold War competition for sympathy around the world and fed anxieties among Americans who wanted to view themselves as a humane people. Americans could not deviate entirely from the norm without a price that they were unwilling to pay.

The process of accommodation, though, was dynamic. External pressures and traditional customs did not fully determine American cultural attitudes on noncombatant immunity, but neither did Americans ignore the pressures and traditions. Unwilling to abandon their new destructive techniques of warfare, Americans reinterpreted noncombatant immunity, which included the critical significance of intention and a shrunken notion of what should remain immune from attack, and optimistically insisted that the new methods could be made to adhere to this idea of legitimate warfare. This reinterpretation was not the invention of a few philosophers or theologians nor was it imposed on the broader public by concerned officials. It emerged from a series of widespread public discussions in the decade following World War II, which scholars and officials shaped but did not dominate.

The interpretation served American interests but also imposed restraints. Americans rejected as illegitimate the intentional killing of innocent noncombatants as a method of warfare. Deliberate extermination remained an atrocity in the eyes of most. This limitation provided a few genuine protections for civilian populations caught in the midst of American wars. It mitigated the violence of the Korean War to a small, but substantive, degree by helping to slow the escalation of the war and by prompting official and private American aid to suffering Korean civilians. Although it is difficult to measure precisely, the norm against intentionally killing noncombatants also predisposed individuals serving in the U.S. armed forces to avoid harming civilians, even though this inclination could be overridden by circumstance. In addition, this aversion to extermination became an added, if peripheral, consideration in American leaders' consideration of the use of nuclear weapons. The new conception of noncombatant immunity continued to cause public controversy throughout the Vietnam War and in American wars after the end of the Cold War and to demand the attention of officials who worked to maintain the country's international reputation.

Although noncombatant immunity retained some cultural power among Americans and constrained U.S. violence in limited ways, the norm also served to rationalize harm to noncombatants. When Americans believed that their use of force conformed to the new interpretation, noncombatant immunity worked to justify the violence. The ambiguities at the heart of the idea of noncombatancy, the questions of who was innocent in war and what should be spared to prevent suffering, eased the reinterpretation of the norm and made optimistic denial easier. The faith that Americans could control the violence of war and spare noncombatants was so strong that some even believed that nuclear weapons, a prime symbol of the age of mass killing, could be tamed. Many of the optimists believed out of ignorance that the violence could be controlled. They did not realize the destruction that American firepower could and did inflict on civilians. However, the expansive definitions of what constituted a "military target" assisted those who were in a position to understand the potential for devastation, such as military leaders, to avoid dwelling on harm to civilians. When virtually all physical structures could be seen as "military targets" as the American prosecution of the Korean War demonstrated, U.S. soldiers could more easily view their use of force as discriminate. They could protect their sense of self as military professionals who waged war against military targets and not against civilians.

Americans' reinterpretation of noncombatant immunity was certainly neither monolithic nor all-pervading. Most Americans spent little or no time thinking about the dilemma of noncombatant immunity and massively destructive war or did not bother to attempt to reconcile the two. Even in the public discussions that did address the issues, a few dissenters from the uneasy reconciliation continued to reject categorically either noncombatant immunity or massively destructive war. However, these dissenters were small minorities whose views attracted attention largely because of their unconventionality.

That intent became the moral fulcrum in American attitudes toward noncombatant immunity is understandable. Intention has been of fundamental cultural importance to Americans. Christian notions of evil and sin have weighed intentions heavily. American law has viewed premeditation as the most crucial aggravating circumstance in determining criminal punishment and has placed a special emphasis on punishing conspiracy to commit crimes.

Yet more than the heavy weighting of intention within American cultural traditions explains the increased importance of intention for thinking about noncombatant immunity. The very nature of the trend toward increasingly uncontrollable military firepower has widened the cultural space for the significance of intention. When wars were fought with spears and clubs, the ease with which these weapons could be directed against a specific target left little room for questions of intention. In face-to-face warfare, warriors attacked individuals that they could identify as combatants or as bystanders. Mistakes could be made, but these occurred under unusual circumstances such as in combat at night or in fog. In most close fighting, intention was manifest in action. Either warriors killed noncombatants purposefully or they spared them. With the introduction of weapons that killed over long distances and devastated great areas, intent no longer clearly followed from action. Common and widespread unintended destruction became plausible. The great acceleration of this trend toward uncontrollable firepower in the twentieth century contributed to making intention crucial to Americans' thinking about noncombatant immunity after World War II. Americans rationalized harm to noncombatants from violence that they could not control as collateral damage, a tragedy in war, but not a crime.

The significance that intent has attained in the discourse on harming civilians has brought new problems. The difficulty of distinguishing results from intentions has contributed to misunderstanding and bad feelings between the military and its critics. Those especially critical over the issue of harm to civilians point to the deaths and devastation resulting from the use of American weapons and condemn the armed forces for attacking civilians. Soldiers, thinking of their intentions to avoid harm to noncombatants, respond that they do not attack civilians. With the loss of nuance in often-heated exchanges, both sides can understandably see the other as mendacious, which leads to the further deterioration of dialogue.

Moreover, the centrality of intention has contributed to a complacent stance toward the problem of collateral damage. Intent is simply a state of mind. The intention not to harm noncombatants has no direct connection to actually keeping them from harm. An interpretation of noncombatant immunity that weighs intentions so heavily imposes only the requirement of right thinking and some evidence of that right thinking such as warnings or relief aid for civilians. It does not necessarily prevent the killing of civilians by American weapons. As a consequence, Americans have spent more time thinking about their good intentions than about how they could prevent more civilian deaths from their wars. The combination of the cultural importance of intention with weapons, the devastating effects of which are difficult to control, has been and will continue to be a dangerous mix for noncombatants.

Since the end of World War II, Americans have backed away from visions of total war. In struggling to distinguish legitimate violence in war from atrocity, Americans have clung to the norm of noncombatant immunity tenaciously. Most have refused to advocate the intentional killing of civilians in war for any reason, yet the practical protections from harm that noncombatants have received from these sentiments have had severe limits. American firepower devastated Korea; nuclear weapons were incorporated into the U.S. arsenal and targeted on Soviet cities; and collateral damage persists as a regular feature of American uses of force. The tradition of noncombatant immunity has proven resilient in one of the greatest challenges it faced to its continued existence, but it has often been inadequate in keeping civilians from harm.

Select Bibliography

Abbreviations

AHTL   Andover Harvard Theological Library, Cambridge, MA.
DDEL   Dwight D. Eisenhower Library, Abilene, KS.
FRUS   *Foreign Relations of the United States.*
GUL   Georgetown University Library, Washington, DC.
HLSL   Harvard Law School Library, Cambridge, MA.
HSTL   Harry S. Truman Library, Independence, MO.
LC   Library of Congress, Washington, DC.
NA   National Archives I and II, Washington, DC and College Park, MD.
NHC   Naval Historical Center, Washington, DC.
OA   Operational Archives, Naval Historical Center, Washington, DC.
PPP   *Public Papers of the Presidents of the United States.*
RG   Record Group.
SPC   Swarthmore Peace Collection, Swarthmore College, Swarthmore, PA.

Manuscript Collections and Government Records

Andover Harvard Theological Library, Cambridge, MA. Joy, Charles R. Papers.
Dwight D. Eisenhower Library, Abilene, KS.

>   Dulles, John Foster. Papers.
>   Jackson, C. D. Papers.
>   National Security Council Series. Ann Whitman File.
>   Operations Coordinating Board Central File. National Security Council Staff. White House Office.
>   Subject Subseries. National Security Council Series. Office of the Special Assistant for National Security Affairs. White House Office.

Harvard Law School Library, Cambridge, MA. Leach, W. Barton. Papers.
Harry S. Truman Library, Independence, MO.

>   Finletter, Thomas K. Papers.
>   Psychological Strategy Board Files. Staff Members and Office Files.
>   Selected Records Relating to the Korean War.
>   Symington, W. Stuart. Papers.

Library of Congress, Washington, DC.

>   Ickes, Harold L. Papers.
>   LeMay, Curtis E. Papers.
>   Vandenberg, Hoyt S. Papers.

National Archives I & II, Record Groups, Washington, DC and College Park, MD.

>   Army Staff. RG 319.
>   Atomic Energy Commission. RG 326.
>   Department of State. RG 59.
>   Far East Command. RG 349.
>   Headquarters, U.S. Air Force. RG 341.
>   Joint Chiefs of Staff. RG 218.
>   Joint Congressional Committee on Atomic Energy. RG 128.
>   Office of the Secretary of Defense. RG 330.

Office of the Secretary of the Air Force. RG 340.
Office of the Secretary of the Army. RG 335.
Supreme Commander Allied Forces, Pacific. RG 331.
United States Army Commands, 1942 –. RG 338
United States Information Agency. RG 306.
U.S. Eighth Army. RG 500.

Naval Historical Center, Operational Archives, Washington, DC. Ofstie, Ralph A. Papers. Operational Archives.
Swarthmore Peace Collection, Swarthmore College, Swarthmore, PA.

Fellowship of Reconciliation-USA Papers.
Peacemakers Papers.
War Resisters League Papers.

Government Publications

Congressional Record.
Public Papers of the Presidents of the United States.
U.N. Security Council Official Records.
U.S. Department of the Army. Inspector General. *No Gun Ri Review.* January 2001. <www.army.mil/nogunri>.
U.S. Department of State Bulletin.
U.S. Department of State. Foreign Relations of the United States.
U.S. House. Committee on Armed Services. *The National Defense Program — Unification and Strategy: Hearings.* 81st Cong., 1st sess.
U.S. Senate. Committee on Armed Services. *The Military Situation in the Far East: Hearings.* 82nd Cong., 1st sess.
U.S. Senate. Committee on Foreign Relations. *Geneva Conventions for the Protection of War Victims: Hearings.* 84th Cong., 1st sess.
———. *The Genocide Convention: Hearings.* 81st Cong., 2nd sess.

Newspapers

Baltimore Sun
Boston Post
Chicago Tribune
Cleveland Press
Daily Worker
Detroit News
Houston Chronicle
Los Angeles Times
National Guardian
New York Times
New York Times Magazine
Philadelphia Bulletin
San Francisco Examiner
St. Louis Post-Dispatch
Washington Post

Periodicals

Air Force
Air University Quarterly Review
America
American Legion
American Mercury

Atlantic
Bulletin of the Atomic Scientist
Business Week
Catholic World
Christian Century
Collier's
Commonweal
Fellowship
Fortune
Harper's
Human Events
Life
Marine Corps Gazette
Military Review
Nation
New Republic
Newsweek
Peace Action
Reader's Digest
Saturday Evening Post
Saturday Review of Literature
Scientific American
Time
United States Naval Institute Proceedings
United States News and World Report
Vital Speeches of the Day

Articles and Books

Anders, Roger M., ed. *Forging the Atomic Shield: Excerpts from the Office Diary of Gordon E. Dean.* Chapel Hill, NC: University of North Carolina Press, 1987.

Appleman, Roy. *South to the Naktong, North to the Yalu: June–November 1950.* Washington, DC: Office of the Chief of Military History, Department of the Army, 1961.

Bacevich, A. J. "The Paradox of Professionalism." *Journal of Military History* 61, no. 2 (April 1997): 303–34.

Barlow, Jeffrey. *Revolt of the Admirals: The Fight for Naval Aviation, 1945–1950.* Washington, DC: Naval Historical Center, Department of the Navy, 1994.

Batchelder, Robert C. *The Irreversible Decision, 1939–1950.* Boston, MA: Houghton Mifflin, 1962.

Bernstein, Barton J. "Truman and the A-Bomb: Targeting Noncombatants, Using the Bomb, and His Defending the 'Decision.'" *Journal of Military History* 62, no. 3 (July 1998): 547–70.

Best, Geoffrey. *Humanity in Warfare.* New York: Columbia University Press, 1980.
———. *War and Law Since 1945.* New York: Clarendon, 1994.

Biddle, Tami Davis. *Rhetoric and Reality in Air Warfare: The Evolution of British and American Ideas About Strategic Bombing, 1914–1945.* Princeton, NJ: Princeton University Press, 2002.

Bilton, Michael and Kevin Sim. *Four Hours in My Lai: A War Crime and its Aftermath.* New York: Viking, 1992.

Boyer, Paul. *By the Bomb's Early Light: American Thought and Culture at the Dawn of the Atomic Age.* New York: Pantheon, 1985.
———. *Fallout: A Historian Reflects on America's Half-Century Encounter with Nuclear Weapons.* Columbus, OH: Ohio State University Press, 1998.

Carr, Caleb. *The Lessons of Terror: A History of Warfare Against Civilians, Why It Has Always Failed and Why It Will Fail Again.* New York: Random House, 2002.

Cillessen, Bret J. "Embracing the Bomb: Ethics, Morality, and Nuclear Deterrence in the U.S. Air Force, 1945-1955," *Journal of Strategic Studies* 21, no. 1 (March 1998): 96–134.

Clodfelter, Mark. *The Limits of Air Power: The American Bombing of North Vietnam.* New York: Free Press, 1989.

Crane, Conrad C. *Bombs, Cities, and Civilians: American Airpower Strategy in World War II.* Lawrence, KS: University of Kansas Press, 1993.

————. *American Airpower Strategy in Korea, 1950–1953*. Lawrence, KS: University of Kansas Press, 2000.

Cumings, Bruce. *The Origins of the Korean War*. Vol. 2, *The Roaring of the Cataract, 1947–1950*. Princeton, NJ: Princeton University Press, 1990.

De Groot, Gerald J. *The Bomb: A Life*. Cambridge, MA: Harvard University Press, 2005.

Douhet, Guilio. *The Command of the Air*. Translated by Dino Ferrari. New York: Coward-McCann, 1942.

Elliot, David C. "Project Vista and Nuclear Weapons in Europe." *International Security* 11, no. 1 (Summer 1986): 163–83.

Federal Council of Churches of Christ in America. *The Christian Conscience and Weapons of Mass Destruction*. New York: Department of International Justice and Goodwill, 1950.

————. Commission on the Relation of the Church to the War in the Light of Christian Faith. *Atomic Warfare and the Christian Faith*. New York, 1946.

Field, James A. *The History of United States Naval Operations: Korea*. Washington: U.S. Government Printing Office, 1962.

Ford, John C. "The Morality of Obliteration Bombing." *Theological Studies* 5, no. 3 (September 1944): 261–309.

Forsythe, David P. *Humanitarian Politics: The International Committee of the Red Cross*. Baltimore: Johns Hopkins University Press, 1977.

Franklin, Bruce. *War Stars: The Superweapon and the American Imagination*. New York: Oxford University Press, 1988.

Futrell, Robert. The United States Air Force in Korea 1950–1953. rev. ed. Washington: U.S. Government Printing Office, 1983.

Gaddis, John Lewis, Philip H. Gordon, Ernest R. May, and Jonathan Rosenberg, eds. *Cold War Statesmen Confront the Bomb: Nuclear Diplomacy Since 1945*. Oxford: Oxford University Press, 1999.

Garrett, Stephen A. *Ethics and Airpower in World War II: The British Bombing of German Cities*. New York: St. Martin's, 1993.

Gertsch, W. Darrell. "The Strategic Air Offensive and the Mutation of American Values, 1937–1945." *Rocky Mountain Social Science Journal* 11, no. 3 (1974): 37–50.

Grimsley, Mark and Clifford J. Rogers, eds. *Civilians in the Path of War*. Lincoln, NE: University of Nebraska Press, 2002.

Grossman, Dave. *On Killing: The Psychological Cost of Learning to Kill in War and Society*. Boston, MA: Little, Brown, 1995.

Hammond, Paul Y. *Organizing for Defense: The American Military Establishment in the Twentieth Century*. Princeton, NJ: Princeton University Press, 1961.

Hanley, Charles J., Sang-Hun Choe, and Martha Mendoza. *The Bridge at No Gun Ri: A Hidden Nightmare from the Korean War*. New York: Holt, 2001.

Harris, Robert and Jeremy Paxman. *A Higher Form of Killing: The Secret Story of Chemical and Biological Warfare*. New York: Hill and Wang, 1982.

Hartigan, Richard Shelly. *The Forgotten Victim: A History of the Civilian*. Chicago: Precedent, 1982.

Hastings, Max. *The Korean War*. New York: Simon and Schuster, 1987.

Herken, Gregg. *Counsels of War*. New York: Knopf, 1985.

Hermes, Walter, Jr. *Truce Tent and Fighting Front: October 1951–July 1953*. Washington: Office of the Chief of Military History, Department of the Army, 1966.

Hersh, Seymour M. *My Lai 4: A Report on the Massacre and its Aftermath*. New York: Random House, 1970.

Holmes, Robert L. *On War and Morality*. Princeton, NJ: Princeton University Press, 1989.

Hopkins, George. "Bombing and the American Conscience during World War II." *Historian* 28, no. 3 (May 1966): 451–73.

Johnson, James Turner. *Ideology, Reason, and the Limitation of War: Religious and Secular Concepts 1200–1740*. Princeton, NJ: Princeton University Press, 1975.

————. *Just War Tradition and the Restraint of War: A Moral and Historical Inquiry*. Princeton, NJ: Princeton University Press, 1981.

Kaplan, Fred. *The Wizards of Armageddon*. New York: Touchstone, 1983.

Kaufman, Burton I. *The Korean War: Challenges in Crisis, Credibility, and Command*. Philadelphia: Temple University Press, 1986.

Knox, Donald. *The Korean War: An Oral History*. New York: Harcourt Brace Jovanovitch, 1985.

Laurence, William L. *The Hell Bomb*. New York: Knopf, 1951.

LeBlanc, Lawrence J. The United States and the Genocide Convention. Durham, NC: Duke University Press, 1991.

LeMay, Curtis E. with Mickey Cantor. *Mission with LeMay: My Story*. Garden City, NY: Doubleday, 1965.

MacDonald, Callum A. *Korea: The War Before Vietnam*. New York: Free Press, 1987.

MacIsaac, David. *Strategic Bombing in World War Two: The Story of the United States Strategic Bombing Survey*. New York: Garland, 1976.

McFarland, Stephen L. *America's Pursuit of Precision Bombing, 1910–1945*. Washington, DC: Smithsonian Institution Press, 1995.

Miller, Richard L. *Under the Cloud: The Decades of Nuclear Testing*. New York: Free Press, 1986.

Millis, Walter. *Arms and Men: A Study in American Military History*. New York: Putnam, 1956.

———. *Arms and the State: Civil-Military Elements in National Policy*. New York: Twentieth Century Fund, 1958.

Mossman, Billy C. *Ebb and Flow: November 1950–July 1951*. Washington: U.S. Army Center of Military History, 1990.

Novick, Peter. *The Holocaust in American Life*. Boston, MA: Houghton Mifflin, 1999.

Piccigallo, Philip R. The Japanese on Trial: Allied War Crimes Operations in the East, *1945–1951*. Austin, TX: University of Texas Press, 1979.

Public Papers and Addresses of Franklin D. Roosevelt. Vol. 8. New York: Russell and Russell, 1941.

Quester, George H. *Deterrence Before Hiroshima: The Airpower Background of Modern Strategy*. New York: Wiley, 1966.

Ridgway, Matthew B. *Soldier: The Memoirs of Matthew B. Ridgway*. New York: Harper, 1956.

———. *The Korean War: How We Met the Challenge*. Garden City, NY: Doubleday, 1967.

Roberts, Adam and Richard Guelff, eds. *Documents on the Laws of War*. Oxford: Clarendon, 1989.

Rosenberg, David Alan. "The Origins of Overkill." *International Security* 7, no. 4 (Spring 1983): 3–71.

Ross, Steven T. *American War Plans, 1945–1950*. Portland, OR: Cass, 1988.

Ross, Steven T. and David Alan Rosenberg, eds. *America's Plans for War Against the Soviet Union, 1945–1950*. 15 vols. New York: Garland, 1989–1990.

Schaffer, Ronald. *Wings of Judgment: American Bombing in World War II*. New York: Oxford University Press, 1985.

Schnabel, James F. *Policy and Direction: The First Year*. Washington: Office of the Chief of Military History, Department of the Army, 1972.

Schnabel, James F. and Robert J. Watson. *The Joint Chiefs of Staff and National Policy*. Vol. 3, *The Korean War*. Wilmington, DE: Glazier, 1979.

Schulzinger, Robert D. *A Time for War: The United States and Vietnam, 1945–1975*. New York: Oxford University Press, 1997.

Stueck, William. *The Korean War: An International History*. Princeton, NJ: Princeton University Press, 1995.

Sherry, Michael S. *The Rise of American Air Power: The Creation of Armageddon*. New Haven, CT: Yale University Press, 1987.

Stone, I. F. *The Hidden History of the Korean War, 1950–1951*. New York: Monthly Review, 1952.

Taylor, Telford. *The Anatomy of the Nuremberg Trials: A Personal Memoir*. Boston: Little, Brown, 1992.

Thompson, Reginald W. *Cry Korea*. London: Macdonald, 1951.

Truman, Harry S. *Memoirs*. Vol. 1, *1945, Year of Decisions*. Garden City, NY: Doubleday, 1955.

———. *Memoirs*. Vol. 2, *Years of Trial and Hope*. Garden City, NY: Doubleday, 1956.

Walker, J. Samuel. Prompt and Utter Destruction: Truman and the Use of Atomic *Bombs Against Japan*. Chapel Hill, NC: University of North Carolina Press, 1997.

Walzer, Michael. *Just and Unjust Wars: A Moral Argument with Historical Illustrations*. New York: Basic, 1977.

Weart, Spencer R. *Nuclear Fear: A History of Images*. Cambridge, MA: Harvard University Press, 1988.

Wells, Donald. *The Laws of Land Warfare: A Guide to U.S. Army Manuals*. Westport, CT: Greenwood, 1992.

Wittner, Lawrence. *Rebels Against War: The American Peace Movement, 1933–1983*. rev. ed. Philadelphia: Temple University Press, 1984.

Winkler, Allan M. *Life Under a Cloud: American Anxiety About the Atom.* New York: Oxford University Press, 1993.

Y'Blood, William T., ed. *The Three Wars of Lt. Gen. George E. Stratemeyer: His Korean War Diary.* Washington, DC: Air Force History and Museums Program, 1999.

Yavenditti, Michael J. "The American People and the Use of Atomic Bombs on Japan: The 1940s." *Historian* 36, no. 2 (February 1974): 224–47.

York, Herbert F. *The Advisors: Oppenheimer, Teller, and the Superbomb.* Stanford, CA: Stanford University Press, 1976.

Notes

Chapter 1

1. Ronald Schaffer, Wings of Judgment: American Bombing in World War II (New York: Oxford University Press, 1985), 64, 97, 128–36; Michael S. Sherry, The Rise of American Air Power: The Creation of Armageddon (New Haven, CT: Yale University Press, 1987), 276–77; Wesley Frank Craven and James Lea Cate, eds., The Army Air Forces in World War II, vol. 5 (Washington, DC: Office of Air Force History, 1983), 614–17; Conrad C. Crane, Bombs, Cities, and Civilians: American Airpower Strategy in World War II (Lawrence, KS: University of Kansas Press, 1993), 140.
2. Wendy Doniger with Brian K. Smith, trans., The Laws of Manu, (New York: Penguin, 1991), 137–38; Pramathanath Bandyopadhyay, International Law and Custom in Ancient India (Calcutta: Calcutta University Press, 1920), 104–35; S. V. Viswanatha, International Law in Ancient India (Bombay: Longmans, Green, 1925), 155–57; Indra, Ideologies of War and Peace in Ancient India (Hoshrarpur: Vishveshraranand Institute Publications, 1957), 64–71.
3. Bradley Shavit Artson, Love Peace and Pursue Peace: A Jewish Response to War and Nuclear Annihilation (New York: United Synagogue of America Commission on Jewish Education, 1988), 150–59.
4. Majid Khadduri, War and Peace in the Law of Islam (Baltimore, MD: Johns Hopkins University Press, 1955), 102–107; John Kelsay, "Religion, Morality, and the Governance of War: The Case of Classical Islam," Journal of Religious Ethics 18, no. 2 (fall 1990): 123–39; Fred M. Donner, "The Sources of Islamic Conceptions of War," in Just War and Jihad: Historical and Theoretical Perspectives on War and Peace in Western and Islamic Traditions, ed. James Turner Johnson and John Kelsay (New York: Greenwood, 1991), 52.
5. James A. Aho, Religious Mythology and the Art of War: Comparative Religious Symbolisms of Military Violence (Westport, CT: Greenwood, 1981), 115–16.
6. James Turner Johnson, Just War Tradition and the Restraint of War: A Moral and Historical Inquiry (Princeton, NJ: Princeton University Press, 1981), 127, 131–50; James Turner Johnson, Ideology, Reason, and the Limitation of War: Religious and Secular Concepts 1200–1740 (Princeton, NJ: Princeton University Press, 1975), 7–8, 150–51, 195–203, 227–28, 235–40, 246–53, 263–65.
7. Armstrong Starkey, European and Native American Warfare, 1675–1815 (Norman, OK: University of Oklahoma Press, 1998), 25–26; Patrick M. Malone, The Skulking Way of War: Technology and Tactics Among the New England Indians (Lanham, MD: Madison, 1991), 78; Jill Lepore, The Name of War: King Philip's War and the Origins of American Identity (New York: Vintage, 1999), 8–13, 107–13.
8. Mark Grimsley, The Hard Hand of War: Union Military Policy Toward Southern Civilians, 1861–1865 (Cambridge: Cambridge University Press, 1995), 178–83.
9. Robert Winston Mardock, The Reformers and the American Indian (Columbia, MO: University of Missouri, 1971), 67–72; Helen Hunt Jackson, A Century of Dishonor (Boston: Little, Brown, 1905).
10. Stuart Creighton Miller, "Benevolent Assimilation": The American Conquest of the Philippines, 1899–1903 (New Haven, CT: Yale University Press, 1982), 206–52; Brian MacAlister Linn, The Philippine War, 1899–1902 (Lawrence, KS: University of Kansas Press, 2000), 300–21; Richard E. Welch, Jr., Response to Imperialism: The United States and the Philippine-American War, 1899–1902 (Chapel Hill, NC: University of North Carolina Press, 1979), 133–47.
11. Geoffrey Best, War and Society in Revolutionary Europe, 1770–1870 (New York: St. Martin's, 1982), 53–59, 77–81, 86–91, 155–88, 265–72.

12. Michael Clodfelter, Warfare and Armed Conflicts: A Statistical Reference to Casualty and Other Figures, 1618–1991, vol. 2 (Jefferson, NC: MacFarland, 1992), 707, 713, 715.
13. Geoffrey Best, Humanity in Warfare (New York: Columbia University Press, 1980), 147–57; Adam Roberts and Richard Guelff, eds., Documents on the Laws of War (Oxford: Clarendon, 1989), 52–53.
14. Clodfelter, Warfare and Armed Conflicts, 780–82.
15. John Horne and Alan Kramer, German Atrocities, 1914: A History of Denial (New Haven, CT: Yale University Press, 2001), 229–47.
16. Sherry, The Rise of American Air Power, 12–14.
17. Guilio Douhet, The Command of the Air, trans. Dino Ferrari (New York: Coward-McCann, 1942), 9–10, 20, 57–61, 150.
18. Roberts and Guelff, Documents on the Laws of War, 121–23, 126.
19. Crane, Bombs, Cities, Civilians, 18–27; Schaffer, Wings of Judgment, 23–34; Sherry, The Rise of American Air Power, 49–58.
20. Council on Foreign Relations, The United States in World Affairs: Account of American Foreign Relations 1937 (New York: Harper, 1938), 213; Council on Foreign Relations, The United States in World Affairs: Account of American Foreign Relations 1938 (New York: Harper, 1939), 311; "Barcelona Horrors," Time, March 28, 1938, 16; New York Times, June 13, 1938; Congressional Record, 75th Cong., 3rd sess., vol. 83, pt. 8, 9524–26, 9545; Public Papers and Addresses of Franklin D. Roosevelt, vol. 8 (New York: Macmillan, 1941), 454.
21. Schaffer, Wings of Judgment, 37–38; Sherry, The Rise of American Air Power, 144; Crane, Bombs, Cities, and Civilians, 31.
22. Schaffer, Wings of Judgment, 36, 38.
23. Ibid., 66–67, 103; Sherry, The Rise of American Air Power, 232–35; Crane, Bombs, Cities, and Civilians, 7–8.
24. New York Times, February 25, 1945; Schaffer, Wings of Judgment, 97–100; Sherry, The Rise of American Air Power, 289.
25. Sherry, The Rise of American Air Power, 139–40.
26. Paul Boyer, By the Bomb's Early Light: American Thought and Culture at the Dawn of the Atomic Age (New York: Pantheon, 1985), 22.
27. PPP 1945, 197, 212.
28. The Gallup Poll: Public Opinion, 1935–1971, vol. 1 (New York: Random House, 1972), 521–22; "The Fortune Survey," Fortune, December 1945, 305. Five and a half percent of those polled for the Fortune survey chose "Don't know."
29. Washington Post, August 23, 1945; Louisville Courier-Journal, August 26, 1945; Gallup Poll, vol. 1, 477; New York Times, April 6, 14, 1945.
30. David Lawrence, "What Hath Man Wrought!" U.S. News and World Report, August 17, 1945, 38–39; Boyer, By the Bomb's Early Light, 218; David E. Lilienthal, The Journals of David E. Lilienthal, vol. 2 (New York: Harper and Row, 1964), 271. Also see Lester Nurick, "The Distinction Between Combatant and Noncombatant in the Law of War," American Journal of International Law 39, no. 4 (October 1945): 680–97.
31. "Godless Gotterdammerung," Time, October 15, 1945, 62; Henry Emerson Fosdick, On Being Fit to Live With: Sermons on Post-War Christianity (New York: Harper and Brothers, 1946), 20, 77; Robert C. Batchelder, The Irreversible Decision, 1939–1950 (Boston: Houghton Mifflin, 1962), 170; Federal Council of Churches of Christ in America, Commission on the Relation of the Church to the War in the Light of Christian Faith, Atomic Warfare and the Christian Faith (New York, 1946), 11–13, 19; Lewis Mumford, "Atom Bomb," Air Affairs 2, no. 3 (July 1948): 326–45; A. J. Muste, Not by Might: Christianity, the Way to Human Decency (New York: Harper, 1947), 5–7, 15–17, 149–50.
32. David S. Wyman, "The United States," in The World Reacts to the Holocaust, ed. David S. Wyman (Baltimore: Johns Hopkins University Press, 1996), 705, 715; Peter Novick, The Holocaust in American Life (Boston: Houghton Mifflin, 1999), 63–65.
33. Telford Taylor, The Anatomy of the Nuremberg Trials: A Personal Memoir (Boston: Little, Brown, 1992), 640, 648; Ann Tusa and John Tusa, The Nuremberg Trial (London: Macmillan, 1983), 504; Wyman, "The United States," 718.
34. R. John Pritchard and Sonia Magbunua Zaide, eds., The Tokyo War Crimes Trial, vol. 1 (New York: Garland, 1981), 390; Philip R. Piccigallo, The Japanese on Trial: Allied War Crimes Operations in the East, 1945–1951 (Austin, TX: University of Texas Press, 1979), xi.

35. R. B. Pal, International Military Tribunal for the Far East: Dissentient Judgment (Calcutta: Sanyal, 1953), 620–21.
36. Roberts and Guelff, Documents on the Laws of War, 169–337; New York Times, December 9, 1949. For press reaction, see Chicago Tribune, December 11, 1949; Boston Post, December 10, 1950, Washington Post, January 5, 1950. The editorial pages of nine other major city dailies ignored the new conventions during the fall and winter of 1949. The dailies were New York Times, Los Angeles Times, Philadelphia Bulletin, Detroit News, Baltimore Sun, St. Louis Post-Dispatch, Cleveland Press, San Francisco Examiner, and Houston Chronicle.
37. Lawrence J. LeBlanc, The United States and the Genocide Convention, (Durham, NC: Duke University Press, 1991), 235–38.
38. Richard Shelly Hartigan, The Forgotten Victim: A History of the Civilian (Chicago: Precedent, 1982); Mark Grimsley and Clifford J. Rogers, eds., Civilians in the Path of War (Lincoln, NE: University of Nebraska Press, 2002). See also the popular and polemical history, Caleb Carr, The Lessons of Terror: A History of Warfare Against Civilians, Why It Has Always Failed and Why It Will Fail Again (New York: Random House, 2002).
39. James Turner Johnson, Ideology, Reason, and the Limitation of War: Religious and Secular Concepts 1200–1740 (Princeton, NJ: Princeton University Press, 1975); James Turner Johnson, The Just War Tradition and the Restraint of War: A Moral and Historical Inquiry (Princeton, NJ: Princeton University Press, 1981); Best, Humanity in Warfare; Geoffrey Best, War and Law Since 1945 (Oxford: Clarendon, 1994). The literature on just war theory is vast and generally prescriptive, concerned with how the just war concepts can be applied instead of its history. Michael Walzer, Just and Unjust Wars: A Moral Argument with Historical Illustrations (New York: Basic Books, 1977); Malham M. Wakin, ed., War, Morality, and the Military Profession (Boulder, CO: Westview, 1979); William V. O'Brien, The Conduct of Just and Limited War (New York: Praeger, 1981); Sheldon M. Cohen, Arms and Judgment: Law, Morality, and the Conduct of War in the Twentieth Century (Boulder, CO: Westview, 1989); Robert L. Holmes, On War and Morality (Princeton, NJ: Princeton University Press, 1989); A. J. Coates, The Ethics of War (New York: St. Martin's, 1997); James Turner Johnson, Morality and Contemporary Warfare (New Haven, CT: Yale University Press, 1999); Colm McKeogh, Innocent Civilians: The Morality of Killing in War (New York: Palgrave, 2002).
40. Schaffer, Wings of Judgment; Sherry, The Rise of American Air Power; Crane, Bombs, Cities, and Civilians; Tami Davis Biddle, Rhetoric and Reality in Air Warfare: The Evolution of British and American Ideas About Strategic Bombing, 1914–1945 (Princeton, NJ: Princeton University Press, 2002).
41. Gerald J. De Groot, The Bomb: A Life (Cambridge, MA: Harvard University Press, 2005); Boyer, By the Bomb's Early Light; Allan M. Winkler, Life Under a Cloud: American Anxiety About the Bomb (New York: Oxford University Press, 1993); Spencer R. Weart, Nuclear Fear: A History of Images (Cambridge, MA: Harvard University Press, 1988); Michael J. Yavendetti, "The American People and the Use of Atomic Bombs on Japan: The 1940s," Historian 36, no. 2 (February 1974): 224–47.
42. Guenter Lewy, America in Vietnam (New York: Oxford University Press, 1978); George McT. Kahin, Intervention: How America Became Involved in Vietnam (New York: Knopf, 1986).
43. George E. Hopkins, "Bombing and the American Conscience during World War II," Historian 28, no. 3 (May 1966): 451–73; Hartigan, The Forgotten Victim, 1–10; Schaffer, Wings of Judgment, 3, 217–18; H. Bruce Franklin, War Stars: The Superweapon and the American Imagination (New York: Oxford University Press, 1988), 105; Paul Boyer, Fallout: A Historian Reflects on America's Half-Century Encounter with Nuclear Weapons (Columbus, OH: Ohio State University Press, 1998), 12.

Chapter 2

1. Carl A. Spaatz, "Air Power in the Atomic Age," Collier's, December 8, 1945, 11–12, 83.
2. W. Stuart Symington, "Our Air Force Policy," Vital Speeches of the Day, July 1, 1949, 567–70.
3. William Bradford Huie, "The Facts Which Must Prevent War," Reader's Digest, January 1949, 23–30.

4. Transcript, Ray Henle, "Three-Star Extra," ABC, January 25, 1949, 6:45 p.m., box 106, Unclassified General Correspondence, RG 128, NA.
5. U.S. News and World Report, October 7, 1949, 30–33. Also see R. E. Lapp, Must We Hide? (Cambridge, MA: Addison-Wesley, 1949), 5, 70–73, 140–41.
6. Washington Post, March 15, 1949.
7. A Washington Post editorial condemning the UP story as warmongering equated the seventy targets with cities. Washington Post, March 15, 1949. The notion of targeting seventy Russian cities did not disappear from the press quickly, appearing in articles months after the initial report. D. V. Gallery, "An Admiral Talks Back to the Airmen," Saturday Evening Post, June 25, 1949, 25, 136–38; Philadelphia Bulletin, August 13, 1949; Los Angeles Times, October 6, 1949; "Atomic Threat," U.S. News and World Report, October 7, 1949, 20–21.
8. The official definition of strategic air warfare was: "Air combat and supporting operations designed to effect, through the systematic application of force to a selected series of vital targets, the progressive destruction and disintegration of the enemy's war-making capacity to a point where he no longer retains the ability or the will to wage war. Vital targets may include key manufacturing systems, sources of raw materials, critical material, stock piles, power systems, transportation systems, communication facilities, concentrations of uncommitted elements of enemy armed forces, key agricultural areas, and other such target systems." Memorandum, Ofstie to OP-05, November 10, 1948, box 3, Ralph A. Ofstie Papers, Operational Archives, Naval Historical Center (Hereafter OA, NHC).
9. U.S. House, Committee on Armed Services, Investigation of the B-36 Bomber Program: Hearings, 81st Cong. 1st sess., 1949, 126–27; J. M. Spaight, "A Matter of Nomenclature," Air University Quarterly Review 3, no. 2 (fall 1949): 24–29.
10. Hoffman Nickerson, "No Separate Air Force," Harper's, December 1942, 11; Hoffman Nickerson, Arms and Policy, 1939–1944 (New York: Putnam's, 1945), 267–98.
11. B. H. Liddell Hart, The Revolution in Warfare (New Haven, CT: Yale University Press, 1947), x, 34–36, 71–77, 83–95; J. F. C. Fuller, The Second World War, 1939–45: A Strategic and Tactical History (New York: Duell, Sloan, and Pearce, 1949), 220–31, 384–90, 402–408; P. M. S. Blackett, Fear, War, and the Bomb (New York: Whittlesey, 1949), 13–15, 39–44, 77.
12. Conference minutes, July 7, 1949, box 2389, 514.2, Central Decimal Files 1945–1949, RG 59, NA. For how the Soviets used this line of propaganda for domestic consumption, see airgram, Moscow Embassy to Secretary of State, July 12, 1949, box 2389, 514.2, Central Decimal Files 1945–1949, RG 59, NA.
13. For example, the New York Times ran three short wire service dispatches on the affair which included the nature of the Soviet resolution but little else. New York Times, July 8, 20, August 10, 1949.
14. Washington Post, January 10, 23, 1949; Philadelphia Bulletin, August 13, 1949; New York Times, May 22, 1949; Hanson W. Baldwin, "What Kind of War?" Atlantic, July 1949, 22–27. At the end of the year Baldwin produced a short book in which he pronounced the destruction of Hiroshima and Nagasaki with the atomic bomb as one of the great mistakes of the war. Hanson W. Baldwin, Great Mistakes of the War (New York: Harper, 1949). Walter Lippmann, "The Russian-American War," Atlantic, July 1949, 17–21. Also see William H. Hessler, "The A-Bomb Won't Do What You Think," Collier's, September 17, 1949, 16–17, 72; William H. Hessler, Operation Survival: America's New Role in World Affairs (New York: Prentice-Hall, 1949).
15. Spaight gave Hoffman Nickerson and his references to "baby-killing" as an example of such a critic.
16. J. M. Spaight, Air Power Can Disarm: A Sequel to Air Power and the Cities, 1930 (London: Air League of the British Empire, 1948), 9–14, 164–68; Stefan T. Possony, Strategic Air Power: The Pattern of Dynamic Security (Washington: Infantry Journal Press, 1949), 48–62.
17. David MacIsaac, Strategic Bombing in World War Two: The Story of the United States Strategic Bombing Survey (New York: Garland, 1976), 100–102, 141–42.
18. Alfred Hassler, "Execution with a Straight Face," Fellowship 15, no. 2 (February 1949): 14–17; Walter M. Horton, "The Revolutionary Years," Christian Century, April 13, 1949, 490–92; James E. Kelly, "If Atom Bombs Should Fall," Catholic World, October 1949, 28–33; "Churchill and Amsterdam," Christian Century, April 20, 1949, 488; "Jesuit Editor Protests Plans for Atomic Bombing," Christian Century, September 17, 1949, 1028; "Atomic Slaughter," America, August 13, 1949, 516; "Alternative to Strategic Bombing," America, September 3, 1949, 573–74.

19. Memorandum, Pace to Truman, April 5, 1949, Subject File, President Harry S. Truman's Office Files, microfilm collection, (Bethesda, MD: University Publications of America, 1989); Congressional Record, 81st Cong., 1st sess., vol. 95, pt. 12, A337; ibid., pt. 6, 8407; New York Times, June 28, 1949.

20. W. Barton Leach to Ernest S. Griffith, February 7, 1950, box 59, Leach Papers, HLSL; memorandum, [Leach] to Thomas K. Finletter, May 6, 1950, box 52, Leach Papers, HLSL.

21. Alfred F. Kalberer to Leo, November 9, 1949, box 16, Formerly Classified General Correspondence 1950–1952, Public Information Division, Office of Information Services, RG 340, NA.

22. Steven L. Rearden, The Formative Years, 1947–1950, vol. 1 of History of the Office of the Secretary of Defense, ed. Arthur Goldberg (Washington: Historical Office, Office of the Secretary of Defense, 1984), 354–57.

23. "Why the Navy Wants Big Aircraft Carriers," U.S. News and World Report, May 20, 1949, 24–28; D. V. Gallery, "An Admiral Talks Back to the Airmen," Saturday Evening Post, June 25, 1949, 25, 136–38.

24. House Committee on Armed Services, The National Defense Program — Unification and Strategy: Hearings, 81st Congress, 1st sess., 1949, 41–43, 50–52.

25. Ibid., 55–56, 102.

26. Ibid., 183–89.

27. Ibid., 190, 192. "Impressions of Today's Hearings," October 11, 1949, box 7, Files of Senate Investigations August–October 1949, Executive Office, Office of the Deputy Chief of Staff for Operations, RG 341, NA.

28. He may have been thinking of the 1923 Hague Air Warfare Draft Rules, which attempted to limit the aerial bombardment of cities but were never adopted.

29. National Defense Program, 238–40, 246, 273–74, 338, 340, 346.

30. Ibid., 349–62.

31. Radford rejected the suggestion that the mass bombing of cities might be necessary to win a war because he claimed that the bombing of cities was an inefficient method for defeating an opponent. Ibid., 80–81, 106.

32. Ibid., 178, 216–17; New York Times, October 17, 1949.

33. Ibid., 212, 217.

34. Generalizations about newspapers in this chapter are based on the examination of the news and editorial coverage from twelve American newspapers. For each newspaper, editorial pages and columns were examined for the entire months of October and November and full news coverage was examined from October 7 to October 23. The twelve daily newspapers surveyed for this study were the New York Times, Chicago Tribune, Los Angeles Times, Philadelphia Bulletin, Detroit News, Baltimore Sun, St. Louis Post-Dispatch, Cleveland Press, Washington Post, Boston Post, San Francisco Examiner, and Houston Chronicle. One daily newspaper was selected from each of the eleven largest cities in the United States according to the 1950 census. The Houston Chronicle was added to the sample to provide more regional balance, Houston being the third largest city in the south behind Baltimore and Washington and fourteenth largest city in the country. Most of the newspapers selected were the dailies with the largest circulation in their city. The New York Times and Washington Post were selected over dailies with significantly larger circulation because of the prestige of the papers and to prevent the sample from overrepresenting papers from the McCormick and Hearst newspaper chains. The Boston Post was selected over a paper with a slightly larger circulation to prevent overrepresentation of the Hearst chain. The sample contains one daily each from the Hearst, McCormick, and Scripps-Howard newspaper chains. The twelve newspapers in this sample had a combined average weekday circulation of approximately 4.9 million and average Sunday circulation of approximately 6.8 million in 1950. N. W. Ayer and Son's Directory of Newspapers and Periodicals, 1950 (Philadelphia: N. W. Ayer and Son, 1950).

35. New York Times, October 8, 10–14, 17, 1949; Washington Post, October 8, 11–14, and 17, 1949; Baltimore Sun, October 8, 10, 12–14, 1949. The editorial pages of the Washington Post and Baltimore Sun had expressed concern over the current conception of strategic bombing in early October even before the admirals' testimony. Washington Post, October 3, 1949; Baltimore Sun, October 3, 1949. U.S. News and World Report also gave the admirals' criticism of attacking noncombatants a prominent place in its coverage of the hearings. "Why Navy Officers Risk Careers," U.S. News and World Report, October 14, 1949, 22–23.

36. St. Louis Post-Dispatch, October 7, 11–13; Philadelphia Bulletin, October 7, 11–13, 1949; Cleveland Press, October 7, 11–13, 1949.
37. St. Louis Post-Dispatch, October 12, 1949.
38. Detroit News, October 12, 1949; Houston Chronicle, October 12, 1949.
39. New York Times, October 12, 1949; Washington Post, October 12, 1949. A Time magazine article on the hearings included Ofstie's picture with the pictures of three of the Navy's top leaders and war heroes, Halsey, Denfeld, and Blandy. "Facts and Fears," Time, October 24, 1949, 26–27.
40. St. Louis Post-Dispatch, October 23, 1949; Detroit News, October 13, 1949.
41. Washington Post, October 13, 1949; Philadelphia Bulletin, October 13, 1949. An October 13 St. Louis Post-Dispatch editorial also mentioned Halsey's claim that strategic bombing would unite the enemy.
42. Houston Chronicle, October 12, 18, 1949; Los Angeles Times, October 18, 1949; Detroit News, October 13, 21, 1949; Philadelphia Bulletin, October 20, 1949.
43. Philadelphia Bulletin, October 20, 1949.
44. Los Angeles Times, October 8, 12–14, 1949; Boston Post, October 11, 13, 17, 1949; San Francisco Examiner, October 8, 12–14, 17, 1949; Chicago Tribune, October 8, 12, 17 1949.
45. Untitled paper, n.a., n.d., box 5, Files of Senate Investigations August–October 1949, Executive Office, Office of the Deputy Chief of Staff for Operations, RG 341, NA; untitled paper, Orville A. Anderson, n.d., box 7, Files of Senate Investigations August–October 1949, Executive Office, Office of the Deputy Chief of Staff for Operations, RG 341, NA.
46. National Defense Program, 402–403.
47. Ibid., 413.
48. Ibid., 433–34.
49. Ibid., 434.
50. Ibid., 436.
51. National Defense Program, 453–58, 480; untitled draft paper, W. Barton Leach, October 10, 1949, box 7, Symington Papers, HSTL; Jeffrey G. Barlow, Revolt of the Admirals: The Fight for Naval Aviation, 1945–1950 (Washington, DC: Naval Historical Center, Department of the Navy, 1994), 257; Washington Post, October 10, 1949; New York Times, October 12, 1949.
52. Joint Committee on Atomic Energy, "Notes on Closed Meeting Held October 14, 1949," October 15, 1949, Unpublished United States House Hearings, microfiche collection (Bethesda, MD: Congressional Information Service, 1992).
53. National Defense Program, 346.
54. Ibid., 74–75, 212.
55. Ibid., 421, 463–64, 509.
56. Ibid., 238–39.
57. Ronald Schaffer, Wings of Judgment: American Bombing in World War II (New York: Oxford University Press, 1985), 89, 140–41.
58. National Defense Program, 520–23.
59. Ibid., 536.
60. PPP, 1949, 509, 511; Truman to Overton Brooks, October 27, 1949, Subject File, Truman's Office Files; "Overnight Information Policy Guidance No. 309 for INP, IBD, and Occupied Areas," October 14, 1949, box 90, Lot 52D335, International Information Activities 1930–1953, RG 59, NA.
61. New York Times, November 30, 1949; Philadelphia Bulletin, October 12, 1949; Washington Post, October 23, 1949.
62. New York Times, October 27, November 17, 1949; Washington Post, October 3, 13, 19, 29, 1949. Symington's reassurance that the Air Force did not favor the mass bombing of civilians attracted a significant amount of attention in the press. New York Times, October 19, 1949; Washington Post, October 19, 1949; Baltimore Sun, October 19, 1949; Philadelphia Bulletin, October 18, 1949; St. Louis Post-Dispatch, October 18, 1949; Boston Post, October 19, 1949; Los Angeles Times, October 19, 1949.
63. One letter to the editor of the Cleveland Press supporting the ban said, "Think of the destruction the bomb could do, the killing of innocent people." Cleveland Press, October 6, 1949.
64. Chester I. Barnard, "Arms Race v. Control," Scientific American, November 1949, 11–13; Detroit News, October 13, 21, 1949.

65. "If New Wars Come, They Will Be More 'Total' Than Ever," Saturday Evening Post, November 19, 1949, 10.
66. New York Times, December 23, 1949; transcript, "What Should the Free World Do About the Atomic Bomb?" ABC, 8:30 p.m., October 25, 1949, box 48, Years in the House 1940–1952 series, Henry M. Jackson Papers, University of Washington Library; St. Louis Post-Dispatch, October 12, 1949.
67. "The Shape of Things," Nation, October 15, 1949, 357; Baltimore Sun, October 23, 1949; Philadelphia Bulletin, October 12, 21, 1949; Detroit News, October 22, 1949; Cleveland Press, October 19, 26, 1949; Ray Holland, Jr., "The Unification Row," Collier's, December 31, 1949, 26–27; "Committee Room Campaign," Commonweal, October 21, 1949, 28–29; "Morals and the Bomb," Commonweal, October 28, 1949, 59–60.
68. Washington Post, November 13, 1949.
69. "Why Navy Officers Risk Careers," U.S. News and World Report, October 14, 1949, 22–23; "How Should U.S. Be Defended? Military Chiefs in a Muddle," U.S. News and World Report, October 21, 1949, 14–17; "Next War: Hand to Hand," U.S. News and World Report, October 28, 1949, 16–17; "Storm over the Pentagon," Newsweek, October 17, 1949, 23–27; "Undress Parade," Newsweek, October 24, 1949, 23–24.
70. Los Angeles Times, October 28, 1949; Boston Post, October 21, 1949.
71. "Revolt of the Admirals," Time, October 17, 1949, 21–23; "Facts and Fears," Time, October 24, 1949, 26–27; "The Incorrigible and Indomitable," Time, October 31, 1949, 13–15.
72. San Francisco Examiner, October 13, 1949; Fletcher Pratt, "War in the Pentagon III," Nation, January 7, 1950, 10–12.
73. St. Louis Post-Dispatch, October 18, 20, 21, 23, November 23, 1949.
74. Ibid., October 20, 1949; Detroit News, October 20, 1949.
75. Washington Post, October 11, 1949.
76. Carl Kaysen, "Military Importance of the Atomic Bomb," Bulletin of the Atomic Scientist, December 1949, 340–43.
77. New York Times, October 19, 1949. For the sole exception in the twelve newspapers and numerous periodicals examined, see the brief mention of a comment by Representative Kilday. Washington Post, October 12, 1949.
78. New York Times, October 17, 1949. Similar articles appeared on October 17, 1949 in the Washington Post, Baltimore Sun, Los Angeles Times, San Francisco Examiner, and St. Louis Post-Dispatch.
79. Daily Worker, October 12–14, 1949.
80. Ibid., October 19, 1949.
81. San Francisco Examiner, October 18, 1949.
82. Ibid., December 18, 1949.
83. Chicago Tribune, October 23, November 6, 15, 1949.
84. MacIsaac, Strategic Bombing in World War Two, 119–35.
85. Memorandum, Ofstie to Deputy Chief of Naval Operations for Air, September 26, 1947, box 3, Ofstie Papers, OA, NHC; memorandum, Ofstie to Chief of the Bureau of Aeronautics, June 21, 1948, box 3, Ofstie Papers, OA, NHC; memorandum, Ofstie to Radford, August 31, 1949, box 4, Ofstie Papers, OA, NHC; Ofstie to Halsey, September 23, 1949, box 4, Ofstie Papers, OA, NHC.
86. Memorandum, Ofstie to P. E. Pihl, October 14, 1948, box 3, Ofstie Papers, OA, NHC; memorandum, Ofstie to OP-05, November 10, 1948, box 3, Ofstie Papers, OA, NHC; memorandum, Ofstie to OP-05, April 29, 1949, box 4, Ofstie Papers, OA, NHC.
87. Memorandum, Ofstie to Chairman of General Board, April 8, 1948, box 3, Ofstie Papers, OA, NHC.
88. John W. Dower, War Without Mercy: Race and Power in the Pacific War (New York: Pantheon, 1986), 35–36, 85.
89. Memorandum, Ofstie to Arleigh A. Burke, September 14, 1949, box 4, Ofstie Papers, OA, NHC.
90. Ofstie to Field, October 13, 1949, box 4, Ofstie Papers, OA, NHC.
91. Ofstie to Gallery, October 14, 1949, box 4, Ofstie Papers, OA, NHC.
92. Daily Worker, October 31, 1949.
93. S. Arthur Devan, "Planning National Defense, 1950 to 1970," Public Affairs Bulletin No. 75, September 1949, Legislative Reference Service, Library of Congress, 43, 46, 54, 56. A copy can be found in box 59, Leach Papers, HLSL.

94. Leach to Ernest S. Griffith, February 7, 1950, box 59, Leach Papers, HLSL; Griffith to Leach, February 23, 1950, box 59, Leach Papers, HLSL.
95. Orvil A. Anderson, "Air Warfare and Morality," Air University Quarterly Review 3, no. 3 (winter 1949): 5–14.
96. John J. Wood, "The Morality of War," Air University Quarterly Review 4, no. 1 (summer 1950): 31–42.
97. Philip Schwartz, "Bombing Accuracy," Ordnance 34, no. 178 (January–February 1950): 230–33; New York Times, January 3, 1950.
98. Press release, Public Information Office, Headquarters, Eighth Air Force, December 12, 1949, box 15, Formerly Classified General Correspondence 1950–1952, Public Information Division, Office of Information Services, RG 340, NA. For another example, see Robert J. Seabolt, "Why Emphasize Air Power?" Air University Quarterly Review 3, no. 3 (winter 1949): 2–3.
99. Alexander P. de Seversky, Air Power: Key to Survival (New York: Simon and Schuster, 1950), 66–69. The chapter suggests that it was written in part as a response to the Navy's criticism of strategic bombing. It included a reference to disagreeing with the Navy's recent commendation of bombardment as immoral.
100. Alexander P. de Seversky, Victory Through Air Power (New York: Simon and Schuster, 1942), 8–12.
101. Alexander P. de Seversky, "Atomic Bomb Hysteria," Reader's Digest, February 1946, 121–26.
102. Paul Y. Hammond, "Super Carriers and B-36 Bombers: Appropriations, Strategy, and Politics," in American Civil-Military Decisions: A Book of Case Studies, ed. Harold Stein (Tuscaloosa, AL.: University of Alabama Press, 1963), 465–567; Keith D. McFarland, "The 1949 Revolt of the Admirals," Parameters 11, no. 2 (1981): 53–63; Phillip S. Meilinger, "The Admirals' Revolt of 1949: Lessons for Today," Parameters 19, no. 3 (September 1989): 81–96; Warren A. Trest, "View From the Gallery: Laying to Rest the Admirals' Revolt of 1949," Air Power History 42, no. 1 (spring 1995): 17–29; Barlow, Revolt of the Admirals.

Chapter 3

1. Washington Post, December 1, January 2, 4, 6, 1950; St. Louis Post-Dispatch, January 4, 5, 1950; Houston Chronicle, January 7, 10, 1950.
2. GAC report, October 30, 1949 reprinted in Herbert F. York, The Advisors: Oppenheimer, Teller, and the Superbomb (San Francisco, CA: W. H. Freeman, 1976), 150–59.
3. Dubridge to Lilienthal, December 5, 1949, box 8, Combined Policy Committee, Office of the Assistant Secretary of Defense for Atomic Energy, RG 330, NA.
4. Memorandum, AEC to President, November 9, 1949, FRUS 1949, vol. 1, 576–85.
5. R. G. Hooker, Jr., "The Moral and Ideological Implications of U.S. Policy on the Use of the Atomic Weapon," December 15, 1949, box 6, Lot 64D563, Subject Files, Policy Planning Staff 1947–1953, RG 59, NA.
6. Memorandum, Hickerson, January 11, 1950, FRUS 1950, vol. 1, 10; memorandum, Kennan, January 20, 1950, FRUS 1950, vol. 1, 22–44.
7. Memorandum, Nitze, December 19, 1949, FRUS 1949, vol. 1, 610–11.
8. Memorandum, James E. Webb to Nitze, December 3, 1949, FRUS 1949, vol. 1, 599–600; Dean Acheson, Present at the Creation: My Years in the State Department (New York: Norton, 1969), 346, 348.
9. Memorandum, Strauss to Truman, November 25, 1949, FRUS 1949, vol. 1, 596–99.
10. McMahon to Truman, November 21, 1949, FRUS 1949, vol. 1, 588–95.
11. Memorandum, Bradley to Johnson, November 23, 1949, FRUS 1949, vol. 1, 595–96; Bradley to Johnson, January 13, 1950, FRUS 1950, vol. 1, 503–11.
12. PPP 1950, 138.
13. The Gallup Poll: Public Opinion, 1935–1971, vol. 2 (New York: Random House, 1972), 888; Washington Post, February 1, 1950; Houston Chronicle, February 1, 1950; Baltimore Sun, February 1, 1950; San Francisco Examiner, February 1, 8, and 17, 1950; Boston Post, February 2, 1950; Los Angeles Times, February 10, 1950; New York Times, February 5, 1950.
14. Washington Post, December 1, 1949, January 25, 1950; "Hydrogen Bomb: Next Superweapon?" U.S. News and World Report, January 13, 1950, 21–22; Washington Post, January 25, 1950; "The Hydrogen Bomb," Life, January 30, 1950, 23; Baltimore Sun, February 2, 1950; Los Angeles Times, February 2, 1950.

15. Transcript, Drew Pearson, ABC, 6:00 p.m., January 15, 1950, box 106, Unclassified General Correspondence, RG 128, NA; "Guilt," Commonweal, January 27, 1950, 428–29; "The Root of Our Moral Crisis," Christian Century, March 8, 1950, 294–95; National Guardian, February 8, 1950; Detroit News, February 5, 1950; Philadelphia Bulletin, February 11, 26, 1950; St. Louis Post-Dispatch, February 18, 1950.
16. U.S. Senate, Committee on Foreign Relations, The Genocide Convention: Hearings, 81st Cong., 2nd sess., 1950, 309–10, 469–70; St. Louis Post-Dispatch, February 1, 1950; Philadelphia Bulletin, February 1, 1950; Chicago Tribune, February 2, 1950; Los Angeles Times, February 2, 1950; Congressional Record, 81st Cong., 2nd sess., vol. 96, pt. 14, A1767.
17. Washington Post, February 9, 1950; New York Times, February 24, 1950; Daily Worker, February 9, 1950.
18. New York Times, February 3, 1950; message, Tokyo Embassy to Secretary of State, February 8, 1950, box 3173, 711.5611, Central Decimal Files 1950–1954, RG 59, NA.
19. New York Times, February 12, 1950. See also New York Times, February 6, 1950; Washington Post, February 4 and 15, 1950; St. Louis Post-Dispatch, February 4, 1950; National Guardian, March 8, 1950; Westbury Quarterly Meeting of the Religious Society of Friends to Truman, February 4, 1950, box 3173, 711.5611, Central Decimal Files 1950–1954, RG 59, NA; Ruth Thomas to Truman, January 30, 1950, box 6, Subject Files 1946–1950, Office Files of David E. Lilienthal, RG 326, NA; Beretam Fox et al. to Lilienthal, February 13, 1950, box 6, Subject Files 1946–1950, Office Files of David E. Lilienthal, RG 326, NA.
20. Respectively, 30 percent, 9 percent, and 10 percent.
21. The other answers garnering more than 5 percent were 19 percent for "use only in self-defense" and 7 percent for "none of our business." "Popular Attitudes Toward Some Questions on the Atomic Bomb," February 20, 1950, box 7, Lot 57D688, Office of the Special Assistant to the Secretary for Atomic Energy 1944–1952, RG 59, NA.
22. Wallace Carroll, "It Takes a Russian to Beat a Russian," Life, December 26, 1949, 80–88. Also see Washington Post, December 27, 1950.
23. David Lawrence, "The Battle Against Fear," U.S. News and World Report, March 17, 1950, 37; Washington Post, February 25, 1950.
24. "WRL Statement on the Hydrogen Bomb," 1950, box 10, series B, War Resisters League Papers, SPC; Paul Scherer et al., "Statement on the Hydrogen Bomb Issue," January 27, 1950, box 3, series A-4, section II, Fellowship of Reconciliation-USA Papers, SPC; "An Adequate and Moral Program of National Defense," Special Supplement, Peacemaker 1, no. 11 (March 15, 1950), Peacemakers Papers, SPC.
25. New York Times, September 3, 1948.
26. Ibid., February 27, 1950.
27. Bible News Flashes, February 1950, 6–9, The Right Wing Collection of the University of Iowa Libraries, 1918–1977, microfilm collection (Glen Rock, NJ: Microfilming Corporation of America, 1977), B7.
28. New York Times, February 4, 1950; "The Urge to Do Something," Time, February 13, 1950, 15; "The Soul-Searchers Find No Answer," Life, February 27, 1950, 37–40.
29. New York Times, February 15, March 22, 1950.
30. Ibid., January 18, 26, February 5, 26, 1950; "Hydrogen Age ... Whither America?" Newsweek, February 13, 1950, 17–20; Houston Chronicle, February 10, 1950.
31. New York Times, February 4, 1950; "The H-Bomb," Commonweal, February 17, 1950, 499.
32. New York Times, January 29, April 15, June 20, 1950; Lewis L. Strauss, "Some A-Bomb Fallacies Are Exposed," Life, July 24, 1950, 81–90.
33. George Fielding Eliot, "What the Russian 'A-Bomb' Means to You," American Legion, February 1950, 16–17, 54–55.
34. Memorandum, Borden to Cole, July 24, 1950, box 62, Declassified General Subject Files, RG 128, NA; Congressional Record, 81st Cong., 2nd sess., vol. 96, pt. 16, A5316–8.
35. Millard E. Tydings, "World Disarmament," Vital Speeches of the Day, March 1, 1950, 290–95; New York Times, February 5, 1950; St. Louis Post-Dispatch, February 1, 2, 1950; Detroit News, February 6, 12, 19, 20, 27, 1950; Cleveland Press, February 7, 1950.
36. "The Hydrogen Bomb," New Republic, February 13, 1950, 5–8; Freda Kirchwey, "Some Other Choices," Nation, February 11, 1950, 121–22; "Hydrogen Bomb Brings Another Day of Judgment," Christian Century, February 1, 1950, 131; "Alternative to Atomic Chaos,"

Christian Century, February 15, 1950, 199–200; Walter M. Horton, "War Can Be Overcome," Christian Century, April 12, 1950, 459–61; New York Times, February 13, 1950.

37. "H-Bomb: Prelude to What?" America, February 11, 1950, 541; Philadephia Bulletin, February 6, 1950.

38. New York Times, February 5, 1950.

39. Ibid., February 13, 1950; Hans A. Bethe, "The Hydrogen Bomb," Bulletin of the Atomic Scientists, April 1950, 99–104, 125; Hans A. Bethe, "The Hydrogen Bomb II," Scientific American, April 1950, 18–23.

40. Washington Post, February 4, 1950; Philadelphia Bulletin, February 4, 1950; Cleveland Press, February 4, 1950; St. Louis Post-Dispatch, February 4 and 5, 1950; New York Times, February 5, 1950; Chicago Tribune, February 5, 1950; Baltimore Sun, February 5, 1950; Detroit News, February 5, 1950; Boston Post, February 5, 1950; Los Angeles Times, February 5, 1950; San Francisco Examiner, February 5, 1950.

41. New York Times, February 20, March 14, 1950; St. Louis Post-Dispatch, February 1, 1950; Philadelphia Bulletin, February 8, 1950; Houston Chronicle, February 7, 1950.

42. "Record of the Meeting of the State-Defense Policy Review Group," February 27, 1950, FRUS 1950, vol. 1, 168–75; memorandum, Kennan, January 20, 1950, FRUS 1950, vol. 1, 22–44.

43. William L. Laurence, The Hell Bomb (New York: Knopf, 1951), 68–70, 72–74, 105.

44. William L. Laurence, "The Truth About the Hydrogen Bomb," Business Week, June 24, 1950, 17–19, 90–94; New York Times, June 30, 1950. William Borden shared Laurence's belief that the hydrogen bomb could be an important tactical weapon. Memorandum, Borden to Cole, July 24, 1950, box 62, Declassified General Subject Files, RG 128, NA.

45. "What About the H-Bomb?" Life, January 8, 1951, 57–60; James R. Newman, "'Destroy Them with a Mighty Destruction,'" New Republic, January 22, 1951, 18–19; "Books," New Yorker, January 27, 1951, 79–80; Roy Gibbons, "Greatest Peril Since the 'Black Death,'" Chicago Tribune Magazine of Books, January 28, 1951, 3. For the openly skeptical reviews, see William A. Higinbotham, "The H-Bomb and the Clouded Future," New York Times Book Review, January 7, 1951, 3, 20; "Books in Brief," Nation, February 17, 1951, 160; Gerald Wendt, Atomic Energy and the Hydrogen Bomb (New York: Medill McBride, 1950), 130.

46. "Our Standpat Atomic Policy," America, February 18, 1950, 570; "Reservoir of Christian Hope," America, February 18, 1950, 572.

47. Edward A. Conway, "A Moralist, a Scientist, and the H-Bomb," America, April 8, 1950, 9–11; letter to editor, America, May 27, 1950, 256. For Connell's original article, see Francis J. Connell, "Is the H-Bomb Right or Wrong?" Sign, March 1950, 11–13, 71. Connell's views did receive a little exposure in the national press. The UP offered a story which mentioned that the hydrogen bomb could be used in a just war. St. Louis Post-Dispatch, February 1, 1950.

48. New York Times, February 10, 1950; "Limits on the Atom Bomb," U.S. News and World Report, March 17, 1950, 28–32; Los Angeles Times, February 15, 1950.

49. Nitze to Dean Rusk, January 30, 1950, box 114, Lot 66D95, Records relating to State Department Participation in the Operations Coordinating Board and the NSC 1947–1963, RG 59, NA; memorandum with attachment, James S. Lay to NSC, January 26, 1950, box 45, Lot File 61D167, Policy Planning Staff, 1935–1962, RG 59, NA; Department of Defense, Semiannual Report of the Secretary of Defense, July 1 to December 31, 1949 (Washington: U.S. Government Printing Office, 1950), 63–64.

50. Letter with attachment, Pike to President, May 26, 1950, box 1, White House Correspondence 1947–1950, Office Files of David E. Lilienthal, RG 326, NA; memorandum with attachment, Lay to R. Gordon Arneson et al., June 7, 1950, box 12, Lot 71D163, Subject Files of the Special Assistant for Atomic Energy and Aerospace 1950–1966, Office of the Deputy Assistant Secretary for Political-Military Affairs, RG 59, NA; letter with attachment, Carlton Savage to R. Gordon Arneson, June 13, 1950, box 7, Lot 64D563, Subject Files, Policy Planning Staff, RG 59, NA; "Overnight Information Policy Guidance No. 382," n.d., box 90, Lot 52D335, Records Relating to International Information Activities 1930–1953, RG 59, NA; "Overnight Information Policy Guidance No. 383," February 1, 1950, box 90, Lot File 52D335, Records Relating to International Information Activities 1930–1953, RG 59, NA.

51. JCS 1477/1, "Overall Effect of Atomic Bomb on Warfare and Military Organization," October 30, 1945, 4, in America's Plans for War Against the Soviet Union, 1945–1950, ed. Steven T. Ross and David Alan Rosenberg, vol. 1 (New York: Garland, 1989–90); JWPC 486/7,

"Guidance for Mobilization Planning as Effected [sic] by the Use of Atomic Weapons," July 29, 1947, 24, 70–73, in America's Plans for War, vol. 5; JCS 1952/1, "Evaluation of Current Strategic Air Offensive Plans," 6–8, in America's Plans for War, vol. 9; JIC 329, "Strategic Vulnerability of the USSR to a Limited Air Attack," November 3, 1945, in America's Plans for War, vol. 1; JWPC 416/1, "Military Position of the United States in the Light of Russian Policy," January 8, 1946, 36, in America's Plans for War, vol. 1; JSPG 496/4, "Broiler," February 11, 1948, 176, 178–79, in America's Plans for War, vol. 6; JCS 1953/1, "Evaluation of Effect on Soviet War Effort Resulting from the Strategic Air Offensive," May 12, 1949, 95, in America's Plans for War, vol. 11.

52. JCS 1953/1, "Evaluation of Effect on Soviet War Effort Resulting from the Strategic Air Offensive," May 12, 1949, 16–17, in America's Plans for War, vol. 11. For another example of this attitude, see JCS 1952/1, "Evaluation of Current Strategic Air Offensive Plans, 6–7, in America's Plans for War, vol. 9.

53. JCS 2081/1, "Implications of Soviet Possession of Atomic Weapons," February 21, 1950, 51, in America's Plans for War, vol. 11; JWPC 486/7, "Guidance for Mobilization Planning as Effected [sic] by the Use of Atomic Weapons," July 29, 1947, 68–70, in America's Plans for War, vol. 5; JCS 1953/1, "Evaluation of Effect on Soviet War Effort Resulting from the Strategic Air Offensive," May 12, 1949, 180–81, in America's Plans for War, vol. 11. It should be noted that the quoted study was an analysis of the impact of a Soviet atomic attack on the United States.

54. JCS 1953/1, "Evaluation of Effect on Soviet War Effort Resulting from the Strategic Air Offensive," May 12, 1949, 180–81, in America's Plans for War, vol. 11; JWPC 486/7, "Guidance for Mobilization Planning as Effected [sic] by the Use of Atomic Weapons," July 29, 1947, 71, in America's Plans for War, vol. 5; JSPG 496/4, "Broiler," February 11, 1948, 16, in America's Plans for War, vol. 6; JCS 1920/5, "Dropshot," December 19, 1949, in America's Plans for War, vol. 14.

55. New York Times, May 3, 1950; David P. Forsythe, Humanitarian Politics: The International Committee of the Red Cross (Baltimore: Johns Hopkins University Press, 1977), 118–19.

Chapter 4

1. Teletype conference, Frank Pace et al. and MacArthur et al., June 27, Documentary History of the Truman Presidency, ed. Dennis Merrill, vol. 18, (Bethesda, MD: University Publications of America, 1997), 53–60.

2. Message, JCS to MacArthur, June 29, 1950, FRUS 1950, vol. 7, 240–41.

3. Draft notes on June 29, 1950 White House defense meeting, box 71, Elsey Papers, HSTL; memorandum of conversation, Philip C. Jessup, June 29, 1950, box 4263, 795.00, Central Decimal Files 1950–1954, RG 59, NA; message, Warren R. Austin to Acheson, June 27, 1950, FRUS 1950, vol. 7, 208–209. A Saturday Evening Post article from November 1951 about the June 29 meeting claimed that the president had placed the restrictions on North Korean targets to insure the bombing would not be indiscriminate. Beverly Smith, "Why We Went to War in Korea," Saturday Evening Post, November 10, 1951, 22–23, 76–88. There is some disagreement in the sources about what exactly happened at the June 29 NSC meeting. Truman's memoirs claimed that Pace suggested the limitations on operations in North Korea, but this is clearly contradicted by the contemporary accounts of the meeting. Harry S. Truman, Memoirs, vol. 2, Years of Trial and Hope (Garden City, NY: Doubleday, 1956), 341. The official Air Force history claims that the restrictions were placed on the bombing of North Korea out of humanitarian considerations, but the evidence it offers does not support this claim. Humanitarian considerations may have been in the back of Truman's mind in the June 29 meeting, but the contemporary accounts of the meeting gave no indication of this and Truman's memoirs did not explain his motivation this way. Robert Futrell, The United States Air Force in Korea 1950–1953, rev. ed. (Washington, DC: U.S. Government Printing Office, 1983), 41–42.

4. O'Donnell to LeMay, July 11, 1950, box 65, series B, LeMay Papers, LC.

5. Stratemeyer to O'Donnell, July 11, 1950, box 103, Series B, LeMay Papers, LC; HQ USAF, An Evaluation of the Effectiveness of the United States Air Force in the Korean Campaign (Barcus Report), vol. 5, 2, box 906, Project Decimal Files 1942–1954, Directorate of Plans, Office of the Deputy Chief of Staff for Operations, RG 341, NA; Charles J. Bondley, Jr., to LeMay, July 16, 1950, box 65, series B, LeMay Papers, LC.

6. U.S. Senate, Committee on Armed Services, The Military Situation in the Far East: Hearings, 82nd Cong., 1st sess., 3063, 3072–73; Curtis E. LeMay with MacKinley K. Cantor, Mission with LeMay: My Story (Garden City, N.Y.: Doubleday, 1965), 382.

7. Message, Moscow Embassy to Secretary of State, June 30, 1950, box 4263, 795.00, Central Decimal Files 1950–1954, RG 59, NA; message, London Embassy to Secretary of State, July 1, 1950, box 4264, 795.00, Central Decimal Files 1950–1954, RG 59, NA.; New York Times, July 4, 11, 12, 14, 18, 26, 1950; message, Moscow Embassy to Secretary of State, July 14, 1950, box 4265, 795.00, Central Decimal Files 1950–1954, RG 59, NA; message, Moscow Embassy to Secretary of State, July 17, 1950, box 4265, 795.00, Central Decimal Files 1950–1954, RG 59, NA; Daily Worker, July 4-6, 10, 12, 14, 17, 18, 20, 24–28, 31, 1950; United Nations Security Council Official Records, August 8, 1950, 5th year, 484th mtg., S/PV.484, 20. The Soviet Union also led a campaign among Communist countries to raise relief funds for the Korean victims of American "terror bombing." "From Korea Bulletin 1 August 1950," box 1, Korean War Communiques and Press Releases 1950–1951, Office of the Chief of Information, RG 319, NA; New York Times, August 3, 1950. Seoul City Sue, the English-speaking commentator for North Korean radio broadcasts to U.N. forces, excoriated the U.S. Air Force for promiscuous bombing of schools and the strafing of farmers. Message, CINCFE to UEPC/Department of the Army, August 8, 1950, box 199, 311.5, Classified Decimal File 1950, Office of the Chief of Information, RG 319, NA.

8. United Nations Security Council Official Records, July 31, 1950, 5th year, 479th mtg., S/PV.479, 4–7; "Weekly Information Policy Guidance, No. 18," August 2, 1950, box 101, Lot 60D262, Bureau of Public Affairs 1944–1962, RG 59, NA; press release, "Relief and Support of Civilian Population of Korea," August 2, 1950, Press Conferences of the Secretaries of State, 1922–1973, microfilm collection (Wilmington, DE: Scholarly Resources, 1973).

9. Message, CINCFE to Department of the Army, August 11, 1950, box 155, 091.412, Decimal Files March 1950–1951, Office of the Assistant Chief of Staff for Operations, RG 319, NA; "Report of the First Month of Operations FEAF Bomber Command," August 13, 1950, box 65, series B, LeMay Papers, LC; message, JCS to CINCFE, August 15, 1950, box 87, Vandenberg Papers, LC; HQ USAF, An Evaluation of the Effectiveness of the United States Air Force in the Korean Campaign (Barcus Report), vol. 5, 102–103, box 906, Project Decimal File 1942–1954, Directorate of Plans, Office of the Deputy Chief of Staff for Operations, RG 341, NA. The FEAF dropped 200,000 more warning leaflets on September 20.

10. Memorandum of conversation, Philip C. Jessup, August 18, 1950, box 4267, 795.00, Central Decimal Files 1950–1954, RG 59, NA; memorandum of conversation, George W. Perkins, August 18, 1950, box 4267, 795.00, Central Decimal Files 1950–1954, RG 59, NA; notes on Cabinet meeting, James E. Webb, August 18, 1950, box 4267, 795.00, Central Decimal Files 1950-1954, RG 59, NA; message, New Delhi Embassy to Secretary of State, August 18, 1950, box 4267, 795.00, Central Decimal Files 1950–1954, RG 59, NA; New York Times, August 19, 25, 1950; message, New Delhi Embassy to Secretary of State, August 29, 1950, box 4268, 795.00, Central Decimal Files 1950–1954, RG 59, NA. Concern about British and Indian opinion was reflected in the American press. St. Louis Post-Dispatch, July 2, 1950; "Key to Conflict … and Its Significance," Newsweek, August 28, 1950, 20–21; "North Korean Toll," Newsweek, September 4, 1950, 16. By October, the New York Times was reporting Pakistani criticism of American bombing in Korea. New York Times, October 11, 1950.

11. New York Times, September 3, 1950. See also "Report of the United Nations Command Operations in Korea," U.S. Department of State Bulletin, October 2, 1950, 534–40; "Fifth Report of the U.N. Command Operations in Korea," U.S. Department of State Bulletin, October 16, 1950, 603–606.

12. "North Korea Slanders U.N. Forces to Hide Guilt of Aggression," U.S. Department of State Bulletin, September 18, 1950, 454; message, State Department to Certain American Diplomatic and Consular Officers, September 7, 1950, box 2238, 511.00, Central Decimal Files 1950-1954, RG 59, NA; "Overnight Information Policy Guidance, No. 535," September 6, 1950, box 91, Lot 52D335, International Information Activities 1930–1953, RG 59, NA. The State Department sent another message on the importance of these themes to diplomatic posts in the East Asia a week later. Message, State Department to Certain American Diplomatic and Consular Officers, September 14, 1950, box 2237, 511.00, Central Decimal Files 1950–1954, RG 59, NA. The State Department became involved in other efforts to shape the way the military depicted its use of force in Korea. The Singapore embassy had reported that Communist propaganda about bombing Korean cities and burning villages was having

some effect there. The U.S. Information Service suggested that Air Force press releases stress accuracy instead of tonnage delivered in its bombing and point out the military nature of the targets. Subsequently, the Public Affairs Bureau of the State Department coordinated public information efforts with the Air Force in order to emphasize the accuracy and effectiveness of air operations. Message, Singapore Embassy to Secretary of State, August 18, 1950, box 4267, 795.00, Central Decimal Files 1950–1954, RG 59, NA; message, "Far East Annex to Weekly Information Policy Guidance, Nr. 22," August 30, 1950, box 2237, 511.00, Central Decimal Files 1950–1954, RG 59, NA; "Far East Annex to Weekly Information Policy Guidance, Nr. 23," September 7, 1950, box 2237, 511.00, Central Decimal Files 1950–1954, RG 59, NA; message, CG FEAF to CS USAF, September 9, 1950, box 4, Public Information Division, Office of Information Services, RG 340, NA; memorandum, Lauris Norstad to Secretary of the Air Force, September 14, 1950, box 22, Norstad Papers, DDEL; message, Norstad to Stratemeyer, September 21, 1950, box 22, Norstad Papers, DDEL.

13. "Korean Release, No. 551," October 13, 1950, box 2, Korean War Communiques and Press Releases 1950–1951, Office of the Chief of Information, RG 319, NA.

14. Examples include "Far East Command Communique, No. 177," July 31, 1950, box 1, Korean War Communiques and Press Releases 1950–1951, Office of the Chief of Information, RG 319, NA; "Far East Command Communique, No. 196 and 197," August 3, 1950, box 1, Korean War Communiques and Press Releases 1950–1951, Office of the Chief of Information, RG 319, NA; "Korean Release Unnumbered," August 10, 1950, box 1, Korean War Communiques and Press Releases 1950–1951, Office of the Chief of Information, RG 319, NA; "Korean Release, No. 278," August 20, 1950, box 1, Korean War Communiques and Press Releases 1950–1951, Office of the Chief of Information, RG 319, NA; "Korean Release, No. 332," August 28, 1950, box 1, Korean War Communiques and Press Releases 1950–1951, Office of the Chief of Information, RG 319, NA; "Korean Release, No. 355," August 31, 1950, box 1, Korean War Communiques and Press Releases 1950–1951, Office of the Chief of Information, RG 319, NA; "Korean Release, No. 370," September 3, 1950, box 2, Korean War Communiques and Press Releases 1950–1951, Office of the Chief of Information, RG 319, NA; "Korean Release, No. 415," September 11, 1950, box 2, Korean War Communiques and Press Releases 1950–1951, Office of the Chief of Information, RG 319, NA. The press releases were regularly printed in the New York Times.

15. "Korean Release, No. 348," August 30, 1950, box 1, Korean War Communiques and Press Releases 1950–1951, Office of the Chief of Information, RG 319, NA.

16. "Far East Command Communique, No. 151," July 27, 1950, box 1, Korean War Communiques and Press Releases 1950–1951, Office of the Chief of Information, RG 319, NA; "Far East Command Communique, No. 159," July 29, 1950, box 1, Korean War Communiques and Press Releases 1950–1951, Office of the Chief of Information, RG 319, NA; "Far East Command Communique Unnumbered," August 4, 1950, box 1, Korean War Communiques and Press Releases 1950–1951, Office of the Chief of Information, RG 319, NA; "Korean Release, No. 242," August 12, 1950, box 1, Korean War Communiques and Press Releases 1950–1951, Office of the Chief of Information, RG 319, NA; "Korean Release, No. 315," August 26, 1950, box 1, Korean War Communiques and Press Releases 1950–1951, Office of the Chief of Information, RG 319, NA.

17. "Korean Release Unnumbered," August 9, 1950, box 1, Korean War Communiques and Press Releases 1950–1951, Office of the Chief of Information, RG 319, NA.

18. "Korean Release, No. 221," August 8, 1950, box 1, Korean War Communiques and Press Releases 1950–1951, Office of the Chief of Information, RG 319, NA; "Korean Release, No. 222," August 8, 1950, box 1, Korean War Communiques and Press Releases 1950–1951, Office of the Chief of Information, RG 319, NA; "Korean Release, No. 291," August 22, 1950, box 1, Korean War Communiques and Press Releases 1950–1951, Office of the Chief of Information, RG 319, NA.

19. "Far East Command Communique, No. 65" July 12, 1950, box 1, Korean War Communiques and Press Releases 1950–1951, Office of the Chief of Information, RG 319, NA; "United Nations Command Communique Unnumbered," August 20, 1950, box 1, Korean War Communiques and Press Releases 1950–1951, Office of the Chief of Information, RG 319, NA; "Korean Release, No. 310," August 25, 1950, box 1, Korean War Communiques and Press Releases 1950–1951, Office of the Chief of Information, RG 319, NA; "Korean Release, No. 388," September 6, 1950, box 2, Korean War Communiques and Press Releases 1950–1951, Office of the Chief of Information, RG 319, NA; "Korean Release, No. 398,"

September 8, 1950, box 2, Korean War Communiques and Press Releases 1950–1951, Office of the Chief of Information, RG 319, NA; "Korean Release, No. 405," September 9, 1950, box 2, Korean War Communiques and Press Releases 1950–1951, Office of the Chief of Information, RG 319, NA; "Korean Release, No. 408," September 10, 1950, box 2, Korean War Communiques and Press Releases 1950–1951, Office of the Chief of Information, RG 319, NA; "Overnight Information Policy Guidance, No. 549," September 16, 1950, box 91, Lot 52D335, Records Relating to International Information Activities 1930–1953, RG 59, NA; "Korean Release, No. 502," September 27, 1950, box 1, Korean War Communiques and Press Releases 1950–1951, Office of the Chief of Information, RG 319, NA; "Far East Annex to Weekly Information Policy Guidance, No. 26," September 28, 1950, box 2237, 511.00, Central Decimal Files 1950–1954, RG 59, NA; "Special Information Policy Guide on Korea, No. 22," September 28, 1950, 511.00, Central Decimal Files 1950–1954, RG 59, NA.

20. Harold H. Martin, "How Our Air Raiders Plastered Korea," Saturday Evening Post, August 5, 1950, 26–27, 88–90; New York Times, September 15, 1950; Los Angeles Times, August 1, 1950. For additional statements that advocated the discriminate use of force and condemned attacks on civilians, see San Francisco Examiner, July 24, 1950; Eugene E. Wilson, "Hope in the Air," Vital Speeches of the Day, December 1, 1950, 119–22.

21. "The Korean War," Newsweek, July 10, 1950, 18; "Battle of Korea," Time, July 17, 1950, 18; "The Korean War," Newsweek, July 17, 1950, 14–16; "The Air War," Time, July 24, 1950, 26; "The Korean War," Newsweek, July 24, 1950, 15–16; "The Air War," Time, July 31, 1950, 20; "The Korean War," Newsweek, July 31, 1950, 21; "The Air War," Time, August 7, 1950, 19; "The Air War," Time, August 14, 1950, 15; "The Korean War," Newsweek, August 28, 1950, 17–18.

22. "The Korean War," Newsweek, July 17, 1950, 14–16; "The Korean War," Newsweek, July 24, 1950, 15–16.

23. "Little Man & Friends," Time, July 10, 1950, 9–10; "The Korean War," Newsweek, July 31, 1950, 21.

24. "The Korean War," Newsweek, August 21, 1950, 21.

25. Lawrence H. Hammer to Acheson, July 18, 1950, box 4265, 795.00, Central Decimal Files 1950–1954, RG 59, NA; Robert A. Graham, "'Strategic Bombing,'" America, September 9, 1950, 612; "Brickbat," Air Force 33, no. 11 (November 1950): 6.

26. Henry Beston, "Soliloquy on the Airplane," Human Events 7, no. 42 (October 18, 1950): 1–4; Henry H. Klein, "Peace and Prosperity — Or War and Destruction," Women's Voice, October 26, 1950, The Right Wing Collection of the University of Iowa Libraries, 1918–1977, microfilm collection (Glen Rock, NJ: Microfilming Corporation of America, 1978), W35.

27. Washington Post, August 17, September 12, 1950.

28. "Annex to Summary of Air Situation in Korea, August–December 1950," vol. 1, box 209, Korean Daily Reports April 1951–July 1953, Office of the Deputy Director for Estimates, Directorate of Intelligence, Office of the Deputy Chief of Staff for Operations, RG 341, NA; U.S. Department of the Army, Inspector General, No Gun Ri Review, January 2001, <www.army.mil/nogunri>, 137. An extensive investigation by the Department of Defense was unable to uncover any written Air Force policies on protecting civilians. "Out of Korea by Christmas?" U.S. News and World Report, September 29, 1950, 16–19; message, CG FEAF to CG FAF, September 20, 1950, box 905, Project Decimal File 1942–1954, Directorate of Plans, Office of the Deputy Chief of Staff for Operations, RG 341, NA; New York Times, January 10, 1951. See also, New York Times, July 5, 1950.

29. "Out of Korea by Christmas?" U.S. News and World Report, September 29, 1950, 16–19; HQ USAF, An Evaluation of the Effectiveness of the United States Air Force in the Korean Campaign (Barcus Report), vol. 5, 9, box 906, Project Decimal File 1942–1954, RG 341, NA; FEAF HQ conference transcript, January 6, 1951, box 905, Project Decimal File 1942–1954, Directorate of Plans, Office of the Deputy Chief of Staff for Operations, RG 341, NA. See also Walter Karig, "Korea — Tougher to Crack than Okinawa," Collier's, September 23, 1950, 24–25, 69–70.

30. Mission report, Thirty-fifth Fighter Bomber Squadron, July 31, 1950 <www.henryholt.com/nogunri>; Operations report summary, U.S.S. Valley Forge, July 25, 1950 <www.henryholt.com/nogunri>; memorandum, Turner C. Rogers to Timberlake, July 25, 1950, <www.henryholt.com/nogunri>. See also mission report, Thirty-fifth Fighter Bomber Squadron, July 20, 1950 <www.henryholt.com/nogunri>.

31. Interview transcript of K. H. Muse, January 5, 1951, box 905, Project Decimal File 1942–1954, Directorate of Plans, Office of the Deputy Chief of Staff for Operations, RG 341, NA; Walter Karig, Malcolm W. Cagle, and Frank A. Manson, Battle Report, vol. 6 (New York: Reinhart, 1952), 111–12.

32. No Gun Ri Review, 33–35.

33. Robert L. Bateman, No Gun Ri: A Military History of the Korean War Incident (Mechanicsburg, PA: Stackpole, 2002), 71–75; Charles J. Hanley, Sang-Hun Choe, and Martha Mendoza, The Bridge at No Gun Ri: A Hidden Nightmare from the Korean War (New York: Henry Holt, 2001), 79–80.

34. No Gun Ri Review, 36; New York Times, September 1, 1950.

35. No Gun Ri Review, 23–24.

36. The Pulitzer Prize winning journalists later published a much more extensive version of their findings in Hanley, Choe, and Mendoza, The Bridge at No Gun Ri.

37. Ibid., i–ii, 139–41, 153, 147, 190.

38. Ibid., i, vii, ix–x, xiv–xv, 131–32.

39. Ibid., x–xiii, xv, 26–27, 185–90.

40. Muccio to Rusk, July 26, 1950, box 4266, 795.00, Central Decimal Files 1950–1954, RG 59, NA. The letter resides in a collection of State Department documents on the Korean War which, according to the No Gun Ri Review's appendix on records research, the Pentagon investigation did not examine. It is unlikely that representatives of the South Korean government would have objected to talk of harsh actions against their own citizens at this meeting. On July 25, the AP reported that the government had announced it would execute all civilians found "making enemy-like action" in the war zone, which included leaving their houses at any time except during a designated daily two-hour period. New York Times, July 26, 1950.

41. No Gun Ri Review, 35, 37; journal, HQ Twenty-fifth Infantry Division, July 26, 1950 <www.henryholt.com/nogunri/documents.htm>.

42. O. H. P. King, Tail of the Paper Tiger (Caldwell, ID.: Caxton, 1961), 358–59; Roy Appleman, South to the Naktong, North to the Yalu (Washington, DC: Office of the Chief of Military History, Department of the Army, 1961), 291.

43. Korea — 1950 (Washington, DC: Office of the Chief of Military History, Department of the Army, 1952), 82.

44. Washington Post, December 6, 2000; No Gun Ri Review, 37.

45. Washington Post, September 30, 1999.

46. "Men at War: The Ugly War," Time, August 21, 1950, 20–22; John Osborne, "Report from the Orient: Guns Are Not Enough," Life, August 21, 1950, 77–85. The No Gun Ri Review mentioned Osborne's article but did not include the anecdote about shooting civilians presumably because it was not directly related to the incident at No Gun Ri. No Gun Ri Review, 36–37. An AP report from August also said that peasants were walking into mines that American forces had planted and that other civilians were being cut down in battle. New York Times, August 19, 1950.

47. Communications log, First Battalion, Eighth Cavalry Regiment, First Cavalry Division, August 9, 1950 <www.henryholt.com/nogunri/documents.htm>; journal, First Cavalry Division Artillery Command, August 29, 1950 <www.henryholt.com/nogunri/documents.htm>; journal, HQ Sixty-first Field Artillery Battalion, August 29, 1950 <www.henryholt.com/nogunri/documents.htm>; journal, Thirty-fifth Infantry Regiment, Twenty-fifth Infantry Division, August 17, 1950 <www.henryholt.com/nogunri/documents.htm>.

48. See, for example, the descriptions of the burning of villages and towns with incendiaries by Navy and Air Force planes. Message, CINCFE to UEPC/Department of the Army, July 30, 1950, box 200, 311.5, Classified Decimal File 1950, Office of the Chief of Information, RG 319, NA; message, Commander, Task Force 77 to Seventh Fleet, September 3, 1950, box 905, Project Decimal File 1942–1954, Directorate of Plans, Office of Deputy Chief of Staff for Operations, RG 341, NA; transcript of interview with Lt. Col. Dean E. Hess, November 3, 1950, box 905, Project Decimal File 1942–1954, Directorate of Plans, Office of Deputy Chief of Staff for Operations, RG 341, NA.

49. William T. Y'Blood, ed., The Three Wars of Lt. Gen. George E. Stratemeyer: His Korean War Diary (Washington, DC: Air Force History and Museums Program, 1999), 236–37.

50. Ibid., 253–55.

51. Douglas MacArthur, Reminiscences (New York: McGraw-Hill, 1964), 366; Conrad C. Crane, American Airpower Strategy in Korea, 1950–1953 (Lawrence, KS: University of Kan-

sas Press, 2000), 46; memorandum of conversation, Muccio, November 17, 1950, FRUS 1950, vol. 7, 1175; Stratemeyer Diary, 258–61.

52. Stratemeyer Diary, 256–57; message, Stratemeyer to Vandenberg, November 5, 1950, box 86, Vandenberg Papers, LC.

53. Futrell, U.S. Air Force in Korea, 221–23, 226; Stratemeyer Diary, 269; interview transcript from Ninety-eighth Bomb Group, November 30, 1950, box 905, Project Decimal File 1942–1954, Directorate of Plans, Office of the Deputy Chief of Staff for Operations, RG 341, NA. One daily operations report recorded that B-26 fighter-bombers had "burned" twelve enemy-held towns in North Korea including Ssongwangan, which was "completely destroyed." "Annex to Air Situation in Korea, August–December 1950," vol. 1, November 10, 1950, box 209, Korean Daily Reports April 1951–July 1953, Office of the Deputy Director for Estimates, Directorate of Intelligence, Office of the Deputy Chief of Staff for Operations, RG 341, NA.

54. Stratemeyer Diary, 371–72; Crane, American Airpower Strategy in Korea, 63.

55. New York Times, January 16, 1951.

56. Radio broadcasts to North Korea by the Psychological Warfare Branch of the U.N. Command that warned civilians away from military targets in the summer of 1950 defined the term explicitly. One broadcast said they were "railroads and railroad facilities, docks and harbors, bridges, power plants, factories helping the war, ships and boats, airfields, supply warehouses" and another said they were "marshalling yards, bridges, heavy industries, chemical plants, power plants and similar installations." Transcript, "Voice of the Free Peoples of World," July 23, 1950, box 2539, 511.95, Central Decimal Files 1950–1954, RG 59, NA; transcript, "Voice of the Free Peoples of World," August 22, 1950, box 155, 091.412, Decimal Files March 1950–1951, Office of the Assistant Chief of Staff for Operations, RG 319, NA. For other definitions of military targets early in the war, see the instructions to MacArthur discussed earlier in the chapter.

57. "Summary of First Two Months of Naval Activity in the Korean War," n.d., box 2, Korean War Communiques and Press Releases 1950–1951, Office of the Chief of Information, RG 319, NA; "Korean Release, No. 778," January 2, 1951, box 3, Korean War Communiques and Press Releases 1950–1951, Office of the Chief of Information, RG 319, NA; "Korean Release Unnumbered," December 2, 1951, box 5, Korean War Communiques and Press Releases 1950–1951, Office of the Chief of Information, RG 319, NA; memorandum to Schmelz, October 31, 1951, box 15, Formerly Classified General Correspondence, Public Information Division, Office of Information Services, RG 340, NA; Wiley D. Ganey to LeMay, September 7, 1952, series B, box 65, LeMay Papers, LC.

58. "Ninth Report: For the Period November 1–15, 1950," U.S. Department of State Bulletin, January 8, 1951, 47–50.

59. See the press releases printed daily in the New York Times starting with "Korean Release, No. 627," November 9, 1950. By spring 1951, references to supply centers or areas as the targets for U.N. air attacks were frequent in the releases. Releases December 1950–December 1951 are also in boxes 2–3, Korean War Communiques and Press Releases 1950–1951, Office of the Chief of Information, RG 319, NA. The terms like supply center were not only used by the military for public consumption. Similar terms were used in internal documents by American officers. Message, G-2, Department of the Army to USCINCEUR et al., November 24, 1952, box 756, Chronological File 1949–June 1954, Office of Security Review, Office of the Assistant Secretary of Defense for Legislative and Public Affairs, RG 330, NA.

60. Memorandum, Office of the Chief of Information, HQ FEC to Public Information Office, FEAF, August 1, 1951, box 36, Office of the Chief of Information, Office of the Chief of Staff, Supreme Commander for the Allied Powers, RG 331, NA.

61. New York Times, November 9, 1950.

62. Chicago Tribune, November 8, 1950; St. Louis Post-Dispatch, November 8, 1950; Detroit News, November 8, 1950; Philadelphia Bulletin, November 8, 9, 1950; Los Angeles Times, November 8, 9, 1950; San Francisco Examiner, November 8, 9, 1950; Houston Chronicle, November 8, 9, 1950; Washington Post, November 8–10, 1950; Baltimore Sun, November 8–10, 1950; Boston Post, November 8–11, 1950; New York Times, November 9, 1950; Cleveland Press, November 9, 1950. Of the twelve daily newspapers surveyed, only the Detroit News and Cleveland Press did not label Sinuiju a supply base or similar term. Two newspapers of those surveyed printed reports before the Sinuiju strike that U.N. planes had begun to burn villages in North Korea to flush out Communist soldiers who had been dressing as

civilians and hiding in the villages. Detroit News, November 7, 1950; St. Louis Post-Dispatch, November 7, 1950. The Boston Post included this report in its coverage of the Sinuiju bombing on November 8.

63. Philadelphia Bulletin, November 9, 1950; St. Louis Post-Dispatch, November 9, 1950; Detroit News, November 9, 1950; Houston Chronicle, November 9, 1950.
64. Cleveland Press, November 9, 1950; Detroit News, November 10, 1950; New York Times, November 10, 11, 1950; Chicago Tribune, November 11, 1950; Los Angeles Times, November 11, 1950; San Francisco Examiner, November 11, 1950; Boston Post, November 11, 13, 1950; Baltimore Sun, November 11, 13, 1950; Washington Post, November 11, 13, 1950; Philadelphia Bulletin, November 12, 1950; St. Louis Post-Dispatch, November 13, 1950; Houston Chronicle, November 13, 1950. One exception to referring to the targets as supply centers or with similar terms was a brief reference to "Villages were fired, big towns smashed" in a Houston Chronicle article. Houston Chronicle, November 10, 1950. Four newspapers of the ones surveyed briefly mentioned the firebombing of Kanggye that occurred before the Sinuiju attack. New York Times, November 6, 1950; Baltimore Sun, November 6, 1950; Philadelphia Bulletin, November 6, 1950; Boston Post, November 6, 1950.
65. National Guardian, November 22, 1950.
66. Karig, Cagle, and Manson, Battle Report, 151, 205.
67. New York Times, March 30, 1951; "Korean Release Unnumbered," December 17, 1951, box 5, Korean War Communiques and Press Releases 1950–1951, Office of the Chief of Information, RG 319, NA; "Korean Release Unnumbered," December 19, 1951, box 5, Korean War Communiques and Press Releases 1950–1951, Office of the Chief of Information, RG 319, NA.
68. Message, CINCFE to Department of the Army, September 23, 1950, box 727, Korean Message File June 1950–May 1954, Far East and Pacific Branch, Office of the Deputy Chief of Staff for Operations, RG 319, NA; message, CG FEAF to CG FAF and CG BOMCOM, September 27, 1950, box 905, Project Decimal File 1942–1954, Directorate of Plans, Office of Deputy Chief of Staff for Operations, RG 341, NA; message, CG FEAF to CG EUSAK, September 28, 1950, box 905, Project Decimal File 1942–1954, Directorate of Plans, Office of Deputy Chief of Staff for Operations, RG 341, NA; message, I Corps to CG EUSAK, November 8, 1950, box 710, Security Classified Correspondence, Adjutant General Section, RG 500.
69. New York Times, January 4, 25, 1951; Donald Knox, The Korean War: An Oral History (New York: Harcourt Brace Jovanovitch, 1985), 573, 659; Crane, American Airpower Strategy in Korea, 67; Billy C. Mossman, Ebb and Flow: November 1950–July 1951 (Washington, DC: U.S. Army Center of Military History, 1990), 201, 226.
70. George Barrett, "That's the Way the Ball Bounces," New York Times Magazine, November 23, 1952, 14–15, 66–67, 69.
71. "Korean Releases No. 787 and No. 788," January 5, 1951, box 3, Korean War Communiques and Press Releases 1950–1951, Office of the Chief of Information, RG 319; letter, E. F. LaClare, November 16, 1950, box 22, Formerly Classified General Correspondence, Public Information Division, Office of Information Services, RG 340; New York Times, March 30, 1951; Max Hastings, The Korean War (New York: Simon and Schuster, 1987), 168; interview transcript from Ninety-eighth Bomb Group, Medium, November 30, 1950, box 905, Project Decimal File 1942–1954, Directorate of Plans, Office of Deputy Chief of Staff for Operations, RG 341, NA.
72. New York Times, March 1, 1951.
73. Mossman, Ebb and Flow, 196, 202, 204; Matthew B. Ridgway, The Korean War: How We Met the Challenge (Garden City, NY: Doubleday, 1967), 95–96; message, EUSAK to X Corps et al., January 1, 1951 <www.henryholt.com/nogunri/documents.htm>; journal, HQ Second Battalion, Eighth Cavalry Regiment, January 3, 1951 <www.henryholt.com/nogunri/documents.htm>; memorandum to CO Thirty-eighth Infantry, June 29, 1951 <www.henryholt.com/nogunri/documents.htm>.
74. Knox, The Korean War, 657.
75. Raymond S. Sleeper, "Korean Targets for Medium Bombardment," Air University Quarterly Review 4, no. 3 (spring 1951): 18–31. Also see Hamilton DeSaussure, "International Law and Aerial Bombing," Air University Quarterly Review 5, no. 3 (fall 1952): 22–34.
76. Thomas to Truman, May 14, 1951, Correspondence File, President Harry S. Truman's Office Files, 1945–1953, microfilm collection (Frederick, MD: University Publications of

America, 1989); Truman to Thomas, May 17, 1951, Correspondence File, Truman's Office Files.

77. New York Times, October 14, 15, 1951; Thomas to Lovett, October 15, 1951, Correspondence File, Truman's Office Files; Thomas to Truman, October 15, 1951, Correspondence File, Truman's Office Files; Truman to Thomas, October 17, 1951, Correspondence File, Truman's Office Files; Denver Post, October 18, December 13, 1951; Thomas to Gilpatric, December 6, 1951, box 15, General Correspondence, Public Information Division, Office of Information Services, RG 340, NA.

78. New York Times, January 19, 1951; Green Bay Press-Gazette as quoted in "'Keep Your Shirt On,'" Time, December 18, 1950, 76; "A-Bomb Will Not Beat China," U.S. News and World Report, December 8, 1950, 23.

79. Congressional Record, 81st Cong., 2nd sess., vol. 96, pt. 12, 16050; New York Times, April 19, November 14, 1951; Robert A. Taft, "The Korean War and MacArthur Dismissal," Vital Speeches of the Day, May 1, 1951, 420–22; Carl Spaatz, "The Airplane Is Our Hope Now," Newsweek, December 11, 1950, 33. Also see "If Peace in Korea Fails," U.S. News and World Report, January 25, 1952, 16.

80. Eugene R. Guild to Wayne Aspinall, March 2, 1951, Right Wing Collection, F47; Fighting Homefolks of Fighting Men Newsletter, January 13, 1955, Right Wing Collection, F47.

81. Memorandum of conversation by Acheson, January 7, 1952, box 70, Acheson Papers, HSTL.

82. "The General Sows Confusion," Nation, April 28, 1951, 388–89; "The Three Chinas," Christian Century, May 16, 1951, 605–607; "Would Air-Sea Action Against the Chinese Mainland Serve Our Real Objectives in Asia?" Life, February 11, 1952, 26; Facts Forum News, March 1953, Right Wing Collection, F9; New York Times, May 20, 1951.

83. Committee on Foreign Relations, Military Situation in the Far East, 43, 82–83, 194, 219, 397–398, 1362–1363. For other expressions of concern over noncombatant immunity at the hearings, see ibid., 613, 1245–46, 1470–71, 3299–3301. MacArthur's comments about his revulsion at the destruction in Korea were popular with the weekly news magazines. See "The MacArthur Hearing," Time, May 14, 1951, 20; "What MacArthur Believes in … and Why He Believes It's Best," Newsweek, May 14, 1951, 26–28.

84. Eighth Fighter-Bomber Wing, "Songs of the Eight Fighters," n.d., box 15, Formerly Classified General Correspondence, Public Information Division, Office of Information Services, RG 340, NA.

85. Melvin B. Voorhees, Korean Tales (New York: Simon and Schuster, 1952), 45–47.

Chapter 5

1. Thomas Parrish, The Cold War Encyclopedia (New York: Holt, 1996), 342.

2. Information memorandum No. 86, 1950, box 4, Files of Francis H. Russell 1945–1953, Office of Public Affairs, Office of the Assistant Secretary of State for Public Affairs, RG 59, NA; Carlton Savage, "Stockholm Resolution to Outlaw Atomic Weapons," June 8, 1950, box 7, Lot 64D563, Subject Files, Policy Planning Staff 1947–1953, RG 59, NA; "Soviet Peace Petition," July 12, 1950, Press Conferences of the Secretaries of State, 1922–1973, microfilm collection (Wilmington, DE: Scholarly Resources, 1973); New York Times, October 17, 24, 1950.

3. Memorandum, Nitze to Secretary of State, July 17, 1950, with attachment Carlton Savage, "The Question of U.S. Use of Atomic Bombs in Korea," July 15, 1950, box 7, Lot 64D563, Subject Files, Policy Planning Staff 1947–1953, RG 59, NA; memorandum, Stefan T. Possony to Walter B. Putnam, July 27, 1950, box 906, 385.2, Project Decimal Files 1942–1954, Directorate of Plans, Office of Deputy Chief of Staff for Operations, RG 341, NA.

4. New York Times, July 13, 16, 21, 1950.

5. The editorial pages and columns of eleven daily newspapers were examined from July 1 to August 31, 1950. The newspapers were the New York Times, Chicago Tribune, Philadelphia Bulletin, Detroit News, Los Angeles Times, Baltimore Sun, St. Louis Post-Dispatch, Cleveland Press, Washington Post, San Francisco Examiner, and Houston Chronicle.

6. Saturday Evening Post, August 5, 1950, 10; Chicago Tribune, July 15, 1950; Detroit News, July 29, 1950; Boston Post, July 18, 1950; Philadelphia Bulletin, July 14, 1950. Also see Daily Worker, July 27, 1950; "America Mustn't Open the Way to Atomic Conflict,"; Carl Spaatz, "Some Answers to Korean Questions," Newsweek, July 31, 1950, 19; "The War in Cicero," Time, July 31, 1950, 12; "Atomic Weapons and the Korean War," Bulletin of the Atomic Scientist, July 1950, 194, 217. For expressions of concern in newspaper columns and special

features, see Los Angeles Times, July 16, 1950; Philadelphia Bulletin, July 29, 1950; San Francisco Examiner, August 8, 1950; St. Louis Post-Dispatch, August 16, 1950; Telford Taylor, "Not the A-Bomb Alone but All Armaments," New York Times Magazine, August 27, 1950, 13, 50–54. For letters to the editor expressing concern, see St. Louis Post-Dispatch, July 27, August 2, 13, 16, 1950; Cleveland Press, August 2, 1950; Baltimore Sun, August 3, 1950; New York Times, July 13, August 6, 1950; San Francisco Examiner, August 9, 1950; Washington Post, August 9, 1950; Detroit News, August 16, 1950.

7. Detroit News, July 31, August 11, 16, 1950; Washington Post, August 4, 1950.
8. New York Times, July 27, 1950.
9. Robert Barrat, "Peace, Peace, When There Is No Peace," Commonweal, August 18, 1950, 455–58.
10. Gordon C. Zahn, "Morality and the Bomb," Commonweal, September 8, 1950, 536; Gordon C. Zahn, "The A-Bomb: Moral or Not?" Commonweal, September 29, 1950, 606–607.
11. Francis J. Connell, "A Reply," Commonweal, September 26, 1950, 607–608.
12. Joseph T. Mangan, "An Historical Analysis of the Principle of Double Effect," Theological Studies 10 (1949), 41–61; John C. Ford, "The Morality of Obliteration Bombing," Theological Studies 5, no. 3 (September 1944): 289; Robert L. Holmes, On War and Morality (Princeton, NJ: Princeton University Press, 1989), 193–96.
13. Memorandum, Planning Adviser, Bureau of Far Eastern Affairs to Assistant Secretary of State for Far Eastern Affairs, November 8, 1950, FRUS 1950, vol. 7, 1098–1100; memorandum, Director of the Policy Planning Staff, November 4, 1950, FRUS 1950, vol. 7, 1041–42.
14. PPP 1950, 727.
15. Ibid, fn 3.
16. Concern about the negative political effects of harming noncombatants with the use of atomic weapons in East Asia continued to be an issue for American officials throughout the Korean War. See memorandum, Carlton Savage, May 23, 1951, FRUS 1951, vol. 1, 834–37; "Staff Study on Use of Atomic Weapons in Korea," n.d., box 907, 385.2, Project Decimal File 1942–1954, Directorate of Plans, Office of the Deputy Chief of Staff for Operations, RG 341, NA; memorandum, Psychological Warfare Division to War Plans Division, May 13, 1952, box 907, 385.2, Project Decimal File 1942–1954, Directorate of Plans, Office of the Deputy Chief of Staff for Operations Division, RG 341, NA; memorandum, Director of Intelligence to Director of Plans, May 19, 1952, box 907, 385.2, Project Decimal File 1942–1954, Directorate of Plans, Office of Deputy Chief of Staff for Operations, RG 341, NA; Frank Pace, Jr. interview, Harry S. Truman Presidential Oral History Collection, microfilm collection (Bethesda, MD: University Publications of America, 1990), 137–40.
17. "How About the Bomb?" Time, December 18, 1950, 50; Information Paper, No. 389, December 8, 1950, Office of Intelligence Research, box 3, Lot 57D459, Bureau of Public Affairs 1944–1962, RG 59, NA; New York Times, December 2, 5, 1950; message, New York to Secretary of State, December 1, box 8, Selected Records Relating to the Korean War, HSTL; memorandum of conversation, Eleanor Roosevelt, December 1, 1950, FRUS 1950, vol. 1, 116.
18. New York Times, December 2, 7, 1950; "How About the Bomb?" Time, December 18, 1950, 50.
19. Washington Post, December 4, 1950; Chicago Tribune, December 13, 1950; Michael Amrine, Edward A. Conway, and Murray S. Levine, "One More Question, Mr. President!" America, December 16, 1950, 329–30; Cleveland Post, December 1, 1950. For letters to the editor, see Cleveland Press, December 4, 1950; Washington Post, December 6, 7, 1950; Baltimore Sun, December 7, 9, 1950; St. Louis Post-Dispatch, December 8, 1950; New York Times, December 10, 1950.
20. New York Times, December 5, 1950; Cleveland Press, December 11, 1950; Washington Post, December 14, 1950; Hazel Felman Buchbinder, "For a War on War," Saturday Review of Literature, January 27, 1951, 24; James C. Jones, Jr., "All's Quiet on the Home Front," American Legion 52, no. 2 (February 1952): 20–21, 57–60.
21. The specific poll numbers were France: 48 percent unjustified, 25 percent justified, 27 percent no opinion; West Germany: 44 percent unjustified, 18 percent justified, 38 percent no opinion; Italy: 54 percent unjustified, 14 percent justified, 32 percent no opinion; Sweden: 61 percent unjustified, 34 percent justified, 5 percent no opinion; Great Britain: 45 percent unjustified, 41 percent justified, 14 percent no opinion. International Public Opinion Research, Inc. "Views of Western European Nations on Use of the Atomic Bomb," October 16, 1950, box 3, Lot 57D459, Bureau of Public Affairs 1944–1962, RG 59, NA.

22. "Survey of Western European Opinion on the Atom Bomb as an Immoral Weapon," February 13, 1951, Office of Intelligence Research, box 7, Lot 57D688, Special Assistant to the Secretary for Atomic Energy 1944–1952, RG 59, NA.

23. Erik Von Kuehnelt-Leddihn, "The Constant Shadow," Commonweal, July 7, 1950, 311–12.

24. Congressional Record, 82nd Cong., 1st sess., vol. 97, pt. 1, 62–64; U.S. Senate, Committee on Foreign Relations and Committee on Armed Services, Assignment of Ground Forces of the United States to Duty in the European Area: Hearings, 82nd Cong., 1st sess., 755, 785.

25. New York Times, September 29, 1949; David Lawrence, "Who Is the 'Quarterback'?" U.S. News and World Report, December 9, 1949, 34–35.

26. "Weird Machines of 'Next' War," U.S. News and World Report, May 12, 1950, 18–19; "Improve Means of Destroying Targets," Air Force 33, no. 6 (June 1950): 35, 37; Richard Wilson, "Atomic Weapons ... Will Save Money — They May Stop War," Look, October 10, 1950; W. R. Kintner and D. P. Yeull, "The A-Bomb Goes Tactical," Marine Corps Gazette 34, no. 10 (October 1950): 22–26.

27. New York Times, May 7, June 8, 12, 13, August 20, 1950.

28. J. Robert Oppenheimer, "Comments on the Military Value of the Atom," Bulletin of the Atomic Scientist, February 1951, 43–45. Apparently, Oppenheimer agreed with Admiral Ofstie's arguments about the immorality and imprudence of city bombing as Oppenheimer quoted them in his speech and article. On Oppenheimer's aversion to the idea of killing noncombatants, see memorandum for the files, J. Kenneth Mansfield, June 15, 1951, box 41, Declassified General Subject Files, RG 128, NA.

29. New York Times, February 6, 9, March 12, 1951; "'A Kinda Flash,'" Time, February 5, 1951, 11; "What Our New Army Can Do," U.S. News and World Report, February 9, 1951, 20–27; Vannevar Bush, "The Defense of the Free World," Vital Speeches of the Day, March 15, 1951, 329–30.

30. "Strong & Weak Bombs," Time, February 12, 1951, 58; "Army, Navy, Air Can Use A-Bomb," U.S. News and World Report, January 26, 1951, 16–17; New York Times, January 30, February 4, 7, 1951; "Atomic Tests Light Up Four States," Life, February 12, 1951, 25–27; "How Little A-Bombs May Work," Life, February 26, 1951, 50; "Our Triple-Threat Atomic Weapons," Reader's Digest, April 1951, 29–30.

31. David E. Lilienthal, "Can the Atom Bomb Beat Communism?" Collier's, February 3, 1951, 14–15, 66–68; David E. Lilienthal, "When and Where Do We Drop the A-Bomb?" Collier's, March 10, 1951, 30–31, 63–64.

32. Federal Council of Churches of Christ in America, The Christian Conscience and Weapons of Mass Destruction (New York: Department of International Justice and Goodwill, 1950). For endorsements and further discussion of the Dun commission report, see Religious and Welfare Committee of the New York Committee on Atomic Information, "Ethical-Military Aspects of Atomic Energy," February 14, 1951, box 13, Amrine Papers, GUL.

33. George M. Houser, "Can Politics Be Moral Now?" Christian Century, April 4, 1951, 425–27; Stewart Meacham, "Another Look at the Dun Report," Christian Century, May 23, 1951, 633–34; "Statement by National Council F.O.R. Dealing with Dun Commission Report on 'The Christian Conscience and Weapons of Mass Destruction,'" December 1950, box 4, series A-2, section II, Fellowship of Reconciliation-USA Papers, SPC. For an expanded critique by Georgia Harkness, see Georgia Harkness, "A Second Look at the Dun Report," Christian Century, October 17, 1951, 1186–88.

34. Executive Committee of the American Council of Christian Churches, "Mass Weapons of Destruction," January 5, 1951, The Right Wing Collection of the University of Iowa Libraries, 1918–1977, microfilm collection (Glen Rock, NJ: Microfilming Corporation of America, 1978), A81.

35. Sam Bradford, "Should the United States Use the Atomic Bomb?" n.d., attached to Harold T. Dibble to Truman, January 31, 1951, box 3174, 711.5611, Central Decimal Files 1950–1954, RG 59, NA.

36. New York Times, May 13, 15, 19, 24, June 7, 15, July 1, 1951; "Atomic Bomb over Nevada," Life, July 16, 1951, 50.

37. New York Times, August 25, 26, September 11, 1951.

38. Charles J. V. Murphy, "The War We May Fight," Life, May 28, 1951, 76–95; "New Atomic Weapons Now Aim at Mass Armies," Newsweek, August 20, 1951; New York Times, September 9, 11, 1951.

39. David Alan Rosenberg, "Toward Armageddon: The Foundation of United States Nuclear Strategy, 1945–1961," Ph.D. diss., University of Chicago, 1983, 171; A. J. Bacevich, The Pentomic Era: The U.S. Army Between Korea and Vietnam (Washington: National Defense University Press, 1986), 82.

40. David Alan Rosenberg, "The Origins of Overkill: Nuclear Weapons and American Strategy, 1945–1960," International Security 7, no. 4 (spring 1983): 22.

41. Congressional Record, 82nd Cong., 1st sess., vol. 97, pt. 9, 11496–99; ibid., pt. 10, A5936–8. For press attention that McMahon's statements received, see New York Times, September 13, 19, 1951; "Fantastic Weapons," Life, September 24, 1951, 121–33; "Cut-Rate Defense," Time, October 1, 1951, 18–19.

42. U.S. House, Subcommittee of the Committee on Appropriations, Second Supplemental Appropriation Bill, 1952: Hearings, 82nd Cong., 1st sess., 3; Roger M. Anders, ed., Forging the Atomic Shield: Excerpts from the Office Diary of Gordon E. Dean (Chapel Hill, N.C.: University of North Carolina Press, 1987), 276–85.

43. "What Stalin's A-Bomb Means to the West and Its Defense," Newsweek, October 15, 1951, 23–24; "Varieties of Atom Bombs," Scientific American, November 1951, 32. The AP and UP wire services both distributed reports on the speech.

44. "Our New Atomic Power," Life, October 22, 1951, 38; New York Times, October 7, 1950; Edward A. Conway, "The Case of the Tactical Atom," America, October 20, 1951, 66–68. Although it did not directly mention Dean's speech, another article appeared in the Baltimore Sun Sunday Magazine arguing that new guided missiles and plentiful tactical atomic weapons could put an end to the mass bombing of cities and civilians. Michael Amrine, "No More Mass Bombing?" Baltimore Sun Sunday Magazine, November 4, 1951, 7–9, 23–24.

45. Dean went over parts of his speech with Admiral Sidney Souers, Truman's national security advisor, but others in the administration believed Dean to be expressing his own thinking. Concern about using nuclear weapons primarily against military targets did appear to have been an issue of interest among several members of the AEC in 1951. Thomas E. Murray wrote a letter to President Truman about the issue in April, and Sumner Pike was reported to be "intensely interested in the psychological implications of atomic energy" in a memorandum about Dean's speech. Anders, Forging the Atomic Shield, 173; memorandum, Bill Korns to John Sherman, October 9, 1951, box 2, Psychological Strategy Board, Staff Members and Office Files, HSTL; Murray to Truman, April 11, 1951, box 5, Executive Secretary Subject Files, NSC Staff, DDEL.

46. "Notes on Conversation with Oren Stephens regarding propaganda treatment of 'novel weapons,'" n.d., with attachments memorandum, Charles P. Arnot to O. C. Anderson, October 8, 1951, and memorandum, Llewellyn White to Charles P. Arnot, October 8, 1951, box 37, Psychological Strategy Board, Staff Members and Office Files, HSTL; New York Times, October 6, 1951.

47. Congressional Record, 82nd Cong., 1st sess., vol. 97, pt. 10, 12866–70; transcript, "Man of the Week," CBS, October 14, 1951, box 107, Unclassified General Correspondence, RG 128, NA.

48. Congressional Record, 82nd Cong., 1st sess., vol. 97, pt. 10, 12938; New York Times, October 12, 1951. They included Edwin C. Johnson, Harry P. Cain, Bourke B. Hickenlooper, Albert Gore, Zales N. Ecton, and Wayne Morse. New York Times, October 6, November 1, 10, 25, 1951.

49. New York Times, October 24, 29, 31, November 1, 10, 1951; "Atomic Artillery Tests," Newsweek, October 22, 1951, 25–26; "Exercise Desert Rock," Time, November 12, 1951, 21–22; "New Weapon for the GIs," Life, November 12, 1951, 38–39; Richard L. Miller, Under the Cloud: The Decades of Nuclear Testing (New York: Free Press, 1986), 122; Anders, Forging the Atomic Shield, 161.

50. Collier's, October 27, 1951.

51. Memorandum, Edward Barrett to Sitrick, October 2, 1951, box 87, Lot 53D11, International Information Activities 1930–1953, RG 59, NA.

52. Harold H. Martin, "Are Our Big Bombers Ready to Go?" Saturday Evening Post, December 30, 1950, 18–19, 65–67; Francis V. Drake, "The Facts About Strategic Bombing, Reader's Digest, July 1951, 55–60.

53. New York Times, March 30, 1951.

54. Project Vista had been another sign of the growing interest in tactical nuclear weapons in 1951. The scientific and technical study completed under the auspices of the California

Institute of Technology for the government concluded that the tactical employment of atomic weapons held outstanding promise for defending Western Europe. David C. Elliot, "Project Vista and Nuclear Weapons in Europe," International Security 11, no. 1 (summer 1986): 163–83.

55. New York Times, June 5, 1952; press release, June 14, 1952, box 181, Unclassified General Correspondence, RG 128, NA.

56. R. C. Weller, "Pyrrhic Victory?" Air University Quarterly Review 5, no. 2 (spring 1952): 77–82; Ralph E. Williams, Jr. "National Security and Military Policy," United States Naval Institute Proceedings 77, no. 3 (March 1951): 235–45; S. R. Shaw, "Wrong Target," Ordnance 35, no. 185 (March–April 1951): 471–78.

57. "Summary of Remarks at a Meeting with an Advisory Group of Business Leaders in Washington," June 26, 1952, box 13, Finletter Papers, HSTL. In an earlier speech Finletter came closer to justifying attacks on civilians. His speech to an American Legion post in Memphis touched upon the question of retaliation against nuclear attack. He said: "We are all, I am sure, horrified at our possible use of such devastating power. We would be less horrified, I think, if some atomic bombs started dropping on our cities." Press release, November 12, 1951, box 1, Formerly Classified General Correspondence, Public Information Division, Office of Information Services, RG 340, NA.

58. Memorandum, Jesse D. Willoughby to Parks, May 28, 1951, box 214, 470, Classified Decimal File 1952, Office of the Chief of Information, RG 319, NA; Anders, Forging the Atomic Shield, 159; memorandum, "Miss J." to Dorn, October 15, 1951, with attachments "A Presentation to the Army Policy Council on 'Public Information Program, Tactical Employment of Atomic Weapons,'" n.d., "Draft Staff Study: Public Information Policy on Tactical Employment of Atomic Weapons," n.d., "Public Information Plan, Tactical Employment of Atomic Weapons," n.d., and "Draft Press Interview by the Secretary of the Army on the Subject of Tactical Employment of Atomic Weapons," n.d., box 204, 008, Classified Decimal File 1951, Office of the Chief of Information, RG 319, NA; New York Times, November 28, 1951.

59. For example, see New York Times, June 17, 1951; Walter Lippmann, "Total War and Co-Existence," Reader's Digest, September 1951, 97–98.

60. For example, see Stewart Alsop and R. E. Lapp, "The Grim Truth About Civil Defense," Saturday Evening Post, April 14, 1951, 163; PPP 1951, 265–69.

61. Stewart Alsop, "The British and the Bomb," Bulletin of the Atomic Scientist, June 1951, 164.

62. JCS 2056/7, "Target Selection for the Strategic Air Offensive," August 12, 1950, in America's Plans for War, vol. 15; Rosenberg, "The Origins of Overkill," 16–18, 37; memorandum, LeMay to Vandenberg, January 15, 1951, box 197, series B, LeMay Papers, LC; LeMay diary, January 23, 1951, box 103, series B, LeMay Papers, LC; LeMay to E. Moore, March 3, 1951, box 197, series B, LeMay Papers, LC; Barry H. Steiner, Bernard Brodie and the Foundations of American Nuclear Strategy (Lawrence, KS: University of Kansas Press, 1991), 101.

63. Psychological Strategy Board, "Staff Study on Publicity with Respect to Novel Weapons," November 14, 1951, box 12, Subject File of the Special Assistant for Atomic Energy and Aerospace 1950–1966, Office of the Deputy Assistant Secretary for Politico-Military Affairs, RG 59, NA; memorandum, Edmond L. Taylor to R. B. Allen, February 13, 1952, box 37, Psychological Strategy Board, Staff Members and Office Files, HSTL.

64. NSC 126, "Report to the National Security Council by the Psychological Strategy Board," February 28, 1952, FRUS 1952–54, vol. 2, 869–72; memorandum, C. B. Marshall to John H. Ferguson, November 27, 1951, box 2, Lot 62D333, Psychological Strategy Board Working File 1951–1953, Executive Secretariat, RG 59, NA; memorandum, Bohlen to Edward Barrett et al., December 6, 1951, box 2, Lot 62D333, Psychological Strategy Board Working File 1951–1953, Executive Secretariat, RG 59, NA.

65. Ellis M. Zacharias, "Absolute Weapons ... More Deadly than the Atom," U.N. World, November 1947, 13–15; New York Times, September 10, 1949, July 26, October 22, 1950; Anton J. Carlson, "The Scientists' Responsibility," Nation, special supplement, May 20, 1950, 493.

66. Committee on Biological Warfare, Research and Development Board, "Report on International Aspects of Biological Warfare," October 14, 1947, box 206, 385.2, Central Decimal Files 1948–1950, RG 218, NA; Walter Millis, ed., The Forrestal Diaries (New York: Viking, 1951), 399.

67. William M. Creasy, "Presentation to the Secretary of Defense's Ad Hoc Committee on CEBAR," January 27, 1950, box 61, Lot 57D688, Special Assistant to the Secretary for Atomic Energy Matters 1944–1952, RG 59; William M. Creasy, "Presentation to the Secretary of Defense's Ad Hoc Committee on CEBAR," February 24, 1950, box 207, 385.2, Central Decimal Files 1948-1950, RG 218, NA; "Report of the Secretary of Defense's Ad Hoc Committee on Chemical, Biological, and Radiological Warfare," June 30, 1950, box 204, Decimal File July–December 1950, Correspondence Control Section, Office of the Administrative Secretary, RG 330, NA; JCS Decision on JCS 1837/26, "A Memorandum by the Joint Advanced Study Committee on Biological Warfare," February 25, 1952, with enclosure "Study by the Joint Advanced Study Committee on Biological Warfare," n.d., box 152, 385.2, Central Decimal Files 1951–1953, RG 218, NA. The Air Force consultant Stefan Possony also lauded the propaganda benefits of radiological weapons that could be used for area denial instead of destruction and which could allow a the United States to fight "a war without casualties." The British military likewise praised biological weapons because of their capacity to incapacitate enemy forces in friendly or neutral countries without the attendant physical destruction of nuclear or conventional weapons. Memorandum for the record, Byron K. Enyart, October 6, 1952, box 37, Psychological Strategy Board, Staff Members and Office Files, HSTL; Stefan T. Possony, "An Outline of American Atomic Strategy in the Non-Military Fields," November 18, 1952, box 37, Psychological Strategy Board, Staff Members and Office Files, HSTL; Report of Chiefs of Staff Committee, Biological Warfare Report 1950–1951, January 1952, box 4, BW-CW General Decimal Files 1952, Office of Deputy Chief of Staff for Operations, RG 341, NA.
68. New York Times, April 18, 1950, February 9, 1952.
69. New York Times, April 23, November 1, 1950, November 23, 1951; Louis N. Ridenour, "How Effective Are Radioactive Poisons in Warfare," Bulletin of the Atomic Scientist, July 1950, 199–202; 224; David B. Parker, "War Without Death," Coronet, July 1950, 93–98; "Radiological Warfare," Officers' Call 2, no. 6: 1–12; Washington Star, April 27, 1953.
70. Department of Defense Directive, "700.01-1S-Policy on Chemical, Biological, and Radiological Warfare," November 28, 1951, box 152, 385.2, Central Decimal Files 1951–1953, RG 218, NA; memorandum for the record, Harold Berzof, October 21, 1952, box 6, 381, BW-CW General Decimal Files 1952, Office of Deputy Chief of Staff for Operations, RG 341, NA; memorandum, Office of the Chief of Psychological Warfare to Office of the Chief of Information, July 26, 1954, box 15, 311.25, Decimal Files, Confidential Correspondence 1951–1954, Office of the Chief of Special Warfare, RG 319, NA; "Copy for the Basis of the Narration of the Chemical Corps' TV Film, Suggested Title: The Chemical Corps' Role in National Defense," n.d., box 15, 311.25, Decimal Files, Confidential Correspondence 1951–1954, Office of the Chief of Special Warfare, RG 319, NA.
71. New York Times, November 7, 1955.
72. Paul Boyer, By the Bomb's Early Light: American Thought and Culture at the Dawn of the Atomic Age (New York: Pantheon, 1985); Allan M. Winkler, Life Under a Cloud: American Anxiety About the Bomb (New York: Oxford University Press, 1993); Spencer R. Weart, Nuclear Fear: A History of Images (Cambridge, MA: Harvard University Press, 1988); Michael J. Yavendetti, "The American People and the Use of Atomic Bombs on Japan: The 1940s," Historian 36 (February 1974): 224–47.

Chapter 6

1. New York Times, June 10, 1951.
2. New York Times, August 2, 9, 1951; "Statistical Tabulation Explaining the Overall Status of Damage Suffered During the Course of the War of June 25, 1950," August 12, 1952, box 4283, 795.00, Central Decimal Files 1950–1954, RG 59, NA; Alan R. Millett, "Casualties," Encyclopedia of the Korean War, ed. Spencer C. Tucker et al. (Santa Barbara, CA: ABC-CLIO, 2000), 100–101; Conrad C. Crane, American Airpower Strategy in Korea, 1950–1953 (Lawrence, KS.: University of Kansas Press, 2000), 168; David Rees, Korea: The Limited War (New York: St. Martin's, 1964), 460–61; Bruce Cumings, The Origins of the Korean War, vol. 2, The Roaring of the Cataract, 1947–1950 (Princeton, NJ: Princeton University Press, 1990), 748; Charles R. Joy, "May Discursive Report: Korea," June 6, 1952, box 48, Joy Papers, AHTL.

3. For examples, see "Does U. S. Face Endless War in Korea?" U.S. News and World Report, May 4, 1951, 22–23; "Korean War: The Big Losers," U.S. News and World Report, July 13, 1951, 19–20; "Tragedy of Korea," Newsweek, July 9, 1951, 30; "The Forgotten People," Time, July 16, 1951, 22–24.

4. United Nations Document S/2203, June 19, 1951; New York Times, July 3, 1951; "Charges of Atrocities in Korea Called Propaganda to Discredit U.N. Action," U.S. Department of State Bulletin, July 30, 1951, 189–90.

5. Message, CINCUNC to JCS, July 29, 1951, box 33, Geographic File 1951–1953, RG 218, NA; message, CINCUNC to JCS, August 14, 1951, box 33, Geographic File 1951–1953, RG 218, NA; message, CINCUNC to Dept of the Army for G3 and JCS, August 15, 1951, box 33, Geographic File 1951–1953, RG 218, NA. The Soviet press regularly complained about U.S. bombing of nonmilitary targets in Korea and the State Department kept the United Nations Command abreast of Soviet agitation on the issue. Alexander Werth, "What Russia Tells Itself," Nation, September 16, 1950, 247–48; message, Moscow Embassy to Secretary of State, August 12, 1951, box 4275, 795.00, Central Decimal Files 1950–1954, RG 59, NA; message, Secretary of State to SCAP, August 16, 1951, box 4275, 795.00, Central Decimal Files 1950–1954, RG 59, NA; New York Times, September 23, 1951.

6. Frederick J. Libby, "Plans for Peace," Peace Action 17, no. 9 (September 1951): 2; Alfred Hassler, "Cops in Korea," Fellowship 16, no. 9 (September 1950): 4–8; Alfred Hassler, "Call Off the Cops!" Fellowship 17, no. 3 (March 1951): 1–5. For other expressions of skepticism from peace activists, see Helen Mears, "The Voices of America," Fellowship 17, no. 9 (September 1951): 6–7; "Is There a Lesser Evil?" n.d., box 3, series A-5, section II, Fellowship of Reconciliation-USA Papers, SPC.

7. "Faith, Morals and War," Christian Century, April 4, 1951, 422–23; "Korea Must Be Rebuilt," Christian Century, August 8, 1951, 907–908; H. C. Francis, "Modern War," Commonweal, February 16, 1951, 470–72; S. D. Newberry, "Delectable Slaughter," Catholic World, May 1952, 127. Also see "Outlook for Korea," Commonweal, November 28, 1952, 187; "Not Inconvenienced," Christian Century, March 11, 1953, 292.

8. I. F. Stone, The Hidden History of the Korean War (New York: Monthly Review Press, 1952), 143, 179, 236, 256–58, 265.

9. Reginald W. Thompson, Cry Korea (London: Macdonald, 1951), 42, 44, 53–54, 74, 89, 91, 114, 125, 143, 148.

10. For a report of the American consulate in Toronto on the obscurity of Stone's book, see message, U.S. Consulate General, Toronto to State Department, May 14, 1953, box 2248, 511.00, Central Decimal Files 1950–1954, RG 59, NA.

11. Freda Kirchwey, "Liberation by Death," Nation, March 10, 1951, 215–16. See also Walter Sullivan, "Rebuilding Shattered Korea," Nation, February 2, 1952, 107–109.

12. Harold L. Ickes, "Sherman's Hell; Korea's Hell," New Republic, March 3, 1951, 18; Emil Sekerak to Harold Ickes, March 5, 1951, box 462, Ickes Papers, LC. See also E. J. Kahn, Jr., "Letter from Korea," New Yorker, April 21, 1951, 122–25.

13. Washington Post, February 24, 1951; New York Times, March 3, 1951.

14. New York Times, January 6, 1951, June 25, 1952; Robert A. Taft, A Foreign Policy for Americans (Garden City, NY: Doubleday, 1951), 12; Upton Sinclair radio scripts, August 20 and September 3, 1950, The Right Wing Collection of the University of Iowa Libraries, 1918–1977, microfilm collection (Glen Rock, NJ: Microfilming Corporation of America, 1977), C35.

15. New York Times, April 7, 1951; Ben C. Limb, "The Pacific Pact," Foreign Affairs 29, no. 4 (July 1951): 545.

16. New York Times, August 2, 1951; Newsweek, July 9, 1951, front cover.

17. Message, CINCFE to Department of the Army, September 23, 1950, box 727, Korean Message File June 1950–May 1954, Far East and Pacific Branch, Office of the Deputy Chief of Staff for Operations, RG 319, NA; Roy Appleman, South to the Naktong, North to the Yalu (Washington: Office of the Chief of Military History, Department of the Army, 1961), 670; Albert E. Cowdrey, The Medics' War (Washington: Center of Military History, United States Army, 1987), 327; George Barrett, "Preview in Korea — The Task of Relief," New York Times Magazine, August 19, 1951, 10; New York Times, July 14, 1951; "Reports of U.N. Command Operations in Korea: 58th Report for the Period November 16-30, 1952," U.S. Department of State Bulletin, May 11, 1953, 692–93; Division of Public Studies, Office of

Public Affairs, "American Opinion" Memorandum, August 19, 1952, box 136, Lot 56D508, Bureau of Public Affairs 1944–1962, RG 59, NA.

18. "Korean Release, No. 761," December 29, 1950, box 2, Korean War Communiques and Press Releases, 1950–1951, Office of the Chief of Information, RG 319, NA; Ashley Halsey, Jr., "Miracle Voyage Off Korea," Saturday Evening Post, April 14, 1951, 17; message, X Corps to CINCFE, December 22, 1950, box 729, Security-Classified Correspondence 1950, Adjutant General Section, RG 500, NA; James A. Field, The History of United States Naval Operations: Korea (Washington: U.S. Government Printing Office, 1962), 304; Robert Futrell, The United States Air Force in Korea 1950–1953, rev. ed. (Washington: U.S. Government Printing Office, 1983), 269.

19. New York Times, November 12, 1950, April 27, August 2, September 1, November 18, 20, December 15, 1951; W. J. McWilliams to Matthew J. Connelly, August 29, 1951, box 1285, Official File, HSTL; Congressional Record, 82nd Cong., 1st sess., vol. 97, pt. 8, 11199; "Information Bulletin No. 61," July 12, 1952, box 1, Unit Histories and Command Reports, Public Information Office, Far East Command, RG 349, NA.

20. New York Times, November 10, December 12, 1952; PPP 1950, 710–11; message, CG UNCACK 820th AU to CO Civil Assistance Section, Eighth Army (ADV), December 5, 1951, box 37, Subject File 1949–1951, Office of the Chief of Information, Office of the Chief of Staff, Supreme Commander for the Allied Powers, RG 331, NA; draft manuscript, Charles R. Joy, "CARE in Korea," n.d., box 29, Joy Papers, AHTL; Charles R. Joy, "News Release #52," June 12, 1952, box 48, Joy Papers, AHTL; Charles R. Joy, "News Release #45," May 15, 1952, box 48, Joy Papers, AHTL.

21. "Koreans Desperately Need Help Now," Christian Century, December 27, 1950, 1542–43; "Relief Can Be Sent to Korea," Christian Century, January 10, 1951, 37; "Help for the Children of Stricken Korea," Christian Century, December 31, 1952, 1515; New York Times, January 28, March 7, 10, July 16, 30, August 27, September 9, October, 22, November 21, 24, 1951, April 2, August 23, October 17, November 3, 1952, March 26, 29, April 3, 1953.

22. Edward S. Skillin, "New Hope for Korea," Commonweal, July 25, 1952, 383–85; New York Times, May 11, 1951; "Information Bulletin No. 61," July 12, 1952, box 1, Unit Histories and Command Reports, Public Information Office, Far East Command, RG 349, NA.

23. Message, Commanding General Eighth Army to Department of Army, November 20, 1950, box 196, 311.5, Classified Decimal File, Chief of Information, RG 319, NA; "Far East Annex to Weekly Information Policy Guidance, No. 41," January 12, 1951, box 2239, 511.00, Central Decimal Files 1950–1954, RG 59, NA; message, State Department to Pusan Embassy, February 14, 1951, box 2539, 511.95, Central Decimal Files 1950–1954, RG 59, NA; "Far East Annex to Weekly Information Policy Guidance No. 70," August 8, 1951, box 36, Foreign Information Policy Guidance, Office of the Chief of Information, Office of the Chief of Staff, Supreme Commander for the Allied Powers, RG 331, NA; press release, "Personnel in Alaska and Fort Devers Contribute to Korean Orphans," July 10, 1952, box 1, Unit Histories and Command Reports, Public Information Office, Far East Command, RG 349, NA; "Press Advisory Division Censorship Criteria," box 35, Subject File 1949–1951, Chief of Information, Office of Chief of Staff, Supreme Commander for the Allied Powers, RG 331, NA.

24. New York Times, December 25, 1950, January 19, February 11, June 16, 1951, November 4, 1952, January 14, May 25, 1953; San Francisco Examiner, December 1, 1950; "Waifs of War," Time, January 1, 1951, 16; "The Greatest Tragedy," Time, January 15, 1951, 23–24; "Helping the Hopeless," Time, January 29, 1951, 31; Bill Stapleton, "Little Orphan Island," Collier's, July 14, 1951, 51; Michael Rougier, "The Little Boy Who Wouldn't Smile," Life, July 23, 1951, 91–98; James Finan, "Voyage from Hungnam," Reader's Digest, November 1951, 111–12; "Christian Soldiers," Time, June 15, 1953, 75–76.

25. Nora Waln, "Our Softhearted Warriors in Korea," Saturday Evening Post, December 23, 1950, 28–29, 66–67; New York Times, July 30, 1951.

26. William L. Worden, "The Cruelest Weapon in Korea," Saturday Evening Post, February 10, 1951, 26–27, 134–36. For another example of the contrast between harsh actions and good intentions, see Melvin Russell Blair, "A Christmas Story … from the Front Lines in Korea," Saturday Evening Post, December 22, 1951, 8, 54.

27. Christopher Rand, "Letter from Korea," New Yorker, March 1, 1951, 107–16.

28. Harold H. Martin, "The Pious Killer of Korea," Saturday Evening Post, July 21, 1951, 26–27, 87–90.

29. Norman Cousins, "The Age of the Big Trap," Saturday Review of Literature, February 10, 1951, 22–23; "A Place to Intervene," Commonweal, June 1951, 276; "Korea Must Be Rebuilt," Christian Century, August 8, 1951, 907–908; "Korea Must Be Rebuilt — A Task for the U.N.," Bulletin of the Atomic Scientist, August 1951, 194–95; Norman Cousins, "One Sunday Afternoon," Saturday Review of Literature, October 20, 1951, 22–23; Walter Sullivan, "Rebuilding Shattered Korea," Nation, February 2, 1952, 107–109.
30. Hanson H. Hathaway, "Korean Relief," Red Cross Magazine, November 1951, 3–9.
31. Michael Rougier, "The Little Boy Who Wouldn't Smile," Life, July 23, 1951, 91–98.
32. John Denson, "Bitter Week End in Seoul," Collier's, January 27, 1951, 13–15, 74–76; "Forgotten People," Time, July 16, 1951, 22–24; St. Louis-Post Dispatch, December 15, 1950; New York Times, December 19, 1950. Also see, New York Times, January 10, 1951.
33. George Barrett, "The Pak Saga," New York Times Magazine, May 6, 1951, 10, 28–29.
34. Memorandum, Lucius Battle to Secretary of State, January 19, 1951, FRUS 1951, vol. 7, 102–105; New York Times, August 28, 1951; PPP 1950, 675, 686, 742, 757; "Overnight Information Policy Guidance, No. 621," January 5, 1951, box 91, Lot 52D335, Records Relating to International Information Activities 1930–1953, RG 59, NA; "Far East Annex to the Weekly Information Policy Guidance No. 71," August 11, 1951, box 2241, 511.00, Central Decimal Files 1950-1954, RG 59, NA; "Far East Annex to the Weekly Information Policy Guidance No. 72," August 17, 1951, box 2241, 511.00, Central Decimal Files 1950–1954, RG 59, NA; "Overnight Information Policy Guidance No. 801," September 17, 1951, box 91, Lot 52D335, Records Relating to International Information Activities 1930–1953, RG 59, NA; "Resolution Adopted by ECOSOC on November 7, 1950," U.S. Department of State Bulletin, November 27, 1950, 859–862; "Relief and Rehabilitation of Korea," U.S. Department of State Bulletin, January 22, 1951, 146–149. For further public attributions of blame to the Communists for the civil destruction in Korea by civilian officials and members of the military, see "North Korea Slanders U.N. Forces to Hide Guilt of Aggression," U.S. Department of State Bulletin, September 18, 1950, 454; Willis G. Carter, "Strategic Bombardment and National Objectives," Air University Quarterly Review 4, no. 3 (spring 1951): 5–14.
35. William L. Worden, "What Must We Do About Korea Now?" Saturday Evening Post, December 15, 1951, 32–33, 93–101. For another example, see New York Times, December 29, 1950.
36. New York Times, January 18, 1952; Harold E. Fey, "Let the Churches Help Korea!" Christian Century, February 13, 1952, 190–92; Charles R. Joy, "CARE Conference Report: Korea, Summary of Activities from December 1st, 1951 to August 1st, 1952," box 48, Joy Papers, AHTL.
37. Edgar S. Kennedy, Mission to Korea (London: Derek Verschoyle, 1952), 108–109.
38. New York Times, December 13, 1950, January 3, August 9, 1951.
39. Ibid., December 15, 1950.
40. Ibid., July 21, 29, 1951.
41. E. J. Kahn, Jr., "Letter from Korea," New Yorker, June 30, 1951, 60–66; William L. Worden, "What Must We Do About Korea Now?" Saturday Evening Post, December 15, 1951, 32–33, 93–101.
42. New York Times, December 9, 1949, July 5, 1950.
43. Ibid., July 15, 1950.
44. Memorandum of conversation, "Relations of International Committee of the Red Cross with Unified Command in Korea," February 14, 1951, box 4380, 800.571, Central Decimal File 1950–1954, RG 59, NA; memorandum of conversation, "Relations of International Committee of the Red Cross with Unified Command in Korea," 3:00 p.m., February 14, 1951, box 4380, 800.571, Central Decimal File 1950–1954, RG 59, NA; memorandum, Charles Runyon to Louis J. Halle, June 28, 1954, with attachments "Background memorandum Concerning the Application of the 1949 Geneva Conventions," n.d., letter, Hickerson to Secretary of Defense, November 21, 1951, letter, William C. Foster to Secretary of State, February 15, 1952, letter, Hickerson to Secretary of Defense, April 21, 1952, and letter, Marshall S. Carter to Secretary of State, May 15, 1952, box 75, Lot 61D53, Bureau of Public Affairs 1944–1962, RG 59, NA; memorandum, Robert M. Lee to Hoyt Vandenberg, January 31, 1952 with attachments memorandum, Pace to Secretary of Defense, January 11, 1952, and "Extract of Report by Chief Physician on Hospital Ship 'Jutlandia,'" box 903, 383.6, Project Decimal File 1942–1954, Directorate of Plans, Office of Deputy Chief of Staff for Operations, RG 341, NA; message, Tokyo Embassy to Secretary of State, December 5, 1951,

box 4380, 800.571, Central Decimal Files 1950–1954, RG 59, NA; message, CG KCOMZ to CINCUNC, July 30, 1952, box 808, Security Classified General Correspondence 1952, Adjutant General Section, RG 500, NA.

45. Paul Ruegger, "Press Conference Statement," April 9, 1951, box 4380, 800.571, Central Decimal Files 1950–1954, RG 59, NA; New York Times, July 23, September 27, 1952; K. R. Kreps to Secretary of State, April 20, 1951, box 879, 014, Project Decimal File 1942–1954, Directorate of Plans, Office of Deputy Chief of Staff for Operations, RG 341, NA.

46. New York Times, June 25–27, 1952; "Why the British Were Not Told of Plans to Bomb Power Plants," Newsweek, July 7, 1952, 32–35; "Irresponsible Ally?" Time, July 7, 1952, 26–27; message, PsyWar to CINCFE, June 28, 1952, box 4276, 795.00, Central Decimal Files 1950–1954, RG 59, NA; message, PsyWar to CINCFE, June 29, 1952, box 4276, 795.00, Central Decimal Files 1950–1954, RG 59, NA; "Supplement to Weekly Foreign Information Policy Guidance, No. 116," n.d., box 1, Confidential Weekly Foreign Information Policy Guidance Papers July 1950–July 1952, Office of the Secretary of the Army, RG 335, NA.

47. United States Strategic Bombing Survey, "The Effects of Strategic Bombing on Japanese Morale," June 1947, Final Reports of the United States Strategic Bombing Survey 1945–1947, microfilm collection (Washington, DC: National Archives, 1975), 132–33; Ronald Schaffer, Wings of Judgment: American Bombing in World War II (New York: Oxford University Press, 1985), 141–42; Michael S. Sherry, The Rise of American Air Power: The Creation of Armageddon (New Haven, CT: Yale University Press, 1987), 312. The FEAF under General George Kenny also issued warnings to target cities in Japan before air attacks. Crane, American Airpower Strategy in Korea, 13.

48. Paul Boyer, By the Bomb's Early Light: American Thought and Culture at the Dawn of the Atomic Age (New York: Pantheon, 1985), 194–95.

49. Bonner Fellers, Wings for Peace: A Primer for a New Defense (Chicago: Regnery, 1953), 92; "Why Soviet Avoids Big War: Fear of A-Bomb, U.S. Industry," U.S. News and World Report, August 25, 1950, 11–12.

50. New York Times, July 13, 1950, October 12, 1951; San Francisco Examiner, August 9, 1950; Detroit News, August 16, 1950; Congressional Record, 82d Cong., 1st sess., vol. 97, pt. 10, 12938; Collier's, October 27, 1951.

51. HQ USAF, An Evaluation of the Effectiveness of the United States Air Force in the Korean Campaign (Barcus Report), vol. 5, 102–103, box 906, Project Decimal File 1942–1954, Directorate of Plans, Office of the Deputy Chief of Staff for Operations, RG 341, NA; transcripts, "Voice of the Free Peoples of World," July 7–9, 11, 12, 15, 16, 19, 20, 21, 23, 26, 1950, box 2539, 511.95, Central Decimal Files 1950–1954, RG 59, NA; United Nations Security Council Official Records, September 7, 1950, 5th year, 497th mtg., S/PV.497, 11–13.

52. "Policy Directive, No. 60," August 25, 1951, box 21, General Correspondence 1952, Psychological Warfare Section, General Headquarters, Far East Command, RG 338, NA; "Twenty-seventh Report of the U.N. Command Operations in Korea," U.S. Department of State Bulletin, October 29, 1951, 708–11; "Reports of the U.N. Command Operations in Korea," U.S. Department of State Bulletin, December 24, 1951, 1028–34.

53. Memorandum, D. N. Yates to Deputy Chief of Staff for Operations, September 17, 1951, with attachment "Recommendation to the Air Staff: Political and Psychological Warfare," September 1, 1951, box 14, Formerly Classified General Correspondence 1947–1952, Public Information Division, Office of Information Services, RG 340, NA; Harold C. Stuart, "The New Look in Korea," Air Force 34, no. 12 (December 1951): 71. Also see an Air Force officer's mention of the warning program in Korea, Raymond S. Sleeper, "Korean Targets for Medium Bombardment," Air University Quarterly Review 4, no. 3 (spring 1951): 18–31.

54. First Radio Broadcast and Leaflet Group, "Plan for Psychological Warfare Operations Designed to Support the United Nations Air Force," June 12, 1952, box 20, General Correspondence 1952, Psychological Warfare Section, General Headquarters, Far East Command, RG 338, NA; "Plan for Psychological Warfare Operations in Support of Air Attack Program," July 7, 1952, box 7, General Correspondence 1952, Psychological Warfare Section, General Headquarters, Far East Command, RG 338, NA; "Monthly Report for August 1952," box 14, General Correspondence 1952, Psychological Warfare Section, General Headquarters, Far East Command, RG 338, NA; "Report of the U.N. Command Operations in Korea," U.S. Department of State Bulletin, January 26, 1951, 155–59; "Psychological Warfare Weekly Bulletin," n.d., box 20, General Correspondence 1952, Psychological Warfare Section, General Headquarters, Far East Command, RG 338, NA; Crane, American

Airpower Strategy in Korea, 122–25; message, CINCFE to PsyWar, October 9, 1952, box 759, Chronological File 1949–June 1954, Office of Security Review, Office of the Assistant Secretary of Defense for Legislative and Public Affairs, RG 330, NA; "Reports of U.N. Command Operations in Korea: Sixty-Fifth Report for the Period March 1–15, 1953," U.S. Department of State Bulletin, July 13, 1953, 52–53.

55. New York Times, July 12, 16, 31, 1952.
56. St. Louis Post-Dispatch, August 5, 1952; Los Angeles Times, August 5, 1952; Washington Post, August 6, 1952.
57. Baltimore Sun, August 6, 1952; "Remarks on Warnings to North Korean Cities on Bombing," August 7, 1952, box 13, Finletter Papers, HSTL; New York Times, August 8, 1952; "U.S. Air Power Rising in Korea," U.S. News and World Report, September 19, 1952, 44–47.
58. Message, Circular #123, August 5, 1952, box 2245, 511.00, Central Decimal Files 1950–1954, RG 59, NA; message, Secretary of State to Tokyo Embassy, August 13, 1952, box 808, Security Classified General Correspondence 1952, Adjutant General Section, Eighth Army 1944–1956, RG 500, NA.
59. Message, CINCFE to JCS, July 21, 1951, box 33, Geographic File 1951–1953, RG 218, NA; message, JCS to CINCFE, July 25, 1951, box 33, Geographic File 1951–1953, RG 218, NA; message, CINCFE to JCS, August 15, box 33, Geographic File 1951–1953, RG 218, NA.
60. New York Times, August 12, 13, 18, 20, 22, 23, September 1, 1952; message, PsyWar to CINCFE, August 5, 1952, box 4283, 795.00, Central Decimal Files 1950–1954, RG 59, NA; message, Paris Embassy to Secretary of State, August 6, 1952, box 4283, 795.00, Central Decimal File 1950–1954, RG 59, NA; message, Olso Embassy to State Department, August 21, 1952, box 4283, 795.00, Central Decimal File 1950–1954, RG 59, NA; memorandum, Louis T. Olom to Joseph B. Phillips, August 21, 1952, box 1, Coordinator for Psychological Intelligence, RG 306, NA; Daily Worker, August 6, 7, 1952. See also a letter to the editor which called the bombing of the seventy-eight cities genocide. Louisville-Courier, August 23, 1952.
61. "The Right Track," Time, July 21, 1952, 32; message, PsyWar to CINCFE, August 9, 1952, box 808, Security Classified General Correspondence 1952, Adjutant General Section, Eighth Army 1944–1956, RG 500, NA; "Will Bombing End Korean War?" U.S. News and World Report, September 12, 1952, 13–15; "Truth About the Air War," U.S. News and World Report, November 7, 1952, 20–21; Carl Spaatz, "Stepped-Up Bombing in Korea," Newsweek, August 18, 1952, 27.
62. For a version of the AP story, see St. Louis Post-Dispatch, August 5, 1952. For a version of the UP story, see Los Angeles Times, August 5, 1952.
63. New York Times, August 5, 6, 8–10, 19, 21, 29, 30, September 14, 20, October 3, 5, 1952.
64. Washington Post, August 6, 1952; New York Times, August 16, 24, 1952.
65. "Report on Psychological Warfare Operations during the Korean Conflict," n.d., box 904, 384.6, Project Decimal File 1942–1954, Directorate of Plans, Office of the Deputy Chief of Staff for Operations, RG 341, NA; "Report of U.N. Command Operations in Korea," U.S. Department of State Bulletin, December 1, 1952, 886; "Report of U.N. Command Operations in Korea," U.S. Department of State Bulletin, December 15, 1952, 961; "Reports of U.N. Command Operations in Korea," U.S. Department of State Bulletin, December 29, 1952, 1037; "Report of U.N. Command Operations in Korea," U.S. Department of State Bulletin, January 26, 1953, 158; "Report of U.N. Command Operations in Korea," U.S. Department of State Bulletin, February 9, 1953, 229; "Report of U.N. Command Operations in Korea," U.S. Department of State Bulletin, February 16, 1953, 280.
66. "Rear Area Effects of Plan 'Strike,'" September 6, 1952, box 21, General Correspondence 1952, Psychological Warfare Section, General Headquarters, Far East Command, RG 338, NA.
67. Brooks E. Kleber and Dale Birdsell, The Chemical Warfare Service: Chemicals in Combat (Washington, DC: Office of the Chief of Military History, 1966), 628, 630–35; Louis F. Fieser, The Scientific Method: A Personal Account of Unusual Projects in War and in Peace (New York: Reinhold, 1964), 36, 52–53; memorandum, A. S. Merrill to Joint Security Control, March 24, 1945, box 764, Chronological File 1949–June 1954, Office of Security Review, Assistant Secretary of Defense for Legislative and Public Affairs, RG 330, NA.
68. Futrell, U.S. Air Force in Korea, 692.
69. Fieser, Scientific Method, 27–29.
70. Message, Radio-TV Branch, Public Information Office to Joint Armed Forces Public Information Office, February 9, 27, March 12, April 17, May 1, 22, June 4, 11, July 16, 1951, box

54, General Decimal File, Office of Public Information, Office of the Assistant Secretary of Defense for Legislative and Public Affairs, RG 330, NA; New York Times, July 10, 1950; Walter Karig, "Korea — Tougher to Crack than Okinawa," Collier's, September 23, 1950, 24–25, 69–70; "'Goop' Bombs Prove Effective Against Russian T-34 Tank," Air Force 33, no. 12 (December 1950): 34.

71. John Denson, "Captain Thach's Phantom Carrier," Collier's, October 14, 1950, 52–56; New York Times, February 9, 1951; Washington Post, February 24, 1951; "Air Warfare Pays Off in Korea," U.S. News and World Report, February 9, 1951, 19. Also see E. J. Kahn, Jr., "Letter from Korea," New Yorker, May 12, 1951, 94–101.

72. Manchester Guardian, March 1, 1952; New York Times, April 28, 1952; Parliamentary Debates Commons, 1951–1952, vol. 500, col. 848–49, 1425–26, vol. 501, col. 446–49, vol. 501, col. 1367; New York Times, June 5, 1952; message, New York to Secretary of State, August 1, 1952, box 4283, 795.00, Central Decimal File 1950–1954, RG 59, NA; pamphlet, "Napalm," n.d., box 60, series D, Friends Committee on National Legislation Papers, SPC. The Manchester Guardian published a second editorial on napalm in May which disputed Birch's defense of napalm use. Manchester Guardian, May 15, 1952.

73. Evaluation Branch, Requirements Division, Office of the Chief of Psychological Warfare, "Communist Charges of the Use of 'Horror' Weapons by the United States," September 4, 1952, box 1, Secret Correspondence 1951–1954, Office of the Chief of Special Warfare, RG 319, NA; message, PsyWar to CINCFE, August 5, 1952, box 808, Security-Classified Correspondence, Adjutant General Section, RG 500, NA; Daily Worker, August 20, 21, 1952.

74. "Air Staff Summary Sheet: Official Air Force Position on the Use of Napalm," August 7, 1952, box 65, 471.6, Operations General Decimal File 1952, Office of Deputy Chief of Staff for Operations, RG 341, NA; memorandum, Thomas D. White to Willis S. Matthews, September 20, 1952, with attachment "Use of Napalm in FEAF," n.d., box 5, Chairman's Files of General Bradley 1949–1953, RG 218, NA; Omar N. Bradley to William Elliot, September 24, 1952, box 5, Chairman's Files of General Bradley 1949–1953, RG 218, NA; memorandum, Arno H. Luehman to Robert Whitney Burns, August 12, 1952, with attachments "Background," n.d., and "Quote by General Twining," n.d., box 65, 471.6, Operations General Decimal File 1952, Office of Deputy Chief of Staff for Operations, RG 341, NA; New York Times, August 19, 1952; message, Circular 307, September 17, 1952, box 2245, 511.00, Central Decimal Files 1950–1954, RG 59, NA.

75. E. J. Kahn, Jr., The Peculiar War: Impressions of a Reporter in Korea (New York: Random House, 1951), 131–32.

76. New York Times, May 13, 1952; "Korean Christians Are Troubled in Spirit," Christian Century, December 31, 1952, 1515; "A Time of Horror," Christian Century, May 14, 1952, 581–82; National Guardian, August 21, 28, 1952.

Chapter 7

1. "What It Can Do," Newsweek, September 14, 1953, 42.
2. "The Evolution of Foreign Policy," U.S. Department of State Bulletin, January 25, 1954, 107–10; Richard H. Immerman, John Foster Dulles: Piety, Pragmatism, and Power in U.S. Foreign Policy (Wilmington, DE: Scholarly Resources, 1999), 83.
3. "A Plea for Another Great Debate," New York Times Magazine, February 28, 1954, 24–26; New York Times, March 30, 1954; "Eisenhower's Real Decision," New Republic, January 11, 1954, 9–10; Christopher Emment, "The President and the Atom," Commonweal, February 12, 1954, 466–69; George R. Fairlamb to Dulles, February 24, 1954, box 2564, 600.0012, Central Decimal Files 1950–1954, RG 59, NA.
4. "L Panel Meeting," July 11, 1952, box 24, Psychological Strategy Board, Staff Member and Office Files, HSTL; New York Times, April 22, June 25, August 30, 1952, February 14, March 9, 17, 21, June 20, July 18, 1953; Omar Bradley, "Soldier's Farewell," Saturday Evening Post, August 29, 1953, 22–23, 46–49.
5. Log of C. D. Jackson, April 22, 1953, box 68, C. D. Jackson Papers, DDEL; message, Circular 959, March 17, 1953, box 2247, 511.00, Central Decimal Files 1950–1954, RG 59, NA; Ad Hoc Committee of the NSC Planning Board on Armaments and American Policy, "Interim Report," May 8, 1953, FRUS 1952–1954, vol. 2, 1150–60; press release of letter, Edward Teller to Sterling Cole, July 31, 1953, box 517, Unclassified General Correspondence, RG 128, NA; "The President and the Bomb," Life, October 19, 1953, 38.

6. PPP 1953, 815; New York Times, December 15, 1953; transcript of CBS press conference, January 4, 1954, box 106c, Unclassified General Correspondence, RG 128, NA; press conference minutes, February 2, 1954, Public Statements by the Secretaries of Defense, microfilm collection (Frederick, MD: University Publications of America, 1982). Also see Department of State press release, "Strategic Concept," December 21, 1954, box 80, Correspondence Series, Speech Series, Personal Papers of John Foster Dulles (Wilmington, DE: Scholarly Resources, 1995).

7. Robert A. Divine, Blowing on the Wind: The Nuclear Test Ban Debate, 1954–1960 (New York: Oxford University Press, 1978), 3–7, 30.

8. New York Times, April 1, 1954; memorandum, Jackson to Dulles, April 9, 1954, box 49, Jackson Papers, DDEL.

9. U.N. Disarmament Commission Official Records: Supplement for April, May, and June 1954, DC/44 and Corr. 1; message, Cairo Embassy to State Department, April 10, 1954, box 3147, 711.5611, Central Decimal Files 1950–1954, RG 59, NA; Jules Moch, "Banning the Bomb," Nation, May 15, 1954, 418–19; New York Times, May 12, October 1, 1954; J. Alvarez Del Vayo, "H-Bomb and Diplomacy," Nation, April 10, 1954, 293–94; Robert Strausz-Hupe, "Europe's 'Neutralism' Rests on Belief That Nobody Could Win An Atomic War," Saturday Evening Post, April 10, 1954, 12.

10. Chester Bowles, "Our Present Foreign Policy," Commonweal, April 30, 1954, 92–93; New York Times, March 28, April 7, August 18, 1954. Lewis Mumford, In the Name of Sanity (New York: Harcourt, Brace, 1954), 65, 161, 170–71, 231. Also see "H-Bomb Reactions," Commonweal, April 16, 1954, 27–28; "Prayer," Christian Century, April 21, 1954, 487.

11. "America's Responsibility," Nation, May 1, 1954, 392; A. J. Muste, "H-Bomb Statement," n.d., box 3, series A-4, section II, Fellowship of Reconciliation-USA Papers, SPC; John M. Swomley to Eisenhower, n.d., box 3, series A-4, section II, Fellowship of Reconciliation-USA Papers, SPC; Alfred Hassler, "The Race That Ends in Death," Fellowship 20, no. 7 (July 1954): 3–9; George MacLeod, "Showdown for the Church," Fellowship 20, no. 7 (July 1954): 13–16; Wyman Spalding, "Decision at 60,000," Fellowship 20, no. 7 (July 1954): 51–52; "We Could Do Without It!" Fellowship 20, no. 7 (July 1954): 53–55.

12. "FOR Ads" flyer," n.d., box 3, series A-5, section II, Fellowship of Reconciliation-USA Papers, SPC; Alfred Hassler, "The Conscientious Combatant," n.d., box 3, series A-5, section II, Fellowship of Reconciliation-USA Papers, SPC.

13. "America Plans No Wanton Destruction," Air Force 38, no. 2 (February 1955): 29; "Nuclear War," Commonweal, April 30, 1954, 83–84.

14. Otto P. Weyland, "Can Air Power Win 'Little Wars'?" U.S. News and World Report, July 23, 1954, 54.

15. Dale O. Smith, "The Morality of Retaliation," Air University Quarterly Review 7, no. 3 (winter 1954–55): 55–59.

16. Charles J. V. Murphy, "Is the H-Bomb Enough?" Fortune, June 1954, 102–103, 246–54.

17. Richard S. Leghorn, "No Need to Bomb Cities to Win Wars," U.S. News and World Report, January 28, 1955, 78–94; George C. Reinhardt and William R. Kintner, "The Tactical Side of Atomic Warfare," Bulletin of the Atomic Scientist, February 1955, 53–58; Robert C. Richardson III, "Will Nuclear Weapons Be Used?" Air University Quarterly Review 7, no. 3 (winter 1954–55): 3–14. See also Thomas R. Phillips, "The Atomic Revolution in Warfare," Bulletin of the Atomic Scientist, October 1954, 315–17; "Nuclear War," Commonweal, November 12, 1954, 157–58; T. F. Walkowicz and William Pfaff, "Nuclear War," Commonweal, December 10, 1954, 279–83.

18. Transcript, NBC-TV, "Meeting the Press," February 6, 1955, box 106, Unclassified General Correspondence, RG 128, NA; memorandum, H. Schuyler Foster to Carl W. McCardle, February 9, 1955, box 42, Lot 57D688, Office of the Special Assistant to the Secretary for Atomic Energy and Outer Space, RG 59, NA.

19. Dulles memorandum of March 6, 1955 conversation with the president, March 7, 1955, box 3, White House Memoranda Series, Dulles Papers, DDEL; Dulles memorandum of March 7, 1955 conversation with the president, March 7, 1955, box 3, White House Memoranda Series, Dulles Papers, DDEL.

20. "Report from Asia," U.S. Department of State Bulletin, March 21, 1955, 459–60; New York Times, March 9, 1955; memorandum, S. Everett Gleason, March 10, 1955," March 11, 1955, box 6, NSC Series, Ann Whitman File, DDEL.

21. Press conference minutes, March 15, Press Conferences of the Secretaries of State 1922–1973, microfilm collection (Wilmington, DE: Scholarly Resources, 1982); PPP 1955, 332, 357; memorandum of telephone call between Dulles and Nixon, March 16, 1955, box 3, Telephone Call Series, Dulles Papers, DDEL; New York Times, March 20, 1955.

22. Memorandum, Richard Hirsch, March 10, 1955, box 9, Operations Coordinating Board Central File, NSC Staff, DDEL; memorandum, Richard Hirsch to E. B. Staats, March 16, 1955, box 9, Operations Coordinating Board Central File, NSC Staff, DDEL; "Courses of Action to Achieve Better Public Understanding of the Varying Effects of Sizes and Types of Nuclear Weapons," March 25, 1955, box 9, Operations Coordinating Board Central File, NSC Staff, DDEL.

23. New York Times, March 13, 16, 17, 20, 21, 24, April 21, 1955; Ernest K. Lindley, "A Fine Atomic Distinction," Newsweek, March 21, 1955, 36; "Nuclear Wars Can Be Small," Life, July 25, 1955, 26; "New Tactics for Limited Warfare," Life, July 25, 1955, 70–83. Also see "Asia," Newsweek, March 21, 1955, 40; F. H. Drinkwater, "The Morality of Nuclear War," Commonweal, March 18, 1955, 623–27.

24. For example, see Neal Rosendorf, "John Foster Dulles' Nuclear Schizophrenia," in Cold War Statesmen Confront the Bomb: Nuclear Diplomacy Since 1945, ed. John Lewis Gaddis, Philip H. Gordon, Ernest R. May, and Jonathan Rosenberg (Oxford: Oxford University Press, 1999), 62–86.

25. Rosendorf, "John Foster Dulles' Nuclear Schizophrenia," 65; John Foster Dulles, War or Peace (New York: Macmillan, 1950), 262; John Foster Dulles, "March 10, 1950 Address to Executive Club of Chicago," Executives' Club News, March 17, 1950, The Right Wing Collection of the University of Iowa Libraries, 1918–1977, microfilm collection, (Glen Rock, NJ: Microfilming Corporation of America, 1978), E9.

26. Rosendorf, "John Foster Dulles' Nuclear Schizophrenia," 65; John Foster Dulles, "A Policy of Boldness," Life, May 19, 1952, 146–60.

27. Memorandum of discussion, S. Everett Gleason, February 12, 1953, FRUS 1952–1954, vol. 15, 770; memorandum of conversation, March 6, 1953, box 3174, 711.5611, Central Decimal Files 1950–1954, RG 59, NA; memorandum of discussion, S. Everett Gleason, April 7, 1953 FRUS 1952–1954, vol. 15, 827.

28. Townsend Hoopes, The Devil and John Foster Dulles (Boston: Little, Brown, 1973), 277–78; John Newhouse, War and Peace in the Nuclear Age (New York: Knopf, 1988), 104.

29. "Radio and Television Report to the Nation," July 22, 1957, box 113, Correspondence Series of the Speech Series of the Personal Papers of John Foster Dulles (1888–1959), microfilm collection (Wilmington, DE: Scholarly Resources, 1995); Dulles news conference, April 1, 1958, box 125, Personal Papers of John Foster Dulles.

30. Andrew P. N. Erdmann, "'War No Longer Has Any Logic Whatever'" in Gaddis et al., Cold War Statesmen Confront the Bomb, 87–119; Campbell Craig, Destroying the Village (New York: Columbia University Press, 1998).

31. Erdmann, "'War No Longer Has Any Logic Whatever,'" 117.

32. Dwight D. Eisenhower, Crusade in Europe: A Personal Account of World War II (Garden City, NY: Doubleday, 1948), 443. See also Eisenhower's reference to the atomic bomb as that "awful thing." Stephen E. Ambrose, Eisenhower, Vol. 1 (New York: Simon and Schuster, 1983), 513.

33. New York Times, July 21, 1950, January 13, 1952.

34. David Alan Rosenberg, "Toward Armageddon: The Foundation of United States Nuclear Strategy, 1945–1961," Ph.D. diss., University of Chicago, 1983, 221.

35. Memorandum, Robert Cutler to Charles E. Wilson, March 21, 1953, FRUS 1952–1954, vol. 15, 815; memorandum of discussion, S. Everett Gleason, May 7, 1953, FRUS 1952–1954, vol. 15, 977; memorandum of discussion, S. Everett Gleason, May 14, 1953, FRUS 1952–1954, vol. 15, 1014.

36. Campbell Craig, Destroying the Village, 60–61.

37. Memorandum of conference, Goodpaster, May 24, 1956, FRUS 1955–1957, vol. 19, 312.

38. Memorandum of discussion, S. Everett Gleason, May 28, 1957, FRUS 1955–1957, vol. 19, 499–504; NSC 5707/8, FRUS 1955–1957, vol. 19, 509–24; Craig, Destroying the Village, 55–67.

39. Memorandum, Joseph Hanson to Gerard C. Smith et al., March 15, 1955 with attachment "Edward Murrow Excerpts," CBS broadcast, March 10, 1955, 7:45 p.m., box 342, Lot

57D688, Office of the Special Assistant to the Assistant Secretary for Atomic Energy and Outer Space, RG 59, NA; New York Times, March 10, 17, 20, December 5, 1955.

40. New York Times, January 24, April 1, 1954, March 17, 1955; Hanson Baldwin, "War or Peace," New York Times Magazine, April 18, 1954. Baldwin also shared his views that nuclear war was unwinnable at the October 1955 annual meeting of the Association of the U.S. Army. "Panel Discussion," Army Combat Forces Journal 6, no. 4 (November 1955): 65–66.

41. Press release, "Remarks by Secretary of the Air Force Thomas K. Finletter at the Annual Banquet of the New York Patent Law Association," February 26, 1952, box 23, Formerly Classified General Correspondence Files, Public Information Division, Office of Information Services, RG 340, NA; Thomas K. Finletter, "Deterrent Force," Vital Speeches of the Day, July 1, 1952, 560–63; transcript of Air War College lecture, Thomas K. Finletter, "The Air Force Task in Provision for National Security," n.d., box 2, Formerly Classified General Correspondence Files, Public Information Division, Office of Information Services, RG 340, NA; Thomas K. Finletter, Power and Policy: U.S. Foreign Policy and Military Power in the Hydrogen Age (New York: Harcourt, Brace, 1954), 49–50.

42. Josephine V. Cowin to Dulles, February 25, 1954, box 3063, 700.5611, Central Decimal Files 1950–1954, RG 59, NA; David W. Wainhouse to Cowin, March 13, 1954, box 3063, 700.5611, Central Decimal Files 1950–1954, RG 59, NA; "Infoguide: Atomic General," April 9, 1954, box 762, Chronological File, 1949–June 1954, Office of Security Review, Office of the Assistant Secretary of Defense for Legislative and Public Affairs, RG 330, NA.

43. Ernest Haveman, "Toughest Cop of the Western World," Life, June 14, 1954, 133–47; New York Times, October 22, 1953; Curtis E. LeMay, "We Must Avoid the First Blow," U.S. News and World Report, December 9, 1955, 46.

44. R. C. Lindsey, "Briefing on Air Force Concepts," April 23, 1954, box 56, General Correspondence, Correspondence Control Section, Office of the Administrative Secretary, RG 330, NA.

45. Leghorn, "No Need to Bomb Cities to Win Wars," 78–94 ; "Nuclear War," Commonweal, November 12, 1954, 157–58; "Can We Defend Ourselves?" Commonweal, April 8, 1955, 15–16; "Nuclear War IV," Commonweal, October 22, 1954, 55–56; Walkowicz and Pfaff, "Nuclear War," 279–83.

46. New York Times, January 4, July 15, 18, 1955; Colonel Shillelagh, "… trouble with cavalry is …," Army Combat Forces Journal 5, no. 6 (January 1955): 34–36; Matthew Ridgway, "My Battles in War and Peace," Saturday Evening Post, January 28, 1956, 34–35, 72–78; Matthew B. Ridgway, Soldier: The Memoirs of Matthew B. Ridgway (New York: Harper, 1956), 275; A. J. Bacevich, "The Paradox of Professionalism: Eisenhower, Ridgway, and the Challenge of Civilian Control, 1953–1955," Journal of Military History 61, no. 2 (April 1997): 303–34.

47. Memorandum by Jesse M. MacKnight, May 18, 1954, box 75, Lot 61D53, Bureau of Public Affairs 1944–1962, RG 59, NA; memorandum of meeting by Louis J. Halle, June 10, 1954, box 76, Lot 61D53, Bureau of Public Affairs 1944–1962, RG 59, NA; memorandum, Charles Runyon to Louis Halle, June 25, 1954, box 75, Lot 61D53, Bureau of Public Affairs 1944-1962, RG 59, NA; memorandum, Charles Runyon to Louis Halle, June 28, 1954, with attachment "Background Memorandum Concerning the Application of the 1949 Geneva Conventions," n.d., box 75, Lot 61D53, Bureau of Public Affairs 1944–1962, RG 59, NA; U.S. Senate, Committee on Foreign Relations, Geneva Conventions for the Protection of War Victims: Hearings, 84th Cong., 1st sess.; New York Times, July 7, 1955.

Chapter 8

1. "Defense Arrangements of the North Atlantic Community," U.S. Department of State Bulletin, July 9, 1962, 64–69; Fred Kaplan, Wizards of Armageddon (New York: Simon and Schuster, 1983), 201–19, 232–47, 258–85; Gregg Herken, Counsels of War (New York: Knopf, 1985), 78–81, 150–52; Lawrence Freedman, The Evolution of Nuclear Strategy, 2nd ed. (London: Macmillan, 1989), 227–44.

2. Thomas E. Murray, Nuclear Policy for War and Peace (Cleveland: World, 1960), 29, 61.

3. S. T. Cohen, The Neutron Bomb: Political, Technological, and Military Issues (Cambridge, MA.: Institute for Foreign Policy Analysis, 1978), 55–62.

4. Herken, Counsels of War, 168–69.

5. U.S. Senate, Committee on Armed Services, Military Procurement Authorization, Fiscal Year 1964, 88th Cong., 1st sess., 106.

6. Report, F. P. Serong to Paul D. Harkins, October 1962, History Backup Files, microfilm collection, The War in Vietnam: Papers of William C. Westmoreland (Bethesda, MD: University Publications of America, 1993); memorandum, John K. Boles, September 2, 1965, History Files, Papers of William Westmoreland.

7. Daniel C. Hallin, The "Uncensored War": The Media and Vietnam (Berkeley, CA: University of California Press, 1989), 105–10.

8. Hallin, The "Uncensored War," 154–58; Peter Braestrup, Big Story: How the American Press and Television Reported and Interpreted the Crisis of Tet 1968 in Vietnam and Washington, Vol. 1 (Boulder, CO: Westview, 1977), 232–86.

9. Tom Wells, The War Within: America's Battle Over Vietnam (Berkeley, CA: University of California Press, 1994), 84–86; Robert D. Schulzinger, A Time for War: The United States and Vietnam, 1941–1975 (New York: Oxford University Press, 1997), 237.

10. Westmoreland to Commander, All Subordinate Units, July 7, 1965, History Files, Papers of William Westmoreland; "Combat Operations Minimizing Non-Combatant Battle Casualties," MACV Directive 525-3, September 7, 1965, History Files, Papers of William Westmoreland; memorandum, George M. Gallagher, September 15, 1965, History Files, Papers of William Westmoreland; "Tactics and Techniques for Employment of U.S. Forces in the Republic of Vietnam," MACV Directive 525–4, September 17, 1965, History Files, Papers of William Westmoreland; "Synopsis of Tactical Air Firepower Study," n.d., History Files, Papers of William Westmoreland; "Combat Operations Control, Disposition, and Safeguarding of Vietnamese Property, Captured Materiel and Food Supplies," MACV Directive 525-9, April 10, 1967, 2021 (MACJ4-Logistics), MACV Historical Office, microfilm collection, Records of the Military Assistance Command Vietnam (Bethesda, MD: University Publications of America, 1988); Division Order 003330.2, August 9, 1967, attachment to August 1967 Command History of the First Marine Division, microfilm collection, Records of the U.S. Marine Corps in the Vietnam War (Bethesda, MD: University Publications of America, 1990); Appendix 10 to Annex A to Ninth Infantry Division Field SOP, attachment to Major General George G. O'Connor, U.S. Army Senior Officer Debriefing Report, February 23, 1968, microfilm collection, U.S. Armed Forces in Vietnam 1954–1975 (Frederick, MD: University Publications of America, 1983).

11. John Schlight, The War in South Vietnam: The Years of the Offensive, 1965–1968 (Washington, DC: Office of Air Force History, 1988), 258–59; Mark Clodfelter, The Limits of Air Power: The American Bombing of North Vietnam (New York: Free Press, 1989), 85, 97, 128, 164, 190.

12. Wells, The War Within, 205; William M. Hammond, Public Affairs: The Military and the Media, 1962–1968 (Washington, DC: U.S. Army Center of Military History, 1988), 136–37.

13. MACV Directive 525-3, September 7, 1965, History Files, Papers of William Westmoreland; Guenter Lewy, America in Vietnam (New York: Oxford University Press, 1978), 235.

14. "Remarks by General W. C. Westmoreland to Correspondents," September 13, 1966, History Files, Papers of William Westmoreland; PPP 1967, vol. 1, 351.

15. Lewy, America in Vietnam, 446–53.

16. Seymour M. Hersh, My Lai 4: A Report on the Massacre and its Aftermath (New York: Random House, 1970), 44–75; Michael Bilton and Kevin Sim, Four Hours in My Lai: A War Crime and its Aftermath (New York: Viking, 1992), 102–62.

17. William C. Westmoreland, A Soldier Reports (Garden City, NY: Doubleday, 1976), 378.

18. Bilton and Sims, Four Hours in My Lai, 356–66.

19. Ibid., 345.

20. Hersh, My Lai 4, 153.

21. Bilton and Sim, Four Hours at My Lai, 345.

22. Lawrence Freedman and Efraim Karsh, The Gulf Conflict 1990–1991: Diplomacy and War in the New World Order (Princeton, NJ: Princeton University Press, 1993), 302.

23. See, for example, Los Angeles Times, January 17, 19, 1991; Atlanta Journal and Constitution, January 18, 1991; Boston Globe, January 19, 1991; Washington Post, February 20, 1991.

24. Needless Deaths in the Gulf War: Civilian Casualties During the Air Campaign and Violations of the Laws of War (New York: Human Rights Watch, 1991), 6.

25. See, for example, Los Angeles Times, January 17, 1991.

26. New York Times, February 15, 1991; Atlanta Journal and Constitution, February 15, 1991.

27. See the references to "collateral devastation" and "collateral effects of damage" in discussions of nuclear attacks before the term became a standardized technical expression, JCS

1953/1, "Evaluation of Effect on Soviet War Effort Resulting from the Strategic Air Offensive," May 12, 1949, 16, 26, 95–96, in America's Plans for War, vol. 11. By the mid-1960s, the term had taken on a more general meaning within the military. See, for example, the term's use by the chairman of the JCS in memorandum, Earle G. Wheeler to Secretary of Defense, February 25, 1965, Vietnam Special Subjects: National Security File, 1963–1969, microfilm collection (Frederick, MD: University Publications of America, 1987).

28. Morton H. Halperin, Limited War in the Nuclear Age (New York: John Wiley and Sons, 1963), 108; George H. Quester, Deterrence Before Hiroshima: The Airpower Background of Modern Strategy (New York: Wiley, 1966), 23, 26, 63, 131, 157, 166, 168.

29. New York Times, September 12, 1974, May 12, 1976, May 4, 1985; Washington Post, November 14, 1980, August 9, 1981.

30. Trevor N. Dupuy, Curt Johnson, and Grace P. Hayes, Dictionary of Military Terms: A Guide to the Language of Warfare and Military Institutions (New York: Wilson, 1986), 51; Lesley Brown, ed., The New Shorter Oxford English Dictionary, vol. 1 (Oxford: Clarendon, 1993), 438; Anne H. Soukhanov, ed., Encarta World English Dictionary (New York: St. Martin's, 1999), 357; Richard Bowyer, ed., Dictionary of Military Terms (Chicago: Fitzroy Dearborn, 1999), 39; Elizabeth J. Jewell and Frank Abate, eds., The New Oxford American Dictionary (New York: Oxford University Press, 2001), 335.

31. Newsday, October 9, 2001; San Diego Union-Tribune, October 18, 2001; New York Times, March 22, 25, 29, April 3, 5, 7, 10, 2003; Washington Post, March 29, 2003; Wall Street Journal, April 1, 2003, Christian Science Monitor, April 7, 2003.

32. Newsday, October 9, 2001; New York Times, October 14, 2001, March 20, 24, 29, 31, April 2, 3, 2003; Washington Post, March 24, 2003; Wall Street Journal, April 1, 2003; Christian Science Monitor, April 7, 2003.

33. Charles Plater, ed., A Primer of Peace and War: The Principle of International Morality (New York: Kenedy, 1915); Franziskus M. Stratmann, The Church and War (New York: Kenedy, 1928); Cyprian Emanuel, The Ethics of War, Committee on Ethics Pamphlet, no. 9 (Washington, DC: Catholic Association for International Peace, 1932); John Kenneth Ryan, Modern War and Basic Ethics, (Milwaukee: Bruce, 1940); John C. Ford, "The Morality of Obliteration Bombing," Theological Studies 5, no. 3 (September 1944): 261–309.

34. John Courtney Murray, Morality and Modern War (New York: Church Peace Union, 1959); William J. Nagle, Morality and Modern Warfare: The State of the Question (Baltimore: Helicon, 1960); Joseph C. McKenna, "Ethics and War," American Political Science Review 54 (September 1960): 647–58; G. E. M. Anscombe and Walter Stein, Nuclear Weapons: A Catholic Response (New York: Sheed and Ward, 1961).

35. Ralph Luther Moellering, Modern War and the American Churches: A Factual Study of the Christian Conscience on Trial from 1939 to the Cold War Crisis of Today (New York: American, 1956); Roland H. Bainton, Christian Attitudes Toward War and Peace: A Historical Survey and Critical Re-Evaluation (New York: Abingdon, 1960); Paul Ramsey, War and the Christian Conscience: How Should Modern War Be Conducted Justly? (Durham, NC: Duke University, 1961).

36. Murray, Nuclear Policy for War and Peace; Robert W. Tucker, The Just War: A Study in Contemporary American Doctrine (Baltimore: Johns Hopkins, 1960).

37. See, for example, Ralph B. Potter, War and Moral Discourse (Richmond, VA: John Knox, 1969); James Turner Johnson, Ideology, Reason, and the Limitation of War: Religious and Secular Concepts 1200–1740 (Princeton, NJ: Princeton University Press, 1975); Michael Walzer, Just and Unjust Wars: A Moral Argument with Historical Illustrations (New York: Basic, 1977); Sheldon M. Cohen, Arms and Judgment: Law, Morality, and the Conduct of War in the Twentieth Century (Boulder, CO: Westview, 1989); Robert L. Holmes, On War and Morality (Princeton, NJ: Princeton University Press, 1989).

38. F. H. Drinkwater, "War and Conscience," Commonweal, March 2, 1951, 511–14. See also Michael De La Bedoyere, "Pacifism and the Christian Conscience," Commonweal, December 21, 1951, 271–73; "War and Conscience," Commonweal, January 18, 1952, 375–78.

39. U.N. General Assembly, "Respect for Human Rights in Armed Conflicts," Resolution 2444, December 19, 1968; U.S. Department of the Army, The Law of Land Warfare, Field Manual 27-10, Change No. 1, July 15, 1976; Adam Roberts and Richard Guelff, eds., Documents on the Laws of War, (Clarendon: Oxford, 1989) 415, 455.

40. Micheal Clodfelter, Warfare and Armed Conflicts: A Statistical Reference to Casualty and Other Figures, 1618–1991, vol. 2 (Jefferson, NC: MacFarland, 1992), 780–82.

41. Henry L. Stimson, "The Decision to Use the Atomic Bomb," Harper's, February 1947, 97–107; Harry S. Truman, Memoirs, vol. 1, 1945, Year of Decisions (Garden City, NY: Doubleday, 1955), 417; Barton J. Bernstein, "The Struggle over History: Defining the Hiroshima Narrative," in Judgment at the Smithsonian: The Bombing of Hiroshima and Nagasaki, ed. Philip Nobile (New York: Marlowe, 1995), 137–42, 178–85; J. Samuel Walker, Prompt and Utter Destruction: Truman and the Use of Atomic Bombs Against Japan (Chapel Hill, NC: University of North Carolina Press, 1997), 98–110, 116–19n.
42. Bernstein, "The Struggle over History," 206–40.
43. See, for example, memorandum, John K. Boles, September 2, 1965, History Files, Papers of William Westmoreland.
44. William V. O'Brien, "The Meaning of 'Military Necessity' in International Law," World Polity 1 (1957), 109–76.

Index